The Divine Kingship in Ghana and Ancient Egypt

The Divine Kingship in Ghana and Ancient Egypt

EVA L. R. MEYEROWITZ

© *Eva Leonie Lewin-Richter Meyerowitz* 1960

2018 BLP REPRINT EDITION

WWW.BLACKLEGACYPRESS.ORG

ISBN: 978-1-63652-430-6

Contents

PREFACE AND ACKNOWLEDGMENTS	page 15
LIST OF ABBREVIATIONS	19

I. THE DIVINE KING, THE INCARNATION OF THE GOD OF HIS CLAN — 23

Akan:

 Introduction: The Falcon Clan People — 23

  1. The Supreme Mother-goddess — 26
  2. The Clan-goddess, the Manifestation of the Supreme Mother-goddess — 27
  3. The Divine Queen-mother, the Incarnation of the Goddess of her Clan — 28
  4. The Divine King, the Incarnation of the God of his Clan — 29

Egypt:

 Introduction: The Falcon Clan People — 31

  1. Hathor in her Role as Clan and Supreme Mother-goddess — 31
  2. Horus, the Son of Hathor — 35
  3. Horus the Elder, Son of Hathor — 37
  4. The Divine King Osiris, Incarnation of Horus the Elder — 44
  5. Horus, Son of Isis — 47
  6. The Divine Pharaoh, the Incarnation of Horus, Son of Isis — 49
  7. The Divine Queen, the Incarnation of Isis — 52

II. THE DIVINE KING, THE INCARNATION OF THE SKY FERTILITY-GOD OF THE STATE — 59

CONTENTS

Akan:

1. The Father and Craftsman Creator-god Odomankoma Bore-Bore .... page 59
2. The Sky Fertility-gods 61
3. The Bull-god Buru 63

Egypt:

1. The Father and Craftsman Creator-god Ptah 64
2. The Sky Fertility-gods 72
3. The Bull-god Apis 76
4. The Bull-god Min 79

III. THE DIVINE KING, THE INCARNATION OF THE SUN-GOD 85

Akan:

1. The Sun-god Nyankopon 85
2. The King, the Son of the Sun-god 86
3. The King as the Incarnation of the Sun 88

Egypt:

1. The Sun-gods: Atum, Re-Atum, Amen-Re and Aton 90
2. The King as the Son of the Sun-god 93
3. The King as the Incarnation of the Sun 96

IV. THE DIVINE KING, THE INCARNATION OF THE DIVINE PROCREATOR OF HIS LINEAGE 98

Akan:

1. The *Ntoro* Cult, the Cult of the Begetter 98

Egypt:

1. The Khamutef Cult, the Cult of the Begetter 100

V. THE KING'S POTENCY: THE KRA AND THE KA 103

Akan:

1. The Concept of the *Kra* 103
   (a) The *Kra* of the Commoner 103
   (b) The *Kra* of the King 105
2. The *Akrafohene*, the Priest of the King's *Kra* 106
3. The Ritual in the *Kra Fieso* 107

CONTENTS

Egypt:
 1. The Concept of the *Ka*   page 109
  (*a*) The *Ka* of the Commoner   109
  (*b*) The *Ka* of the King   111
 2. The *Anmutef*, the Priest of the King's *Ka*   114
 3. The Ritual in the *Pa Dwat*   115
 4. Nehebkau, the Uniter of *Kas*   118

VI. THE KING'S SUPPORTERS, THE ROYAL ANCESTORS   121

Akan:
 1. Man's Immortal, Self-existing Elements after Death   121
  (*a*) The *Kra*, the Representative of his Personality   121
  (*b*) The Heart, the Representative of his Emotions   122
  (*c*) The *Honhom*, the Divine Soul   122
  (*d*) The *Saman*, the Spiritualised Body   123
  (*e*) The *Sunsum*, the Shadow Soul   124
  (*f*) The *Sasa*, the Personification of his Energy   124
  (*g*) Reincarnation   124
  (*h*) The *Honhom Nipadua*, the Transfigured Spirits   124
  (*i*) The Name   125
  (*k*) The Body   125
 2. The Royal Ancestral Spirits, the Royal Ancestors   126
 3. The Chapel of the Stools   127
 4. The Custodian of the Chapel of the Stools   128
 5. The Ritual in the Chapel of the Stools   129

Egypt:
 1. Man's Immortal Self-existing Elements after Death   130
  (*a*) The *Ka*, the Representative of his Personality   130
  (*b*) The Heart, the Representative of his Emotions and his Conscience   131
  (*c*) The *Ba*, the Divine Soul   131
  (*d*) The *Sahu*, the Spiritualised Body   132
  (*e*) The *Khaibit*, the Shadow Soul   132

CONTENTS

  (f) The *Sekhem*, the Personification of his
    Energy   *page* 132
  (g) Reincarnation   132
  (h) The *Akhu*, the Transfigured Spirits 133
  (i) The Name   134
  (k) The Body   134

 2. The Royal Ancestral Spirits, the Royal Ancestors   135
 3. The Dual Shrines   136
 4. The Custodian of the Dual Shrines   138
 5. The Royal Standards   138
 6. The Ritual in the Dual Shrines   140

VII. THE REJUVENATION OF THE KING'S DIVINE AND LIFE-GIVING POWER ON NEW YEAR'S DAY IN SPRING   142

 Akan:

  1. The *Nyanku Sai* Festival, the King's Reinstatement as Lawful Ruler of the Land 142
  2. The *Apo* Festival, the Rejuvenation of the King's solar *Kra*   146
  3. The Festival of the God of the Land, Taa Kese 149

 Egypt:

  1. The *Sed* Festival, the King's Reinstatement as Lawful Ruler of the Land   151
  2. The *Nehebkau* Festival   163
   (a) The Uniting of the *Kas*   163
   (b) The Rebirth of the Sun-god incarnate in the King   165
  3. The Festival of the God of the Land, Tatjenen   168

VIII. THE REJUVENATION OF THE KING'S PERSON ON NEW YEAR'S DAY IN AUTUMN   171

 Akan:

  1. The *Aferehyia Dwaree*, the King's Death and Rebirth   171

 Egypt:

  1. The Min-Khamutef Festival, the King's Death and Rebirth   177

CONTENTS

IX. THE KING'S DEATH   *page* 186

    Akan:

        1. The King's Death   186
        2. The King's Burial   194
        3. The King's Funeral Rites   196
        4. The King's Ascension and Transfiguration   200

    Egypt:

        1. The King's Death, Burial, and Funeral Rites   204
        2. The King's Ascension and Transfiguration   213

X. THE ROYAL SUCCESSION   216

    Akan:

        1. The Selection and Enstoolment Rites   216

    Egypt:

        1. The Accession and Coronation Rites   222

XI. DIFFUSION   228

    APPENDIX   236

    INDEX   240

Illustrations

1. The late Queen-mother of Asante, Nana Kwadu Yiadom *facing page* 36
2. The Queen-mother of Bono-Takyiman, Nana Afua Abrafo 36
3. Head of the goddess Hathor 37
4. The Falcon-god Soker and Hathor 44
5. The Pharaoh Ramses II 45
6. The Egyptian Queen Teta-Shery 45
7. Small brass mask representing an Akan Sky fertility-deity 64
8. Pendants in gold from Baule 65
9. Osiris enthroned within a shrine 80
10. *Ka* and *Hemsut* deities from a relief at Deir el Bahri 81
11. The Asantehene, Otumfor Sir Osei Agyeman Prempeh II 112
12. The Bono-Takyimanhene, Nana Akumfi Ameyaw III 113
13. The *Anmutef* priest 128
14. Isis and Nephthys adoring the Sun-god Re *following page* 128
15. The Weighing of the Heart in the Hall of Judgement 128
16. *Ba* bird visiting a mummy *facing page* 129
17. Two scenes from the *Sed* festival 144
18. Scenes from the Min-Khamutef festival 145
19. *Adosowa*, the effigy of a deceased Akan king 196
20. The brother of Nana Akumfi Ameyaw III lying in state 197
21. The *Gyaasehene*, Nana Yaw Atow of Bono-Takyiman 204
22. Nana Akumfi Ameyaw III performing a ritual dance 205

ILLUSTRATIONS

Figures in the Text

1. The ancient sceptre of the Akan Queen-mother   *page* 28
2. The Falcon Horus crouching on a dome-shaped cone   36
3. The Falcon Horus-Shu-Onuris crouching on a truncated cone   36
4. The Horus falcon walking on a crescent moon   36
5. The *Djed* emblem of Osiris   68
6. The Akan *Djed*   69
7. The unidentified animal of the god Set   74
8. The *Sankofa* bird   91
9. Painting on a potsherd from the Naqada period   231

Maps

1. Map showing the migration of the Akan Falcon clan people   *page* 25
2. Map of Ancient Egypt   33

Preface and Acknowledgments

This is the fourth volume of the series of which the first, *The Sacred State of the Akan*, gives a picture of the old Akan civilisation. The second, *Akan Traditions of Origin*, deals with the early history of the people who now call themselves Akan. The third, *The Akan of Ghana, Their Ancient Beliefs*,[1] showed the development of their religion. The fourth, here presented, *The Divine Kingship in Ghana and Ancient Egypt*,[2] attempts to show that Akan religion, which includes the cult of the divine king and the main features of their social organisation, is largely derived from Ancient Egypt.

The matter published in this book arose out of my field-work on the Gold Coast in 1945-6 which was financed by the Colonial Development and Welfare Fund, and in 1949-50 by a grant from the University College of the Gold Coast. I was fortunate in that I was able to work in what is now called Ghana at a time when many of the people who were custodians of the old traditions were still alive and still felt the importance of their responsibility for the preservation of the traditions entrusted to them. The years 1936-45 I spent at Achimota. There I had ample opportunity for travel, not only through the Gold Coast repeatedly, but to various parts of West Africa and the French Sudan. These travels have been of great value to me. I gained from them a clear idea of the geographical features of this part of Africa, and acquaintance with the many tribes that inhabit it.

Finding myself in a matrilineally organised society I was as a

---

[1] Originally entitled *The Akan Cosmological Dogma*.
[2] Originally entitled, in the preface to *The Akan of Ghana*, *The Akan Divine Kingship and its Prototype in Ancient Egypt*.

PREFACE AND ACKNOWLEDGMENTS

woman able with greater ease to enter into closer association with the people. Moreover, I had the good fortune to discover the one section of the Akan people that had preserved the past with more completeness and in greater detail than any other. This section was the Bono-Takyiman—now styled Tekyiman-Brong—whose aristocracy once ruled the Bono Kingdom which was destroyed by the Asante (Ashanti) about 1740. Their ancestors founded the first Akan civilisation south of the Black Volta River (*c.* 1295). The Bono Kingdom became the wealthiest and most civilised among all the Akan states, including Asante. I had an opportunity to be of help to the Bono-Takyiman in the political sphere, and mainly as the result of this help, I gained their confidence to the extent that they entrusted me with secrets of their traditions which they had kept strictly to themselves in the past. I have had ample opportunity moreover to judge of the truth, and weigh the value, of their statements.

The more I became acquainted with Akan beliefs and customs, the more I realised that they were not isolated phenomena. It became clear to me that they were ultimately based upon those of Ancient Egypt. Time and place and historical change had so modified these religious forms as to produce effects which made them not indeed repetitions of the Egyptian example but obvious derivations from it.

This book was in part financed by Rhodes University, Grahamstown, South Africa, which awarded me a Hugh Le May Fellowship for the year 1954. I wish to record here my deep gratitude to the Academic Council of Rhodes University for the support that enabled me to carry out my researches and write up my material.

I desire to thank here once more the Academic Board of the University College of Ghana for the grant awarded me for fieldwork in 1949–50. Further, my most sincere thanks are due to Nana Akumfi Ameyaw III, Omanhene of Bono-Takyiman (Tekyiman-Brong), the Queen-mother Nana Afua Abrafi, and the Elders and people of Takyiman for all their assistance and enthusiastic support in my work. The late Mr. J. A. Ankomah, Inspector of N.A. Police, was a brilliant and most devoted interpreter, as was also Mr. D. K. Owusu when he accompanied me.

When I started to write my book I had the great good fortune to meet the late Professor H. Frankfort, author of *Kingship and the Gods*. My outline of the scope and trend of my work gained from him generous encouragement for which I was deeply grateful. To my great regret he never saw the completed volume. I missed the benefit of his criticism which would have been especially valuable on those points where our conclusions differed. Those drawn from the Akan, amongst whom Ancient Egyptian religious thinking is still alive, may well differ from what the scholar can deduce from extant material available for study.

I must thank Miss Sheila Maritz of St. Mary's Hall, Rhodes University, for the care she lavished on me during my stay in Grahamstown, and Miss A. Currie for her kindness and help in the improvement of my style. An untidy manuscript was left behind when I had to leave for South Africa in 1958. I owe deep gratitude to Mrs. Beatrice Hooke for taking charge of it and preparing it for press, and later for reading the proofs. I am indebted also to Miss D. Marshall for compiling the index.

Looking back over the years during which I have been engaged on this work, I feel that there are two people in Ghana without whose help my books would never have been realized. Until I met Dr. J. B. Danquah my knowledge of Akan customs and beliefs was mainly derived from Capt. R. S. Rattray's books *Ashanti*, *Art and Religion in Ashanti*, and others. He presented a picture of an intelligent but primitive African people whose religion had no discernible system. I am indebted to Dr. Danquah, author of *The Akan Doctrine of God* (1944), for showing me that the facts were otherwise.

The other person to whom I am deeply indebted is Mr. Kofi Antubam, now a well-known painter in Ghana, who accompanied me on my first trip in 1945–6. His great service to me was not merely that he proved to be a first-rate interpreter but also that he made me acceptable to his people. His insistence that I could be entrusted with their secret traditions enabled me to obtain information that otherwise would have been denied to me. If he had not prepared the way it would never have been possible for me to collect much of the best material on my second trip in 1949–50.

EVA L. R. MEYEROWITZ

Cape Town, 1958

List of Abbreviations

No attempt has been made to include in this list of abbreviations any books or articles except those actually used in writing this book. The titles of more recent books and articles infrequently referred to are given in full in the footnotes.

Ak. of Ghana—see Meyerowitz.
Ak. Trad.—see Meyerowitz.
Baumgärtel, *Cultures*—E. Baumgärtel, *The Cultures of Pre-historic Egypt*, London, 1947.
von Bissing-Kees, *Re-Heiligtum*—*Das Re-Heiligtum des Königs Ne-Woser-Re*, herausgegeben von F. W. von Bissing. Vols. I, II, and III. Berlin, 1905, 1923, and 1928.
von Bissing-Kees, *Untersuchungen*—F. W. von Bissing und Hermann Kees, *Untersuchungen zu den Reliefs aus dem Re-Heiligtum des Rathures*, München, 1922.
Borchardt, *Neuserre*—L. Borchardt, *Das Grabdenkmal des Königs Ne-user-Re*, Leipzig, 1907.
Borchardt, *Sahure*—L. Borchardt, *Das Grabdenkmal des Königs Sahu-Re*, Leipzig, 1910, 1913.
Breasted, *Ancient Records*—J. H. Breasted, *Ancient Records of Egypt*, I–V, Chicago, 1906–7.
Brugsch, *Ägypt*—H. Brugsch, *Die Ägyptologie*, 1891.
Brugsch, *Geogr. Inschr.*—H. Brugsch, *Geographische Inschriften altägyptischer Denkmäler*, Leipzig, 1857–60.
Brugsch, *Rel.*—H. Brugsch, *Die Religion und Mythologie der alten Ägypter*, Leipzig, 1885–8.
Budge, *Fetish*—E. A. W. Budge, *From Fetish to God in Ancient Egypt*, London, 1934.
Budge, *Gods*—E. A. W. Budge, *The Gods of the Egyptians*, vols. I and II, London, 1904.
Budge, *Osiris*—E. A. W. Budge, *Osiris and the Egyptian Resurrection*, vols. I and II, London, 1911.

LIST OF ABBREVIATIONS

Dümichen, *Geogr. Inschr.*—J. Dümichen, *Geographische Inschriften altägyptischer Denkmäler*, Leipzig, 1863-5.
Erman-Blackman, *Literature*—A. Erman, *The Literature of the Ancient Egyptians*. Translated into English by A. M. Blackman, London, 1927.
Erman, *Memph. Theol.*—A. Erman, *Ein Denkmal memphitischer Theologie*, Berlin, 1911.
Erman, *Religion*—A. Erman, *Die Religion der Ägypter*, Berlin und Leipzig, 1934.
Fakhry, *Kheruef*—Ahmed Fakhry, 'A Note on the Tomb of Kheruef at Thebes', in *Ann. Serv.*, XLIII (1943) pp. 449-508.
Frankfort, *Kingship*—Henri Frankfort, *Kingship and the Gods*, Chicago, 1948.
Grapow, *Urkunden*—H. Grapow, *Religiose Urkunden*, Leipzig, 1915.
Gauthier, *Fêtes*—H. Gauthier, *Les Fêtes du dieu Min*, Le Caire, 1931.
Gauthier, *Personnel*—H. Gauthier, *Le Personnel du dieu Min*, Le Caire, 1931.
Gayet, *Louxor*—Gayet, *Le Temple de Louxor*, 1894.
Hierakonpolis—J. E. Quibell and F. W. Green, *Hierakonpolis*, vol. I, London, 1900.
Hopfner, *Tierkult*—Th. Hopfner, *Der Tierkult der alten Ägypter*, Wien, 1913.
Jacobsohn, *Dogm. Stell.*—H. Jacobsohn, *Die dogmatische Stellung des Königs in der Theologie der alten Ägypter*, Ägyptol. Forschung, Heft 8, 1939.
JEA—*Journal of Egyptian Archaeology*, London, 1914-.
Jéquier, *Pepi II*—G. Jéquier, *Le monument funéraire de Pepi II*, vol. II, Le Caire, 1938.
JNES—*Journal of Near Eastern Studies*, Chicago, 1942-.
Junker, *Hathor-Tefnut*—H. Junker, *Der Auszug der Hathor-Tefnut aus Nubien*, Berlin, 1911.
Junker, *Onuris*—J. Junker, *Die Onurislegende*, Wien, 1917.
Kees, *Götterglaube*—H. Kees, *Der Götterglaube im alten Ägypten*, Leipzig, 1941.
Kees, *Lesebuch*—H. Kees, *Religionsgeschichtliches Lesebuch*, Tübingen, 1928.
Kees, *Opfertanz*—H. Kees, *Der Opfertanz des ägyptischen Königs*, Leipzig, 1912.
Kees, *Totenglauben*—H. Kees, *Totenglauben und Jenseitsvorstellungen der alten Ägypter*, Leipzig, 1926.
Mercer, *Études*—S. A. B. Mercer, *Études sur les Origines de la Religion de l'Égypte*, London, 1929.
Mercer, *Horus*—S. A. B. Mercer, *Horus, Royal God of Egypt*, Grafton, Mass., 1942.

LIST OF ABBREVIATIONS

Mercer, *Pyr.*—S. A. B. Mercer, *The Pyramid Texts*, vols. I, II, III, and IV, 1952.
Mercer, *Rel.*—S. A. B. Mercer, *The Religion of Ancient Egypt*, London, 1949.
Meyerowitz, Eva L. R.—*The Akan of Ghana: Their Ancient Beliefs*, London, 1958.
Meyerowitz, Eva L. R.—*Akan Traditions of Origin*, London, 1952.
Meyerowitz, Eva L. R.—*The Sacred State of the Akan*, London, 1951.
Moret, *Rituel*—A. Moret, *Le Rituel du Culte divin journalier en Égypte*, Paris, 1902.
Moret, *Royauté*—A. Moret, *Du caractère religieux de la royauté pharaonique*, Paris, 1902.
Naville, *Deir el Bahri*—E. Naville, *The Temple of Deir el Bahri*, I, II, III, 1896–1913.
Naville, *Osorkon*—E. Naville, *The Festival Hall of Osorkon II, in the great Temple of Bubastis*, London, 1892.
Nelson, *Medinet Habu*—H. H. Nelson, *et al.*, *Medinet Habu*, Chicago, 1930.
Otto, *Stierkulte*—E. Otto, *Beiträge zur Geschichte der Stierkulte in Ägypten*, Leipzig, 1938.
Petrie, *Koptos*—W. M. F. Petrie, *Koptos*, London, 1896.
Petrie, *Egypt*—W. M. F. Petrie, *The Making of Egypt*, London, 1939.
Petrie, *Royal Tombs*—W. M. F. Petrie, *The Royal Tombs of the First Dynasty*, London, 1900.
Röder, *Urkunden*—G. Röder, *Urkunden zur Religion der alten Ägypten*, Jena, 1915.
Sacred State—see Meyerowitz.
Schäfer, *Mysterien*—H. Schäfer, *Die Mysterien des Osiris in Abydos unter König Sesostris III*, Leipzig, 1904.
Sethe, *Dram. Texte*—K. Sethe, *Dramatische Texte zu altägyptischen Mysterienspielen*, vols. I and II, Leipzig, 1928.
Sethe, *Pyr.*—K. Sethe, *Die altägyptischen Pyramidentexte*, Leipzig, 1908–22.
Sethe, *Memph. Theol.*—K. Sethe, *Das 'Denkmal memphitischer Theologie', der Schabakostein des Britischen Museums*, Leipzig, 1928.
Sethe, *Untersuchungen*—K. Sethe, *Untersuchungen zur Geschichte und Altertumskunde Ägyptens*, Leipzig, 1896 ff.
Sethe, *Urgeschichte*—K. Sethe, *Urgeschichte und älteste Religion der Ägypter*, Leipzig, 1930.
Speiser, *Origins*—E. A. Speiser, *Mesopotamian Origins*, Philadelphia, 1930.
Wainwright, *Sky Rel.*—G. A. Wainwright, *The Sky Religion in Egypt*, Cambridge, 1938.

CHAPTER I

The Divine King, the Incarnation of the God of his Clan

AKAN
Introduction: The Falcon Clan People

In the past the greatest and most important Akan kingdom in the territory which is now called Ghana was Bono; in modern times it is Asante (Ashanti). Bono was founded about 1295 and soon became powerful owing to its wealth in gold; in 1740 it was conquered by the Asante, who had established their kingdom in the forest zone to the south of it.[1] Bono then ceased to exist; its territories, in the form of a number of vassal states, were incorporated in Asante. One of these was the Bono-Takyiman state which was created in 1748; the Asante permitted its kings and queen-mothers to be chosen from princes and princesses of the Bono royal line; their descendants still rule the state today. Bono-Takyiman gained its independence in 1951; it is now called Tekyiman-Brong.

More than a thousand years ago the ancestors of the kings and queen-mothers of Bono, Asante, and Bono-Takyiman, who belong to the Ayoko clan whose totem is the falcon, ruled over a kingdom called Diadom or Djadum, literally, 'Dia (or Dja) Confederation', which was situated in the region west of the Tibesti mountain range that separates the Sahara from Nubia. Following the disturbances caused by the Arab conquest of North Africa in the seventh and eighth centuries, princes and princesses of the Dia dynasty emigrated. They were accompanied by a large number of people and they settled along the Niger bend in the region roughly

---

[1] For details see *Ak. Trad.*, pp. 29 ff.

between Djenné and Timbuktu. Either they were incorporated into an already existing Dia kingdom or confederation, or possibly they were among its founders.

In Dia or Dja near Timbuktu, the predecessors of the Bono and Bono-Takyiman kings and queen-mothers founded Diala, the capital of a city state of the same name; the predecessors of the Asante kings and queen-mothers founded, it is believed, Diana.[1] When, at the beginning of the eleventh century, Islamised Tuaregs from the Sahara conquered the kingdom, the falcon clan people, being unwilling to accept Islam, migrated, accompanied by thousands of their subjects. The Diala people finally founded the first Gbon or Bono kingdom in the region between the Red and White Volta Rivers among the Mo, Grusi-speaking aboriginals, whom they colonised. When the first Bono kingdom was conquered, rather less than 300 years later, by the ancestors of the present rulers of Mossi, princess Ameyaa together with her three sons and a large following left. They sought refuge in Gbon-Dja (*anglicé* Gonja, a state in the Northern Territories of Ghana) which had been founded at an earlier date by Gbon peoples from Dia on the Niger bend. Desiring to found their own state, however, they soon moved farther south and founded the second Gbon or Bono kingdom south of the Black Volta River about 1295. The princess Ameyaa, later called Ameyaa Kese, 'the Great', and her third son, Asaman, became the first queen-mother and king of the new state.

When the Diana people left the Niger bend region they took a different route. Led by a prince, a son of the queen-mother Nyamkomaduewuo, they moved south and settled west of the Black Volta River. There they founded the Gbona or Bona kingdom (now in the French Ivory Coast) which still borders on Gonja in the west.[2] About the year 1600 the Bona kingdom was conquered by the Mande; a princess, Ankyeo Nyame, was unwilling to remain at the court and left with some followers and went to Bono. Her daughter Bempomaa, wishing to rule over a state of her own, moved farther south and finally founded Asiakwa, a city state within the Akwamu kingdom (south-eastern Ghana). Her great-grandson

---

[1] In the dynastic name of the Asante kings, Diara-Korono, Diara is used and not Diana. However Diala, Diara, and Diana all mean 'Dia people'. The Akan today only use *na* with the significance of descendants, but the Diula (or Diala) who have remained in the Djenné region still use all three suffixes. The name Djenné is derived from Diani or Djani.

[2] *Ak. Trad.*, p. 104.

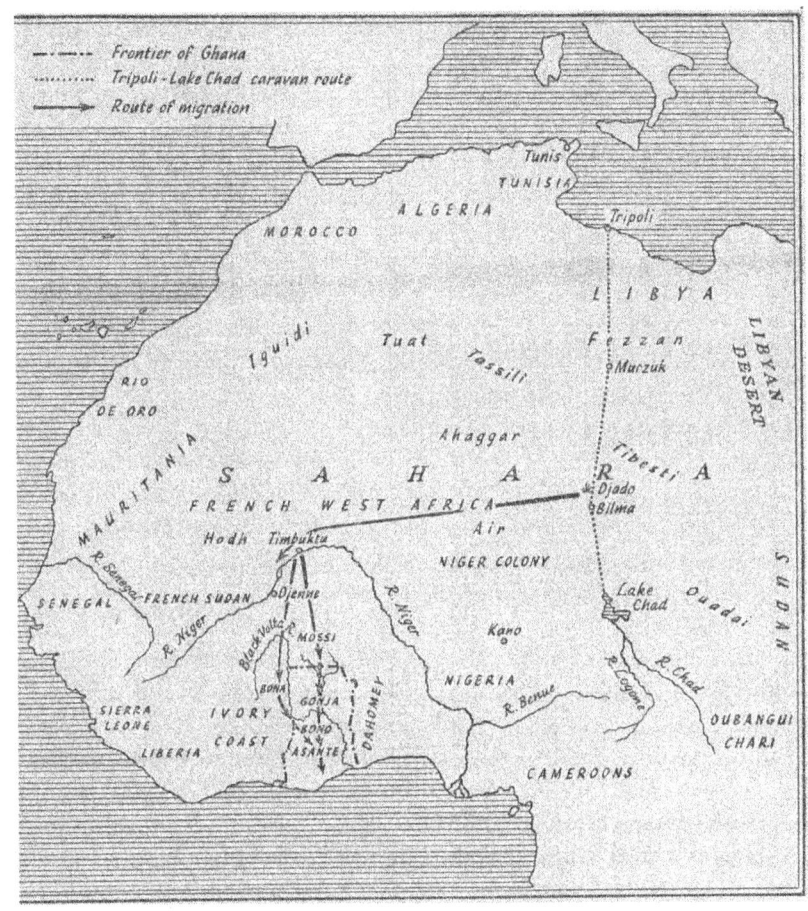

Map showing the Migration of the Akan Falcon Clan People

Osei Tutu became chief of the Kumasi state in 1699 and in 1701 made himself king of Asante, then a confederation of seven autonomous states.[1] His successor Opoku Ware conquered Bono in 1740.

The medieval Dia or Dja can be identified with the Za or Zagha (*gha* the plural suffix) who, from Ethiopia, from the beginning of our era onwards conquered large parts of the Sudan, the

---

[1] ibid., pp. 107 ff.

Sahara and North Africa.[1] They may have had a South Arabian origin.

In most of the conquered territories, especially at Diadom in the eastern Sahara, the Dia or Zagha constituted the royal clan in a confederation largely composed of three groups of people: the Libyans (Berbers), the Gara or Kora (among them the descendants of the Garamantians of antiquity), and the Tuareg who, since 2000 B.C., if not earlier, had formed confederated states with the other two peoples in various regions.[2] In the Dia kingdom on the Niger a fourth people was incorporated—Sudanese negroes of whom many had been colonised by North African and Saharan, as well as Nubian Libyans, probably long before the beginning of our era.

The Saharan Libyans called themselves Gban or Gwan in the Niger bend region. When they moved farther south and settled in the territories around the Black, Red, and White Volta Rivers, Gban and Gwan came to be pronounced Gbon and Gwon.[3] The names 'Bono' and 'Bona' are derived from Gbon and mean literally 'confederation or state (which is implied) of Gbon descendants (na or no)'.

The totem of the clan of the kings and queen-mothers of Bono and Bona in the past, and of Bono-Takyiman and Asante, was the falcon; the deity of their clan was incarnate in that bird. As it was the custom for clanspeople to identify themselves with their totem, the falcon clan people had to reign supreme, as their bird reigns in the sky, pursuing its prey with patience and endurance and never giving up till it has achieved its aim. It is therefore not surprising that the falcon clan people in Ghana, though small in numbers, created among dozens of Akan states the two most powerful and highly civilised kingdoms—Bono and Asante.

1. *The Supreme Mother-goddess*

The great deity worshipped by the ancestors of the Akan was visible as the moon and was personified as a moon Mother-goddess. She was self-begotten, self-produced, and self-born, eternal and

---

[1] For details see the author's 'The Akan and Ghana', in *MAN*, vol. LVII (1957), pp. 86–7.

[2] See p. 232 in this vol.

[3] Other variations are still preserved in names of Akan clans, states, and towns. The meaning of the name 'Akan' is not known; most probably its original form was A' Kpan (*A* being the noun prefix). A' Kpan in western Twi, the language of the Akan, corresponds to A'Gban in other dialects.

infinite, and first brought forth without the help of a male partner the firmament with its stars and the sun. She was *Atoapoma*—the Ever-ready-shooter—for she gave life by shooting the life-giving rays of the moon (fire) into men and beasts on earth. The power or spirit of the lunar fire which animated the blood and gave it life was and is still called the *kra*. The idea that life-blood is fire is not, after all, so far-fetched since oxygen is burnt in our blood as long as we are alive.

The Great Mother was venerated not only as the giver of life but also as the giver of death. She was *Odiawuono*, literally the 'Killer Mother'; the *kra*, the spark of life which she gave, she also took away again, and it returned to her after death to unite again with her lunar *kra*. Thus she became the mother of the dead and ruled not only the sky and earth but also the underworld, envisaged as barren soil in which the dead lay buried.

2. The Clan-goddess, the Manifestation of the Supreme Mother-goddess

Occasionally a woman in the dim past was possessed by the *kra*, the life-giving spirit of the moon Mother-goddess, and in that ecstatic state gave life to an *obosom*. The *obosom* represented the visible manifestation of the *kra*, the life-giving force of the supreme deity, the moon. *Obosom*, to quote an informant, 'is a small part of the deity's *kra* power in manageable size'. In the past the *obosom* was personified as a goddess and given a name, so that people might address her in prayer.

The goddess usually revealed herself to the people whom the woman had gathered around her, in times of need when there was a food shortage, for example, or when water could not be found, or when the people had to flee from an enemy. Then an antelope, a wild pig, a falcon, a leopard or some other animal would guide them to more fertile earth or to water, or would lead them to safety by taking them to a ford across a river, or to a cave where they could hide. This animal, called the *akyeneboa*, was thereupon venerated as divine, for it 'masked' (*kyene*: to mask) the goddess, and was the form she assumed when she wanted to show herself to her people. The people consequently identified themselves with the animal and adopted its characteristics; it became *ahoboa*—'the beast within oneself'. Should the *akyeneboa* happen to have been a leopard, the people became aggressive and bloodthirsty; if a sheep, then they became gentle and unwarlike; if a falcon, then the people practised patience and endurance in achieving their aim, both believed to be characteristics of this bird as it stalks its prey.

The Elder Woman, regarded as divine, gave life not only to a goddess incarnate in an animal, but also to a clan, for her people who identified themselves with the sacred animal now formed a distinct social group, and the *akyeneboa* became the totem animal. When the people of a clan united with another one, a state came into being under the rule of the Elder Woman who, one assumes, either had the stronger personality, or 'owned' the greater deity. To form a single people clan exogamy was introduced. This meant that sexual intercourse between members of a clan, now declared to be kinsmen, came to be regarded as incest and was punished by death or expulsion from the state.

3. *The Divine Queen-mother, the Incarnation of the Goddess of her Clan*

The state of the Elder Woman, originally a confederation of two clans, became in time a confederation of three or more clans each owning a city and a number of villages; seven was finally the desired number. The Elder Woman then became an *ohemmaa*,

Fig. 1
The ancient sceptre of the Akan Queen-mother, called Nyansa Pow, *the 'knot of Wisdom' (from a gold weight)*

(For details see p. 230, n. 2.)

literally 'female king' which is now generally translated as 'queen-mother', and she owned the state as a 'mother owns a child'. She was divine, for the life-giving *kra* of the founder of the state (herself the descendant of the founder of the clan) was within her, and with it she was able to give 'life' and maintain the 'life' in her state. She was also a priestess and was in charge of the cult of her clan's goddess, now the goddess of the state. The goddess was worshipped generally in a sacred grove in which a tree, usually a fig-tree, was venerated as the abode of the deity and the resting-place for her *kra*. It was the function of the goddess to act as an intermediary between the queen-mother and her people and the supreme Mother-goddess, who was regarded as too great to be approached directly. The clan's head-women ruled the people of their clan but served on the queen-mother's council (Fig. 1. The Queen-mother's sceptre). They were the priestesses of their deity.[1]

4. *The Divine King, the Incarnation of the God of his Clan*

In the course of time, owing to circumstances dealt with in Chapter II, the supreme moon Mother-goddess, the genetrix of the universe, came to be regarded as bi-sexual. Her male aspect, when thought of separately, was personified as a moon-god, her son, who like herself gave 'life'. At the same time the concept of the goddess was enlarged. She was no longer worshipped exclusively as a mother but also as a young woman, personified as her daughter, who received her life-giving power (*kra*) from the moon but her procreative force from the planet Venus. She became the sister and wife of the god. The clan *obosom* or goddess, who was still regarded as the manifestation of the supreme goddess, was now also envisaged either as bi-sexual or as a goddess and a god. They were worshipped above all as Sky fertility-deities, and as such were manifested in vegetation; by this period agriculture had become the people's main preoccupation.

On earth the queen-mother, divine because of her life-giving lunar *kra*, chose her brother or son as king to personify the god of her clan and state. Like the queen-mother he was divine thanks to his inherited lunar *kra*, and acted as the intermediary, and thus a priest, between his people and the supreme moon-god. When in time the priest-king was given secular power, a council of clan chiefs came into being, presided over by the king. This was exactly similar to the council of the head-women of the clans, presided over by the queen-mother. The king, however, acted solely as an executive; the

[1] For greater detail on this early period (Cult Type I) see *Ak. of Ghana*, ch. I.

queen-mother, as owner of the state, reserved for herself the last word in all matters of policy.

The clan goddess, being regarded solely as the manifestation of the supreme goddess, had the power of her life-giving *kra* renewed once a year, for it was believed that *kra* power fades. This was done originally by sacrificing the *akyeneboa*, the animal which personified her; the *kra* of the goddess, rejuvenated through union with the lunar *kra* of the Mother-goddess, was then resurrected in another younger animal of the same species.[1] When the clan goddess became bi-sexual the king and the queen-mother personified the clan's deity, and the king, in his role as executive for the queen-mother, was chosen to suffer the fate of the sacred animal and was sacrificed to rejuvenate his life-giving power. Since, however, a queen-mother had only a limited number of close male relatives, a proxy, the 'bearer of his *kra*' (*okra*), generally took his place.[2] After his death the king was reborn to the queen-mother who, in the rite, personified the moon Mother-goddess. In another rite he then performed with her (now personifying Venus) a sacred marriage.[3] In the first union, in which the lunar *kra* of the king-god again became one with that of the moon Mother-goddess in heaven, *kra* power was revivified; in the second, the sacred marriage, *sunsum* (generative force) was restored. It had been discovered that the union of the sexes was necessary for procreation.

The bi-sexual Supreme Being of the Akan is now called Nyame, a name derived probably from *nyam* ('shining', 'bright'), a reference to the firmament; her male aspect is personified as Nyankopon, literally the 'alone great Nyame', a name he no doubt acquired when the male *kra* became incarnate in the sun, whose life-giving power came to be regarded as greater than that of the moon.

[1] This rite has survived in one place and is described in *Ak. of Ghana*, pp. 38 ff.

[2] Among the ancient peoples the divine king was usually sacrificed every seven, nine, or twelve years. The Akan do not remember whether their ancestors also had this custom or not. For the *okra* and the development of these rites, see *Ak. of Ghana*, pp. 52 ff.

[3] If the king was the son of the queen-mother, a proxy was substituted for one party; if they were sister and brother, they may originally have performed the marriage. There is no memory of this but the king's skeleton is rubbed with the juice of a plant which is called *bedewonua*—'Desire your sister.'

EGYPT

Introduction: The Falcon Clan People

Ancient traditions make it clear that the falcon clan people who worshipped the great Mother-goddess Hathor and her son Horus entered Egypt from western Asia in groups independent of each other. Three of these groups became of historical importance: that represented by Horus the Elder, son of Hathor, whose people originated from Punt (Punt I was situated in southern Arabia, Punt II in Nubia); they were followed, or preceded, also in prehistoric times, by a second group from Punt whose people worshipped Min-Horus, son of Hathor. The third group came via Syria into Egypt under the leadership of chiefs or kings, the last of which in Egypt was deified as Osiris, son of Hathor. Details are given in the following sections of this chapter. There can be little doubt that these groups were segments of a matrilineal clan, for succession in its royal lineage was in the female line and Hathor and Horus are typical representatives of matrilineal deities.

1. Hathor in her Role as Clan and Supreme Mother-goddess

It would appear that the falcon clan people in Egypt established their first city state in a region on the east bank of the Nile, where they founded a town near the modern Atfih, called Aphroditopolis[1] by the Greeks, which is traditionally regarded as the home of Hathor. There may of course have been settlements previously founded by extended families of the falcon clan in other parts of Egypt, but among matrilineals it is the *piesie* which is important: the first city state, however small, founded by the clan's leader, ultimately descended from the divine founder of the clan.

Hathor is said to have been brought forth by the Mother-goddess Nut as a black, or reddish-black, child,[2] a reference whose meaning is clear only if we relate it not to the goddess but to the people she

---

[1] Aphroditopolis was situated in the XII *nome*, the Greek word for city state. J. Cerny, *Ancient Egyptian Religion*, pp. 18, 19, says 'the *nome* were clearly the last remnants of small independent city states'; he should have added 'and of dependent city states which formed part of confederations headed by great kings in prehistoric times and in the Old Kingdom'.
[2] Junker, *Hathor-Tefnut*, p. 15; Junker, *Onuris*, p. 76.

THE INCARNATION OF THE GOD OF HIS CLAN

represented. 'Brought forth' suggests that Hathor's people did not settle on virgin land but on land already owned by the people of the Mother-goddess Nut. Hathor's people, according to texts, came from Punt; the original Punt is believed to have been situated along the South Arabian coast,[1] the second in Nubia, in the desert east of the Nile.[2] In the first Punt Hathor's people, red-skinned,[3] may have incorporated in their clan a subject race, a small swarthy people whom the Greeks in a later age called the Eastern Aethiopians; in mythology they appear as the descendants of the Aethiop Memnon.[4] In the second Punt the falcon clan people absorbed 'negroes' into their society, for in a Denderah text Hathor is called '... in this thy name: Negress'.[5] The falcon clan people who worshipped Min-Horus, and who also came from Punt, called their god 'Strong Horus who subjected the "negroes" and who is first in Nubia'.[6] At the annual festival of Min a 'negro' used to recite ritual formulae so that the worshippers of Min should never forget their past victories.[7]

Hathor, according to a Denderah text, flew from Punt to Egypt in the shape of a female falcon.[8] But as the 'Lady of Punt'[9] or 'from Punt', she was envisaged as a lioness.[10] The falcon, in which she was incarnate, was emblematic of her clan; the lioness indicated to the Egyptians that Hathor's people came from Punt, since Punt in Nubia was ruled by a royal lineage of a lion clan.[11] Hathor's people must therefore have been composed, in accordance with the law of exogamy, of people whose mother was of the falcon clan[12] and whose father was from the lion clan or some other clan in the confederation. The supreme Mother-goddess of the Punt kingdom or

---

[1] Brugsch, *Ägypt.*, p. 23; Morgan, *Préhistoire*, p. 252.
[2] *Hathor-Tefnut*, p. 26.
[3] Brugsch, p. 22. The Egyptians distinguished four races: red-skinned people from the southern Arabian coast who came to dominate Egypt; a yellow race in the east of Egypt, black-skinned negroes, and a white-skinned people, the Libyans.
[4] F. W. König, *Die Geschichte Elams*.
[5] Dümichen, *Hist. Inschr.* II, 57 d; Junker, *Hathor-Tefnut*, p. 18.
[6] Gauthier, *Fêtes*, p. 202.
[7] ibid., pp. 158, 199. These so-called negroes were not true negroes. See Junker, 'The First Appearance of Negroes in History', *JEA* (1921), pp. 121 ff.
[8] *Hathor-Tefnut*, p. 12.
[9] *Onuris*, p. 73.
[10] Hathor as lioness deity of Philae, *Hathor-Tefnut*, pp. 15, 34; *Onuris*, p. 73.
[11] The true ruler of Punt a lion, *Hathor-Tefnut*, pp. 15, 16, 24.
[12] A child always belongs to the clan of its mother.

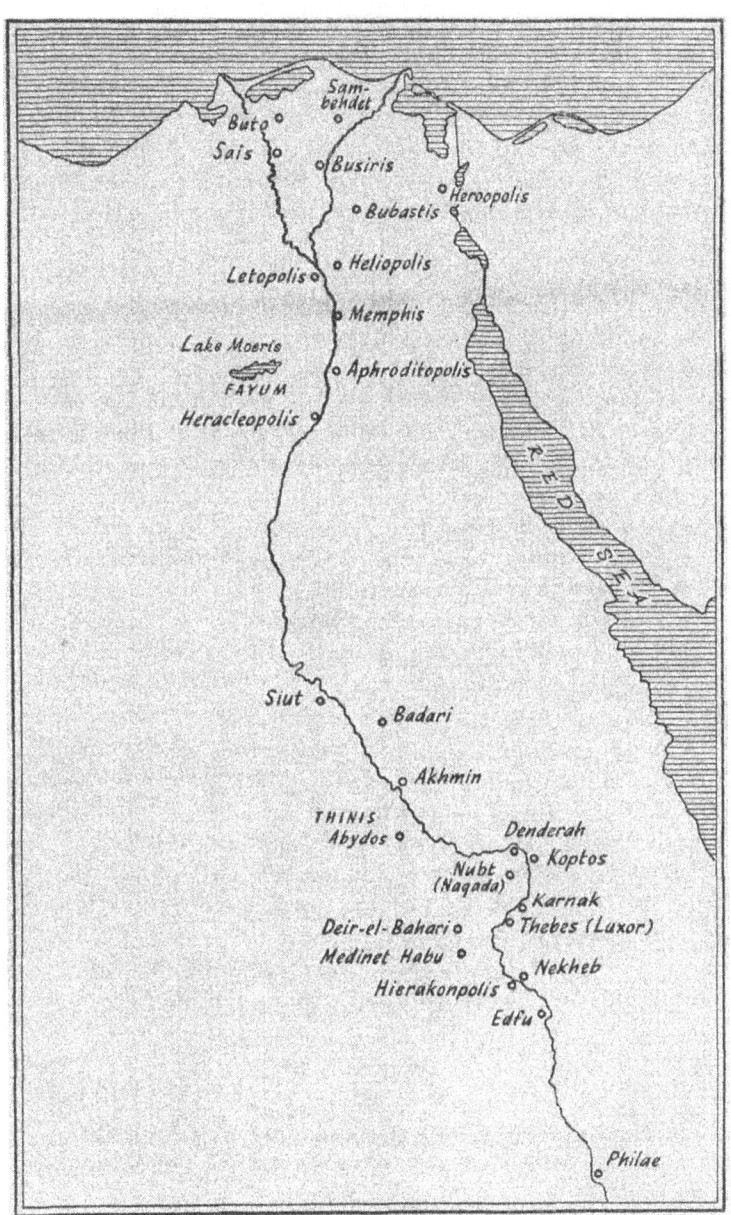

Ancient Egypt

confederation of clans was the lioness-deity Tefnut[1] who, when her cult was introduced into Egypt in prehistoric times, became one of the greatest of all deities. In the historic period she was overshadowed by Hathor, who became the supreme Mother-goddess owing to the political supremacy of her people. Tefnut, who gradually declined in significance, was finally completely identified with Hathor.

The Mother-goddess Hathor, like Tefnut and Nut, was a moon-goddess. She was venerated as the goddess of the west because the lunar month started with the first appearance of the crescent in the western sky. She is sometimes depicted carrying in her hand a notched palm-branch with which she kept count of the days of the lunar year. At Denderah she is called the 'Mistress of the Beginning of the Year'.[2] The palm-tree was her abode and thus sacred to her (the palm symbolised the moon Mother-goddesses throughout the ancient East; this was so with the Akan also.)[3] As the goddess of the night sky Hathor was also regarded as the mother of the sun to which she gave birth in the eastern sky.

Hathor, like Tefnut and other goddesses, was the 'Lady of the Flame'[4]—the flame representing the fire of the moon and sun. As 'Lady of the Flame' she gave birth and destroyed the enemies of her people. As giver of birth she was a *hemsut* goddess:[5] *hemsut* is the word for the female *ka*, which is identical with the Akan female *kra*. When the Mother-goddess became bi-sexual, the *kra* also became bi-sexual; *she* gave birth through the power of her female *kra*, *he* gave life through his male *kra*, or generative power.

Hathor as 'Mother of the Dead' and the 'Lady of the Underworld' played an important part in connection with the welfare of the dead, whom she is said to have received in the west, where the sun sets and where the new moon first becomes visible. Hathor as a clan-goddess was incarnate in the falcon, but in her form of Sky fertility-goddess, or Venus, she was incarnate in the cow. She is generally depicted with the full moon between cow horns, sometimes with a star on the tip of each horn, or with the sun disk

---

[1] The 'Kingdom of Tefnut', with certain priestesses of Thebes, its heiresses, is mentioned on inscriptions at Thebes from the 25th and 26th dynasties (see Sethe, *Urgeschichte*, p. 62, n. 2).
[2] Mariette, *Denderah*, 1873, p. 207.
[3] *Sacred State*, p. 73, *Ak. of Ghana*, pp. 48, 134 n. 4, 135 n. 1.
[4] *Onuris*, p. 110; *Hathor-Tefnut*, p. 34.
[5] Depicted as such in Pl. 10.

between cow horns when she was viewed as the mother of the sun. As such her abode became the sycamore fig-tree; at Memphis it was called the 'Living Body of Hathor'. (see also Pl. 4).

Hathor's male aspect was personified as Horus. As among the Akan, the god was regarded as the son of the Mother-goddess and as such a moon-god and god of the night sky. The Sky fertility-god Horus became the husband of the goddess and the sacred marriage between Hathor and Horus was still celebrated annually at Edfu in historic times. Owing to historical and political circumstances the clan-goddess Hathor became the supreme Mother-goddess, first of the prehistoric states founded by the falcon clan people (see next sections) and later of the 'Two Lands', historic ancient Egypt.

2. Horus, the Son of Hathor

More information is available about Horus than about any other god embodied in an animal, owing to the fact that he became the dynastic god after the unification of the country in historic times. His name, hr (Greek: Horus) was written in earliest times with the crouching falcon, showing that the god was identified with the bird.[1] The crouching falcon, however, had a different meaning from that of the falcon standing upright, which came to symbolise not only Horus but also the Pharaoh who was his incarnation.

Among the Akan the crouching falcon, in contrast to the upright one, represented the Mother-goddess of the falcon clan. In the Bono-Takyiman state, the royal spokesman acting as intermediary between the king and the queen-mother still carries a golden staff surmounted by a male and a female falcon.[2] The female falcon *osansa*, (reputed to be small and fast-flying, probably *Falco peregrinus*) sitting on two eggs represents the falcon moon Mother-goddess, the deity of the clan; the two eggs represent her two children, the queen-mother and the king. The tall upright falcon (*akroma*, a bigger and heavier species of hawk) is placed above the female on a perch and represents the god of the falcon dynasty. He is, however, no longer a moon- but a sun-god. In Egypt also the proud upright falcon came to represent the solar Horus. The crouching falcon of prehistoric times must originally have been

[1] Mercer, *Horus*, pp. 96, 97.
[2] For illustration see *Sacred State*, Pl. 29; the staff surmounted by the male and female falcons is on the extreme right.

bi-sexual and personified the lunar 'female Horus', that is to say, Hathor.[1]

On a limestone relief found at Hierakonpolis, Horus (Heru-Nub) is shown crouching on a dome-shaped cone (Fig. 2) and Horus-Shu-Onuris crouching on a truncated cone (Fig. 3). Among the Akan the cone and the truncated cone represent shrines for the *kras* of deities and, from the period of Cult Type II onwards, were used in addition to the tree in the sacred grove.[2] Both Horuses were

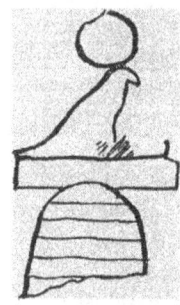

Fig. 2
The falcon Horus crouching on a dome-shaped cone. Hierakonpolis, *I*, Pl. XLVI, fig. 7

Fig. 3
The falcon Horus-Shu-Onuris crouching on a truncated cone, wearing the Upper and Lower Egyptian Crown. Hierakonpolis, *I*, Pl. XLVI, fig. 11

Fig. 4
The falcon Horus walking on a crescent moon. Hierakonpolis, *I*, Pl. XIX, fig. 1

moon-gods.[3] Horus (Heru-Nub) of Hierakonpolis or Nekhen was probably the god of the founders of the city and was venerated by the early dynastic Horus kings, who resided in Hierakonpolis; Horus-Shu-Onuris was the god of another section of the falcon clan which in prehistoric times had founded El Khab on the opposite bank of the Nile.[4] There are said to be twenty-three falcon-gods in all, who perhaps represent the various peoples of this scattered clan.

[1] Kees, *Lesebuch*, p. 37.
[2] p. 62. see also *Ak. of Ghana*, pp. 49, 50, Pls. 37, 38, 39, 41.
[3] For the lunar Horus see Mercer, *Horus*, p. 111; for Horus-Shu-Onuris, Junker, *Onuris*, p. 136.
[4] Junker, *Hathor-Tefnut*, p. 4.

TWO AKAN QUEEN-MOTHERS

1. The late Queen-mother of Asante, Nana Kwadu Yiadom. Her attendants have a lunar swastika engraved into their short-cropped hair. (From a postcard; permission to use the photograph was given to me in 1946.)

2. The Queen-mother of Bono-Takyiman (Tekyiman-Brong), Nana Afua Abrafo in ochre-coloured mourning cloth.

3. Head of the goddess Hathor with cow's ears and a head-dress ending in spirals which symbolise her as a goddess of birth and creation. (For a Hathor head of this type in gold decorating an Akan ceremonial gun see *Sacred State*, Pl. XXX.) (Reproduced by courtesy of the Trustees of the British Museum.)

THE INCARNATION OF THE GOD OF HIS CLAN

The falcon-god was always the same Horus but emphasis was placed on different traits in his character owing largely to the history of the people who worshipped him.[1]

Some scholars see in the crouching falcon the mummified sacred hawk of later times. The mummification of sacred animals was a more elaborate form of the custom, practised in the prehistoric period, of burying animals in cemeteries, carefully wrapped up in mats and linen. It recalls the Akan custom of burying animals which personify clan deities (totem animals). These also are carefully wrapped up and the same rites are performed for them as for members of the clan to which they belong; they are then buried in a part of the clan's cemetery. Live falcons, which, until recently, were kept by the kings and queen-mothers at Takyiman, were mummified in a primitive way when they died. Their bodies were dried, encased in white clay, wrapped in white cloth and placed in coffins decorated with divine symbols. The birds were given a royal funeral and buried, according to their sex, either in the king's or the queen-mother's cemetery.

In Egypt the *ka* had the same nature and function as the *kra*. When a prince in Egypt succeeded to the throne, the *ka* symbol was enclosed in his Horus name. This was to show that the Pharaoh was the incarnation of the immortal *ka* of Horus, the god of his clan and lineage. The falcon-god Horus was thus the totem of a matrilineally organised clan, and the animals buried or mummified by the Egyptians originally, if not also later, represented clan deities. Further, as has been shown, the crouching falcon referred to Horus the lunar clan deity or 'Female Horus'; the upright falcon of later times to Horus the dynastic god, first lunar, then solar and incarnate in the Pharaoh.

5. *Horus the Elder, Son of Hathor*

In the minds of the Egyptians the 'time of the gods' or the 'time of the god' had really existed. The particular gods they thought of were Atum, Geb, Osiris, Horus and, most often, Re. Nor by this term do the Egyptians always mean a vague reference to time immemorial.[2] It was believed that the gods had lived on earth and had actually ruled over it, or more precisely over Egypt. Indeed, the

[1] And, furthermore, to the planet, other than the moon, which gave them their *ka* and thus their character (Cult Type II), see pp. 60, 61.
[2] cf. Cerny, *Ancient Egyptian Religion*, London, 1952, p. 46.

priest Manetho of Sebennytos, who in Ptolemaic times wrote a history of Egypt in Greek, and the fragmentary papyrus from about the time of Ramses II (now preserved in the Turin Museum) prefix the lists of human kings with a list of gods. They are accompanied by numbers which, in the papyrus, indicate the years of their lives, and in Manetho the length of their reigns. It is evident that the earlier kings, whose names had been forgotten, were represented collectively by the god whom they had incarnated during their reigns. The later ones, who were recalled by their own names, were mentioned individually. The gods thus symbolised dynasties of city states, or, more probably, the confederations of pre-dynastic city states, which in the course of time became part of either the Lower or the Upper Egyptian kingdom.

The dynasties of Lower and Upper Egypt, which preceded the historical one of the Pharaohs, would seem to have been listed in the so-called Great Ennead of Heliopolis. Much time and labour have been spent in attempting to discover the primitive nucleus of the Ennead, which is clearly historical; I shall try to substantiate my theory in the following passages. At the head of the Ennead stood Atum, who was regarded as the first living man-god,[1] that is to say, a king who was the incarnation of a god. From him issued (the dynasties of) Shu and Tefnut (from Punt, see last section), who became the parents or predecessors of (the dynasties of) Geb and Nut, who in turn preceded (the dynasties of) Osiris, Isis, Set, and Nephthys. Horus, son of Isis, incarnate in the Pharaohs, is sometimes mentioned as the tenth god.

Originally it would seem that the city states were each ruled by a divine woman or queen-mother and a *saru*, a council of men,[2] headed by an elder, whose office may have been in many ways similar to that of the *Korontihene* of the Akan. The *Korontihene* in the past was the ruler of the men and the administrator of the state; he was not divine as he had not the life-giving power of the queen-mother,[3] who may or may not have shared her office with a life-

---

[1] Budge, *Gods*, II, p. 349.
[2] A. Moret, *Des Clans aux Empires*, 1923, p. 163.
[3] For the *Korontihene* as the ruler of men before kingship was introduced, see *Ak. of Ghana*, p. 51. The *Korontihene*'s office is still in existence. He came from a different clan from that of the queen-mother. In Egypt the office of vizier (*T'ate*), governor, leader of Government approximated to that of the *Korontihene*, and the elder, or chief of the *saru*, may have been his predecessor in prehistoric times.

THE INCARNATION OF THE GOD OF HIS CLAN

giving priest-chief, her brother or son, but who had originally no secular power. The insistence of the Egyptians on the 'Great Throne of Atum'[1] right through the ages suggests that the divine priest-chiefs, incarnations of the ichneumon god Atum,[2] were the first who actually ruled as divine kings. That their kingdom was a confederation of matrilineal clans is suggested by the legends which tell of some events connected with Atum's reign (see below). The capital was probably Pa Atemt; in the Bible the town is called Pithom; the Greeks at a much later date called it Heroonpolis.[3] It was situated on the large canal which ran from the Red Sea to the Nile, not far from the Sinai Peninsula. The Greeks described the place as the 'Gate to the East'.[4]

One of the clans in Atum's confederation must have been that of the Mother-goddess Hathor and her son Horus the Elder (Haroeris), for Horus the Elder was regarded as a son of Atum (*Pyr.* 881b, 874b) before the Ennead (i.e. the dynasties) existed.[5] Two other clans, possibly the original ones, whose people had formed the confederation with those of Atum, were represented by the lion-god Shu and the lioness-goddess Tefnut (i.e. lion clan); for the earliest

---

[1] Ramses II addressing himself to his deceased father says, 'while I shine as Re for the people, being upon the Great Throne of Atum as Horus, son of Isis', after Breasted, *Ancient Records*, III, par. 272.

[2] Sethe, *Urgeschichte*, par. 116, p. 96, believes the cult of Atum in the form of an ichneumon to be of a late period; on the contrary, it ought to go back to the earliest times. If Atum was still worshipped in that form, one can presume that people of the ichneumon clan were still in existence, and continued the ancient worship which the priests and their theology had left untouched. Evidence that the ichneumon was the sacred animal of the god is clear from the story that Atum changed himself into this animal in a fight against a snake in order to help his people, a common action of a clan god. The snake with which Atum is sometimes identified was probably that of the aboriginal clanspeople, owners of the land on which Atum's people built their state. A snake god Quertet was worshipped at Pa Atemt, the capital of Atum's state (Budge, *Gods*, II, p. 353).

[3] Budge, loc. cit.

[4] Sethe, op. cit., p. 87, believes in a Heliopolitan kingdom that preceded that of the Pharaohs. So far all archaeological evidence is lacking since excavations carried out by Schiaparelli and others at Heliopolis speak against this theory (Baumgärtel, *Cultures*, p. 51). Pa Atemt (Heroonpolis), however, seems to have preceded Heliopolis, where from the 2nd or 3rd Dynasty onwards Re-Atum was worshipped, as the capital of a kingdom that was ruled by kings in whom the solar god Atum was incarnate.

[5] Mercer, *Pyr.*, IV, p. 181. Mercer, in *Literary Criticism of the Pyramid Texts*, 1956, p. 47, attributes this text to the Horus kings of Upper and Lower Egypt before the unification of the country, that is to say, to a later date.

THE INCARNATION OF THE GOD OF HIS CLAN

triad was formed by Atum, Shu, and Tefnut. A Pyramid text (*Pyr.* 447) reads as follows: 'O Atum, together with the two lions, ye double power of the gods, yourselves, who created yourselves, that is Shu together with Tefnut [who] created the gods, begat the gods and established the gods.'

'Created, begat and established the gods' can be interpreted as referring to the setting-up and acknowledging of clan gods, whose people had come to settle and thus joined the confederation. Tefnut was called 'the daughter of Atum without a mother' (*Pyr.* 1248); she was therefore not 'brought forth' by Atum's mother and wife, as was Hathor by Nut. Shu, however, was 'flesh and bone of Re'[1] (Atum); his mother was the goddess Iusaaset, the mother and wife of Atum.[2] The lion clan was represented by two different deities, who were, no doubt, the same deity under different names,[3] since they possessed 'one soul between them'. This suggests that their people came to Pa Atemt from different places. According to all the traditions Tefnut's people came from Punt, and those of Shu may have come with Atum's people (flesh and bone, i.e. twin clans) possibly from Syria or Palestine. Atum has many of the characteristics of a patrilineal god; the matrilineal peoples, represented by the goddesses Tefnut, Iusaaset, Hathor and so forth, who were evidently stronger, may have supplied the framework of the state;[4] the divine kingship thus grew out of patrilineal and matrilineal concepts of the state and its ruler.[5]

---

[1] Budge, Hymn to Shu, *Fetish*, pp. 418, 419.

[2] Budge, *Gods*, II, p. 354.

[3] Tefnut's original name may have been Tefent (Tefen with west Semitic feminine ending *t*). The name Tefent instead of Tefnut appears in the 'Legend of Shu and Geb when they reigned as Kings on Earth'. Shu is called Tefen in *Pyr.* 317; Shu may have been the title of the god or perhaps the name of the first divine king of the lion clan who incarnated the god.

[4] Matrilineal gods are invariably the sons and husbands of goddesses. Atum had no mother; he is said to have risen out of the primeval watery abyss and to have created himself by uttering his own name. These features, if not his own, he would seem to have adopted from the great creator-god Nun who sometimes takes the place of Atum at the head of the Heliopolitan Ennead. On the other hand, he had wives, the above-mentioned goddess Iusaaset the mother of Shu, and Nebt-hetep, who was a cow-goddess (Budge, *Gods*, I, 354). These so-called wives can be regarded as the goddesses of clans who came under the supremacy of the ruling clan, for which there are many examples (see Neith and Nephthys as wives of Set, also Nekhbet was a wife of Set and so forth).

[5] For the ideas which contributed to the creation of the divine kingship see *Ak. of Ghana*, pp. 51 ff.

THE INCARNATION OF THE GOD OF HIS CLAN

According to legend, a war broke out in the distant past and Atum was forced to flee from his enemies.[1] Shu, faithful, defeated them twice but not, it would seem, before he and Thoth (ape clan)[2] had brought the 'angry Tefnut' back from Punt. She apparently had run away and her people had refused to fight.[3] According to another version Shu and Tefnut brought the 'angry Hathor' back from Punt.[4] When victory was finally achieved, 'Atum spoke to his son Shu: Thou hast destroyed my enemies. My members have grown again because my children [i.e. clans in the confederation], who had been distant from me, have returned to me.'[5] The hero who brought back the goddesses was called Onuris; his name is said to mean 'He who brought back the distant ones'.[6] He was depicted as either Shu or Horus the Elder; more evidence of the close connection between the lion and the falcon clan people.

The Atum kingdom was eventually destroyed by Shu. According to the 'Legend of Shu and Geb when they reigned as Kings on Earth',[7] Shu one day left Memphis,[8] possibly the capital of his city state, to visit his father Re (i.e. Atum). He crossed the Nile and established himself on the throne of Atum at Aat Nebes, then the residence of the kings. Desert hordes destroyed the place and at a later date Geb invaded the kingdom of Shu. (There is reason to

---

[1] Junker, *Hathor-Tefnut*, pp. 4 ff.

[2] Junker, *Onuris*, p. 95. Thoth from Pnubs situated behind Punt was incarnate in the ape.

[3] Among the Akan it sometimes happened in the past that a clan, dissatisfied with the conduct of affairs, simply packed up and left, and in the case of war refused to fight. An example is the revolt of the people on the outbreak of war between the Bono and the Asante in 1740. Many clan chiefs ruling towns and villages took their people, those of their own clan and others, with them and migrated to other lands (*Ak. Trad.*, p. 42). When, after the war, the king of the newly created Bono-Takyiman state, the successor state of Bono, asked them to return, only a few chiefs with a few of their people obeyed.

[4] Junker, *Onuris*, p. 132. There was further the 'angry Sekhmet' and the 'angry Nekhbet'. Sekhmet was a lioness-goddess and probably represented another branch of the lion clan, Sekhmet being another name for Tefnut, with whom she was identified.

Sekhmet's people settled chiefly at Memphis, capital of a city state, whose god was Ptah, and Sekhmet became the wife of Ptah (see p. 40 n. 4). The vulture-goddess Nekhbet became the guardian deity of Upper Egypt; her people settled mainly at Nekheb.

[5] *Onuris*, p. 132.   [6] ibid., p. 131.   [7] In Budge, *Fetish*, pp. 438 ff.

[8] Prehistoric Memphis is believed to have been Hininsu which the Greeks called Herakleopolis. It was situated some twenty miles south of historic Memphis.

believe that the people of Geb also came from Punt, see below.) Shu was defeated by Geb and 'went up to heaven with his followers'. Tefnut fought on after Shu's death but Geb 'laid hands upon her with great violence at Pkharti, and a very great commotion took place in the palace'. Geb then established himself as king.

Evidence of Shu's kingly character is confirmed in other contexts for he is called the 'hero' in a late inscription found at El-Arish,[1] and when he succeeded Atum as a great king he drew up a list of *nomes* and cities which had been founded or conquered by his ancestors and himself.

Geb's kingly character is also emphasised; the 'throne of Geb' continued to play a prominent part in historic Egypt; even the deceased Pharaohs occupied the 'throne of Geb' in heaven.[2] He is generally depicted as a goose or as a bearded man with a goose's head; that is to say, the kings who incarnated Geb were of the goose clan. The queens who incarnated Nut, on the other hand, were of the bee clan[3] and came from Punt in Nubia. Geb says to Nut in a text: 'Thou wert powerful in the body of Tefnut, before thou wert born',[4] meaning before Nut became a state goddess and 'appeared as queen'.[5] Nut originally seems to have been the same goddess as the Libyan Nit, Greek Neith, whose queens, also of the bee clan, founded or settled in Sais in Lower Egypt. Also Geb is the only one among the gods who is represented wearing the phallic sheath, which is regarded as a Libyan article of attire,[6] and with the Lower Egyptian crown, the crown of Neith.

Geb in the myths became an earth-god, barley was grown 'on the ribs of Geb'.[7] He was particularly concerned with the division of the land of Egypt; for instance, he acted as arbiter in the struggle between Horus and Set, that is between the kings incarnating the gods Horus and Set; he is envisaged here as the king who owned the lands before them (see below). As a Sky fertility-god Geb was

---

[1] Röder, *Urkunden*, p. 150.

[2] Sethe, *Urgeschichte*, par. 74; Erman-Blackman, *Literature*, p. 143.

[3] Sethe, op. cit., par. 82.

[4] A. Rusch, 'Die Entwickelung der Himmelsgöttin Nut zu einer Totengottheit', *Mitteilungen der Vorderasiatischen-Ägyptischen Gesellschaft*, 27 Jahrgang, 1922. In the Pyr. Texts, Ut. 684, Tefnut is regarded as the mother of Nut.

[5] Rusch, second verse.

[6] E. A. W. Budge, *The Greenfield Papyrus in the British Museum*, 1912, Pl. 1, p. 106.

[7] Sethe, op. cit., IV, p. 146 (14).

incarnated in the bull (*Pyr.* 316a), the counterpart of Nut as the 'Great Wild Cow'.

The Mother-goddess Nut was, like Tefnut and Hathor, a heaven goddess, and, like them, was the mother of the sun. In the Pyramid texts Nut rather than Hathor looks after the deceased Pharaohs, protects them and assists them in their resurrection. No doubt this was because Nut, as the supreme goddess of a kingdom which was inherited by Horus kings, was still regarded in later times as having precedence over Hathor.

The Geb-Nut dynasty was followed by one which worshipped Horus the Elder (Haroeris). According to *Pyr.* 466a 'Horus is of the seed of Geb'; in other words, the Geb kings were succeeded by a chief of the falcon clan (whose ancestors one may assume had founded Aphroditopolis) who had made himself king. The transfer of power seems to have been accompanied by violence, for some texts refer to a blood bath at Memphis (Herakleopolis),[1] then capital of Upper Egypt (see next section), and in historic times Pharaoh as Onuris-Horus is depicted as a lion killing the goose (namely Geb) before the god Harendotus (Horus the avenger of his father).[2]

In the most ancient texts Horus the Elder was called 'Lord of Letopolis',[3] a town north-east of the historic Memphis and the main centre of his cult. His birth-place is said to have been Kus near Nubt (Ombos);[4] Nubt was the capital of a confederation whose state god was Set. At Kus the 'Lord of Letopolis' butchered Set;[5] at Kus Horus the Elder was called for the first time 'Lord of the South'.[6] In *Pyr.* 242 the deceased Pharaoh is identified with the Sun-god and Horus the Elder of Kus as supreme over the gods and unites the lands and heavens under his leadership.

At some time, either before or after the victory in the south, the kings incarnating Horus the Elder invaded the delta region from Letopolis and conquered the Lower Egyptian kingdom which had been founded at Sais. Horus the Elder was consequently given the title 'Horus of Libya who lifts his arm'[7] since Lower Egypt was then predominantly inhabited by Libyans. In the *Sed* festival depicted on the walls of the Sun temple of Ne-Woser-Re, Horus of Libya represents Lower Egypt together with Neith, and the Pharaoh receives from him the *was* sceptre, in addition to the crook and flail,[8] evidence of the historical importance of the god.

[1] *Onuris*, p. 38.   [2] ibid., pp. 3, 4.   [3] ibid., p. 41.   [4] ibid., pp. 33, 34.
[5] ibid., p. 41.   [6] ibid., p. 34.   [7] Mercer, *Études*, p. 24.   [8] See p. 161.

4 The Divine King Osiris, Incarnation of Horus the Elder

There is reason to believe that Osiris and his followers—Osiris here representing the first chief or king of an Osirian line—came to Egypt from Syria and that his people brought with them a higher culture and civilisation than was extant at that time in the Nile valley.[1]

All traditions make the divine Osiris, the last of his line, king; his regal character is most striking; he is most commonly represented as a bearded man, crowned in various ways. He was also depicted as a falcon; his two sisters, Isis and Nephthys, were, if not in human shape, portrayed as falcons. Osiris was regarded as a son of Hathor (*Pyr.* 466a) and in some representations the *menat*, an ornament sacred to Hathor, hangs from his back. The god incarnate in Osiris was undoubtedly Horus and, as we shall see, the lunar Horus the Elder.

All the legends, supported by modern research, connect Osiris, more precisely the Osirians, from the beginning with the eastern delta and the town where the god Anzti was worshipped (later called Busiris by the Greeks). It would seem that the Osirians first settled there.[2] In a Pyramid text (614) it is said, 'Horus has made thee (Osiris) to live in this thy name Anzti.' This passage, in other words, states that Osirian kings, incarnations of Horus, succeeded kings of a dynasty who incarnated the ram-god Anzti.[3]

At some time the Osirians, or more probably only a prince and princess with followers, left the eastern delta region to settle elsewhere. The evidence suggests that they went to Siut in Upper Egypt, then capital of a city state whose kings incarnated the wolf-god Upwaut, the 'Opener-of-the-Ways'. The title of the god indicates that the wolf clan people had opened up virgin land for cultivation,[4] and thus were the first settlers in the land.

---

[1] Osiris is said by Plutarch to have taught agriculture, promulgated a code of laws etc.; cf. Budge, *Fetish*, p. 177.

[2] Frankfort, *Kingship*, p. 200, however, argues differently and believes Abydos to have been the original centre of Osiris worship.

[3] The crown of Anzti or Andjeti consisted of two feathers on the horizontal horns of an extinct species of ram. Anzti (alone among the *nome* symbols) was of human shape and appeared with feathers, crook, and flail as did Osiris. It is, therefore, widely believed that Osiris derived these attributes from a deified delta king.

[4] For the role of Upwaut at the *Sed* festival as 'Opener' of the land, see p. 155 ff.

4. Illustration from the Papyrus of Ani. On the left the Falcon god Soker wearing the crown and insignia of Osiris. In the centre Hathor as goddess of Birth and Rebirth, symbolised by the hippopotamus. In her right hand she carries a flame, fire from the moon; she is seen wearing the moon disk between cow horns. In her left hand she carries the ankh, the symbol for life. In front of her is a table with offerings, destined for the *ka* of the deceased scribe Ani. On the right Hathor, symbolised by the cow as Queen of the Underworld, appears out of the funerary mountain of western Thebes. The cow decorated with the eight-petalled flower and the papyrus plants indicates that she is also the goddess of procreation and generation. In the corner below the tomb of Ani. (Reproduced by courtesy of the Trustees of the British Museum.)

5. The Pharaoh Ramses II wearing the White Crown with the uraeus, the symbol of royalty, and holding the crook and flail of Osiris in his hands. (Reproduced by courtesy of the Trustees of the British Museum.)

6. The Egyptian Queen Teta-Shery, wearing the vulture head-dress of the goddess Mut and the uraeus (broken off). (Reproduced by courtesy of the Trustees of the British Museum.)

THE INCARNATION OF THE GOD OF HIS CLAN

In the *Memphite Theology* II Geb calls Horus 'That heir, the son of my son, the Upper Egyptian Wolf, the Opener-of-the-body, Upwaut.' The meaning of the pronouncement made by Geb can only be that a king, incarnating the wolf-god Upwaut, opened the body (i.e. the royal lineage) of the falcon clan, and produced Horus, a falcon-wolf king, who finally succeeded to the throne of Geb. This assumption is supported in various ways. In a Pyramid text (2108a) it is said of Osiris 'adorned as a god, thy face a wolf, Osiris'. Further, Pharaoh's Upper Egyptian Royal Ancestors, the 'Souls of Nekhen' are depicted with the heads of wolves, and not falcon-headed like those of Lower Egypt, the 'Souls of Pe', for which there must be some reason, since they also were of the falcon clan. Moreover, the standard of Upwaut shows a protuberance, the so-called *shedshed*, and Upwaut is called 'Lord of the *Shedshed*'.[1] The *shedshed* probably represents a womb encasing a foetus[2] and would thus illustrate Upwaut as the 'Opener-of-the-body'.[3] The Osirian falcon king at the head of an Upwaut state would naturally incarnate the wolf-god, in addition to Horus, whose worship now became a private affair in the royal lineage. The king embodying several gods is one of the principles of the dogma of the divine kingship and is, in many cases, based on political expediency.[4]

From Siut the Osirian kings then managed, either by agreement or intrigue, to make themselves rulers of the kingdom. No texts seem to exist which refer to the transfer of power, which is curious, since the circumstances accompanying the succession of the previous dynasties were so well remembered. The succession then, from the Horus kings, 'the seed of Geb', to the Horus-Upwaut kings of the Osirian line must have taken place without incident; possibly the line of Horus the Elder had no suitable heir. In the Heliopolitan Ennead Horus the Elder is not mentioned, which may suggest that the dynasty represented by Horus the Elder and the Osirian dynasty were regarded as one, since the kings of both lines incarnated this god, the god of their lineage.

The conquest by Horus the Elder of the Set country in the south and of Lower Egypt in the north, was possibly carried out by Osirian

[1] *Pyr.* 5394, 800a, 1036a.
[2] A. Moret, *Mystères égyptiens*, 1913, pp. 79–80, 82.
[3] The princess whose body Upwaut opened to produce the heir to the throne seems to have been represented at the *Sed* festival by the 'divine mother of Siut'. See p. 156.
[4] Hocart, *Kingship*, p. 20.

kings, since Osiris is usually credited with having been the first king who ruled over a united Egypt. The end of the Osirian kingdom was caused through Set; according to the legends the last Osiris was murdered by the Set king, and this had important repercussions on the history of ancient Egypt.

The divine king Osiris was deified after his death; all the powers attributed to the various gods he had incarnated in life, the lunar Horus the Elder, Anzti, Upwaut, Anubis, the city god of Abydos, and so forth, were ascribed to him. Thus he came to be worshipped by the people as a moon-god, 'Osiris the Moon'. He was the 'power and influence that emanated from the moon'[1] and in spring the Egyptians celebrated the festival called 'The Entrance of Osiris into the Moon'. His soul (*ba*) became incarnate in the lunar Apis, a Sky fertility-god, who caused the Nile flood to fertilise the land of Egypt.[2] Osiris also became incarnate in a special form of Horus called Soker or Sokaris, who was the 'Great Lord, the Lord of the Sky'.[3] Soker was sometimes depicted in the form of a crouching falcon, or as a man with the head of a falcon (Pl. 4). In the Pyramid texts the name Soker appears only as another name for Osiris, and in Ptolemaic times the two were completely identified. Soker was especially worshipped at Abydos in the temple of Osiris. In Memphis he had his own temple; according to a legend Osiris was drowned at Memphis by Set, and Soker means 'the coffined one'.[4] The annual festival at Memphis, in which the barque containing the coffin of the god was borne on a sledge in solemn procession, possibly re-enacted the death of Osiris. At Memphis too Osiris was worshipped in his form of Ptah-Soker-Osiris; Ptah was the state god of Memphis and in historic times stood in a special relationship to the Pharaohs.[5] Soker was regarded as a son of Horus,[6] which can only mean that Osiris-Soker was the son or successor of Horus the Elder, or of the kings who incarnated this god before Osiris.

The dead king-god Osiris was venerated above all as the ancestor of the Pharaohs who, in the historic period, succeeded him as rulers over a united Egypt. They did not incarnate Horus the Elder but.

---

[1] For Osiris the moon see Budge, *Osiris*, I, chapter xii. The quotation is from Plutarch.
[2] For details on Apis see pp. 76 ff.
[3] Naville, *Deir el Bahri*, II, p. 11.
[4] Erman, *Memph. Theol.*, pp. 15c–19; Sethe, *Memph. Theol.* I, pp. 37 f.
[5] See p. 67.
[6] Mercer, *Rel.*, p. 154.

Horus, son of Isis and Osiris, that is to say, the reborn Horus the Elder.

5. Horus, Son of Isis

The events after the death of Osiris were recorded, at a much later date, on the so-called Metternich stela.[1] Other material appertaining to it was preserved in stories woven round Osiris and in allusions handed down in the Pyramid texts. The legend told on the Metternich stela is roughly as follows:

Isis, sister and wife of the murdered Osiris, was captured and imprisoned by Set. Thoth arranged for her escape and sent seven scorpions to guard and defend her. When Isis reached the town of Per Sui at the edge of the papyrus swamps in the Nile delta region, she was given a hostile reception by a woman, whereupon her scorpions killed this woman's child. Later, however, Isis restored it to life. Finally, in a thicket of papyrus near Kheb or Chemnis, Isis brought forth Horus. Set thereupon sent a scorpion and Horus was killed. Isis, in despair, appealed to the god Re and Thoth was allowed to bring Horus back to life.

The events may be interpreted thus: Isis, the queen-mother or reigning queen, was taken prisoner after the murder of Osiris, but managed to escape with the help of the chief or king of the Thoth clan. We cannot be sure whom the seven scorpions symbolised; their names are given and since there are seven of them and a matrilineal state is generally a confederation of seven clans, they may have represented the followers of Isis from the various clans[2] who were willing to fight for her. The hostile woman and her child in the delta region almost certainly symbolised a queen-mother and her state,[3] who was defeated by the followers of Isis; later Isis restored the city state. The 'bringing forth' of Horus probably signifies that Isis rallied her followers around her and gave life to a new confederation with a Horus king at its head, but she was defeated by Set who had sent an army against her. The people of Thoth for a second time helped Isis and saved Horus, that is to say,

---

[1] Budge, *Fetish*, pp. 491 ff.
[2] Isis was a scorpion-goddess, no doubt in her form of 'Lady of the Flame', a title she shared with Tefnut and Hathor. Scorpion bites burn; Hathor and Nephthys, sister of Isis, were also scorpion-goddesses. Hopfner, *Tierkult*, p. 164.
[3] Among the Akan, as will be remembered, the queen-mother owns the state as if it were her child (p. 28).

the young state founded by Isis, the nucleus of the Lower Egyptian Horus kingdom of history.

There is good reason to assume that Pe became the capital of the kingdom of Isis; it means 'seat' or 'throne'. Pe was founded near Buto, the old Lower Egyptian capital, where the cobra-goddess Wadjet was worshipped. This goddess became the protectress of the shrines of the 'Souls of Pe'—later Pharaoh's falcon-headed Lower Egyptian Royal Ancestors who were descended from the divine Isis.

Before the Horus kings could rule in peace at Pe the struggle with Set had to be brought to a satisfactory conclusion. Thoth would appear to have played a prominent role as arbiter in the legal dispute between the two. This famous contest has been preserved in the *Memphite Theology* of the Thinite period. In the Pyramid texts it is very often referred to and forms a large part of the 'Contendings of Horus and Set' in the Chester Beatty Papyrus, No. 1 of the Ramesside Period. The main bone of contention seems to have been Set's claim to the territories of Osiris, including Lower Egypt. Plutarch (I.O., 54), on the other hand, records that the issue in question was the legitimacy of Horus, who was said to have been posthumously born. The two questions are closely related, the second, no doubt, arising from the first. *Pyr.* 93 bears witness to the association of Horus (son of Isis) with Lower Egypt, and that of Set with Upper Egypt.[1] The position would appear to have been that, before the union of the Two Lands by Menes, there had been a Lower Egyptian state ruled by Horus kings descended from Isis, and an Upper Egyptian state that had been ruled by a Set dynasty until some time before the union. Menes, the founder of a united Egypt, was called the 'Thinite' probably because he came from Thinis near Abydos. Manetho records that ten falcon kings had ruled there in pre-dynastic times.[2] They probably were the descendants of Nephthys, sister of Osiris and Isis; her name means 'Lady of the House' or 'Palace'.[3] In the myths she was the 'wife of Set'; wife,

---

[1] Arguments for and against Horus and Set as gods of Lower and Upper Egypt respectively have been summarily dealt with by Mercer, *Rel.* in the chapter on Horus and Set. My own views on the subject I have, I hope, made clear in the Egyptian sections of this chapter.

[2] Mercer, *Études*, p. 35.

[3] Moreover Nephthys is named in the Heliopolitan Ennead, the nucleus of which, I maintain, was historical, the gods and goddesses representing dynasties.

In a text Nephthys says to Osiris: 'Thy little son Horus born of two sisters' (i.e. Isis and Nephthys). G. D. Hornblower ('The Egyptian Fertility Rite',

in this context, would indicate that heiress princesses descended from Nephthys had to marry the Set kings, a political measure among matrilineals to tie vassal states to the reigning house.

Menes the Thinite, possibly a son of the Set king, which would account for Set's friendly role at the time of the unification of the Two Lands, conquered Lower Egypt, ruled by the descendants of Isis, because the Lower Egyptians refused a peaceful settlement. The battles that ensued are recorded on the Narmer (Greek, Menes) Palette. The last of these would appear to have taken place in or near Sambehdet in the most northernly part of the eastern delta. In Graeco-Roman times the insistence on the importance of Sambehdet in the unification of Upper and Lower Egypt is very marked.[1] A Denderah text describes Sambehdet as the place of 'Uniting the Two Lands'. The Horus who presided over the union was Horus the Behdetite, who became the guardian god of the united kingdom. Hathor, as Hathor the Behdetite, was regarded as his nurse, and Isis as his mother.[2]

6. The Divine Pharoah, the Incarnation of Horus, Son of Isis

Pharaoh's divine ancestry is evident from the following lines (*Pyr.* 466a): 'Thou art Horus, son of Osiris, the eldest god, son of Hathor.' 'Thou art Horus' states that Pharaoh, each Pharaoh, incarnated Horus, the god of the divine lineage of the falcon clan.

postscript, *MAN*, LXIII (1943), p. 16) comments on it as follows: 'A truly astonishing statement offering an excellent example of the wild extravagances found at certain times in a certain kind of priestly utterance.' However, if Nephthys and Isis are viewed as the ancestresses of the dynastic kings in whom Horus was incarnate, the meaning of the priestly statement is clear.

[1] For the role of Sambehdet in Egyptian history see A. H. Gardiner, 'Horus the Behdetite', in *JEA*, XXX (1944).

[2] Mercer, *Rel.*, p. 205, says: 'Hathor's relationship to Horus as mother, wife and nurse is a good example of the general lack of knowledge and systematic thinking among the ancient Egyptians and illustrates the oft-repeated assertion that the Egyptians never forgot old legends but illogically combined them with new ones without being disturbed about inconsistencies.'

It is quite true that the Egyptians never forgot old legends, they were to them historical accounts, and when they added new ones, it invariably made sense. Hathor could not be the mother and wife of Horus the Behdetite because he personified the united Two Lands (he was as such not viewed as a clan god), any more than Hathor could be the mother of Horus, Osiris reborn, personifying Lower Egypt and as such a son of Isis. Thus Hathor, in her form of Behdetite, became the nurse and protectress of the god. Isis was his mother because the Behdetite was a title given to Horus, son of Isis.

'Son of Osiris' can be understood to mean that every Pharaoh was regarded as a descendant of Osiris, the last king of an Osirian dynasty, who, after his death, became the deified ancestor, or 'eldest god' of the dynastic line. Both Horus and Osiris, as an incarnation of Horus, were sons of Hathor, the Mother-goddess and supernatural ancestress of the falcon clan's royal lineages.

Pharaoh's title 'son of Isis' appeared for the first time in the 1st Dynasty[1] and implied that Pharaoh was of the line of Isis, founded by the queen Isis in Lower Egypt after the death of Osiris. The name Isis was written with the symbol of the throne, which in fact she represented. Only by virtue of being a son of Isis was Pharaoh the legitimate ruler of the country. Ramses IV made this clear when he said 'I am a legitimate ruler, not an usurper, for I occupy the place of my Sire, as the son of Isis, since I appeared as king on the throne of Horus.'[2] This suggests that Menes, of the line descended from Nephthys in Upper Egypt, was not regarded as a legitimate successor to the throne of the Two Lands, in spite of his conquest of Lower Egypt. This is borne out by the fact that the title 'Uniter of the Two Lordships' belonged to his wife, the Lower Egyptian queen Neit-Hotep[3] of the line of Isis, whom he married, or made 'queen-mother', so that he might be accepted as king over a united Egypt. The line of Nephthys was no doubt barred from the succession owing to the fact that its rulers had been vassals of the Set kings in the past.

The official titulary of the Pharaoh's 'Horus of Gold' was written by placing the falcon over the sign which stood for gold. Gold refers to Hathor 'the Golden One'; gold was a pre-Heliopolitan representation characteristic of the Lower Egyptian kingdom of Horus,[4] founded by Isis incarnating Hathor. 'Horus of Gold' may therefore represent Pharaoh as 'son of Isis'. Djoser, a king of the 3rd Dynasty, had his full name inscribed upon the gold sign. In his reign Re, the Sun-god, came into prominence and gold is the metal of the sun. The falcon Horus became a solar god and as such a son of the Heliopolitan Hathor; the title 'Horus of Gold' may have assumed a new or additional meaning.

The Nebti title of the Pharaohs relates to the two tutelary goddesses, the vulture-goddess Nekhbet and the cobra-goddess Wadjet

---

[1] Petrie, *Royal Tombs of the earliest Dynasties*, 1900–1, II, Pls. II, nos. 13, 14.
[2] Mariette, *Abydos*, II, 1870–80, Pls. 54, 55.
[3] Morgan, *Préhistoire*, fig. 559.   [4] Mercer, *Pyr.* IV, p. 176.

THE INCARNATION OF THE GOD OF HIS CLAN

(or Edjo). The former was the protectress of Pharaoh's wolf-headed Upper Egyptian Royal Ancestors, the 'Souls of Nekhen', the latter the protectress of Pharaoh's falcon-headed Lower Egyptian Royal Ancestors, the 'Souls of Pe'. The Royal Ancestors were the chief supporters of the Pharaoh in the fulfilment of his function of giving life and maintaining the life in the state; the two goddesses who protected their shrines (*iterty*) thus became of supreme importance. The Nebti title may be regarded as a priestly one, for Pharaoh was the supreme priest of the cult of the Royal Ancestors; it may also have signified that Pharaoh stood at the head of the divine 'Souls', protected by the two goddesses.

The title 'he of the Sedge and the Bee' can be best translated as 'king of Upper and Lower Egypt'. Frankfort,[1] in discussing this title, remarks that 'we do not know what these symbols mean; but their relationship to the two parts of the country is certain'. Among the Akan every kingdom was represented by an animal, and in a few cases also by a plant, as were the small city states of earlier periods. Thus the emblem of the Bono kingdom, whose kings were of the falcon clan, was the parrot; that of the Asante kingdom, whose kings were also of the falcon clan, was the porcupine. The sedge and the bee may therefore be regarded as the emblems of the Upper and Lower Egyptian states. 'Sedge' was the title of the kings of prehistoric Memphis, Hininsu (Greek, Herakleopolis), and it is possible that they wore the high white cap which became the White Crown of Upper Egypt.[2] The first divine king to rule at Memphis-Hininsu incarnated Shu (lion clan). The Shu kings may have supplanted a chief or queen-mother of a sedge clan, in the same way as the Osirian kings supplanted the Anzti kings and took over their regalia.[3]

The sedge, then, represented Upper Egypt and the bee, by analogy, Lower Egypt. The bee was connected with the town of Sais, the seat of the Lower Egyptian kings who worshipped Neith. There was a 'House of the Bee',[4] possibly the residence of the bee kings. When Buto became capital of Lower Egypt the bee remained the symbol of the country; the kings wore the 'crown belonging to the bee'.[5] The Pharaohs, as kings of Lower Egypt, inherited the title 'He of the Bee' and the Red Crown of Neith.

Last in the titulary was the title 'Son of Re', which, when

---

[1] *Kingship*, p. 46.   [2] Mercer, *Études*, p. 34.   [3] See p. 44 n. 3.
[4] Sethe, *Urgeschichte*, par. 81.   [5] ibid., par. 82.

written, was followed by the name that the Pharaoh had received at birth.

Pharaoh's titulary represents a final selection from a variety of titles and designations which had been in use and was standardised before the rise of the 12th Dynasty.

7. *The Divine Queen, the Incarnation of Isis*

In Egypt the queen did not acquire her position by right of marriage but invariably by right of birth, in contrast to the Pharaoh who, on many occasions, only occupied the throne by virtue of his marriage to the queen; the founders of the dynasties are an example of this. Pharaoh, the occupant of the male throne, the 'throne of Horus', stood in a mother-son relationship to the occupant of the female throne personified by Isis in exactly the same way as does an Akan king. Hence the European term 'queen-mother' for the *ohemmaa*, meaning literally 'female king'. In Egypt, as among the Akan, the succession was in the female line; Pharaoh, in general, was the son of a queen or an heiress princess from the line of Isis descended from Hathor.

The queen, as sovereign, incarnated Isis, the mother of Horus who was incarnate in the Pharaoh. Isis, like Hathor, of whom she was the incarnation, was a 'Bestower of Life', a 'Blazing Flame', a 'Vomiter of Fire',[1] and was envisaged as a 'female Horus'.[2] According to Plutarch, Isis represented the 'generative faculty which resides in the moon'. The queen then, like the Akan queen-mother, received her life-giving power from the moon.

In Egypt the matrilineal system, which gave women the power in matters of property and inheritance, lasted until Roman times; it was traditionally based on the example of Isis who had avenged her brother's murder and had continued to reign after his death, conferring benefits on her people.[3] 'For these reasons', says Diodorus Siculus, 'it was appointed that the queen should enjoy greater power and honour than the king, and that among private people the wife should rule over her husband in the marriage contract, the husband agreeing to obey his wife in all things.'[4]

---

[1] In Budge, *Fetish*, p. 200.
[2] G. Röder, *Der Tempel von Dakke*, rev. ed. 1930, p. 167.
[3] A. M. Blackman, 'On the Position of Women in the Ancient Egyptian Hierarchy', *JEA*, VII (1921), pp. 8 f.
[4] In Frazer, *Adonis, Attis and Osiris*, 1914, II, p. 213.

THE INCARNATION OF THE GOD OF HIS CLAN

There is little information about Neit-Hotep, the first queen of the 1st Dynasty, who gave life to the Two Lands and received the title 'Uniter of the Two Lordships'. She had a *ka* name of her own,[1] showing that she incarnated a deity: Isis, the deified ancestress of her lineage, and Hathor, the divine genetrix incarnate in Isis. Fortunately we know a great deal more about Aahmes Nefertari (Aahmes—'the moon is born'), the deified ancestress of the 18th Dynasty who, like Isis, became a goddess. Her titles were the following:[2]

'Royal Daughter; Royal Sister; Great Royal Wife; Royal Mother; Divine Wife of Amen; Divine Mother; Mistress of the Two Lands; Great Ruler, joined to the Beautiful White Crown.'

'Royal Daughter': Aahmes Nefertari was the daughter of the last queen of the 17th Dynasty, Aahotep I (her name means 'delight of the moon'), and her husband Se-khentneb-Ra.

'Royal Sister': she was the sister of Aahmes, the first king of the 18th Dynasty.

'Great Royal Wife': she was the wife, i.e. co-ruler, of her brother Aahmes.[3]

'Royal Mother': she was the mother of Amen-hotep I for whom she reigned until he attained his majority.

'Divine Wife of Amen': she incarnated the goddess Mut, the wife of Amen, the god of the founders of the 17th and 18th Dynasties, state god of Egypt in the Middle Kingdom. Her mummified body wore the crown and the two feathers of the goddess Mut.[4]

'Divine Mother': she incarnated Isis as the occupant of the female throne.

'Mistress of the Two Lands': Nefertari's title as sovereign of Egypt.

'Great Ruler, joined to the Beautiful White Crown': the

---

[1] W. M. F. Petrie, *A History of Egypt*, 1894, p. 38.

[2] Janet R. Buttles, *The Queens of Egypt*, 1908, p. 59.

[3] 'Great Royal Wife' was a title; it did not mean that the queen was the wife of the king. This is evident from the fact that Nefertari's daughter Sat-Amen, who died in infancy, was called 'Royal Sister, Great Royal Wife, Divine Wife'. Also three daughters of Ramses III bore the titles 'Lady of Both Lands' and 'Great Royal Wife'. All these princesses would appear to have been heiress princesses destined to be co-rulers when they came of age (see below in the text). Among the Akan one king can be called the wife of another, which simply means that the alliance between their two states is as close as that between husband and wife. Here the reference must be to the two thrones.

[4] Cairo Museum, Gallery Q, no. 1, 137, Case C.

'Beautiful White Crown' represented Upper Egypt; the dynasty was of Theban origin.

After the death of King Aahmes, Queen Aahmes Nefertari acted as regent for her son and continued to rule after he attained his majority. Maspero[1] comments: 'Nefertari assumed the authority; after having shared the honours for nearly twenty-five years with her husband, she resolutely refused to resign them. She was thus the first of those queens by divine right, who, scorning the inaction of the harem, took on themselves the right to fulfil the active duty of a sovereign.'

Maspero, it seems, has entirely misunderstood the position of an Egyptian queen, because there can be no doubt that queens ruled as occupants of the female throne, 'the throne of Isis'; they were, moreover, senior to the occupant of the male throne, 'the throne of Horus' (the mother-son relationship). A queen, a 'Ruler of all Women'[2] could never have been an occupant of a harem, and the queen, like the Akan queen-mother, had her own court, her own council and women ministers, her own lands and treasury.[3] When Nefertari's son, for whom she had acted as regent, succeeded to the throne, she continued to rule on the female throne. As a sovereign of long experience she probably dominated her son, but that is a different matter.

Aahmes Nefertari was a great life-giver; she was as a result deified like Isis and worshipped as a goddess; her shrine, like that of the gods, was borne in a barque[4] in processions. A special priesthood was attached to her cult which was still in existence six hundred

---

[1] G. Maspero, *Struggle of the Nations*, p. 95.

[2] The title 'Ruler of all Women' was held by Nefert of the 12th Dynasty and Nub-Kha-Es of the 13th among others (Buttles, op. cit., pp. 28, 37).

In one of the Beni Hasan tombs, Chenemhetep, governor of the Oryx *nome*, records the titles of his wife Satab: 'Hereditary Princess, Ruler of all Women'. (Newberry, *Beni-Hasan*, 1893, I, p. 8). That can be taken to mean that his wife was a princess of the Oryx *nome* (i.e. queen-mother) and that she ruled the women of the city state; her husband was governor by virtue of his marriage to her.

Among the Akan each state in a confederation had its own queen-mother, who was descended from the royal lineage of that state and who ruled the women in her domain. The supreme queen-mother ruled the women in her own state; in important matters, however, the queen-mothers of the other states, or their representatives, were summoned to the capital for discussions in the queen-mother's council.

[3] Brugsch, *Ägypt.*, pp. 204–5.

[4] Buttles, p. 59.

years after her death. This is borne out by an inscription of the 21st Dynasty at Karnak, on a relief showing King Herher in adoration before the deities Amen, Mut, Khonsu, and Nefertari. More than thirty such records are in existence at Thebes, Karnak, Edfu, and Abydos which can be dated, besides many other undated examples. Only a queen who gave 'life' in an exceptional way could be revered in this manner. The explanation is that her brother-husband Aahmes, the great Hyksos conqueror, once more established a strong and independent Egypt. His deeds, however, were not enough in this matrilineally organised state; it was also necessary to acknowledge the part played by the divine life-giving woman, who 'brought forth' the state as does a mother her child. Nefertari's cult statue had a black or blueish skin, which is a characteristic of Hathor and Isis. This surely does not mean that they were goddesses of the dead, as some scholars believe, but rather goddesses of the night sky that gives birth to the sun and light.

The Egyptian queen in her role as the 'Great Spouse' or the 'Divine Wife' incarnated, as the wife of Horus, the goddess Hathor (Venus aspect); the title of a queen recorded at Deir-el-Bahari is: 'She, who is united to Horus.'[1] From the Middle Kingdom onwards the queen incarnated the goddess Mut of Thebes, who was identified in the royal cult with Hathor of Heliopolis, the mother-wife of the solar Horus. Even so, the sacred marriage between Horus-Pharaoh and Hathor, personified by the queen or her proxy, continued to be celebrated in the Beautiful Festival of Opet.[2]

In the rites of the sacred marriage among the Akan a wife from the queen's harem, a cross-cousin of the king, took the place of the queen-mother, since the law of exogamy forbade marriage between a man and a woman of the same clan. In Egypt the rite must have been similar, since Pharaoh could not possibly have performed the act with a queen who was his mother; moreover, we are still not certain whether the royal brother-sister marriages were in fact those of brother and sister, the children of one mother.[3] Priestesses, in some cases, would appear to have acted as substitutes for the queen; tombs of priestesses from the 11th Dynasty temple of Mentu-Hetep III near Deir-el-Bahari bore the titles: 'The Royal

[1] Naville, *Deir el Bahri*, II, p. 16.
[2] For the relationship between Pharaoh and Hathor and the sacred marriage between him and the goddess, see Jacobsohn, *Dogm. Stell.*, p. 20.
[3] J. Cerny, 'Consanguineous Marriages in Pharaonic Egypt', *JEA*, IX (1954), pp. 33 ff.

Favourite', 'the Only One', the 'Priestess of Hathor'.[1] These priestesses could never have been Pharaoh's wives or favourites, in the ordinary sense of the word, and they could certainly not have been harem wives as suggested by Naville.[2] As priestesses they would have been attached to the queen's court; had they been wives living in a harem they could never have performed their duties.[3] 'The Royal Favourite' was possibly the title given to a priestess who personified Hathor in the rites of the sacred marriage. The fact that the skeleton of a cow was found in each tomb can be regarded as evidence for this assumption, for a cow representing Hathor would have been sacrificed only once a year during the rites of the New Year festival which commemorated the rebirth of the goddess before her union with Horus.

The queen, who was such by right of birth and not by right of marriage, continued to reign after the death of a Pharaoh who had been her co-ruler.[4] We know of Nefertari that she ruled until her death, as did He-Maat-hap and Mertitefs, the queen of the founder of the 4th Dynasty. On a memorial stone from the temple of Re-Harakhte, Aahmes, a queen of the 18th Dynasty, and her daughter Hatshepsut are portrayed following Thutmosis II. Aahmes, granddaughter of Aahmes Nefertari, wears the crown of a reigning queen; Hatshepsut is given the same titles, but she is not adorned like her mother, although she was the wife of the Pharaoh.[5] This is a clear indication that Hatshepsut did not succeed as queen until after the death of her mother. Meanwhile she acted as her co-ruler and heir-apparent. In the great Akan kingdoms of the past, such as Bono and Asante, each king and queen-mother was served by an heir-apparent with whom they ruled jointly, the heir-apparent

---

[1] Naville, *Deir el Bahri*, II, p. 6.

[2] ibid., p. 7. Naville takes these priestesses to have been princesses because of their elaborate shrines. They were not, however, of the royal lineage though they may have belonged to another line of the falcon clan descended from the old family which provided the priestesses of Hathor. Among the Akan, although a man and a woman of the same clan are not permitted to marry, an exception is made in the case of the kings; they may marry heiresses of their own clan provided they are not descendants of the ancestress of the royal lineage.

[3] Brugsch, *Ägypt.*, p. 204, says that the harem women were called the 'imprisoned'; that is to say, they were not allowed to leave the palace. Similarly, among the Akan, harem women were under the control of eunuchs, who had to take orders from the *Odabeni*, the chief of the royal bed-chamber. See *Ak. of Ghana*, p. 87.

[4] There is very little material on the subject.

[5] Sethe, *Das Hatshepsut Problem*, 1932, p. 96, par. 112.

performing all official duties as well as minor religious functions in order that the sovereigns could devote themselves entirely to the task of giving 'life' to the state. But everything down to the smallest detail was reported to them and they made all the final decisions. This institution must have originated in Egypt, where it was known to have existed, especially during the period of the 17th, 18th and 19th Dynasties.[1]

Hatshepsut reigned not only as queen but also as a king. She acted first as the heir-apparent and co-ruler of her father Thutmosis I because there was no heir; the mother of Thutmosis II, her half-brother, was not of the royal lineage and he had therefore no right to the succession. When her father died (or was deposed as some evidence suggests) Hatshepsut made herself Pharaoh, but, after his marriage to her, she attached Thutmosis II to herself as co-regent. She was later deposed from the male throne and Thutmosis II ruled in her stead; his marriage to Hatshepsut, who still ruled as queen or the co-regent of her mother, made his kingship possible. After his death, she again usurped the male throne and Thutmosis III, her nephew, became her heir-apparent and co-regent until she died.[2] Among the Akan in some states queen-mothers were permitted to occupy both stools, if there was no suitable king, and reigned as queen-mother as well as king.

One more point of interest may be mentioned. A contemporary record from the 6th Dynasty reports that a queen, Queen Amtes, was tried for a crime by one Uni who had been entrusted by Pharaoh Pepi I with this task.[3] Among the Akan also a queen-mother could be tried, but for one crime only, that of high treason. The king placed a body of elders in charge of the trial, and the defender of the queen-mother was usually the high priest of the state god.[4]

---

[1] See p. 226, 227.

[2] This is quite clear from the inscription of Ineni (Breasted, *Ancient Records*, II, pars. 108, 116, 118, 341), where it is clearly stated: 'His son [Thutmosis III] stood in his place as King of the Two Lands, having become ruler upon the throne of the one who begat him. His sister the *divine* consort Hatshepsut, *settled the [affairs] of the Two Lands by reason of her plans*.' A great deal has been written about the Hatshepsut problem by various authors.

[3] Erman, *Inscription Uni II*, pp. 11–13; *ZÄS* (1882), pp. 10, 17.

[4] When I was at Takyiman in 1946 the Queen-mother Akua Dapaa of Bono-Takyiman, was tried for treason; she had attempted to depose the king, having accepted money for it from a foreign power. The trial, in which the king took no part, lasted practically the whole day; she was found guilty and was destooled and exiled.

THE INCARNATION OF THE GOD OF HIS CLAN

Evidence of the importance and high position of the queens of ancient Egypt is found throughout Egypt on temple walls and tombs;[1] on burial stelae and papyrus records; also in the magnificence of their sarcophagi, coffins, and jewels and in the stately ritual which followed them to their tombs, and placed their spirits by the side of the gods in reverence and devotion.

[1] The Pyramid texts are inscribed on the walls of nine pyramids of which three were those of queens—Neit, Aponi, and Oudjabten—who ruled at the same time as Pepi II (Neferkare) of the 5th Dynasty.

CHAPTER II

The Divine King, The Incarnation of the Sky fertility-god of the State

AKAN

1. The Father and Craftsman Creator-god Odomankoma Bore-Bore

The god Odomankoma Bore-Bore presents an anomaly in the Akan cosmological dogma because, unlike the *abosom*, the deities of the clans, he has no part in the *kra*, or life-giving power, of the Universal Genetrix, the supreme Mother-goddess Nyame; nor does he personify her manifestations, but is considered as an independent god in his own right. He is also a creator (*O-dom-anko-ma*: He who alone created the world); but whereas Nyame brought life into being by giving birth, he used his mind and his hands and was envisaged as a divine craftsman or artificer. He created the world by carving or hollowing it out (*bore-bore*) from an inert substance devoid of *kra*. He represented creative intelligence, and is still venerated as the god of *Natura naturata*, the earth with its mountains, plains, seas, rivers and trees, as opposed to Nyame, *Natura naturans*. Odomankoma took his place, theologically, as the co-regent of the Mother-goddess, becoming her executive and administrator, and, in his capacity as her brother or husband, was the 'father-uncle' of the clan *abosom*. His seat, or throne, was the Pole star with which he was identified.

Odomankoma's title *Nna-mmere-son*, literally 'seven-days-times', refers on the one hand to the seven circumpolar stars (*nsoroma-son*) the Bear (Arcturus) which indicate the hours of the night and the seasons. On the other it signifies the seven planets of the ancients: Sun, Moon, Mars, Mercury, Jupiter, Venus and Saturn, and thus the seven-day week, each day of which was, and still is, ruled by a planet. He decreed, it would seem, that the *abosom* no longer received their *kra* exclusively or directly from the moon, but rather from the planet that ruled their weekly natal day. He appointed special officers, the *akragya*, or *kra* progenitors, envisaged as bisexual or as male and female deities, to dispense *kra* for the Mother-goddess: the *akragya* Awo (Moon) on Monday; Abena (Mars) on Tuesday; Aku (Mercury) on Wednesday; Abrao (Jupiter) on Thursday; Afi (Venus) on Friday; Amen (Saturn) on Saturday; and Ayisi (Sun) on Sunday.

The *akragya* still give to the *abosom* born on the day they rule not only their *kra*, but also their *sunsum* (derived from *sunsuma* 'shadow'), 'character', 'personality' and hence 'destiny'. Those born on Monday will have the character of the moon, which is calm, peaceful, cool, protective; those born on Tuesday will become like Mars, fierce and warlike; those born on Wednesday will be wise and learned, like Mercury; those born on Thursday will become great, like Jupiter; those born on Friday, wanderers like Venus, but loving and full of generative force; those born on Saturday, experienced and mature like Saturn; those born on Sunday will be pure, immaculate, and generous like the sun.

Kra and *sunsum* came to be regarded as complementary parts of a whole. The *kra* now represented not only life and life-giving power, but also the immortal soul, the unconscious psyche, the *id* of psycho-analysts, as opposed to the *sunsum*, the ego, the mortal soul, consciousness of self, personality. The people of a clan then ceased to identify themselves with the *akyeneboa*, the totem animal of their *obosom*, which was exclusively associated with the Moon, and identified themselves with the planet of their clan god. Consequently the *kras* of the dead returned to the planet of their clan *obosom*, except for those of the dead queen-mothers and their clans-people, who still returned to the Moon.

The *sunsum*, the mortal soul of a person, changed after death into a *saman*, a shade or spirit body in the likeness of the deceased, or as The *samanfo* (plural of *saman*) went to the *samandow*, the other world, originally imagined as situated beyond the firmament in the outer darkness and approached by the Milky Way (Cult Type II). At a later period this other world was imagined as situated under the earth, presumably in the region through which the sun travels at night (Cult Type III). The maxim 'Odomankoma created Death' implies that he created the other world.

THE INCARNATION OF THE SKY FERTILITY-GOD OF THE STATE

Odomankoma not only created death but actually experienced death himself. This occurred at the time when his 'son', the Sun-god Nyankopon, became supreme; from then onwards Odomankoma lived through him and became his *sunsum* (soul) for the Sun-god was pure *kra*.[1]

2. *The Sky fertility-gods*

In Cult Type II, then, the deities no longer embodied the manifestation of the moon, but might have been that of any of the seven planets. To give one example: Tano (Twumpuduo) of Tuobodom, born on a Monday, is worshipped as a moon-goddess or god; Tano (Taa Kese) of Takyiman, born on Tuesday, as Mars, a war-goddess or god; Tano (Taa Kofi) of Taakofiano, born on Friday, as Venus or Lord of Growth, and Tano (Taa Kora) of Tanobase, born on Saturday, as Saturn 'the great spirit that is everywhere'.

The clan and state deities, moreover, were no longer envisaged as goddesses but as bi-sexual beings; *he* representing the male principle in nature, *she*, as mother and wife, the female principle. Though the deities retained their *akyeneboa*, the sacred animal which gave an indication of their clan origin and continued to represent their *kra*, they acquired additional animals as emblems of their *sunsum*. Tano's *akyeneboa* is the *ewio*, the black duiker antelope (representing night, moon, firmament), but the chief animal associated with his personality is the bush goat, an emblem of sexuality. Tano's main characteristic, therefore, is his power to arouse the sexual urge in man and beast, and thus stimulate procreation. Other animals personifying Tano are the crocodile—male, fierce, aggressive and devouring, but fructifying the waters of the Tano river—and the catfish; these are children of the goddess, symbols of fertility; crocodiles and catfish are fed by the priests at various places on the Tano river.

Tano, who, like all early deities, was originally the goddess of a clan, several centuries ago became the national Sky fertility-deity of the Fante, and when Fante people settled in the Bono kingdom in the second half of the sixteenth century, he/she was given life by their priestess queen-mother Yaa Takyiwaa. At the beginning of the seventeenth century Tano came to be acknowledged as state

---

[1] See also *Sacred State*, pp. 81–3; *Ak. of Ghana*, pp. 46 ff.; J. B. Danquah, *The Akan Doctrine of God*, London, 1944, pp. 59–61.

god/goddess of Bono and, after the destruction of the kingdom, as the state deity of Bono-Takyiman, which he/she still remains.

I call these deities 'Sky fertility-gods' because they all give fertility from the sky; they are all givers of rain and sunshine, thunder and lightning. They fertilise the earth, so that men may live, crops may grow, and herds multiply. They are also givers of children (*Abaama*) but it is *he* not *she*, who now promotes fertility among the women. The so-called *tuobo* display, in which the women showed their genitalia to the deity, was now made to the god, not the goddess. It must have been first officially accepted at that period, although perhaps previously realised, that the union of the sexes was a prerequisite of procreation, for the central rite of the New Year festival ceased to be the death and resurrection of the totem animal, the *akyeneboa*, and became the sacred marriage of the god and goddess, with their death and rebirth. In the cult of the state Sky fertility-*obosom*, the king incarnated the god and the queen-mother the goddess, the mother aspect of the deity; the king's senior wife or queen, as deputy of the queen-mother, represented the Venus aspect; the sacred marriage was performed between the king and the queen. On account of political circumstances, the state gods changed in the course of the centuries, with the result that the succeeding state gods were incarnated in the rites by proxies for the king and queen, who were the chief priests and princesses or priestesses; their rebirth, however, was presided over by the queen-mother.

The Sky fertility-gods were all manifest in vegetation and water-pools, streams, rivers or lakes. Each had an edible plant or crop and a stretch of water in which he/she was incarnate; Tano, for instance, was incarnate in rice and, from the seventeenth century onwards, in yams, and his/her fertile water was the river Tano; Ntoa, an earlier state god of Bono, was incarnate in wild yams and in the various streams near his/her sacred grove.

The shrine or abode of the clan *obosom* or goddess was a tree in the sacred grove; the abode of the bi-sexual Sky fertility-*obosom* was also a tree in the sacred grove and, as well as this, a tree planted in front of the temple hut. Artificial shrines were also erected composed of a conical mound or dome-shaped cone, or truncated cone, on which generally stood a bowl of water from the deity's sacred stream. The mound or cone represented the goddess, the water the god.

THE INCARNATION OF THE SKY FERTILITY-GOD OF THE STATE

In contrast to the clan *abosom* the Sky fertility-gods had a class of priests and priestesses in their service, the *akomfo*, who by going into trances were able to foretell the future. According to a maxim: 'Odomankoma, after he had created Death, created the prophetic priest or priestess'. Odomankoma is further credited with having introduced into the cult the *abrafo*, the masters of ceremonies and reciter priests.[1]

3. The Bull-god Buru

When the ancestors of the Bono people moved into the region between the Black Volta River and the tropical forest (central Ghana) they carried with them the shrine of their former state god Buru or Buru-kpung, Great Buru. The priest who served Buru was Asah or Asaman, a prince of the falcon clan, whose ancestors had ruled the early Bono kingdoms in Mossi and in Diala in Dia on the Niger in the western Sudan. Buru, when consulted by Asaman, advised the people to cease wandering and found towns; the god was consequently honoured with the title Biakuro, 'He who builds towns'. Thereupon Bono-Mansu was founded and became the capital of Bono, a confederation of seven dominant clans, each owning the cities and villages the clanspeople built. Asaman became the first king of Bono and Buru its state god.[2]

Buru's totem animal, indicative of his clan origin, was the mouse: but the mouse clan no longer exists among the Akan. The animal that expressed his *sunsum* (character, personality) as the Sky fertility-deity was the dog (*bodom*) representing the male aspect, and the 'water dog' (*suo-bodom*) which we call the manatee or sea cow, representing the female. The white bull and the black crouching cow personified his/her power of procreation. In the rites of the New Year festival the kings sacrificed and resurrected the divine white bull, the queen-mothers the divine black cow. After the rite the king performed the sacred marriage with his senior wife, the queen, who acted as the queen-mother's deputy. At a later date, when Ntoa and then Tano became state gods, the Bono king and queen-mother continued to incarnate the deity in the rites of the New Year festival.

Buru was born on Tuesday, the day ruled by the planet Mars, hence he/she was violent, hot-tempered and warlike, but the hot

[1] For further details on the period of Cult Type II see *Ak. of Ghana*, ch. II.
[2] *Ak. Trad.*, p. 33.

rays of the sun and the fierce thunderstorms with their beneficial rains fertilised the earth and made the crops grow. The plant in which Buru was incarnate in the Niger country was the *nsana* berry, a small, yellow berry of delicious flavour. In the Bono kingdom maize became the deity's favourite crop. The tree chosen by Buru as his/her abode was the *nampranee* (*gardenia ternifolia*); *nampranee* became one of the titles of the Bono kings. The following maxim is still beaten out on the royal talking drums: '*Osrem dua Nampranee a asee ye nwini* ('Desert tree *Nampranee*, who gives shade'), meaning that the king shelters his people like the tree. Buru's water in which he was incarnate was once the great Niger river in the north; in Bono it is still the small stream that had its source in the caves at Amowi, where Buru, when consulted by Asaman, advised the building of towns and thus became the creator of the Bono kingdom.

EGYPT
1. *The Father and Craftsman Creator-god Ptah*

The name of the god Ptah, who came to play a special role in the cult of the divine Pharaoh, is believed to have been derived from a verb of Semitic origin meaning 'to bore into' or 'to engrave', 'to carve'.[1] Among the signs included in the title of Ptah's priests was one representing a stone-borer.[2] This was an instrument which was evidently used 'to bore into' stone, and may have been originally a fire-drill, since Ptah, according to Manetho, was worshipped as the discoverer of fire (i.e. of fire-making).[3] The Greek writers identified Ptah with their own Hephaistos as the god of fire and the originator of the arts; the Romans identified him with their god Vulcan. Ptah was described as 'He who had fashioned as a smith [using fire in the process] all gods, men and animals in his name';[4] Hephaistos and Vulcan were also smiths and Ptah, like them, 'created the arts'.[5] He was thus envisaged as an artisan, a craftsman creator-god

---

[1] Budge, *Gods*, I, p. 500.
[2] Maj Sandman Holmberg, *The God Ptah*, Lund, 1946, p. 10.
[3] For Ptah the fire-god and the fire-drill see G. St. Clair's *Creation Records*, 1898, pp. 72, 73, 115. Further Sir E. le Page Renouf, *Hibbert Lecture*.
The stone-borer as a sign in the title of Ptah's priest may have symbolised not so much the original fire-drill as the quarry of Tura which belonged to the priests of Ptah, or both.
[4] Holmberg, op. cit., p. 47. Ptah was worshipped as a smith-god at Thebes.
[5] ibid., p. 48.

7. Small brass mask representing an Akan Sky fertility-deity, possibly Ntoa or a divine priest-chief incarnating the god. (Reproduced by courtesy of the Trustees of the British Museum.)

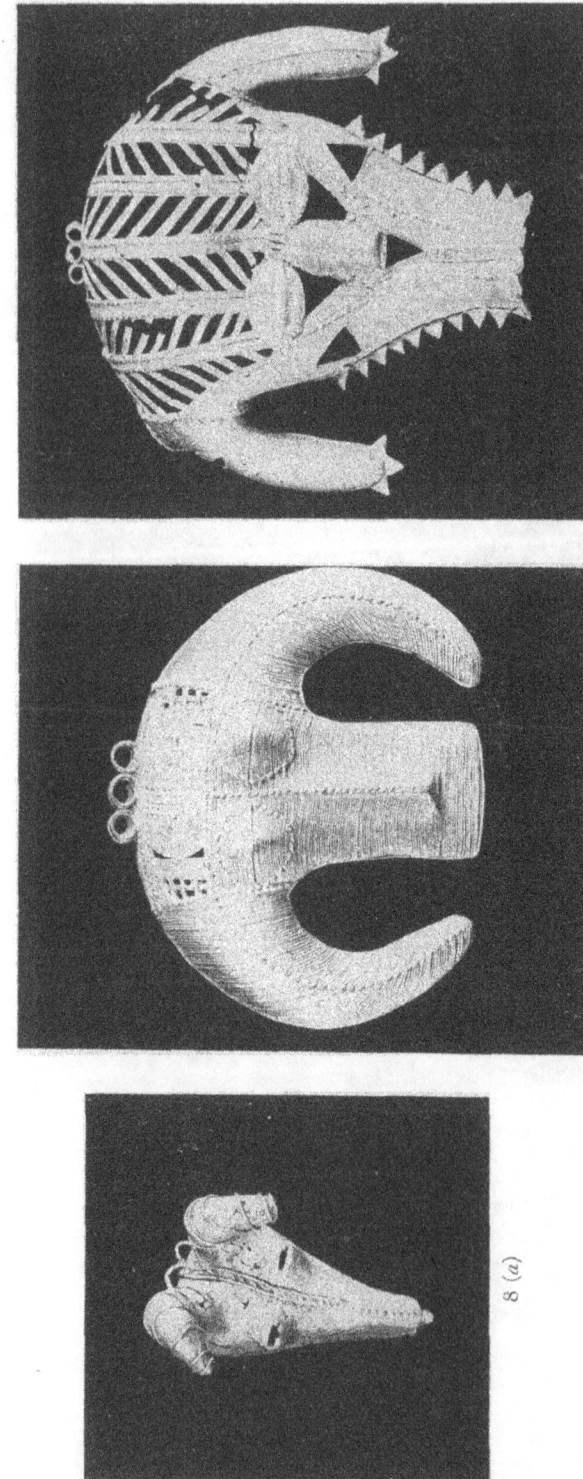

8. Pendants in gold from Baule, an Akan state (now in the French Ivory Coast) which had been founded by Akan about 1730 (a) a goat-god (b) and (c) a ram-god. (Reproduced by courtesy of the Institut Français d' Afrique noire.) These ornaments were possibly worn by the priest-chiefs who incarnated the god.

who had 'fashioned the world with his fingers'[1] and with his mind. This is expressed in the words 'While he thinks (as heart) and commands (as tongue) everything that he wishes.'[2] Ptah thus represented creative intelligence.

The seat or throne of Ptah would appear to have been the Pole star, an hypothesis put forward by St. Clair in *Creation Records*,[3] and confirmed by Akan religious thought, for the craftsman creator-god Odomankoma is the divinity of the Pole star and is evidently in every respect the same god as Ptah (see below). This would also explain why Ptah became the measurer of time, the 'Lord of the Years',[4] for the seven circumpolar stars revolving round the Pole star indicate the hours of the night as well as the seasons.[5] Ptah is often depicted standing on a pedestal in the shape of the sign of *Maat* and was consistently regarded in all periods and at different places as 'the Owner of *Maat*' and 'He who created *Maat*', or the 'Lord of *Maat*', the 'Father of *Maat*'.[6] *Maat* is usually translated as 'Truth', but really means the right order, the established cosmic order.[7]

Ptah also created the sun; this is made clear not only in a number of texts but also in a bas-relief at Philae, which shows Ptah turning the egg of the sun and moon on a potter's wheel, an alternative means of creation to that of the fire-drill.[8] The accompanying inscription reads: 'O, God, architect of the world, thou art without

---

[1] ibid., p. 27, quoting the corrupt text in the tomb of Prince Khetiu at Siut from the 9th or 10th Dynasty. Further 'Inactivity is the abomination of his fingers' (Budge, *Gods*, I, p. 146).
[2] In section V of the *Memphite Theology*; discussed by Frankfort, *Kingship*, pp. 28 ff.
[3] pp. 100 ff.
[4] cf. Holmberg, 'Ptah as Time measurer', op. cit., pp. 68, 75, 76, 77.
[5] For Ptah as 'Lord of the Night' see n. 22.
[6] P. Stolk, *Ptah*, Ein Beitrag zur Religionsgeschichte des alten Ägyptens, 1911, p. 21.
[7] Frankfort, *Kingship*, p. 51, ch. IV, n. 4.
[8] Wiedemann, *Rel.*,p . 132. It is interesting to note that the two eggs are a royal emblem among the Akan. They are depicted as a larger egg containing a smaller one and are called *nkosuano*. Their meaning is said to be: 'When two eggs come together they form what can only be understood by Nyame.' Nyame is here envisaged as Nyame Amowia, the lunar goddess who gave birth to the sun. The concept of the eggs as moon and sun evidently belongs to the Cult Type II period, hence to Odomankoma, but by presenting a larger egg, the moon, to contain a small egg, the sun, the old concept of the moon as the mother of the sun prevailed.

a father, begotten by thine own becoming; thou art without a mother being born through repetition of thyself.' This inference is two-fold; first, to rotation as a means of creation, and second, to the never-ceasing rising and setting of the sun and moon. Ptah, the creator of the sun and moon, also embodied these planets, as is evident from the following text: 'It is thy two eyes that give light' ... 'Thy two eyes that circle day and night; thy right eye is the disk of the sun, thy left the moon. Thy images are the indefatigable ones.'[1] These are the heavenly bodies whose perpetual motion, like that of the circumpolar stars, also indicates the hours of the day and night, the seasons, and the length of the year.

In the *Memphite Theology*, Section V, it is said of Ptah: 'Great and exalted is Ptah who bequeathed his power to all gods and their *kas* through his heart and his tongue . . . and thus the *kas* were made and the *hemsuts* were created—they that make all sustenance and food . . .' The *kas* and *hemsuts* are represented as fully-grown deities in a relief at Deir-el-Bahari (Pl. 10) which shows the birth scenes of Queen Hatshepsut.[2] They appear to be the equivalent of the Akan *akragya*, the seven male and female deities of the planets,[3] created by Odomankoma, who give to the child its life force, *kra*, and *sunsum*, its mortal ego soul and its destiny. There is no direct evidence in any existing text that the *kas* and *hemsuts* gave to a child, as well as its life force, its ego soul called *khaibit* in Egyptian; but Ptah, like Odomankoma the father of gods and men, is referred to as 'the maker of their lives' and he who 'determined their years'; he is emphatically a god of destiny.[4] The concept of the mortal ego soul presupposes the recognition of death, and thus Ptah, like Odomankoma, became the creator of the netherworld and resurrection; he was 'He who has made Eternity'.[5] The following lines are believed to have been spoken by him: 'I am yesterday, today and tomorrow for I am born again and again [the old idea of Ptah being born through perpetual reproduction of himself]. I am the Lord of

---

[1] Gerald Massey, *Natural Genesis*, I, p. 118.

[2] Naville, *Deir el Bahari*, Pl. LIII.

[3] Frankfort, *Kingship*, p. 74, says that six *ka* and six *hemsut* deities are depicted. There are seven of each, nevertheless, because one must include the two cow-goddesses in the scene, who should be Hathor and Isis and almost certainly here represent the *ka* (Isis, throne) and the *hemsut* (Hathor, lineage) of the moon.

[4] Holmberg, pp. 64 ff.

[5] Stock, *Ptah*, p. 21.

Resurrection who cometh forth from the dusk and whose birth is from the House of Death.'[1]

Ptah is often portrayed in mummy form, as in death, and from a number of texts it is clear that at some point he ceased to be a living god or, to be more precise, he ceased to be a fire-god and god of the Pole star, who ruled the sky. Hence we lack all direct evidence of this aspect of his nature. The fact of his death must have been accepted when it was observed that his throne the Pole star, the centre from which all motion proceeded, was no longer stable but shifted in the course of the year, thus noticeably displacing the stars with reference to the sun; but probably far more important was the discovery that the sun was eternal and not created anew each morning. Thus the Sun-god took precedence over the creator of the sun and Ptah was forced to abdicate. He continued to exist, however, as the 'representative' or 'substitute' of Re,[2] the Sun-god, whose cult was established in the reign of the kings of the 2nd Dynasty (approximately 2800 B.C.). Re seems to have symbolised the revolving sun, its apparent path or ecliptic. From the 4th Dynasty onwards the Pharaohs incarnated Re and regarded themselves as the sons of the Sun-god; it is therefore not surprising that Ptah is hardly ever mentioned in Pyramid texts,[3] although the old concept of him as creator or 'father' of the visible sun never became quite obsolete.[4]

Ptah in his double aspect of 'fashioner of new bodies'[5] and 'representative' of the Sun-god, was the chosen god for the 'Opening-of-the-Mouth' ceremony of the deceased Pharaohs. In this rite his

[1] St. Clair, *Creation Records*, p. 275.

[2] Holmberg, pp. 153 ff. Ptah has this epithet on a number of Middle Kingdom stelae from Abydos, and, in the list of Ptah's names in the Ramesseum, his twenty-ninth name is 'Ptah the representative of Re'. In the New Kingdom he came to be regarded as the manifestation of Amun-Re; he was never described as the sun.

[3] In Utterance 320 (Mercer, *Pyr.*, vol. II,) the reference is possibly to Ptah, for the deceased Pharaoh appears as a star regulating the night and sending the hours on their way (also *Pyr.* 515a, b). Then 'N. (i.e. the Pharaoh) is that son of her who knew not that she had borne N. of powerful visage as Lord of Nights.' The only star that 'sends the hours on their way' is the Pole star round which revolve the circumpolar stars. The goddess who did not know that she had borne the 'Lord of Nights' may be either Nut or Hathor, the mother of the deceased Pharaoh, for neither Nut nor Hathor was the mother of a king who incarnated the divinity of the Pole star, i.e. Ptah.

[4] Holmberg, op. cit., p. 153.

[5] Budge, *Gods*, I, p. 501.

ordinary faculties were restored to the dead king to bring him back to life. It was thus a rite of resurrection and immortality. Ptah, the craftsman creator-god, used an iron tool for this purpose. A relief from the New Kingdom shows Horus and Ptah 'opening the mouth' of the dead Osiris.

One may presume that Ptah, after his 'death' or possibly earlier, was fused with various other gods and thus maintained his position as 'Father of the Beginnings'. One of these gods was Nun, the 'old' or 'the oldest', who personified the primeval water regarded as primeval matter pregnant with life.[1] Out of it rose the primeval earth, personified as the god Tatjenen, and Tatjenen finally became a variant name for Ptah as the creator of nature with its perpetual death and rebirth.

A great deal has been written about the *Djed* object of which the significance is obscure. It has, however, generally been agreed that it represented a tree with lopped-off branches, and symbolised the backbone of Osiris (Fig. 5). This interpretation is correct, for this symbol is

Fig. 5

An amulet of Osiris in the form of the Djed. *Mariette,* Denderah, *IV*, 87. *The* Djed *consists here of a triangular cone and the four lopped-off branches of a tree*

also known to the Akan, where it is called *konkom dua kom*, meaning 'tree firmness' (Fig. 6). It refers to the tree of the god, the abode or resting place of his *kra*. Hence this tree, so often filled with divine power, was believed to be more firmly rooted than an ordinary tree, and became a symbol of steadfastness and stability, a support or backbone in times of need for the people who worshipped the god. The god was addressed as *Tweduampon*, meaning 'Lord of the tree [on whom we] lean [and] never fall.'

The same idea would appear to have been expressed on a relief in a tomb from Ramesside times at Denderah, where people are seen in prayer round a being with the body of Osiris and a *djed* for

---

[1] K. Sethe, *Amun und die acht Urgötter in Hermopolis*, 1929, pp. 51, 74.

THE INCARNATION OF THE SKY FERTILITY-GOD OF THE STATE

its head, crowned with the *atef* crown of the dead king. The text is as follows:

> *Worship of thy* ka, *Osiris, Lord of* Djedu,
> *Unifer* [the Good Being], *ruler of the Living.*
> *Hail to thee thou glorious* Djed.[1]

Djedu is the feminine form of *Djed*, and means 'house' or 'abode' of the *Djed*. The 'house' or 'abode' is the tree, and the *Djed* therefore must be the spirit or power of the tree, the *ka* of the god (in this case Osiris) which is addressed in the passage. The *ka* was the divine, immortal part of the mortal king and, as shown, the *ka* of Osiris was that of Horus. The head of the dead king Osiris was here accordingly replaced by a symbol that conveyed steadfastness,

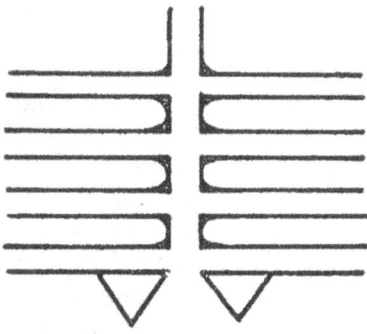

Fig. 6

The Akan Djed as it is engraved on the back of the flat head of some of the akuaba statuettes which symbolise the Mother-goddess. It shows a tree trunk with four lopped-off branches and two triangles which convey that she and her son rule the sky, earth and underworld

reliability, constancy and permanence to the people, who desired support and something on which they could depend.

The *Djed*, an artificial tree,[2] was erected by the Pharaohs on the day preceding the *Sed* festival. Here it also demonstrated to the people that Osiris, whose death and resurrection had been enacted earlier, was nevertheless a god to be relied upon to give help and support in the year to come.

[1] Holmberg, p. 161.
[2] Tree worship in ancient Egypt is well documented.

The *Djed* also symbolised the steadfastness, reliability, and divinity of other gods, for all gods of matrilineally organised peoples have shrines for their *kras* or *kas*. It is curious, however, that the *Djed* is also connected with Ptah, who was unmistakably the god of an originally patriarchal people, since he has no totem animal; nor was he the personified male manifestation of a goddess, and as such her son and husband. It is therefore not surprising to learn that *Djed* was given to Ptah by Thoth, presumably after the god's 'death', to illustrate, so to speak, his divinity. Apart from that he also received it indirectly through Osiris when Ptah-Soker-Osiris were worshipped as one deity at Memphis. In a text from Kheruef's tomb at Thebes there is a passage: 'on the day of the raising of the glorious *Djed* belonging to Ptah-Soker-Osiris'.[1]

Ptah is commonly represented as a man with a shaven head, wrapped up like a mummy. His features are usually very handsome; he was known as 'Ptah with the beautiful face',[2] a reference perhaps to the beauty of nature created by him. On the other hand he is sometimes depicted as an ugly dwarf, as, for instance, in the statuette of him found at Gizeh, now in the Cairo Museum. Ptah in his form of Ptah-Soker was also sometimes depicted as a dwarf, half man and half bird with a sharp beak—Soker was a falcon-god —and his feet pointing in opposite directions.[3] As Ptah-Soker he personified primeval creative power with its inert power of darkness, death, and rebirth. He seems to have survived in that form among the Akan as Sasabonsam, a demi-god and the evil spirit of the primeval forest who causes earthquakes, thunder and lightning; his half-moon-shaped wings, which hang from his raised arms, characterise him as a fertility-god, however. He is usually depicted on ancient gold weights with a birdlike face and, like his sons the *mmoatia* (ugly dwarfs), with feet turned in opposite directions[4] or his legs ending in snakes.[5] Nobody knows where he

[1] Fakhry, *Kheruef*, p. 477.

[2] Holmberg, p. 49.

[3] As illustrated in G. W. Rawlinson, *The History of Herodotus*, 1858, II, p. 434. For an explanation of why the feet point in opposite directions, see St. Clair, *Creation Records*, pp. 273–5.

[4] Four-footed animals representing gods, depicted in the past by the Akan, often have their fore-feet pointing the normal way but their hind-feet pointing backward. They indicate the cardinal points of the compass, east and west, or the sun and moon. For an illustration see *Ak. of Ghana*, fig. 5.

[5] Snakes, among the Akan, are a symbol for death and resurrection. Ptah, in the statuette found at Gizeh, is also holding snakes. The crooked legs of the

dwells; like Ptah-Soker he is a 'dweller in the secret place'[1]—the netherworld. They both seem to express the idea that death gives birth to life or that in death, or death-like primeval matter, is life.

Herodotus (III, 37) reports that an image of Ptah which resembled a pygmy was worshipped in the temple of Hephaistos (Ptah) at Memphis. Moreover, we are told that there was at Memphis a temple of the Cabiri, who were also pygmies, and believed to be sons of Hephaistos. The Cabiri are said to have had some connection with mining.[2] Since Ptah's emblem was the stone-borer and since he was worshipped as a smith at Thebes, this may be an indication that Ptah's people (in western Asia) were the first to mine and work in metals—copper.[3]

Horapallo in his *Hieroglyphica* said that when the Egyptians wished to depict the figure of Hephaistos (Ptah) they drew a scarab and a vulture, and when they wished to represent Athena (Neith) they drew a vulture and a scarab, for they believed the world to be composed of two elements, one male and the other female; these being the only two gods whom they regarded as being both male and female. Among the Egyptians as well as among the Akan the scarab and the vulture symbolised self-begetting, self-creation and self-birth. An Akan maxim says of Odomankoma:

dwarf may have been derived from the outline of the cone or mound (Soker is often depicted as a falcon on a mound). Among the Akan the mound in some regions is called *kanta* and crooked legs *kanto*.

[1] In the Papyrus of Anhai; cf. Budge, *Gods*, I, p. 507.
[2] Holmberg, p. 185.
[3] Ptah's origin was probably in the Caucasus region where metals were first mined and worked. This hypothesis is also supported by other factors.

The craftsman creator-god, whether under the name of Ptah or a different one, was worshipped all over the ancient East. The Syrians of Ugarit knew him as K*t*r and addressed him as Ptah (Mercer, *Pyr.*, IV, p. 204). The Phoenicians called him Kussor. The Sumerians and Babylonians called him Enlil and adored him as the 'Guardian of the Tablets of Destiny'; he sat in 'the council of the seven gods who determine destiny'. He was the 'Lord of the Enlils', the seven stars which are believed by some scholars to have been represented by Arcturus (Supa) and the seven stars of the Plough, which rotate round the Pole star. Enlil's title was Enki, which is usually translated as 'Lord Earth'. He was probably an earth-god in the same sense as Ptah-Tatjenen and Odomankoma, the creator of *natura naturata*. His symbol was most probably, as among the Akan, the open five-fingered hand; on ceramics excavated at Tepe Musyan the five-fingered hand is depicted as well as the three-fingered hand of the Mother-goddess, the genetrix of the universe (see also *Ak. of Ghana*, fig. 2). A study of this most important god is long overdue.

'The animal that symbolises Odomankoma who created the world is the vulture' (*Odomankoma a oboadee, ne kyeneboa ne opete*).

Odomankoma is evidently the same divinity as Ptah who goes back to the dawn of history. The names of both signified 'to bore into' or 'to hollow out', 'to engrave' or 'to carve'. They were both craftsman-gods, who created the visible world with their hands and minds and thus represented creative intelligence. They were both self-begotten, self-created and self-born and, viewed from this angle, they were both bi-sexual.

Odomankoma was the creator of the 'seven times' as god of the Pole star and the seven circumpolar stars; he determined the hours of the night and the seasons and created the seven-day week of which each day was ruled by one of the deities (*akragya*) of the seven planets. Ptah was the ruler of the year and probably also originally the divinity of the Pole star. He created the *kas* and *hemsuts*, the equivalents of the *akragya* of the seven planets. Both were the fathers of gods and men and determined their years and their destiny. Both were creators of evil things,[1] the greatest of which was death. Both created eternity—the netherworld—and thus resurrection in the beyond. Both 'died'; we presume at the time when it was discovered that the sun was not a fire lit by them each morning (with the fire-drill) but eternal. In both cases the Sun-god succeeded them. In the cult of the king as the son of the Sun-god they both came to be regarded as his father, who lived through him. They both, however, continued to be worshipped as the 'Father of the Beginnings'—as the personification of the primeval ocean and the primeval earth and nature with its perpetual death and rebirth.

2. *The Sky Fertility-gods*

Horus was worshipped as a clan-god in prehistoric times, and possibly later as long as the clan system prevailed; and as the dynastic god in historic times; he was also worshipped by the people right through the ages and in many different places as a Sky fertility-god. Like the Akan gods of this type he received his power from one or other of the planets and acquired secondary animals to represent his 'personality'. Thus the 'Red Horus' (Herteshe)

---

[1] Holmberg, p. 64. Evil 'opened its eyes' when Odomankoma created the ego soul (*sunsum*) of man. J. B. Danquah, *The Akan Doctrine of God*, 1944, p. 92.

THE INCARNATION OF THE SKY FERTILITY-GOD OF THE STATE

was identified with Mars; 'Horus the Bull' (Heruka) with Saturn; 'Horus the Scintillating Star' (Hertenen) and 'Horus the Illuminator' (Upsch) with Jupiter.[1] Horus of Edfu received his life-giving power and generative force, his 'personality' from the sun; he was symbolised by the sun disk with the outspread wings of the falcon. At Edfu, on his birthday, he was reborn to his mother Hathor, and his marriage to her was celebrated with the greatest splendour.

The planet of Horus the Elder, the clan and state Sky fertility-god, was the moon. As a Sky fertility-god he was incarnate in the crocodile, signifying male procreative power, and in this form he carried Osiris on his back.[2] He is also found depicted as a falcon-headed crocodile.

The god Set, whose clan animal is still not identified[3] (Fig. 7), was also envisaged as a crocodile; a sacred crocodile was kept in the pool near his famous temple at Nubt. There also existed a crocodile

[1] Budge, *Fetish*, p. 223.
[2] Berlin, Ägyptisches Museum, no. 11496. Cf. Mercer, *Horus*, 114.
[3] Scholars believe it to have been a dog, a pig, a boar, a wart-hog, an ass or an animal of an extinct species. Judging from the animal's greyhound-like appearance, with erect ears and tail and the paws of a cat, it may have been an aardwolf (*proteles christatus*), an animal which is still to be found in the Sudan, East and South Africa. It is pale yellow in colour with black stripes across its body; it lives in caves and roams about at night. It feeds on carcass meat and has all the filthy habits of the hyena. If Set's animal was indeed an aardwolf, this would explain why Set was generally considered to be an evil god, apart from his historical role as the murderer of Osiris.

On the other hand there is ample evidence that Set was incarnate in the pig or boar. In the Book of the Dead (Chapter 112) it is said that Set assumed the form of a black pig and, in this guise, tore out the eye of Horus (Chapter 113). The Egyptians sacrificed a pig to Set once a year, and according to Plutarch (10, 8) a pig was sacrificed to Osiris on the anniversary of the date on which, according to tradition, Osiris himself was killed. According to Herodotus (II, 47) the pig offered in sacrifice at full moon was eaten by the worshippers of the god Bacchus (i.e. Set or Osiris). The pig or boar, then, incarnating Set as well as Osiris, may have stood in the same relation to them as the lion to Horus and other deities whose people came from Punt. The lion indicated to the Egyptians the country of origin of certain clan gods and their people; the pig would therefore indicate the country or the confederation from which the people of Osiris and a branch of the Set clan had come—namely Syria. Set appears as 'brother' of Osiris in Pyramid texts (956–60), in the 'Contendings of Horus and Set' and in the Chester Beatty Papyrus I, etc. The birth-place of Set, the son of Geb and Nut, was in the Fayum according to a British Museum stela (no. 79). Just as the falcon clan people migrated to Egypt in several branches, some via southern Arabia, others via Palestine, so also did the people of Set and Thoth (as ape from Punt, as ibis with Osiris amongst others).

standard of Set,[1] and Horus, as Set's conqueror, was called 'Horus on the crocodile'.[2] Other animals which demonstrated to his people the personality of the god were the hippopotamus and certain fish

Fig. 7

The unidentified animal of the god Set. Sethe, Urgeshichte, *p. 72*

(*oxyrhynchus* and *lepidotus*); they symbolised his female procreative powers in water.[3] The goat symbolised his procreative power on the earth,[4] and the ass, sexual lust and procreation in general;[5] the oryx antelope possibly signified the bi-sexual god's supremacy,[6]

[1] Crocodiles, personifying Set, were hung up on persea trees and tortured, probably to revenge the death of Osiris; the persea tree was sacred to Isis (Hopfner, *Tierkult*, p. 123). The torture must have had the connotation of castration, because Set is represented by the crocodile, the animal which symbolised semen or male procreative power.

[2] Hopfner, op. cit., p. 132.

[3] The hippopotamus was recognised all over Egypt as the animal of Set and is said to have had his bad character (Hopfner, pp. 63–5). But surely the original idea was that of the maternal characteristics of the animal; the hippopotamus-goddess Ta-urt, for instance, was a goddess of birth and also Hathor as such appears as a hippopotamus. See Pl. 4.

Fish were the children of the goddess on account of their numerous eggs (see the fish sacred to Tano, p. 61). They also, like the hippopotamus, came to be regarded, in connexion with Set, as unclean; they were abhorred because, according to Plutarch, the *oxyrhynchus* and the *lepidotus* ate the penis of the murdered Osiris after Set had thrown his body into the Nile (Hopfner, p. 154).

[4] In a text it is said that the companions of Set came, changed themselves into goats and were slaughtered in the rite of the great hoeing of the earth at Busiris (Wainwright, *Sky Rel.*, pp. 52–4). The goat among the Akan symbolises the sexual urge; goats were, no doubt, slaughtered to make the earth fertile. At Busiris, the town of Osiris-Anzti, the sacrifice of the goats of Set took on an additional meaning: the people's revenge on Set for the murder of Osiris.

[5] The ass symbolised procreative power, see Hopfner, op. cit., p. 102. But there may have been some further significance, for the ass is connected with the number 30 (a month? it is not known what 30 stands for). In later times the ass was always regarded as an evil animal and was killed as a representative of Set in the rites connected with Soker-Osiris.

[6] Horus seated on the oryx antelope as victor over Set (Hopfner, p. 100). The oryx antelope among the Akan represents Nyame as the bi-sexual Supreme Being and may have had the same significance in Egypt.

Set's kingly aspect was represented by the bull.[1] His planet was the moon.[2] Set was the typical Sky fertility-god, for he was a god of rain, storm, lightning, thunder, and earthquakes; meteorites and thunder-bolts[3] symbolised his strength, his power to open the earth and to fertilise it, and also his power of destruction.

The Egyptian word for 'god' was *ntr*, pronounced *neter* or *netjer*. The concept of *neter* has been discussed by many scholars but their conclusions as to its significance differ.[4] The hieroglyph is believed to represent either a flag or an axe, which in early times was triangular and later rectangular. A flag would seem a reasonable interpretation only if it represented an axe, for this was the 'regular weapon of the Sky fertility-gods, being equivalent to the meteorite or thunderbolt'.[5] Among the Akan the axe is the sceptre and weapon of the Sky fertility-deities and their representatives on earth, the king and the queen-mother. The triangular axe in silver was the emblem of the queen-mothers of Bono, in gold it was that of the kings. The famous 'Golden Axe' of Asante is still carried

---

[1] Set, 'the Bull of Nubt'. Kings who incarnated a Sky fertility-god did not identify themselves with the totem animal of the god but with the animal that most obviously expressed male potency, force, and strength—the bull. Thus the Osirian kings, or Osiris, incarnated the Apis bull and the Pharaohs the Min bull; the Geb kings the 'Bull of Nut', and the Set kings the 'Bull of Nubt'.

[2] Mercer, *Rel.*, p. 60. As a Sky fertility-god he was also the shadow or cloud that darkened the moon. Compare this with the Akan god Ntoa who, in a litany, is called 'coverer of the *kra*' [of the moon], *Sacred State*, p. 158. The moon was his planet as a clan god; the kings who incarnated Set identified themselves with the moon. The constellation sacred to Set, the Sky fertility-god, was the Great Bear (Mercer, op. cit., p. 54) which indicated the seasons.

[3] Set was worshipped in the form of an iron meteorite in the Cabasite *nome* in Roman times (Mercer, op. cit., p. 54).

[4] Budge, *Gods*, I, p. 66, writes that it is most important to obtain some idea of the meaning of *neter*. It is interesting to note that in Twi, the Akan language, *ntere* means to 'expand'; *ntere-mu* is the expanse of the sky, a word which is also used for the firmament. The Egyptian *neter* and the Twi *ntere* (or *nterew* in other dialects) may be related words; if so *neter* would describe deities which are connected with the expanse of the sky, the atmosphere and the firmament. I am aware that *neter* is now read *nutjer* (Cerny, *Rel.*, p. 19).

Budge, *Fetish*, pp. 41, 204–6, was the first to realise that 'an astral system of religion reigned once in Egypt and has left clear traces, notably in the Pyramid Texts'. The astral system, if one could so describe it, meant only that deities were considered to have received their life-giving power and personality or characteristics from a planet, star or constellation.

[5] Wainwright, 'Some Aspects of Amun', in *JEA*, XX (1934), p. 142. Set's sanctuary at Oxyrhynchus displayed the double axe on Roman coinage, ibid., p. 148. *Sacred State*, p. 59.

before the king on festive occasions. The triangular axe may once have played a similar role in Egypt, for a golden axe and bronze axes were found in the tomb of Queen Aahotep of the 17th Dynasty.[1] The word *neter* thus described the bi-sexual Sky fertility-god and his power of procreation. I have devoted separate sections to the gods Apis and Min, because far more is known of them. Moreover both have been connected with the divine kingship, the former in prehistoric as well as in historic times.

3. *The Bull-god Apis*

The worship of Apis goes back to prehistoric times; the cult of the god was revived by King Kakau (Kaiekhos) of the 2nd Dynasty who dedicated a temple to him at Memphis.[2] This cult lasted until A.D. 362, when the last Apis bull was buried.[3]

Plutarch (10, 43) wrote: 'the bull Apis, held to be an image of the soul of Osiris, was born of a cow, which was believed to have been impregnated by a divine influence emanating from the moon'. Herodotus (III, 28) described Apis as 'the calf of a cow which is incapable of conceiving another offspring', and further, 'that lightning descends upon the cow from heaven and from this it brings forth Apis'. According to Pliny (VIII, 72) the Apis bull had a white spot on its right side in the form of a crescent, and Egyptian bronzes depict the animal with a triangular piece of silver fixed to its forehead. The crescent, no doubt, was a lunar one; among the Akan silver is symbolic of the moon and the triangle is a symbol of the Mother-goddess as ruler over sky, earth, and underworld. Apis, then, was given life by a lunar Mother-goddess, who could of course have only one offspring, for the lunar god was no more than the personification of her male power. The 'Lightning that descends on the cow' may be regarded as a lunar ray;[4] the Akan word for lightning, *sraman*, is derived from *srane*, the moon, and was envisaged originally as a spark, fire, *kra*, from the moon. Scholars agree that Apis

---

[1] H. Brugsch, *Egypt under the Pharaohs*, 1891, p. 117. Probably more examples could be found.

[2] Bernhard Otto, *Beiträge zur Geschichte der Stierkulte in Ägypten*, 1938, p. 5; Sethe, *Urgeschichte*, par. 31. According to Aelian, *De Natura Animalum*, XI, p. 10, the worship of Apis was established by Menes, the first king of the 1st Dynasty. On the other hand Apis is mentioned on the Palermo stone (Rs. 3, 4); cf. Stolk, *Ptah*, p. 12.

[3] Otto, op. cit., p. 20.

[4] According to Hopfner, *Tierkult*, p. 77.

THE INCARNATION OF THE SKY FERTILITY-GOD OF THE STATE

was a lunar god and represented the lunar cycle. The drake seems to have been the totem animal of the clan of the god, since the name Apis is connected with this bird.[1]

Apis in his form of Sky fertility-god, the 'Great God, Lord of the Sky',[2] received his power of generation and procreation from the star Orion, whose appearance heralded the Nile flood that fertilised the land of Egypt.[3] Every Sky fertility-god has a piece of water in which he is manifest; that of Apis was the Nile.

In representations of the bull Apis a rectangular-shaped cloth often covers the back of the animal; it is decorated with lozenges or diamonds. This sign among the Akan is symbolic of fertility; the rectangle may stand for 'house' and could in this context be a reference to the womb of the Mother-goddess. It seems probable that among the Egyptians also the markings on the Apis bull (see also below) were symbolic and expressive of religious ideas. If this assumption is correct then these ideograms preceded the hieroglyphs in Egypt and Apis was worshipped before the latter were invented.[4]

Apis in historic times was chiefly worshipped as the *ba* of the king Osiris;[5] *ba* is usually translated as 'soul' but one in which generative power is inherent. Hence Apis was incarnate in the bull, symbol of male procreative power in gods and kings of the Osirian line.[6] The great Akan kings sacrificed and resurrected the bull of the god whom they incarnated on New Year's Day,[7] a custom which, it would appear, also existed in Egypt. In the Papyrus of Anhai the skin of a white bull with sacred marks is shown hanging from a pole near the shrine of Osiris; the bull's head has been cut off (Pl. 9).[8] This is reminiscent of the white bull which was once

[1] Otto, p. 11.
[2] Otto, op. cit., p. 23; *Serapeum*, III, Pl. 6.
[3] Osiris, as god of the Nile, also received his power from Orion.
[4] For the Akan ideograms see *Sacred State*, Chapter VI.
[5] Apis was also the *ba* of Ptah when the latter was viewed as the 'great Nile'.
[6] The Atum kings, it would appear, were incarnate in the Mnevis bull. When the Osirian kings succeeded to the 'throne of Atum' the Apis bull was brought into a relationship with Atum. Hence such sayings as: 'The living Apis Atum the first form of appearance of Wennofer (i.e. Osiris)'. Mariette, *Sur la Mère*, p. 276; cf. Otto, p. 28. On the other hand the Mnevis bull after death became Osiris-Mnevis; cf. Otto, p. 40. The Mnevis bull of Atum was regarded as the father, that is to say, predecessor of the Apis bull of Osiris; Hopfner, p. 87.
[7] Chapter VIII, 1.
[8] In Budge, *Osiris*, pp. 326 ff. I disagree with Budge and other scholars; the Apis bull was not piebald but white with symbolic marks in black.

ritually killed by the kings of Bono (Asante, Denkyira and so forth); its skin used to be hung up near the shrines of the Royal Ancestors in the Chapel of the Stools; the head of the animal was often placed before the shrine of the founder of the dynasty. The tail was used by the kings as a charm to protect them from evil; they used to carry one of these tails, mounted on a golden handle, when they appeared in public.[1]

The marks on the bull's skin in the Papyrus of Anhai are interesting, for they consist of a *crux decussata* (X) and a black circle, repeated twice (Pl. 9). Among the Akan the *crux decussata* symbolises the lunar Mother-goddess as ruler of the heavens; the black circle would signify the moon whose cycle is complete just before the new crescent appears again. The number two (the symbols appear twice) conveys 'birth' or 'mother and child', and the whole would express the idea that the lunar Mother-goddess gives birth, death, and perpetual rebirth to her son the lunar god. Since Apis was a lunar god the signs are appropriate, especially so on the skin of the dead animal.

After the death of the king Osiris the Apis bull was no longer sacrificed, but was allowed to live as long as 25 years;[2] among the Akan, a divine bull could only be sacrificed by the king who incarnated the god. The Apis bull was given a royal burial[3] and the priests went in search of his successor. When they had found him they fed him for forty days;[4] he was then taken to Memphis, where, as legend has it, Osiris was drowned in the Nile. During these forty days only women were permitted to see him. According to Pliny 'they place themselves before the bull, full in his view, pluck up their coats and expose their persons'. Afterwards they were forbidden to come within sight of the god. This display, in which the women show their genitalia to the god in order to conceive, is also known among the Akan, where it is called *tuobo*.[5] The span of forty

---

[1] The Akan kings still use them on ceremonial occasions. For the bull's tail the tail of the *otromo* antelope may be substituted; this is symbolic of Nyame in her form of the bi-sexual Supreme Being; or a white horse's tail, symbolic of the sun and moon and resurrection with special reference to the Royal Ancestors.

[2] Otto, op. cit., p. 18. The significance of the Apis period is not quite clear.

[3] For the bull's mummification and details of the funeral ceremony see Otto, pp. 21, 22.

[4] Budge, *Gods*, II, p. 348.

[5] *Ak. of Ghana*, pp. 50, 58, 66, 75, 78, 146. In Egypt the ram of Mendes was also thus honoured by the women, see Hopfner, *Tierkult*, p. 95.

days is interesting in view of the fact that the sacred calendar of the Akan, the *Adaduonan*, literally Forty Days,[1] consists of forty-day periods; it may be of Egyptian origin, dating back to early prehistoric times. In Memphis the new Apis was then enthroned under a full moon.[2]

Apis, like the Akan Sky fertility-gods, foretold the future; ancient authors refer to the oracle of the god.[3] He, like the bull-god Min, probably had in his service a class of priests, generally called 'seers' or 'prophets'. They seem to have approximated to the Akan *akomfo*, who go into trances in which they communicate with the deity and see or hear of future events.[4]

4. *The Bull-god Min*

According to traditions preserved in the Min cult, the bull-god Min was brought to Egypt from Punt by falcon clan people who settled at Akhmin and Koptos in Upper Egypt.[5] Min bore the title, 'Lord of the Foreign Mountain Country',[6] and 'Great in the Desert',[7] or the 'First in the Desert',[8] both references to Punt.

So far as the evidence goes, Min was worshipped at Akhmin long before the unification of Egypt; he had, further, a sanctuary at nearby Koptos, which is referred to in the texts as 'the house of Min in the capital of the *nome* (city state) of the two falcons'.[9] Before it, in later times, stood a colossal statue of a falcon. Akhmin was the town of the 'Fiery Bull'.[10] The titles of the chiefs of Akhmin were 'Overseer of the slaughter of the cattle of the harem's people',[11] 'Chief herdsman of the Black Cow of Min'[12] and 'Attendant of the White Bull' (of Min).[13]

'Harem's people' is an expression tentatively used by Gauthier, but I do not agree with his translation of the Egyptian word. The so-called 'harem' was more probably what the Akan call *twemma*

---

[1] See *Sacred State*, IX, section 2. [2] Otto, pp. 15, 16. [3] ibid., p. 26.
[4] *Ak. of Ghana*, pp. 55-8. The *akomfo* are the mouthpiece of the gods. Apis, in a text, is called 'mouth of all people of Pe'. The people of Pe may be regarded as the people who surrounded the 'Souls of Pe', Pharaoh's Lower Egyptian Royal Ancestors, descended from Isis. The Apis priests received through them, among others, knowledge of future events.
[5] See Gauthier, *Fêtes*, p. 199. The ritual formulae recited by the 'negro from Punt' probably contained allusions to past historical events and the migration from Punt into Upper Egypt.
[6] ibid., p. 197. [7] Gauthier, *Personnel*, p. 3. [8] ibid.
[9] Sethe, *Urgeschichte*, pp. 36, 37. [10] *Fêtes*, p. 84 n. 1.
[11] *Personnel*, pp. 54, 55. [12] ibid.
[13] G. A. Wainwright, 'Some Celestial Associations of Min', *JEA* (1935), p. 159.

(literally 'vulva'), which was, and still is in many states, the name for the queen-mother's house, for from her vulva issued the king, the princes, and princesses of the state. The title should therefore be understood to mean 'Overseer (more accurately chief or king in charge) of the sacrifice of cattle (that is to say, the white bull and the black cow of Min) belonging to the people (of the royal lineage) in the queen-mother's (or reigning queen's) house'. The correctness of this interpretation is supported by the fact that, in historic times, the Pharaoh sacrificed the white bull of Min, the Sky fertility-god of the state, on New Year's day in autumn. The rite is depicted on the walls of the temple at Medinet Habu (Pl. 18); the sacrifice of the black cow of Min is merely indicated.[1]

Hathor, 'She who is at the head in the East',[2] was regarded as Min's mother until the 6th Dynasty, if not earlier, when Isis took her place.[3] Min's planet was the moon; in his form of Sky fertility-deity his personality, and so his destiny, were therefore those of the moon. At Panopolis Min was called 'the Fiery Bull at the day of the New Moon which appears in the night of each month',[4] and the 'Fiery Bull, Lord of New Moon day, who appears at the Full Moon.'[5] This would indicate that Min, the new moon, reached his full generative power at full moon. A text on the walls of the monument at Medinet Habu states that the festival of Min took place 'at the time of the procession of the protector of the moon',[6] 'protector' having here, it would seem, the same significance as the Akan *akragya* of the planet moon, who gives *kra* and *sunsum* to those born on Monday and acts as their guardian spirit.

Min, as the Sky fertility-god was the 'king above the clouds'[7] and also the 'opener of the clouds',[8] but above all the god 'who created vegetation and let the herds live'.[9] He was, moreover, a storm and thunder-god and his weapons were meteorites and thunderbolts.[10] His statue was painted black,[11] a reference either to the night sky or to the dark, cloudy, thunder-threatening sky. In the hand of his raised right arm he carried a whip or flail to

---

[1] For details see pp. 181, 182.   [2] *Fêtes*, p. 183.
[3] For Isis as the mother of Min see Kees, *Götterglaube*, Index 'Isis in Koptos'.
[4] Brugsch, *Rel.*, p. 875 (n. 1199).   [5] ibid.   [6] Gauthier, *Fêtes*, pp. 62, 84.
[7] ibid., p. 195, Gauthier quoting the translation by B. Turajeff.
[8] ibid., p. 194.   [9] ibid., p. 235.
[10] G. A. Wainwright, 'The Emblem of Min', in *JEA*, XVII (1931), p. 185 *et passim*.
[11] G. A. Wainwright, 'Some Aspects of Amun', in *JEA*, XX (1934), p. 139.

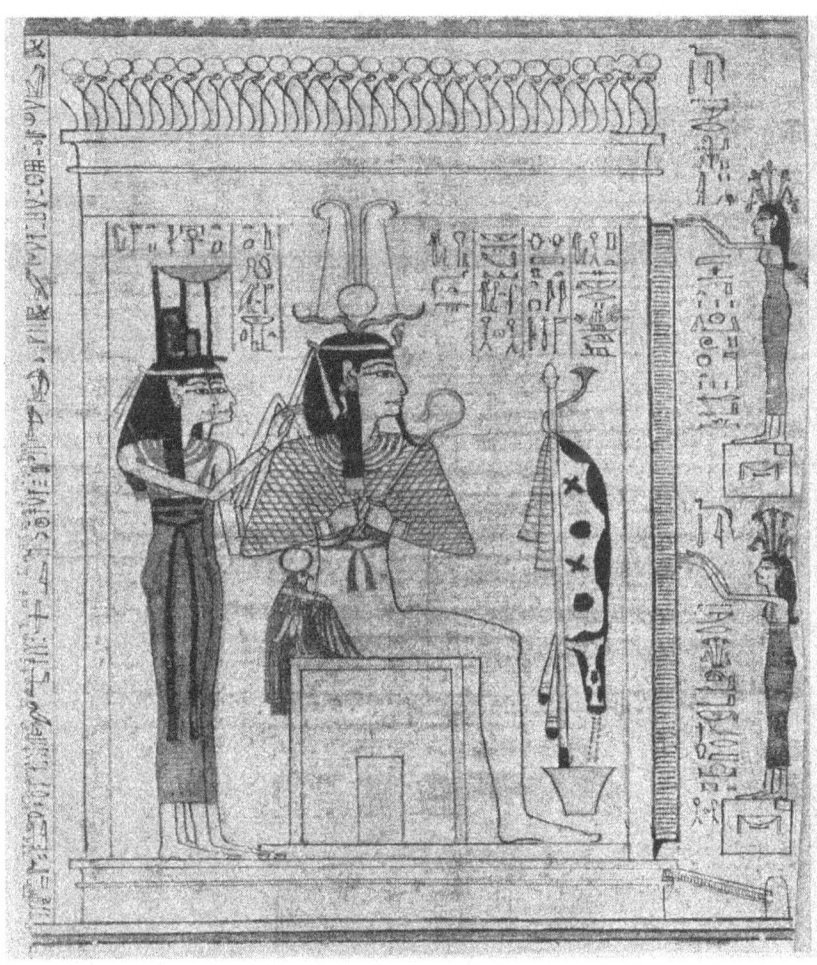

9. Illustration from the Papyrus of Anhai.
Osiris enthroned within a shrine; next to him the falcon Horus, before him the skin of the Apis bull. Behind him are Isis and Nephthys. (Reproduced by courtesy of the Trustees of the British Museum.)

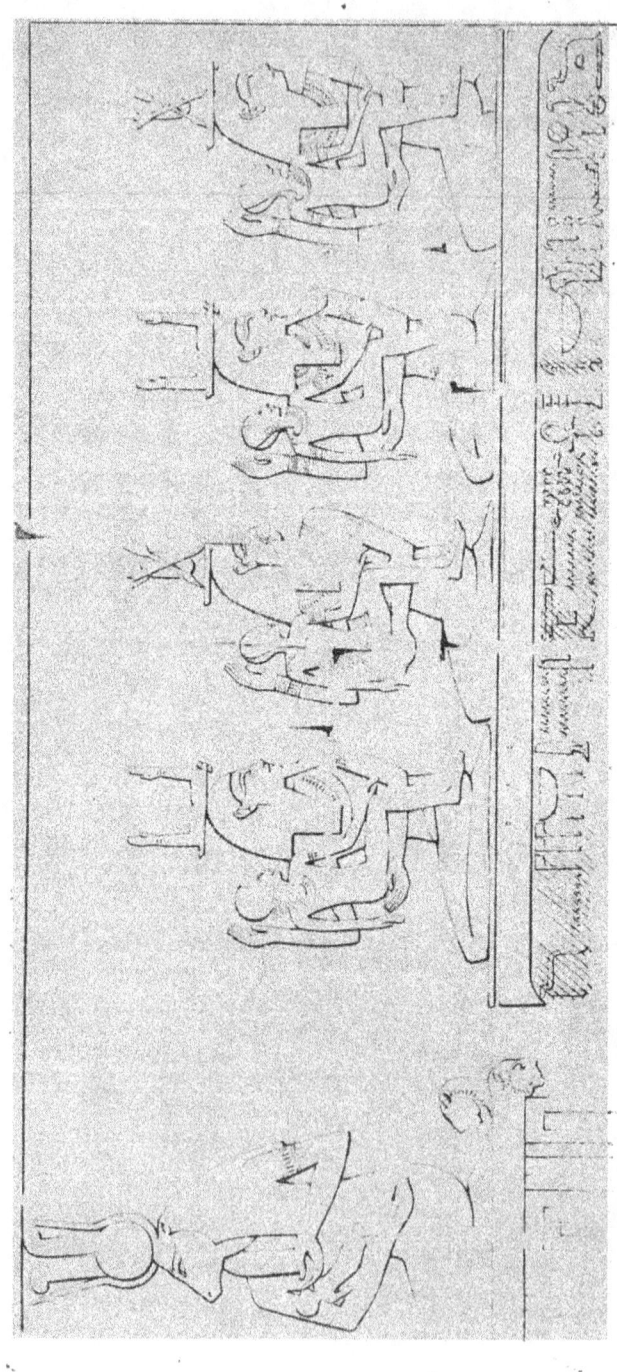

10. *Ka* and *Ḥemset* deities from a relief at Deir el Bahri. They are seen nursing the infant Hatshepsut. The cow goddess with the moon disk between her horns represents either Hathor or Isis. (Naville, *Deir el Bahri* Pl. LIII. Reproduced by courtesy of the Egypt Exploration Society.)

demonstrate his striking power, both beneficent and destructive (Pl. 18); in the earliest representations of Min his head-dress consisted of two upright feathers believed to symbolise his domination of the atmosphere, but since these feathers were also worn by Onuris-Shu-Horus they may have indicated his origin from Punt.[1]

Min was portrayed as an ithyphallic man, and although we cannot be sure that the *tuobo* custom, in which the women showed their genitalia to a god, was performed, several things suggest that it was. Firstly, the custom was known in Egypt and practised before the Apis bull and the ram of Mendes; secondly, Min was called 'the husband' not only of his mother, but of all goddesses and all women. On a stele from Akhmin is written: 'the bull that covers the beautiful women, and gives his semen to gods and goddesses alike'.[2]

Passages on Min monuments refer to the 'divine shadow' of Min, or to 'the shadow of the god'.[3] Gauthier, discussing this, remarks that the shadow of the god is that of the ithyphallic god, the god who begets.[4] The shadow, in the sense of shadow soul, was called *khaibit* by the Egyptians. The concepts of *khaibit* and the *sunsum* of the Akan seem to be the same; *sunsum*, literally 'a kind of shadow', the mortal soul or consciousness of self, the personality, also has the connotation of semen or begetting, because it is passed on to the future child when the father performs the sexual act with its mother; mortal life can only be maintained through procreation.

The Akan Sky fertility-deities, generally manifest in vegetation, each have an edible plant in which they are incarnate. In the case of Min, a Sky fertility-god of the Akan type,[5] it is generally

---

[1] According to Junker, *Onuris*, the two 'high feathers' had the significance of the 'two eyes' meaning sun and moon. The feather crown was also worn by other deities.

[2] *Fêtes*, p. 141.

[3] ibid., p. 154, n. 6.

[4] Gauthier, op. cit., draws attention to the fact that in French the covering of a cow by a bull is called *ombrager*, derived from the word *ombrage* meaning 'shadow'; in German it is *beschatten*, derived from *Schatten* meaning 'shadow'. It shows how widespread this concept must have been since it has left its traces in European languages.

[5] Min resembles most closely Ntoa as worshipped at Wankyi. *Sacred State*, pp. 156 ff. and *Ak. of Ghana*, pp. 59 ff.

assumed that this plant was a certain species of lettuce, believed to stimulate procreation, an allusion to the deity's generative force.[1] Lettuces were carried in a box by priests in the procession at Min's annual festival.[2] Reliefs from the Middle Kingdom show that Min was also incarnate in *emmer* wheat,[3] the earliest cereal grown by the Egyptians, testifying to the great age of the god.

There is some indication that Min from early times was connected with a clan whose totem animal was the bee, for the priests of Min were called 'people of the bee'.[4] The title of Min's high priest at Koptos was 'servant of Horus'[5] and not 'servant of Min', as one might expect: evidence that Min was worshipped as a state god and not as a clan god, the high priest serving the Horus priest-

---

[1] The juice of some species of lettuce is milky, resembling either the flow of milk (female aspect) or semen (male). Cf. L. Keimer in *ZÄS*, LIX, pp. 140 ff.

[2] Note the number of lettuces in illustrations. Among the Akan numbers have a symbolical meaning. See *Sacred State*, VI, p. 2.   [3] See p. 180.

[4] *Fêtes*, p. 247. Min was also sometimes regarded as a bee-god. There was a close connection between Min and Neith of Sais, and also with Nut who seems to have been originally the same deity as Neith. The royal lineages worshipping Neith and Nut had the bee as totem (see p. 51). Nut like Min came from Punt. The original animal in which Min was incarnate, I believe to have been the stag, for on the base of a statue of Min found at Koptos a stag's head on a pole is depicted (Petrie, *Koptos*, p. 7). Moreover the animal of Tanit, the Libyo-Phoenician Neith, was the deer (*Ak. of Ghana*, p. 133), and Neith was the original mother of Min.

When the clan god Min became a state Sky fertility-god he acquired the bull and the ram as personality-expressing animals; thus Min of Koptos and Akhmin was a bull-god and Amun, Amen of Thebes and Baal Hamman, Tanit's son and husband, a ram-god.

The royal lineage of the bee clan may have taken over the worship of Min when that of the stag clan became extinct, in the same way as the royal falcon lineage of Bono took over the worship of the mouse-god Buru, a bull as a Sky fertility-god, after the mouse clan's royal lineage had ceased to exist.

On the base of the above-mentioned statute of Min is also depicted a lioness (cf. G. D. Hornblower, 'Min and his Functions' in *MAN*, September–October 1946, No. 103, p. 118); Petrie believed her to be a hyena (op. cit., p. 7). She, no doubt, represented Tefnut, the lioness, whose people ruled Punt; the flying bird next to the lioness may have been the Horus falcon; elephant and ostrich were possibly the deities of clans formed in Nubia, their people the 'negroes' subjugated by Min. All these animals stand on conical mounds, which characterise them as deities. The jagged beaks of sawfish and pteroceras shells from the Red Sea, also depicted on the base, I regard as expressing Min's power in water, in the same way as the bull-god Buru was symbolised by the manatee or sea-cow.

[5] Wainwright, 'Emblem of Min', p. 191.

chief or king at Akhmin who sacrificed the bull of Min, a royal prerogative.

Gauthier translates 'First Prophet of Min' as 'high priest'.[1] From the term 'prophet' one may assume that the high priest was an *osofo-okomfo*, to use the Akan term, that is to say, one who is able to fall into a trance in order to communicate with the deity. The Egyptian texts mention several prophets in connection with Min: 'prophets, great and pure, chief of the mysteries, in charge of purifications, all confidants of the god, officiating in the sanctuary'[2] and so forth. This description exactly fits the Akan *okomfo*, of whom each great Sky fertility-god has a number; only the high priest, or *osofo-okomfo* can personify the god in the rites.[3] Min also had in his service a reciter priest[4] who sang or read the praises of the god when offerings were made or libations poured out. The Akan call this class of priest *abrafo*. The *abrafo* act as masters of ceremonies and in this role assist the *okomfo* priests when they go into trances during the festivals; they interpret messages from the god when they are unintelligibly delivered, and calm the *okomfo* when necessary. Further, musicians and dancers served the god, among them women who sang and accompanied themselves on the sistrum;[5] the Akan priestesses perform this with rattles on festive occasions.

Even in historic times Min's sanctuary remained the primitive cylindrical hut with the conical thatched roof. In an illustration of it from the 12th Dynasty, Middle Kingdom, the entrance to the hut (almost hidden by the thatch which nearly reaches the ground) is embellished with a portico or pylon.[6] Before it a pole is driven into the ground displaying a pair of bull's horns, symbolic of the god.[7] Between the horns is mounted a spiral, which, among the Akan, is a symbol of birth and creation and would characterise a deity such as *Abaama*, the giver of children.

Wainwright[8] speaks of an omphalos, or conical mound, as being

---

[1] Gauthier, *Personnel*, p. 13.   [2] ibid., p. 10.

[3] For an instance where an *osofo-okomfo* personified the god in the rites, see *Ak. of Ghana* p. 34.

[4] *Fêtes*, pp. 158, 178.   [5] *Personnel*, pp. 86, 91, 92, 113.

[6] *Fêtes*, p. 141. The sanctuary of the Akan god Ntoa at Wankyi is still built in this primitive way, but at Seseman-Nkoranza the building is modernised and consists of a round cement wall with a tall conical tiled roof.

[7] For the significance of the pole see Wainwright, 'Celestial Associations', pp. 163, 167. The Akan, if they use the pole, use it in connexon with Nyame and treat it as an altar, the *Nyame-dua*, see *Ak. of Ghana*, p. 28.

[8] Wainwright, op. cit., pp. 167, 167.

closely associated with the god. The conical mound and the small dome-shaped cones are the traditional shrines of the Akan Sky fertility-deities; these were also used in Egypt for other gods, among them Horus of Hierakonpolis, Soker, Horus Sopdu, Onuris-Shu-Horus, Amun, and Amen of Shiwa (see Fig. 3).

With the unification of Egypt, Min, the god who had, as the Akan say, 'helped to win the victory', became the state god of the Two Lands and incarnate in Pharaoh. On the Palette of Narmer (Menes), which commemorated the victory of the Upper Egyptian king Narmer over the Lower Egyptian people, Min appears for the first time in relation to the Pharaoh. On both sides of the palette a head of Hathor dominates the scenes.[1] On the one side Min's bull attacks an enemy fortress with his powerful horns; on the other the falcon Horus hovers over the severed head of the enemy king. On the Bull palette in the Louvre, dating from the same period, again the bull attacks the enemy and the falcon Horus presides over the scene. The palette and the mace head of Narmer make it clear that he only achieved his victory with the assistance of Min and Horus, who are incarnate in him, the king. Moreover, they show that he was protected by Hathor, the mother of Horus and Min, the divine ancestress of his lineage.

[1] *Hierakonpolis* I, Pl. XXIX.

CHAPTER III

The Divine King, the Incarnation of the Sun-God

AKAN

1. *The Sun-god Nyankopon*

In the past, as the history of Bono and Asante shows, when a kingdom became wealthy and powerful, it must have been felt that the king's status ought to be enhanced and he was thus made, an incarnation of the manifestation of the sun on earth. *Ohene ye awia*—'the king is [the manifestation of] the sun'. It meant that the king was no longer an incarnation of the lunar god, except in certain rituals, but of the solar god, in contrast to the queen-mother, who continued to incarnate the lunar Mother-goddess.

Nyankopon, the personification of the male aspect of the supreme Mother-goddess Nyame, was chosen centuries ago to be the Sun-god, the ancestor and father-god of kings. Nyankopon means 'the alone great Nyame' because the solar *kra* came to be envisaged as greater than the lunar *kra* of the goddess (Cult Type III). Like Nyame he still shows traces of having once been a clan and Sky fertility-god. He is still Nyankopon Kwaame (He of Saturday) because as a Sky fertility-god his birthday was on Saturday. One of his epithets is *Odaa Amen*, of which the meaning has been forgotten. It may be translated either as 'He who rests on Saturday', that is to say, does not show his power on this day (as a sun-god), or 'He who is an adjunct of Amen.' The sense in the latter case may have been that Nyankopon, the shining sun, was an adjunct or successor of Amen, the 'most ancient god', whose planet was Saturn. Nyankopon's secret or strong name is Amen.

Nyankopon's titles as solar god were the following:[1] *Oboade* 'He who created the universe', an epithet he shares with Nyame; *Tetekwaframua* 'He who endureth for ever'; *Atoapoma*, the 'Ever-ready-shooter', that is to say, of the solar *kra*, the life-giving power of the sun, into the universe—also originally one of Nyame's praise names; *Oteanankaduro*, 'He who knows the antidote for the serpent', or death; *Brekyirihunuade*, 'He who sees all and knows all'; and *Nyaamanekose*, 'He in whom one confides troubles', a reference to his being the father-god of the kings, who ask his help in times of need.

Nyankopon, envisaged as the Supreme Being, is symbolised by the bongo antelope (*otromo*). A head-dress of kings and great chiefs, worn during funeral rites, is made from a chaplet of silk, the two ends of which stand upright. This is known as the 'horns of the bongo'. Nyankopon, viewed as the Sun-god, as the giver of the sun's fertility, is symbolised by the ram, and the skin of every white ram of the long-legged Sudanese breed, sacrificed to the Royal Ancestors, is hung up in the Chapel of the Stools where their *kras* are worshipped. Nyankopon as a solar god, fire, is symbolised by the lion; the king in certain rituals sits on the lion-skin; as a solar god with emphasis on the scorching, destructive heat of the sun, he is symbolised by the leopard, the *Gyahene*, which means 'Lord of Fire'. The leopard has become the favourite emblem of the king as war-lord.[2]

2. *The King, the Son of the Sun-god*

The task of the sun-king, like that of the moon-king, was to give and maintain the life of the state. He achieved this through his solar *kra*, which was the *kra* both of the Sun-god, his divine ancestor, and of his Royal Ancestors (*nananom*), the deceased kings, whose *kra* had become one with Nyankopon after death. The kingly solar *kra* can therefore be regarded as an ancestral *kra* reincarnated in the reigning king. He acquired it in a special rite when, after the late king had ascended to heaven, his stool, which had now become the shrine for his *kra*, was brought to his successor; the enstoolment or enthronement ceremony, performed previously, had given him only his secular power to rule the land. He was, however, son of the

---

[1] J. B. Danguah, *Akan Doctrine of God*, pp. 46-8, 53-5.
[2] For further details on Nyankopon see *Sacred State*, pp. 79 ff. and *Ak. of Ghana*, pp. 82 ff.

Sun-god solely with regard to his office; the kingly *kra* descended to him in the male line from his predecessors on the throne; as a man, he remained the son of the lunar Mother-goddess, from whom he was descended in the female line. Constitutionally also, the king continued to be the son of the queen-mother: he could issue decrees only after consultation with her and with his council of elders or ministers. Thus though proclaimed supreme as the incarnation of the Sun-god, he never became an autocrat.

The king was venerated as the fount (*nde nsee*) of everything, above all of truth, justice, wisdom; he was the repository of all authority and power. In reality he delegated all his power to subordinates, but the fiction was maintained. Although he never went to war, all victories were ascribed to his personal valour and superior intelligence; songs credited him with personally slaying the enemy king. He was equally held responsible for national disasters and defeats.

The king devoted himself entirely to the task of giving life, which implied keeping his generative *kra* in a state of perfection and preserving it from all defilement, particularly corpses and menstruating women. Among the Bono, he was forced to live in such seclusion that he left his palace only once a year, on the day of the *Asubo* ceremony, and even then took a road reserved exclusively for the royal procession. His people were not allowed to see him, lest their evil wishes might injure his *kra*. The work of government was undertaken by his heir-apparent, who bore the title '*Dea ote Abakoma Dwa so*' literally 'sitter on the high-born's stool', and ruled publicly like a king. Since in most cases, the king himself had been an heir-apparent, he was familiar with all governmental matters. He kept himself well informed, and gave final decisions on matters of importance.

The king was entirely surrounded by his sons, or the sons of his predecessors, who held all palace offices and posts at court. Of course they served him loyally, because their personal interests were bound up with the throne. In Bono the king had over one thousand wives (3,333 was the desired number) who lived in a harem, supervised by eunuchs. Nearly all came from families who owned stools in the country—that is to say, hereditary offices which their sons and daughters, at the same time the king's sons and daughters, could be chosen to occupy. Thus the king, through his marriages, could attach more closely to himself the clans, vassal states, towns and villages, as well as court officials and palace officers. The king's children who succeeded to the politically important stools, above all those of clans, remained in their mother's clans; the others, including such of the king's children as did not succeed to a chiefly office (and were therefore regarded as commoners), had to join the state-clan (or child-clan) of the royal line which, in Bono, was the Anana. The king himself was obliged to leave his clan after his enstoolment ceremony, for he now belonged to the state, and when he (represented by the heir-apparent) appeared in public, he wore a golden helmet or head-dress surmounted by a golden parrot, the totem of the Anana and emblem of the state.

As the supreme priest of the Sun-god cult, the king venerated his Great Ancestor in the Chapel of the Stools. He also propitiated the Royal Ancestors who had joined the god, after their deaths, in *Nyankopon-kurom*, the 'City of Nyankopon', and who mediated between the Sun-god and the living king. The Sun-god cult was exclusively an ancestor cult in the royal line, for the people continued to worship Nyankopon as the personified male aspect of Nyame.[1]

3. *The King as the Incarnation of the Sun*

Ohene ye awia—'The king is the sun'; for that reason he had to model himself as closely as possible on the sun. Since the sun rose, set, and travelled across the sky with unfailing regularity, the king's day was similarly regulated, even to the times of his walks, his meals and his children's visiting hours. He committed a serious offence if he did not go to bed when the sun set and if he refused certain foods that were intended to make him fat and round like the sun. Even his sexual life was arranged for him, so that he could neither choose a wife from his harem, nor refuse one sent him by the *Odanbeni*, or chief of the royal bed-chamber. This official always had to be a grandson of a king by a mother who was of the royal lineage, and his task was to see that each wife had her turn in the royal bed.

In ancient Bono, the king's day began when the sun rose behind the ruler's head. He slept in a bedroom on the top floor of his three-storied palace, the window of which faced east. The bed was built like a seven-step pyramid; each step was covered with material

[1] For the development of the Sun cult (Cult Type III) see *Ak. of Ghana*, pp. 82 ff.

of a different colour of the rainbow. The rainbow was envisaged as a ladder by which the king could reach his father, the Sun-god, and the Royal Ancestors; or the Royal Ancestors could descend by it to visit him in his sleep. The counterpane and sheets were of yellow silk or brocade, embroidered with gold, symbolic of the sun. His mattress and pillow were stuffed with gold dust that would renew his strength during the night.[1]

All the king's ornaments, eating utensils, and ceremonial instruments were of gold, the metal of the sun. On New Year's day in the evening he appeared as the risen sun on the horizon, his hair and his naked body powdered with gold-dust adhering to grease, wearing a cloth woven of hammered gold thread and his whole person covered with gold ornaments.

After death the king's *kra* was represented in the Chapel of the Stools by a large nugget of gold. His stool, the shrine of his *kra*, was covered with sheet gold and its five columns were filled with gold dust.[2] When the Chapel was closed and the stools lay on their sides so that no evil spirit could sit on them, they were covered with a large yellow cloth, heavily embroidered with gold. The king's coffin was encased in gold on which symbols of heaven were embossed, and his person was covered with gold ornaments.[3]

Whereas the king was revered as the son of the Sun-god, and all his ornaments and ceremonial instruments were of gold, the queen-mother was venerated as the daughter of the moon-goddess, and her ornaments were made of silver, the moon's metal. Since, however, she owned the state and was the king's 'mother', her state swords, the *mmerante*, and her ceremonial smoking pipes (tobacco being sacred to the state deity Ntoa) were made in pairs, one gold and one silver. Like the king she had to live in seclusion, devoting herself entirely to her life-giving function. Her *kra*, like that of the king, was a reincarnated, ancestral one derived from the lunar Mother-goddess and the queen-mothers who had preceded her. The rites she performed in the Chapel of the Stools were identical with those performed by the king in his Chapel. From the time of the Bonohemmaa Gyaasewaa onwards (1656–79), the

---

[1] For greater detail see *Ak. of Ghana*, pp. 86 ff.

[2] From the seventeenth century onwards the stools were no longer covered with sheet gold, but blackened; the five columns were as before filled with gold dust.

[3] For illustrations of royal ornaments in gold, see *Sacred State*.

queen-mother's palace was at Amona, beyond the river Yaa, a few miles north of the capital; but her heiress-apparent remained in Bono-Mansu, deputising for her.

EGYPT
1. The Sun-gods: Atum, Re-Atum, Amen-Re and Aton
(a) Atum

Atum, worshipped as a Sun-god, was not the son of a lunar Mother-goddess but had created himself and was a creator-god in his own right. The priest-chief on earth, who incarnated him, became the 'first living man-god', that is to say, a divine king with secular power; hence the 'throne of Atum' had a special significance and the term was still used in historical times.[1]

Atum's male procreative force was represented by the Mnevis bull, who became the predecessor of the Bull of Geb and the 'father' or predecessor of the Apis bull of Osiris, who was called the 'Living Apis Atum'.[2] Although the kings of the dynasties succeeding that of Atum adopted the bull (the 'Bull of Set', the Min bull etc.), they continued to incarnate the moon-gods of their clan.

(b) Re-Atum

Atum became prominent again in the reign of the 2nd Dynasty kings, but in a new form, as his name Re-Atum indicates. He became even more important in the reign of Djoser, a king of the 3rd Dynasty, *ca.* 2700 B.C. We do not know what caused this renewed interest, but certain events in Djoser's reign may possibly give us some idea. Djoser instituted the civil calendar which was based on the solar year and ousted the lunar calendar until then in use. Djoser, furthermore, was the first king who created for himself a pyramid, a stone building of enormous size, the design of which is supposed to have been based on the pyramidically shaped *ben-ben* stone, the shrine of the Sun-god Re. At the top of this stone, it is said, Re first revealed himself in the form of the *bennu* bird. The Egyptian word *bennu* means 'that which turns back', or 'revolves'.[3] The *bennu* bird seems to be identical with the Akan

---

[1] Thus in the Pyramid texts (*Pyr.* 140 l, ut. 216, ut. 222) at the end of the long coronation hymn Atum figures as the father, that is to say, predecessor on the throne.
[2] See p. 77, n. 6.
[3] Wiedemann, *Rel.*, p. 293.

THE INCARNATION OF THE SUN-GOD

sankofa bird; *sankofa* means 'that which turns back to seize again', that is to say 'revolves' (Fig. 8). The *sankofa* bird is usually depicted with head turned backwards, sitting on a pyramid, or on a step-pyramid and, occasionally, on a truncated three- or four-sided pyramid. It is a royal emblem, the emblem of the sun-kings.[1]

Pliny and Horapallo identified the *bennu* bird with an astronomical cycle. In contrast to Atum, then, the representative of the sun as the creator of the cosmos, Re, who revealed himself as the *bennu* bird, should symbolise the revolving sun—the apparent course of the sun within the year which we call the ecliptic. It would seem

Fig. 8

The Sankofa *bird (from a gold weight)*

therefore that some time during the 2nd Dynasty the discovery was made, or it was officially recognised, that the sun revolved and was eternal. The new concept, however, never entirely displaced the old belief that the sun was borne anew each morning by the Mother-goddess Nut, or that Ptah created the daily sun. The discovery of the course of the sun must have been made at Heliopolis, for its astronomical instruments received divine honours from the hands of the Pharaohs during the *Sed* festival so long as it was celebrated.[2] The priests who made this discovery, or their successors, settled at Heliopolis, the city of the Sun, during the 2nd Dynasty; excavations so far have not shown that Heliopolis existed in

[1] *Sacred State*, Pls. 41, 48, 90.
[2] See p. 166.

91

prehistoric times.¹ Re was fused with Atum and became Re-Atum, and as such combined the characteristics of both Sun-gods.

The Pharaohs did not incarnate Re-Atum, but from the time of Djoser onwards they regarded themselves as sons of Re—'Re, who endureth for ever, and had existed for ever and would exist to all eternity.' Whereas the worship of Re-Atum was in the hands of the priests of Heliopolis, the worship of Re, as the ancestor-god of kings, was in the hands of the Pharaohs. The cult of Re was fused with that of Horus; the life-giving *ka* of the Pharaoh was no longer that of the lunar Horus, but that of the solar Horus, Re-Horus also called Re-Harakhti.²

(c) Amen-Re

In the Middle Kingdom a change took place. Re ceased to be regarded as an aspect of Atum and became merged with Amen, city god of Thebes, at a time when a Theban dynasty ruled Egypt. Amen was originally a Sky fertility-god like Min, with whom he may have shared a common origin, but whereas Min was incarnate in the bull, Amen was incarnate in the ram.³ As a supreme deity he became a creator-god.

Whereas the kings of the Old Kingdom incarnated Re the eternal, revolving sun, the Pharaohs of the Middle Kingdom incarnated Amen-Re, a Sky fertility Sun-god. In the rites of the New Year festival at Thebes the god, represented by the ram, died and was resurrected; the image of Amen was clothed in the skin of the sacrificed beast.⁴

(d) Aton

Amen-hotep IV, Ikhnaton, a king of the 18th Dynasty, reverted to the original conception of Re and reintroduced the god under the name of Aton; the word is believed to mean 'sun' or 'sun disk'. Ikhnaton assumed the office of high priest, calling himself 'First

---

[1] Baumgärtel, *Cultures*, pp. 9 ff.
[2] See *Pyr.* 348, 855.
[3] Amen-Re was sometimes called 'the Beautiful goose' (Hopfner, *Tierkult*, p. 124). The goose for the Egyptians had a strongly erotic character; it was therefore an animal that, like the ram, 'expressed his personality', that is to say, showed him to be a god of love and procreation. Geese were sacrificed in great quantities to Amen (ibid., p. 123), it therefore could not have been the god's totem animal.
[4] J. F. Frazer, *Adonis, Attis, Osiris* (1912), II, pp. 172–3.

Prophet of Re-Harakhti',[1] showing that Aton was the same as Re-Horus incarnated by the Pharaohs in the Old Kingdom. In the early part of the reign of Ikhnaton Aton was actually represented as a man with the head of a falcon above which was a great red disk, adorned with an uraeus in profile. At a later date, it is important to note, no statue of Aton was ever made; his symbol was a disk under the heavens from which shot earthward a number of diverging rays terminating in hands, each one grasping the symbol of life. Aton, in contrast to Amen-Re, a god of procreation, gave life with his *ka* by shooting the life-giving rays of the sun into the universe, going back to an earlier idea of transmitting life from the sky. Ikhnaton established Aton 'the living sole god'[2] to oust the Sky fertility-gods, among whom Amen-Re was the most powerful, for these died annually to be reborn. He also destroyed Re's association with Atum, a primitive creator Sun-god. Aton was Re, the eternal, revolving, life-giving sun. A text expresses it: 'Re the father, who has returned as Aton.'[3] As far as Ikhnaton was concerned Aton and Re were one. Though Ikhnaton abandoned the title 'bodily son of Re' he renounced none of the claims of an Egyptian divine king, and assumed the title 'the son of Re, who lives in truth'.[4] After his death his theology was ignored, for his system was believed to have undermined the unity of his people and the prestige of his country, and he himself was execrated as a criminal.

2. *The King as the Son of the Sun-god*

Pharaoh as the 'Son of Re' embodied the sun on earth and everything was done to maintain this fiction. Because the sun rules supreme in the sky Pharaoh's power over the land and its inhabitants had also to be supreme. In fact, however, he was unable to act in so arbitrary a fashion. He was hailed as the whole source of authority and held responsibility for all official actions, although in practice these were planned and executed by officials to whom he had to delegate his power. He had to maintain *Maat*, that is truth, astronomical truth, the 'cosmic order', hence he was venerated as

[1] A. Moret, *The Nile and Egyptian Civilization*, London, 1927, p. 320.
[2] N. de G. Davies, *The Rock Tombs of Deir el Gebrawi*, London, 1902, IV, Pl. 33.
[3] Gunn, *JEA*, IX (1923), p. 176.
[4] Davies, *JEA*, IX (1923), p. 152.

the fount of all truth and justice and as an integral part of it. It was said of him, 'Thy speech is the shrine of truth (*Maat*)'. *Maat*, personified as a goddess, was regarded as a daughter of the Sun-god Re, whose regular circuit was the most striking manifestation of the established cosmic order. As the sun emerges victoriously each morning, defeating darkness (envisaged as evil), all victories in war and all other great deeds were ascribed to the personal valour and initiative of the Pharaoh; on monuments he is often shown killing in person the enemy king. Since the sun ran its course with unfailing regularity, Pharaoh's life had to mirror the sun. From Diodorus we know that his life was 'as prescribed by a physician', even to the times of his walks and his meals.[1]

From the 4th Dynasty onwards there is evidence that much power in the Two Lands was delegated to the 'Royal Kinsmen', who began more and more to occupy high government offices as well as subordinate positions at court and in the provinces. Many of these, particularly the 'great men of the South', were buried in the burial place of the capital near the king. The names of the 'Royal Kinsmen' were registered in an archive, so that they must have been numerous.

Frankfort prefers to render the word usually translated 'Royal Kinsmen' as 'guardians of' or 'those belonging to' the 'placenta of the king'.[2] All three readings would seem to be correct for 'those who belonged to the placenta of the king' were sons of the living Pharaoh as well as of his predecessor by the hundreds of wives in their harem; the term 'Royal Kinsmen' is therefore appropriate. The placenta was regarded as the dead twin of the Pharaoh because it represented that part of his blood which at birth had not been animated by Hathor. In a matrilineally organised society royal divine blood can only be passed on by women of the royal line, never by the king.[3] His sons, therefore, were not regarded as princes in the line of succession. But Pharaoh's sons would of course be the guardians of the throne, like the *ahenema* of the Akan kings, because their personal interests were bound up with the king's.

The sons of Akan kings were brought up at court and, when they

---

[1] A. Erman, *Life in Ancient Egypt* (ed. Ranke), 1922, p. 67.

[2] *Kingship*, pp. 71 ff.

[3] Among the Akan the placenta is regarded as the twin of the female *kra*. The placentas of the princes and princesses are buried under a palm-tree (moon) on land belonging to the royal lineage.

succeeded to the hereditary offices of their mother's family, they were expected to plead their father's cause and that of the central government with their people. In Egypt also it seems that this was the case. For instance, in the time of the 4th and 5th Dynasties the *nome* chiefs (royal sons as evidence suggests, see below) aided their father in the building of pyramids. The neglect of the *nome* was consequently so great that they, forced no doubt by their people, finally rebelled and regained some of their independence. It is worth while here to deal with this matter in greater detail.

Among the Akan certain work in the state was done by communal labour, and it was the right of the chief, after consultation with his elders, to summon the commoners to build roads and markets, clear virgin forests, drain swamps to gain more farmland, and so forth. The men were not paid because their work was regarded as a means of paying taxes. It may not have been very different in Egypt in the Old Kingdom, since the economy of the country was still largely based on barter. Thus the situation might have arisen that the *nome* chiefs were no longer able to summon their people for work when they were wanted by the Pharaohs to build pyramids. These took years to construct, and for the single task of transporting the blocks of the Great Pyramid, it has been estimated that 100,000 men were annually levied; to this must be added the workers actually engaged in the construction.[1] This meant, of course that there was no further development in the *nome*; in many cases it meant actual neglect, for no repairs could be carried out. All available slave labour was also summoned by the Pharaohs as we know from the Bible. It is no wonder, then, that the 5th Dynasty—each Pharaoh built himself a pyramid of an enormous size—was ousted by the *nome* chiefs. From the beginning of the 6th onwards the chiefs were again buried at home and not near the king, their father; there is also evidence that they could devote themselves more to the welfare of their people. The title 'Governor' or 'Chief' of the *nome* disappeared and was replaced by the title 'Great Prince' or 'Great Lord'. Since, one may assume, by that time the blood of the divine Pharaohs ran in the veins of every one of them, each chief could rightly claim to be a 'son of Re' and a descendant of Osiris, at least on his father's side. Politically, however, they still owed allegiance to the Lord of the land, by whom they had to be confirmed in office. When the 6th Dynasty came to

[1] I. E. S. Edwards, *The Pyramids of Egypt*, London, 1947, pp. 229 ff.

an end the *nomes* (city states) regained complete independence. The Pharaohs of the succeeding dynasty were unable to re-establish a strong central government. Amenemhet, the founder of the 12th Dynasty, was the first to unite Egypt again into a powerful nation.

3. *The King as the Incarnation of the Sun*

The Pharaoh represented the sun on earth; he was the sun; his palace is described as the horizon; when he showed himself he rose, when he died he set. Thus he wears as his diadem the fire-spitting serpent which the Sun-god wears on his forehead and which destroyed his enemies.[1]

Accordingly Amosis I is regarded as the image of Re, whom Re had fashioned.[2] Thutmosis III is spoken of as 'Appearing as king in the ship of millions of years (the Sun-god's boat), as the occupant of the seat of Atum like Re.'[3] Amen-Re is represented as saying to Hatshepsut, who ruled as a Pharaoh: 'Welcome, welcome in peace, beloved daughter of my body, my living image upon earth',[4] and on another inscription Hatshepsut is designated 'the daughter of Amen of his body, the good goddess, mighty of arms, the likeness of Amen-Re his living image upon earth'.[5] She is similarly called 'His [i.e. Re's] living image' on one of her obelisks at Karnak.[6] It is said of Haremhab, 'He is a god, the king of gods—he is Re, his body is the sun.'[7]

The Pharaohs were buried beneath pyramids, the emblem of the Sun-god, the symbol of one of his manifestations, according to *Pyr.* 1652: 'Thou [i.e. the Sun-god] didst appear as the *ben ben* in the House of the *bennu* bird [the Sun temple] in Heliopolis.' Cheops' pyramid was named 'Cheops is one belonging to the horizon', that of Senefru, 'Senefru gleams', that of Sahure, 'The *ba* of Sahure gleams', and that of Meren-Ra, 'Meren-Ra gleams and is beautiful'.[8] Gold is the metal of the sun and gleaming gold, believed to be life-giving, was used in profusion by the Pharaohs.

---

[1] Adolf Erman, *Handbook of Egyptian Religion*, p. 37.
[2] Sethe, *Urgeschichte*, IV, p. 14.
[3] ibid., p. 291.
[4] ibid., p. 279.
[5] ibid., p. 275.
[6] ibid., p. 362.
[7] Dümichen, *Hist. Inschr.* ii, XL e, pp. 15 ff.
[8] For the names of the pyramids see Edwards, *Pyramids*, p. 243.

After death the Pharaoh returned to the sun. When, for instance, Amenemes I died it is said that the 'god entered the horizon'.[1] The horizon meant the sun, which is evident from the following Pyramid text (207–12):

... *Thou risest and settest, thou goest down with Re, sinking in the dusk with Nedy.*
Thou risest and settest, thou risest up with Re and ascendest with the Great Reed Float.
Thou risest and settest; thou goest down with Nephthys, sinking in the dust with the Evening Boat of the Sun.
Thou risest and settest, thou risest up with Isis, ascending with the Morning Boat of the Sun.

Examples in which the Pharaoh is the sun may be multiplied, but these should suffice to illustrate the point.

[1] Hieratische Papyrus aus den Kgl. Museen zu Berlin, BD. V, Leipzig, 1909, R, 6.

CHAPTER IV

The Divine King, the Incarnation of the Divine Procreator of his Lineage

AKAN

1. *The Ntoro Cult, the Cult of the Begetter*

The introduction of the cult of the king as the son of the Sungod was followed in Bono by the introduction of the *Ntoro* cult; this was a further step from matrilineality to patrilineality. In the first-mentioned cult the king received his solar *kra* from the Sun-god through the Royal Ancestors, his titular fathers; in the second he received in addition the *ntoro* spirit from the *Ntoro* god of the royal lineage, also through his titular fathers. The solar *kra*, pure spirit, and the *ntoro* spirit were thus handed down to him through the male line; the lunar *kra*, blood and lineage, as before through the female line.

When the Bonohene Takyi Akwamo (1431–63) introduced the *ntoro* cult, which one may call the cult of the begetter, into his state he chose Buru, the Sky fertility-god of his ancestors, as the *ntoro* of the royal lineage.[1] The great clan chiefs in their turn chose the Sky fertility-gods worshipped by their ancestors as the *Ntoro* gods of their stools, i.e. the clan chiefly lineages.

Bosom Buru (god Buru) or Bosummuru (*mm* is the assimilation of *mb*), the *Ntoro* god, was like his predecessor the Sky fertility-god, envisaged as bi-sexual; whereas the god was incarnate in the king, his divine semen, the goddess was incarnate in the queen-mother, her divine blood. In Bono and Bono-Takyiman the queen-mother received her procreative power, blood, from her titular mothers, her predecessors in office, who were descended from the

---

[1] For greater detail see *Ak. of Ghana*, pp. 108, 109.

INCARNATION OF THE DIVINE PROCREATOR OF HIS LINEAGE

goddess. In the sexual act and in the act of giving birth she incarnated the goddess; the king, who was constitutionally the son of the queen-mother, his titular mother, could thus also claim descent from the goddess in the female line; apart from this he was in fact often her physical son, or the son of one of her predecessors. In Asante, however, where the kings also worshipped Bosommuru as their *Ntoro* god, the princesses, future mothers of kings, had each to marry a cross-cousin of the Bosummuru *ntoro* group, so that the king inherited his *ntoro* spirit from his physical instead of his titular father.

Bosummuru received his *sunsum*, ego, personality, from the planet Mars, and thus was regarded as being hot-tempered, fierce and aggressive. *He* was embodied in the white bull, *she* in the black crouching cow (*Apafram*). In Bono and Bono-Takyiman the god's shrine was a small ceremonial sword,[1] in Asante it was a larger one;[2] both were phallic symbols. The shrines of the goddess were the red *bota* and *bodom* beads, symbolic of blood.[3] Bosummuru's water or semen, that fertilised the land, personified by the goddess, was originally the Niger River, but since this is no longer in Akan territory the legend has arisen that the god's water can no longer be found on this earth; it is with the *Nananom*, the Royal Ancestors in the netherworld (Bono), or with King Adu Gyamfi in the netherworld (Asante).[4] The deity is manifest in maize which was introduced into Bono and Asante at an unknown date.

The *Ntoro* god, like the Sky fertility-god, died annually and was reborn to the Mother-goddess. So also did the king and the queen-mother as personifications of the deity; the queen-mother 'died' in her form of wife of the god; as a mother she resurrected his power. In the sacred marriage that followed, the king and the queen or senior wife (proxy for the queen-mother) celebrated the renewal of their procreative powers.[5] Bosummuru, incarnate in the white bull and the black cow also died annually and was reborn; both animals

---

[1] Illustrated, Pl. 12. In the *Sacred State* I refer to it as a dagger as it is the size of one, but it lacks the sharp point and is therefore better called a ceremonial sword.

[2] Illustrated in *Sacred State*, Pl. 19.

[3] Illustrated ibid., Pl. 95.

[4] Adu Gyamfi was not a king but ruled as acting chief of Kumasi before he enstooled Osei Tutu, who became the first king of Asante in 1699. He is believed to have introduced the *ntoro* cult into this country.

[5] For details see pp. 175 ff.

INCARNATION OF THE DIVINE PROCREATOR OF HIS LINEAGE

were sacrificed in the rites of the New Year festival in autumn[1] and a white bull-calf and a black heifer from the king's sacred herd, born on that day each year, were substituted for them. Maize, in which the deity was incarnate, 'died' annually a natural death and was reborn. But maize was not eaten by the worshippers of the deity, for whom this crop was tabu.[2]

Not only did the king and the queen-mother, the clan chiefs and head women of the clans worship one or other of the twelve *Ntoro* gods of the state, but the commoners also. The *Ntoro* god enshrined in the father gave him status and authority; marriage, hitherto matrilocal, became patrilocal; wives had to acknowledge their husbands as priests of the god. *Rites de passage*, which had been in the hands of the priests of the various gods, were now performed by the father, the head of the family. The principle of the *ntoro* cult was that women were no longer venerated as the only givers of life; men with their divine semen could now claim the same function.[3]

With the *ntoro* cult a double descent system came into being. Men and women belonged as before to the clan of their mothers from which they received their blood, but also to the *ntoro* group of their fathers from whom they received their generative force.[4] The *ntoro* cult was a religious and domestic affair which did not have any important influence on the state organisation.

EGYPT

1. *The Khamutef Cult, the Cult of the Begetter*

The cult of the Khamutef, the begetter and divine procreator, was introduced into Egypt by Thutmosis I, the third king of the 18th Dynasty; from his time onwards the Pharaohs added the title 'Strong Bull'[5] to their *ka* or Horus name; the 'Strong Bull' was,

---

[1] See pp. 175–6.

[2] In the rites of the New Year festival, yams, the favourite crop, take the place of maize, and the first-fruits are offered to Bosummuru and the royal ancestors before people are allowed to eat of them.

[3] For greater detail see *Sacred State*, ch. VII.

[4] According to a saying; 'a man inherits from a man' (not from his father but from male members of his mother's family except procreative *ntoro* power) 'and a woman from a woman'. A girl thus inherits her procreative power from her mother but, since her mother incarnates the goddess of her husband's *ntoro* god as long as she is married, girls belong to the *ntoro* group of their father.

[5] Jacobsohn, *Dogm. Stell.*, p. 58.

in the cult of the king, the Khamutef, the 'Bull of his Mother'. The bull-god who was thus united with Horus was Min (or Amun). Min, originally worshipped at Koptos and Akhmin, became the Sky fertility-god incarnate in the Pharaohs; there is evidence that in the Old Kingdom Min was venerated together with Horus in the Dual Shrines (*Pyr.* 1928 b, c, 1998 a); as the ancestral deity in the Middle Kingdom Min was addressed as 'son of Osiris, born of the divine Isis',[1] epithets which identify him unmistakably with Horus and the living Pharaoh.

Amun, Amen (Greek, Amon) had a common origin with Min and his earliest statues are identical in appearance with those of the latter, being ithyphallic with one arm upraised, and blue-black in colour.[2] He developed on different lines, however, and came to power as a Sky fertility ram-god at Thebes. The 18th Dynasty, being of Theban origin, replaced Min with Amun, and Hathor-Isis with Mut, the consort of Amun; in the texts of the New Kingdom the names are interchangeable.[3]

In Amun Khamutef the powers of three distinct gods were united, as is evident from the ritual of Amenophis I:[4] Amun-Re, the solar creator-god, who was identified with Osiris and the Royal Ancestors; Amun-Apet, the ithyphallic Sky fertility-god identified with Min, and Amun, the bull moon-god equated with the lunar Horus-Min. Amun Khamutef is sometimes referred to as Amun-Re-Khamutef when his aspect as the Great Ancestor is stressed.[5]

The Khamutef, whether Min or Amun in their various forms, died annually to be reborn to his mother, after which he consummated the sacred marriage with her. A text proclaims: 'Amun, bull of his mother (Khamutef), who rejoices in the cow, the husband impregnating with his phallus.'[6]

[1] Erman-Blackman, *Literature*, p. 137; Stela Louvre C. 30.
[2] Mercer, *Rel.*, p. 159 and n. 83.
[3] Jacobsohn, op. cit., p. 18.   [4] ibid., p. 16.
[5] For Amun, viewed as the great-grandfather god, see Jacobsohn, p. 15. Jacobsohn shows that the three forms of Amun are often treated as if they were one person. The *Ntoro* god Bosummuru also has three forms: Buru-kung or Great-Buru, the creator-god; the Sky fertility-god Buru, the son of the former; and Bosummuru, the son or successor of Buru. All three forms of the deity are bi-sexual, hence the Sky fertility-god and the *Ntoro* god are reborn to the Mother-goddess Buru-kung. In Egypt it was the same; Amun, the Sky fertility-god, and Khamutef were both reborn to Mut, see below in the text. These three generations owe their existence to theological development.
[6] H. Grapow, *Die bildlichen Ausdrücke des Ägyptischen*, p. 78.

INCARNATION OF THE DIVINE PROCREATOR OF HIS LINEAGE

In another text it is said: 'Hail to Thee Min who impregnates his mother. How mysterious is that which Thou hast done to her in the darkness.'[1]

On the reliefs at Karnak, in the birth scenes of Hatshepsut, Amun is shown in the act of union with the queen; she must have incarnated Hathor in the act for Hatshepsut is called 'the daughter of the Khamutef, beloved by Hathor'.[2] The death and rebirth of the god, as among the Akan, was identified with that of the king in whom he was incarnate; in the festival depicted at Medinet Habu, that marked the official opening of the harvest season, the white bull, which embodied the god, was sacrificed and, although it is not explicitly stated, there seems to be evidence that the Pharaoh 'died' at that time.[3] On New Year's day the rebirth of Min Khamutef was celebrated, as well as the renewal of the Pharaoh's kingship.

To sum up: In the Khamutef cult the Pharaoh incarnated and identified himself wholly with the 'Strong Bull', the 'Bull of his Mother', a bull moon-god, who was either Min or Amun. Personifying the god in the rite, he 'violates his mother', incarnate in the queen, whether she is Hathor, Isis or Mut, or all three viewed as one goddess, to produce the heir to the throne. The future king thus received his divine blood (i.e. lineage) from Hathor, the genetrix of the falcon clan; or Isis, the genetrix of the dynastic line; or Mut, the genetrix of the 18th Dynasty, the mother and wife of Amun, who was identified with the Heliopolitan Hathor. His generative power, the divine semen, he received from the Khamutef, Min or Amun.

The Khamutef cult and the *ntoro* cult thus have the same object, which is to give greater divinity to the king and to prove his status as the begetter of children, thus making him the queen's equal as the giver of heirs to the throne. Constitutionally, however, the Pharaoh remained the 'son of Isis', analogous with the Akan king, who continued to be the son of the queen-mother; the succession to the throne in Egypt was always in the female line. There is no evidence that the Khamutef cult ever became democratised as did the *ntoro* cult among the Akan, which was responsible for the introduction of a double descent system.

[1] H. O. Lange, *Ein lithurgisches Lied an Min* (Sitz. d. Preuss. Ak. s. Wiss., Berlin), 1927, pp. 331–8.

[2] Jacobsohn, p. 17; Isis too, in her form of Isis of Koptos, is regarded as the Khamutef's mother and wife, and Mut is called the 'female Khamutef'.

[3] See pp. 182, 183.

CHAPTER V

The King's Potency: the *Kra* and the *Ka*

AKAN
1. The Concept of the Kra
(a) The Kra *of the Commoner*

The *kra* in its earliest phase was envisaged as a particle of the life-giving fire of the moon. The supreme Mother-goddess shot it with arrows in the form of rays into the universe. She was called *Atoapoma*—the 'Ever-ready-shooter'.

It is said: *kra ne bogya*—'the *kra* is life blood'. The word *bogya*, 'blood', literally translated means 'fire (*gya*) of the creature (*boa*)' animal and man.[1] The *kra* in man, then, is blood vivified by a spark of fire from the moon (Cult Type I).

In the period of Cult Type II the *kra* came to be envisaged as bi-sexual; its female aspect in man is matter-vivified blood, also the generative power that resides in the blood; its male aspect is spirit, force or power. The *kra* as a spirit is thought to have an independent existence in man, hence it is envisaged as his twin or double. There is a saying: 'But for his *kra* that followed him, he would have died.' Like the moon, the *kra* waxes and wanes; the *kra* is not always at its full power; in a sick man, for instance, it becomes weaker. When a person is stunned by grief or fright and when life appears to have gone from him, people say with pity: 'his *kra* has left him'.

At the same time the concept of the *kra* was extended. By then the *kra* of gods, men, and animals could be the fire of any one of the seven planets; their weekly natal day determined which of them. The *akragya*, or *kra* progenitors, the seven planetary deities, were appointed by Odomankoma to serve as assistants to

---
[1] See also *Sacred State*, p. 70.

the Supreme Being Nyame in giving *kra* (see above, p. 60). At the same time the *kra* was no longer envisaged solely as a life force animating an inert body but came to represent the impersonal and divine soul in god or man, an interpretation which can be roughly equated with Freud's *Id* and Jung's 'unconscious psyche'; the *kra* became man's great reservoir of strength, his sustenance and the source of his energy. It represented his instinctive forces, for the *kra* would act as his guardian spirit and might save him in time of danger. The *kra* became, moreover, the source of man's good and bad fortune, for it was observed that individual fate depends largely on man's uncontrollable impulses.

The *kra*, finally, was thought of as an ancestral spirit which left the Great Ancestress, the Supreme Being, in a farewell ceremony in heaven so that it might be reborn in a child of its mother's family. The word *kra* is said to have been derived from the verb *nkra*, meaning 'to part', 'to take leave'. This expresses the idea that the *kra* of a person has taken leave of the great *kra* of the Supreme Being and will return to her after death. The *kra* when depicted was represented as a stylised figure with a cone- or column-shaped body with arms uplifted and flat outstretched hands, illustrating both its parting from the deity after an embrace and their reunion after death (see *Ak. of Ghana*, Pl. 52).

It is believed that the future child, who is already formed from the blood (*bogya*) of its mother's family and endowed with the *ntoro* spirit of its father, is led by an *akragya* to Nyame and a golden bath is brought in which the *akragya* bathes the child by pouring water over it. Nyame, having uttered the *nkrabea*,[1] the message of destiny, then lets fall a sparkling drop of water from an *adwera* leaf into the child's mouth. This is the 'water of life' (*nkwan suo*), 'the pure water that boils yet does not burn'. It is said to contain a living image of Nyame 'like the figure of a person in a mirror'. The water then penetrates the whole body of the child until it is filled with *honhom* (divine breath)[2] and wakes up alive. The *kra* here has become the 'water of life' but water that still owes its life to a spark of fire from the planets.

Before the child leaves Nyame she gives it the *hyebea*[3] or command to perfect and complete its *kra*, for only a pure and unsullied

---

[1] For the concept of *nkrabea*, see *Sacred State*, p. 87.
[2] For the concept of *honhom*, see p. 122.
[3] For the concept of *hyebea*, see *Sacred State*, p. 87.

kra, consisting entirely of goodness, can become one again with the Supreme Being. Otherwise it must be reincarnated.[1]

After the death of a man offerings are made to his *kra* to ensure that it does not lose its identity, for if so it would be useless as an intermediary between his family and the deity. The *kra* of the deceased, if proved to be worthy, becomes the guardian spirit of the family.

(b) *The* Kra *of the King*

Every man and woman received a *kra*, in the sense of vital force, at birth; it could not give life. But the queen-mother's *kra* could give life for it was the *kra* of her ancestress, the founder of the state, descended from the moon Mother-goddess.

When kingship was instituted,[2] the bi-sexual *kra* was divided between the queen-mother and the king; in her the female lunar *kra* was active, in him the male. The nature of the former was female generative force, divine blood, lineage; that of the latter, male procreative power and spirit. When the Sun cult was introduced the royal *kra* ceased to be lunar and became solar, while that of the queen-mother remained lunar. Finally the rulers' *kra* came to be an ancestral reincarnated *kra*—the king's that of the deceased kings, the Royal Ancestors, descended from the Sun-god, the queen-mother's that of her deceased predecessors in office descended from the moon Mother-goddess. Hence the king was regarded as the son of the Sun-god and the queen-mother as the daughter of the moon-goddess.

It was the duty of the divine king to promote through his *kra* the welfare of the state and to maintain its food supplies on which so much depended. For it to be effective he had to protect it from everything that might damage its power; the greatest dangers to it were death and menstruating women. It was feared that the loss of life blood which is animated by the *kra* might be infectious; therefore the king, and all princes eligible for kingship, were forbidden to go to war, to see a corpse, or to visit a cemetery. They were not permitted to come into contact with menstruating women so that the king's food had to be cooked by men. In addition the king had to be guarded against evil spirits, particularly the *okrabiri*, the *kras*

---

[1] For reincarnation, see p. 124.
[2] Up to the eighteenth century some of the small states were still ruled by queen-mothers without a king.

of deceased wrongdoers, who had been cast out from heaven and could only be redeemed if, through contact with the king's *kra*, they could obtain pardon. The queen-mothers tabooed death solely to protect the life-giving power of their *kra*, as did the princesses eligible for the queen-mother's stool.

2. *The* Akrafohene, *the Priest of the King's* Kra

The divine king's power had to be renewed annually, for it was believed that *kra* power diminishes and full potency must be restored periodically by the supreme deity. To achieve the renewal it was necessary for the king to die so that his *kra* could return to the moon Mother-goddess who would revive its original power. The king himself, however, did not actually die each year—a royal lineage could hardly produce a sufficient number of heirs to make this possible. His death was thus only a ritual one and his *okra*, the 'bearer of his *kra*', acted as a substitute, or 'mock-king' and died instead of his master. The *okra* was usually a youth,[1] whom the king loved deeply and, after the king and the queen-mother, he was regarded as the most sacred person in the state.

In the middle of the seventeenth century the Bono king Akumfi Ameyaw II (1649-59) created the post of *Akrafohene*, 'Chief of the *kra* people', and instituted the *kra* purification ceremony, to be performed regularly every six weeks on a *Fo* or 'Fertile Thursday'. Until this time the kings only purified their *kra* when they felt that its power was diminishing. In the seventeenth century the Bono king's *kra* was essentially the solar *kra* of his Royal Ancestors, the deceased kings. The *kra* purification ceremony was therefore regarded as a funerary rite and, since death was tabu for the king, his place in the ceremony was taken by the *Akrafohene*, 'the bearer of the king's *kra*'.

The *Akrafohene*, a court official, was not sacrificed annually for the king as was the *okra* youth, nevertheless he personified the king in the rite and a criminal was slain.[2] *Akrafo* or *kra* people assisted the *Akrafohene* in sacrificing rams and cooking the offerings to the royal *kra*. At this time the queen-mother too had her *Akrafo-bapanyin* (literally Elder Woman of the *kra* people), who bore her *kra*

---

[1] For details see *Ak. of Ghana*, p. 52.
[2] Apart from the *Akrafohene*, a courtier, the king continued to elect an *okra*, the most beloved of his sons. He was sacrificed at the death of the ruler to follow him into the hereafter.

in the purification rites, and in every way performed the same duties as the *Akrafohene*.[1]

3. *The Ritual in the* Kra Fieso

When the Bono kingdom was still in existence the *Kra Dware*, the purification of the royal *kra*, was performed in the *Kra Fieso*, 'the House of the *kra*', a chapel outside the palace specially designed for this purpose. Today in Takyiman, a bare room in the house of the *Banmuhene*, the priest in charge of the royal cemetery, situated at Hansua, near Takyiman, is used for the rite. The *Kra Dware* has to be performed outside the town because of the death tabu for the king: the purification of his *kra*, which is that of his Royal Ancestors, being regarded as a funerary rite.[2] The rite is also designed to re-animate the *saman*, the resurrected spirit bodies of the Royal Ancestors, and keep them alive. Although their *kra* (life-giving power) is incarnate in the king, the identity of the Royal Ancestors is preserved, so that the king can still address himself to them in prayer.

The Ritual

The *Akrafohene* and the *akrafo*, his assistant priests, get up early in the morning and take a bath. This must be a cold one for the *kras* of the Royal Ancestors are cool (a reference to death);[3] for the same reason they are not permitted to drink alcohol or anything else which may 'heat' their bodies. They all dress in white cloth and then mark their temples, chests, and wrists with three lines of white clay and the *crux decussata* symbol of Nyame, in order to sanctify themselves. White is a substitute for silver and as such is symbolic of the moon, and conveys purity and peace.

When the priests are ready they enter the *kra* room, the floor of which has been strewn with white sand from the sacred stream Adare both to consecrate it and to warn unauthorised persons against entering it. The *Akrafohene* then says a prayer and, dipping *adwera* leaves into a copper jug filled with sacred water (copper is symbolic of fire, blood), sprinkles himself and all those assembled

---

[1] For greater detail see *Ak. of Ghana*, p. 53.

[2] In Asante, however, the *Kra Dware* is performed in the king's bedroom because at night the Royal Ancestors are believed to visit the sleeping king, and at dawn they still hover about. The *Kra Dware* also differs in other points. See, for a description, *Sacred State*, pp. 180 f.

[3] The *kra* is viewed here as the representative of the deceased.

THE KING'S POTENCY

with it, thus blessing their *kras*. Then the female *akrafo* enter; a fire is lit between three pieces of *esa* wood and the offerings already prepared are cooked on it. When everything is ready, the *eto* (mashed yams, kneaded into balls), the meat from a chicken, and hard-boiled eggs broken into pieces, are placed in a large earthenware dish and covered with *adwera* leaves. The *Akrafohene* then sits down with the dish before him on a low table. He takes one of the leaves, dips it into the sacred water, then puts it in his mouth and spits the water over the food, saying '*kosie*' (blessing) three times. He then divides the food into two portions, one of which is placed in a bowl and covered with eggshells and *adwera* leaves. This bowl is placed in a corner of the room so that the *kras* of the Royal Ancestors may partake of the food. Of the other portion, everybody present takes three mouthfuls after the *Akrafohene* has said, 'Be blessed my *kra* (i.e. that of the king whom he personifies in the rite); take this food from my heart.' The rest of the food is given to those waiting outside who wish to share in the sacred meal.

This ceremony is followed shortly afterwards by another. Whereas the first centres on the lunar *kra* of the Royal Ancestors, the aspect of blood and lineage, the second centres on their solar *kra*, the *kra* implicit in kingship. The rite is performed in the courtyard in front of the *kra* chamber; the *Akrafohene*, dressed in the regalia of the king, seats himself on an *asipim* or throne chair and a state umbrella is held over him.

A snow-white, long-legged ram is then brought to him and he pricks its throat three times; one of the *akrafo* then slits the throat of the animal from ear to ear, while another catches the blood in a bowl. This is then given to a woman *okrafo* to boil on a fire that has been lit in the courtyard. When the blood has curdled and thickened, a blood sausage (*bonsua*) is prepared from it. Meanwhile the ram is cut up and a kind of soup, called the *kra suo*, is made from all the parts which are considered to be the seat of life. These include the heart, liver, kidneys, the tail inside the animal (*padua*), the rough and towel-like mouth of the stomach sac (*furu-ano*), and the upper part of the breast (*kokoti*). The rest of the meat is later distributed among the houses of the elders of the state council. When the soup is cooked it is poured together with the meat over seven balls of mashed *eto*; the blood sausage is placed on top.

Everybody then moves into the *kra* chamber. When the *Akrafohene* has seated himself in front of a low table the same ritual is performed as in the first ceremony: the food is blessed, divided into two portions, one share is offered to the Royal Ancestors, the other partaken of by those assembled. The *Akrafohene* then says a long prayer in which he asks the Supreme Being to bless the state, the queen-mother, the elders and all the people. This ends the *Kra Dware*. In the evening the bowls of food offered to the *kras* of the Royal Ancestors are removed by an *okrafo* and given to the women and children of the household to eat.

Throughout the morning, while the ritual is being performed in the *Banmuhene's* house, the Bono-Takyimanhene, dressed in white cloth, sits in the audience courtyard on a stool consecrated with white clay. He has to spend his time in meditation, but later he receives visitors, who have come to greet him. Later in the morning the *akrafo* arrive from Hansua to inform him that the offerings to the Royal Ancestors have been made and that his *kra* is now purified. He gives them a bottle of rum and they leave to pour a libation to the Royal Ancestors in the Chapel of the Stools. When they come back they seat themselves at his feet until the evening, when they return to Hansua. During this time the *Akrafohene*, wearing the king's regalia, sits in the courtyard before the *Kra Fieso*, the children of his house, clad in white, seated at his feet. When the *akrafo* return, he retires and the regalia is restored to the king.

EGYPT

1. The Concept of the Ka

(a) The Ka *of the Commoner*

From the earliest times the Egyptians envisaged the *ka* as vital force, or life itself, and as such it was not confined to the king, nor to man alone, but was found throughout creation. In contrast to the *ka* of the Pharaoh and the reigning queen, the *ka* of the ordinary person was never depicted, no doubt because only the *ka* of the rulers could give 'life'.

Middle and New Kingdom texts indicate that everyone received a *ka* at birth, although its source does not appear to be mentioned. After death ordinary mortals joined their *ka*, and dying is described as to 'going to one's *ka* in heaven'.[1] Here also we lack any further explanation. The Akan mortal also hastens, on his death, to join his *kra* in heaven, which he calls *kra bafano* (*bafano* expressing 'coun-

[1] Kees, *Totenglauben*, pp. 77, 137.

terpart' of the *kra* or 'the very image of one's own *kra*'). The *kra bafano* is the *kra* of the planet from whom, at birth, he received his *kra*, which after death returns to the planet whence it came. The *ka* of the Egyptian almost certainly had a planetary origin, since the *ka* of the Pharaoh originated in the first place from the moon and, at a later period, from the sun.

In the precepts of Ptah-hotep[1] there are references to the *ka* which give some idea as to how it was envisaged by the Egyptians. In precept 7 the guest is enjoined not to cast many glances at his host at table for 'it is an abomination to the *ka* for them to be directed at him', implying that the embarrassment and anxiety caused by this may take away some of the life force of his host. Such anxiety is caused by fear that the guest may not have been given enough to eat and so may feel resentful towards his host. This feeling of resentment is so real that the Akan king himself does not eat or drink without giving a share to those attending him at the time.

In precept 8 it is said 'the washing of the heart shall not be repeated (words said in anger) for that is an abomination to the *ka*'. The Akan believe that anger affects the *kra*, since it induces the harbouring of evil thoughts and ill-feeling; only an uncorrupted *kra* can be reunited with the Supreme Being. The Egyptians held similar beliefs, for the deceased was judged in heaven and, if proved guilty of evil deeds, was not allowed to join 'the *kas* that are in heaven' (*Pyr.* 1220d).

In another precept it is said that all recreation should not be sacrificed to 'too much care for thine house', for 'it is an abhorrence to the *ka* if its time is diminished'; in our parlance: anxiety diminishes the life-force, and may even lead to death, whereas joy and happiness increase it.

The Akan speak of having a lucky *kra*; indeed the word 'luckily', 'fortunately' is expressed by the term *ne kra yiye*. 'Good luck' at a game, for instance, is *nkra ye*. Frankfort[2] points out that in Egypt 'luck', 'fortune' may sometimes be an appropriate translation for *ka*. He gives as an example the phrase 'the Lord of the Two Lands made his *ka*', meaning that the Pharaoh brought good fortune to a man, this not so much, however, by royal favours and gifts as by affecting his vitality, his life-force.

[1] Erman-Blackman, *Literature*.
[2] *Kingship*, p. 69.

Another precept, dealing with a father's conduct towards his son, reads: 'He is thy son whom thy *ka* has begotten for thee; separate not thy heart from him.' Here the *ka*, like the *kra*, is equated with life-force.

The *ka* was depicted in the form of two uplifted arms, the hands flat and outstretched, as is the *kra* among the Akan. The idea that life is transmitted through the embrace of a god was accepted by the Egyptians, as is evident from *Pyr.* 1652: 'Thou [Atum] didst spit out Shu, thou didst spit out Tefnut; Thou didst put thine arms around them with thy *ka*, so that thy *ka* was in them.'[1]

The earlier idea, which never became quite obsolete, seems to have been that *ka* was shot into the universe by the Mother-goddess Neith; her emblem was the two crossed arrows which form the *crux decussata* ($\times$).[2] This emblem is identical with the *hemsut* sign, the symbol for the female *ka*. The hieroglyph *ka.t* designates the female sexual organs.

(b) The Ka of the King

From the earliest phase onwards the Akan queen-mother incarnated the lunar *kra* of the clan goddess, who personified the manifestation of the great moon Mother-goddess. Thanks to her divine *kra* the queen-mother was able to give and maintain the life in her state. When the *kra* came to be envisaged as bi-sexual and kingship was introduced, the queen-mother incarnated solely the female lunar *kra*, the female principle of reproduction; the king incarnated the male aspect. When the cult of the king as son of the Sun-god was finally established the future king still received a lunar *kra* at birth, but when he was enstooled he received in addition a *kra* of a solar nature. It was given to him in a special rite by his predecessor in office at the precise moment when the latter's *kra* had joined the *kras* of the deceased kings, the Royal Ancestors, and that of his Great Ancestor the Sun-god in his city on the sun.

In Egypt the *ka* of the Pharaoh, which was the *ka* of the lunar Horus, had the same function as the *kra* of the Akan king. When the cult of the king as the son of the Sun-god was established, he received in addition a solar *ka*, that of his Royal Ancestors descended

---

[1] Also on many reliefs the Pharaoh is shown being embraced by gods and goddesses.

[2] Note that on reliefs the Pharaoh is sometimes shown shooting an arrow aided by a god, as for instance, Thutmosis III by Set.

from Re-Horus, and, like the Akan king, he acquired it in a special rite after the coronation ceremony.

In the birth scenes of Amenhotep III depicted on the walls of the temple at Luxor, the craftsman creator-god Khnum is shown modelling a homunculus—the future king, while Hathor is making an identical one—the *ka* which gives the future king his life.[1] The *ka*'s nature is fire; the *kas* of the Royal Ancestors, the 'Souls of Pe and Nekhen' are described as 'red as a flame' (*Pyr.* 353) or 'red as fire' (361c, 697a). The flame in Egypt was an emblem of birth, and in the rituals a lamp was lighted whenever there was a reference to the beginning of life.[2] In the reliefs at Luxor which show the queen in the birth scenes, the arms of the two guardian spirits beneath her are raised in the manner of the *ka* symbol, their hands holding the *ankh* sign, the sign of life, while a flame rises above their heads.[3] In a relief at Deir el Bahri the royal infant Hatshepsut is nursed by twelve divinities (see below) in the 'room of fire'.[4] In the Birth temple at Denderah the royal child is presented to Horus in the '*Ka* room of Fire'.[5]

The *ka* is a flame in its most elemental form, but after the introduction of the royal Sun cult its material nature undergoes some change: for Isis, the goddess of the Flame, gives life with milk, and Re with a magical fluid, the *sa* of life. The god Bes and his consort, the hippopotamus-goddess Api, as the guardians of *sa*, both protect birth. The *sa* of life, a fluid, has its origin, however, in the lunar or solar flame. The hieroglyph for the *sa* consists of eight 'luminous knots' or nodes, on an arrow, the ends of which form two additional knots.[6] The *sa* of life seems to be identical with the *nkwan-suo*—'the spark-like water of life' of the Akan; moreover the hieroglyph for the *sa* is found as a gold weight.

In the rendering of the birth scenes of Hatshepsut depicted on the temple walls of Deir el Bahri, twelve divinities identified as *kas*

---

[1] Gayet, *Louxor*, Pl. LXIII and p. 101. At Deir el Bahri (Naville, *Deir el Bahri*, Pl. XLVIII) Khnum creates both homunculi and life is given to them by the birth-goddess Heket. The frog-headed Heket is supposed to have been a form of Hathor and was regarded as the mother of Horus the Elder. At Elephantine she was worshipped as the consort of Khnum, who seems to have been originally the same god as Ptah as he bore many of the titles of this god.

[2] Naville, *Deir el Bahri*, p. 16.

[3] Gayet, *Louxor*, Pl. LXV and p. 103; Moret, *Royauté*, pp. 55, 56.

[4] Moret, op. cit., p. 56.

[5] ibid.

[6] Moret connects the arrow with solar and stellar rays (p. 43, n. 1).

A GREAT AKAN KING

11. The Asantehene, Otumfor Sir Osei Agyeman Prempeh II, sitting on a throne chair, which is decorated with two walking falcons. He wears the triangular breastplate, called *osansatao*, 'the tail of the falcon'. His head-dress consists of a chaplet of silk to which golden triangles are fastened, forming crosses, the crosses symbolise his solar power, the triangles express that he rules for the Mother-goddess incarnate in the queen mother. (From a postcard; permission to use the photograph was given to me by the Asantehene in 1946.)

A GREAT AKAN KING

12. The Bono-Takyimanhene, Nana Akumfi Ameyaw III, sitting on a throne chair, which is decorated with war horns in the shape of crescent moons, symbolising him as the Life-giver to his state and the Destroyer of the state's enemies. He wears the golden *nkanta* necklace which represents the daily sun and the sun below the horizon. In his right hand he holds the Bosummuru sword, encrusted with the blood of the sacrifice.

To the king's right is the *puduo* which contains the gold nuggets, representing the *kras* of the Royal Ancestors. The live parrot at his feet symbolises the state. The leopard-skin characterises him as the Lord of Fire, life-giving to his people, and deadly to his enemies. (Reproduced by courtesy of Nana Akumfi Ameyaw III.)

THE KING'S POTENCY

and *hemsuts* (female *kas*) carry the new-born child so that it may absorb from them vital force, health, joy, good fortune and numerous other blessings. In an adjoining scene the royal child is depicted at the breasts of two cow-goddesses. These fourteen divinities would appear to represent here the equivalent of the Akan *akragya*, the seven male and female divinities of the seven planets, who give *kra* to gods and men on behalf of the Supreme Being Nyame.[1] The Pharaoh is known to have possessed fourteen *kas* compared with the single one of the ordinary mortal.[2] The two cow-goddesses in the scene no doubt represent the moon and are Hathor and Isis, Hathor being the *hemsut* goddess, who gives the child its divine blood and lineage, while Isis, the *ka* goddess, gives the king his throne. Nyame gives the Akan child its destiny; in the relief at Luxor Hathor gives the future king not only his life but also his destiny.[3] This seems to provide evidence that the underlying ideas concerning the *ka* and the *kra* are essentially the same.

The *ka* symbol enclosing the Pharaoh's Horus name is supported by a standard from which arms emerge to hold the staff bearing the king's head and the feather of *Maat*. The arms are those of the king's personified *ka*.[4] The feather of *Maat* the daughter of Re, symbolised truth—the established cosmic order, the regular circuit of the sun on which depend the crops that nourish men and beasts. It is said of Amenhotep I on a relief at Luxor that he strove to 'make the country flourish as in primeval times by means of the design of *Maat*'.[5]

The Pharaoh received his lunar *ka* as we have seen from Hathor and Isis but his solar *ka* from Osiris in a rite which followed his accession to the throne. Osiris in this context represented the Royal Ancestors, for the *ka* of every deceased king united with that of his Royal Ancestors in heaven. According to *Pyr.* 575, 'Horus has arranged with the gods (i.e. the Royal Ancestors) to unite themselves

---

[1] But the *akragya* were created by Odomankoma and their counterparts in Egypt by Ptah, see p. 66.

[2] In Ptolemaic times the Pharaoh was credited with 14 male and 14 female *kas*, in all 28. 28 is a lunar number and represents the days of a lunar month of an early calendar.

[3] Note the Seven Hathors, goddesses of destiny.

[4] See p. 111 for the significance of the arms conveying the idea that *ka* is transmitted by the embrace of a god.

[5] Mariette, *Karnak*, 1875, p. 35.

with Thee', after which the dead Pharaoh assumed the mythological form of Osiris.[1]

The cult of the Pharaoh's *ka* was funerary, which is evident from the rites in the *Pa Dwat* and at the New Year festival. The solar *ka* was, as with the Akan, a reincarnated *ka*, that of the Royal Ancestors, descended from Re-Horus, and represented by Osiris. Through this *ka* in him the Pharaoh was a god:

He is one who illuminates the Two Lands more than the sun disk,
He is one who makes the Two Lands more green than a high Nile.
He has filled the Two Lands with strength and life.
The king is ka.
His mouth is increase.
He is the one creating him who is to be.
He is the Khnum [former] of all limbs,
The begetter who causes the people to be.[2]

2. The Anmutef, *the Priest of the King's* Ka

In ancient Egypt the counterpart of the *Akrafohene* would appear to have been the priest with the title *Anmutef* (or *Inmutef*). At Abydos he was called the 'servant Horus-*Anmutef*'.[3] He purified the Horus *ka* of the Pharaoh and also personified it in certain rites. Accordingly he was regarded as divine, and in a text it is said of him 'that is then the son of a god'.[4]

Moret[5] suggests that the word 'Anmutef' means, by a play on words '(he who wears) the skin of his mother'. He believes this to be so because the most ancient orthography of the word is *Ken-mut* or *Ur-ken-mut*, which reads '(he who wears) the skin of the wolf'. The wolf represents the god Upwaut, who was incarnate in the king Osiris; his descendants, the Pharaoh's Upper Egyptian Royal Ancestors, the 'Souls of Nekhen', were depicted as wolf-headed. Hence their *ka* priest wore the 'skin of the wolf'. Horus-*Anmutef*, wore the 'skin of his mother', namely Hathor, because Horus was incarnate in the Pharaoh.

The *Anmutef* wore a leopard-skin (Pl. 13) which, according to *Pyr.* 219, was the dress of the deceased; leopard-skins belonged to

---

[1] See p. 214.
[2] Erman-Blackman, *Literature*, pp. 84, 85.
[3] Mariette, *Abydos*, I, Pl. 28a.
[4] Moret, *Royauté*, p. 216.
[5] Moret, *Mystères égyptiens* (1923), pp. 75-6.

the equipment of the dead in the most remote period. Among the Akan the leopard is symbolic of fire, he is called the 'Lord of Fire'. Fire is synonymous with the Akan *kra*—the *kra* in gods and men on earth and their resurrected *kra* in heaven. In Asante the *Akrafohene* wears a leopard-skin cap, implying that the *kra* of the living king is solar and lunar in origin. The *ka* of the Pharaoh was also fire, the solar and lunar Horus *ka* of his Royal Ancestors, resurrected in heaven by Hathor the mother of Horus.[1] The leopard-skin worn by the *Anmutef* may have had a significance similar to the leopard-skin cap of the king of Asante's *Akrafohene*. Also, the purification rites for the *ka* of the living Pharaoh were performed in the *Pa Dwat*, 'the House of the Netherworld' which, to all appearances, corresponds to the *Kra Fieso*, the Chapel of the *Kra*. The difference between the *Ken-mut* and the *Anmutef* may have been the same as that between the *okra* of the earliest period and the *okrafo* priest who, in later times became the *Akrafohene*. The former's task was to die for the king on New Year's day, the latter, although he also personified the king's *kra*, was essentially a priest in charge of the purification of the kingly *kra*. The proper counterpart of the *Akrafohene* was the *Sem-Anmutef* in the Middle Kingdom who purified, not the *ka* of Horus incarnate in the Pharoah, but the Horus *ka* of Pharaoh's Royal Ancestors personified by Osiris. Hence the change of name from Horus-*Anmutef* to *SemAnmutef*. The word *Sem* seems to be connected with death.

3. The Ritual in the Pa Dwat

The hieroglyph for the *Pa Dwat* or *Pa Tuat*, 'the House of the Netherworld' is composed of two symbols for 'house' with a five-pointed star between them. The 'houses' indicate that the *Pa Dwat* consisted of two houses or rooms in which the rites were performed, in one for the Pharaoh as king of Upper Egypt, in the other for him as king of Lower Egypt. The five-pointed star symbolised the *Dwat* or netherworld[2] and its ruler Osiris. Among the Akan the five-pointed star, designed in the same way with the fifth point in the centre pointing upwards (★) symbolised the resurrected Royal Ancestors; the rites for their *kras* being the

---

[1] For Hathor as mother of the dead king see Jacobsohn, *Dogm. Stell.*, p. 20.

[2] *Pa Dwat* is more frequently translated as 'House of the Morning' because the ritual took place at dawn, or as the 'Double Rooms of Adoration' by Moret, *Royauté*, p. 212.

THE KING'S POTENCY

same as that of the living king, were performed in the *Kra Fieso* in Bono and now at Takyiman on a Thursday, the day of the planet Jupiter. It is interesting to note that the official name of the king Osiris was written with the same symbols as Jupiter, the 'Star of the Southern Sky'.[1] We do not know whether the ritual for the Pharaoh's kingly *ka*, which was that of his resurrected Royal Ancestors personified by Osiris, was also performed on a Thursday, but there appears to be a definite connexion between Osiris, the planet Jupiter, and *Dwat*, the land of the dead.[2]

The ritual in the *Pa Dwat* was concerned with the re-animation and strengthening of the *ka* of the living Pharaoh. The priest in charge was Horus-*Anmutef* who held the title 'priest in the *Pa Dwat*', or 'He who resides in the *Pa Dwat*', as well as 'he who is master in the *Pa Dwat*'.[3]

On the Egyptian reliefs depicting the ritual[4] appears the Pharaoh (wholly identified with Osiris), sometimes Horus-*Anmutef*, who seems to act as his substitute, and gods and goddesses of the Osirian family: Horus, Thoth, Anubis, and Isis. If one disregards these deities the rest of the ritual was much the same as that performed in the *Kra Fieso*. First came the purification ceremonies executed by

[1] Brugsch, *Ägypt.*, p. 336.
[2] Life in the hereafter and the various 'Lands of the Dead' is discussed by Frankfort, *Kingship*, pp. 112-22. On p. 210 he says:
'The sun seems to enter the earth in the West, and so do the stars. And since the stars are the lights of night, and night belongs to the Netherworld, because life belongs to the day, the word *dat* [or *dwat*] "Netherworld" is written with a star [i.e. the five-pointed star]; the stars are inhabitants of the Netherworld, and consequently they obey Osiris: "The firmament and its stars obey him, and the Great Gates are open to him. There is jubilation for him in the southern sky and adoration for him in the northern sky. The imperishable stars are under his regimen." ' (Cf. Erman-Blackman, *Literature*, p. 42.)
[3] Moret, op. cit., p. 216. Like the *Akrafohene*, the Horus-*Anmutef* priest probably had assistants, for there was a class of priests called 'chiefs of the mysteries in the *Pa Dwat*'.
On p. 232 Moret says that when the Pharaoh was absent the high priest of the temple in which the *Pa Dwat* was situated would deputise for him. This is not likely, since the Horus-*Anmutef* priest conducted the rites and would be the one to deputise for the Pharaoh; possibly being regarded as 'the son of a god' he personified him, as does the *Akrafohene* at Takyiman. On the other hand in Asante, the king was present but took no part, the *Akrafohene* personifying his *kra*. The high priest of the temple very likely played the same role as does the *Banmuhene* priest at Takyiman, in order to witness on behalf of the state that the rites have been properly executed.
[4] It was depicted especially on the walls in front of the sanctuary of Seti I's temple at Abydos, and in the part of the temple at Edfu built by Ptolemy X.

Horus and Thoth (the latter is sometimes replaced by Set); then the ablutions—both these actions are performed by the *Akrafohene*, who personifies the king in the rites before he enters the *Kra Fieso*. Purifications and ablutions among the Akan serve solely to cleanse the *kra* from the defilement of death; in Egypt they had the additional significance of cleansing the body of Osiris which had been defiled through its dismemberment by Set. These ablutions, performed with water from a sacred pool and poured out of golden jugs, re-animated not only the *ka* but also the *sahu*, the resurrected body of Osiris. The ablutions were followed by fumigation with incense and four balls of natron were served to the Pharaoh or his representative to chew.[1]

In subsequent ceremonies the Pharaoh was crowned with the red and white crowns of Lower and Upper Egypt, which were placed on his head by the goddesses Nekhbet and Wadjet. The text attests that the Pharaoh was once more 'on the throne of Horus at the head of the living *kas*',[2] meaning that his *ka* had been purified and could again give 'life'. Furthermore the *sa ankh*, the 'fluid of life', was transmitted to him through the medium of the crowns. (Compare this coronation scene with the appearance of the *Akrafohene* in the regalia of the king.) He was then embraced by a god or goddess, either Horus, Osiris, Amen, or the deity in whose temple the *Pa Dwat* was situated, who also gave him the 'fluid of life'. Sometimes Hathor took the Pharaoh in her arms to give him the breast, so that he could imbibe her *ka* with her milk.

The coronation was followed by a consecrated meal, such as plays such a prominent part in the *Kra Fieso*. There its intention is mainly to re-establish the bond between the Royal Ancestors and the living king, for the kingly *kra* can only live and give life if the *kras* of the Royal Ancestors are kept alive. The Pharaoh expressed the same idea in the following words: 'O, Gods (i.e. the Royal Ancestors), you are safe, if I am safe, your *kas* are safe, if my *ka* is safe at the head of all living *kas*: all live, if I live.'[3]

---

[1] The offering of incense and fumigation with incense are not customary among the Akan, although known and practised in times of epidemics. A vessel containing incense is carried before the king of Asante when he appears in public after the *Adae* rites for the Royal Ancestors have been performed in the Chapel of the Stools.

[2] Moret, op. cit., p. 219. The whole ritual with all its details is described, pp. 212 ff.

[3] ibid., p. 219.

4. Nehebkau, the Uniter of Kas

In Egypt, as among the Akan, two New Year festivals were celebrated, one in spring, on the first day of the first month of the 'Season of Coming Forth', the other in autumn at the end of the Min-Khamutef festival which started the harvest season.

In a text of Seti I it is said of him: 'Thou appearest on the sedan chair of the *Sed* festival like Re on New Year's day.'[1] The reference to Re suggests that New Year's day was connected with a special rising of the sun. As it happens, twice a year the sun rises due east and shines equally on the two hemispheres—in spring on the day of the vernal equinox and in autumn on the day of the autumnal equinox. Among the Bono it was on these two days that the New Year rites were performed which were concerned in the first case with the rebirth of the powers of the Royal Ancestors to revivify their *kras*, and in the second with the ritual death and rebirth of the king himself to rejuvenate his procreative power. The first New Year's day fell at the end of the *Apo* festival in March, the season of sowing and planting; the second at the end of the *Sannaa Kese* festival, at the beginning of the harvest season. The rites on the first day of the *Apo* correspond in many respects to the rites of the Nehebkau festival, and the *Aferihyia Dwaree* of the *Sannaa Kese* festival to the Min-Khamutef harvest festival.[2] In Egypt the two New Year's days were presided over by Nehebkau, who would appear to have been the personification of the equinoxes, symbolic of the death and rebirth of the powers of the Sun-god and his descendants, the Royal Ancestors and the Pharaoh.

Nehebkau is represented on ivory wands as a serpent-headed god, usually grasping two serpents.[3] As one of the gods of the netherworld he is depicted in the *Book of Am Duat* as a huge serpent with two heads on separate necks, the tail also ending in a head.[4] In the Pyramid texts Nehebkau is described as 'having numerous coils'

---

[1] Richard A. Parker, *The Calendars of Ancient Egypt*, 1950, p. 62.

[2] See pp. 171 ff and pp. 177 ff.

[3] London, British Museum, No. 18175. W. M. F. Petrie, *Objects of Daily Use*, Pl. XXXVII, g.

[4] E. A. W. Budge, *The Egyptian Heaven and Hell*, 1906, Pl. XXXV. The two serpents in the first case and the two heads in the second may symbolise the two agricultural seasons; the tail ending in a head, the third season, 'the season of deficiency'. The serpent is a symbol for death and rebirth, see below in the text.

(*Pyr.* 1146). Among the Akan the coil of a serpent forming a spiral symbolises rebirth, or new life after death. In Egypt the symbolism seems to have been the same, for it was said of the deceased Pharaoh Pepi 'he is Nehebkau with numerous coils' and of Meren-Re, 'Meren-Re is a serpent of numerous coils'.[1] In both cases the reference must be to the rebirth of the king in heaven.

In Spell 17 of the Book of the Dead the deceased prays, 'I fly as a hawk, I have cackled like a goose, I live through eternity like Nehebkau',[2] that is to say, being reborn and resurrected in the netherworld his life is eternal.[3] In another spell in the Book of the Dead Nehebkau is referred to as 'that god secret of forms, whose eyebrows are the beams of the balance'.[4] On the days of the equinox the year hangs in the balance, for the sun shines equally on both hemispheres. Nehebkau is also included among the forty-two gods of the netherworld before whom the dead must make their confessions in the trial presided over by Osiris.[5] The forty-two gods most probably represent days of an old forty-two day period calendar, the forerunner of the Akan *Adaduanan* calendar.[6] If this assumption is correct, then Nehebkau in the judicial scene was the representative of the equinoctial day.

Nehebkau is closely connected with the sun, and hence with the two goddesses Bastet and Sekhmet. Bastet, a solar goddess, is a daughter of Re, the 'Lady of the East'; she represents the beneficent powers of the sun. Sekhmet, with whom she is sometimes merged, represents the 'Fiery Dawn'; she is the fiery one emitting flames against her enemies and consequently symbolises the destructive heat of the sun, whose enemies it kills. Nehebkau dwells in the east—the equinoctial sun rises exactly in the east, hence his

[1] A. Shorter, 'The God Nehebkau', in *JEA*, XXI (1935), pp. 41–8. A staff ending in a spiral would seem to have been the god's emblem, for in an illustration in the *Book of Am Duat*, he holds this staff in one hand and a serpent in the other.

[2] E. A. W. Budge, *Book of the Dead*, 1910, section 25.

[3] Shorter, p. 44. In another spell the dead man says, 'O, Nehebkau, I have come unto you, O, ye Gods, that you may deliver me and give to me my splendour for eternity' (i.e. his rebirth).

[4] Shorter, op. cit., p. 43; *Book of the Dead*, Spell 17, section 23; Grapow, *Urkunden*, p. 55.

[5] *Book of the Dead*, negative confession, Ch. CXXIV, para. 2.

[6] See p. 212 and n. 4. For the *Adaduanan* Calendar see *Sacred State*, pp. 143 ff.

connexion with the two goddesses.¹ Also Nehebkau's place is in the solar barque of Re; in the Pyramid texts he assists Re in receiving the dead kings newly arrived among the gods; he announces them to Re and prepares a meal for them.²

Nehebkau has been regarded by Shorter and others as the sinister associate of the Sun-god, which is true of him in some respects, for he is called 'the overthrower of *kas*'³ or 'he who subjugates the *kas*'.⁴ This reference is to New Year's day when Nehebkau deprives the Sun-god (Amen) and the Pharaoh of their *kas*, which, however, he reunites after certain rituals have been performed;⁵ the name Nehebkau also means the 'Uniter of the *kas*'.⁶ He is, too, the 'Bestower of Dignities'⁷ for he returns to the Pharaoh his kingship when he reunites his *ka* with that of the Sun-god and the Royal Ancestors.⁸

¹ Shorter, p. 47, is of the opinion that Nehebkau is an enemy of the Sun-god since he is a serpent-god and Bastet and Sekhmet are known to have been sworn enemies of all serpents. He continues, however, 'alternatively Nehebkau might be associated with Bastet-Sekhmet when identified with the eye of Re in his honourable capacity as servitor of the Sun-god'.
² *Pyr.*, 340b, 346a, 356a, 361a, 1708 c, d.
³ Speleers, *Les Textes des pyramides égyptiennes*, Bruxelles 1923-4, p. 27.
⁴ Shorter, p. 41.
⁵ See p. 167.
⁶ A. H. Gardiner in *JEA*, II (1915), pp. 123, 124; Kees, *Totenglauben*, p. 293.
⁷ Shorter, p. 41. Nehebkau was also 'He who appoints the positions' of the gods and the dead. It is from the equinoctial points that the positions of the sun and moon are measured. The gods are the manifestations of the heavenly bodies and the dead (their *kas*) live on them.
⁸ I wish to add that R. A. Parker, *The Calendars of Ancient Egypt*, says that there is no evidence that the Egyptians knew the equinoxes or, if they did, they disregarded them (par. 235 and F. N. 108).

CHAPTER VI

The King's Supporters, the Royal Ancestors

AKAN

1. Man's Immortal, Self-existing Elements after Death

(a) The Kra, *the Representative of his Personality*

It is believed that when a man dies his *kra* leaves him and makes its way to heaven in a material form exactly resembling the deceased. For forty days, however, it cannot bring itself to leave its familiar surroundings and hovers around the house in an endeavour to protect those whom it must leave behind. But on the fortieth day it must finally depart; to remind it of this, some of the personal possessions of the dead man are left at the entrance gate of the house for the *kra* to take on its journey. During the night friends of the family watch with the mourners, lest the *kra* of the deceased should make an attempt to take the one he loves best into the other world with him.

It is thought that when the *kra* has wandered about for some time, it comes to a hill which must be climbed, and then to the 'River of Life',[1] which must be crossed. Later it reaches another hill on the top of which is a ladder.[2] This it must scale in order to reach the *Osoro Ahemman*, the 'Upper Kingdom'—the confederation of the heavenly bodies, the sun, moon and stars. It then makes its way to *Nyankopon-kurom*, the 'City of Nyankopon' which is on the sun, for it has first to greet the Royal Ancestors, who as representatives of Nyankopon, the Sun-god, rule the heavenly kingdom for him. Before it can remain in heaven, however, the *kra* has to

[1] See the song which mentions the 'River of Life' in *Sacred State*, p. 78.
[2] Small replicas of ladders, cast in brass, are found among the weights formerly used for weighing gold dust.

appear before a court of judgement. Only if the dead man has led a good life may his *kra* go to its *kra bafano*[1] and settle on the planet from which he received it at his birth. It is free to leave if it wishes to do so, especially if it desires to visit the body in the grave, or the shrine erected for his *kra*. All funeral offerings are addressed to the *kras* of the dead, the representatives of their personalities.

(b) The Heart, the Representative of his Emotions

Koma, the heart, is intimately connected with the *kra*. It is the seat of all emotions, passions, and desires, both good and evil. This is illustrated in everyday language: *koma-pa* means cheerfulness, gladness, or contentedness—literally, a good, a joyful heart. *Koma-bone* means badness; the irascible temper of a man is also described thus. Literally translated it means 'evil heart'. *Akoma-di* means anguish of mind, heartache. When a person died far away from home and it was impossible to bring the body back for burial, his heart would be cut out and taken to his home. The heart in this instance stood for the whole personality of the dead man.

(c) The Honhom, the Divine Soul

At the time when the *kra* leaves the dead body, the *honhom*, the divine breath of life (from *home*—to breathe) flies in the shape of a bird to Nyame, the Supreme Being. It is regarded as pure spirit and as a manifestation of the *kra*, for it lives in the *kra* of a man to keep it in existence; it generates life. Everybody has this spirit within him, but it is believed that the majority of people during their life-time are unable to free it from the body for either good or evil purposes. Those people who are able to do so, are described as *bayi-fo* (*ba*—a certain type of spirit;[2] *yi*—release, or liberate; *fo*—people) generally translated as 'witches'. The released spirit then flies like a bird, usually at night; nobody can quite describe its form. It emits fire through the nine doors or openings of the human body: the eyes, nostrils, ears, mouth, anus, the penis of a man, or the vagina of a woman. The *honhom* or *ba*, incorporeal as breath, may therefore become corporeal as half-human, half-bird. Like the *kra* it can roam about at will, visiting the body in the grave or reuniting with the *kra* and other immaterial elements of the deceased (see below) in the shrine erected for him.

---

[1] See pp. 109, 110.
[2] *Ba* is evidently the old Egyptian word for *honhom*, see p. 131.

THE KING'S SUPPORTERS, THE ROYAL ANCESTORS

(*d*) *The* Saman, *the Spiritualised Body*

The *saman* is the spiritualised body of the dead man, his shadow form that goes to live in the *Samandow* or the *Asamanade*, the netherworld. Some believe that this is situated beyond the 'Upper Kingdom' in the outer darkness which is approached by the Milky Way. Others say that it lies below the earth. Wherever it may be only those persons become *saman-fo* (*fo*, people) after death, whose *kra* can prove in the Judgement Hall in the city of the Sun-god that they have not been criminals on earth. These seem to fall into three classes: first, criminals whose bodies on earth were burned, so making their resurrection in the *Samandow* impossible; these after death become *okrabiri* (literally black or dark *kras*), who roam about on earth and cause lightning to strike houses, earthquake damage and so forth. The second are *atofo*, or transgressors, believed to have been punished by sudden death at the hand of the gods. They are condemned to live in utter darkness in the *Asramenta* (eclipse of the moon). From time to time they call through their *kra* (the imperishable soul) to their king on earth to grant them pardon, for without this they cannot be granted absolution by the Royal Ancestors who act for the Sun-god. Thirdly, other sinners and wrong-doers become *saman-tenten*, or wait-about-spirits, homeless on earth. They may be seen sitting at cross-roads, weeping, trying to find their way back to life, so that they may undo the sins they committed during their life-time.

The dead who have been resurrected as *saman-fo* can leave the netherworld if they feel so inclined and reunite with their *kras*. They may do this either in the Upper Kingdom, in their bodies in the grave, or in the shrine erected for the *kra* where it is invoked and offerings are made to it. The *saman-fo* accept libations of rum or gin, and the royal *saman-fo* the blood of human sacrifices;[1] they eat the food offered to the *kra* as well as other foodstuffs which they can collect. They sip the alcohol out of corn-beer and palm-wine, and for this reason these liquids become slimy when left uncovered during the night.

---

[1] Captured kings or great chiefs were sacrificed over the stools of the Royal Ancestors in the Chapel of the Stools and the head severed from the body so that the blood might be spilt over the stools to give the king's *saman* life. Blood is tabu for the *kra* of the dead. The blood sausage, which is made from the boiled blood of sacrificed rams, must therefore also be destined for the *saman*.

(e) The Sunsum, *the Shadow Soul*

The *sunsum* is the shadow or aura about a man's personality or his consciousness of self. The frailty of the *sunsum* can be seen from a line in a very ancient song called *Owuo Papa*, the Death Fan: 'With no more force than the wind stirred by a fan, death can at any time blow the *sunsum* into the other world.'[1] When the *sunsum* has left the dead body it is thought to attach itself first to the *kra* and, after the trial of the dead man, to the *saman*, or to be absorbed by the *saman*.

(f) The Sasa, *the Personification of his Energy*

Sasa or *sesa* is the energy or power of a person, and after death it represents the immaterial personification of his power. Some of the *saman-fo* are invested with it, others are not. In addition the *sasa* may be the revengeful spirit of the dead person; the *sasa* of the victims of human sacrifice, for instance, is greatly feared, as is that of powerful animals killed in the hunt. Executioners and hunters therefore have special charms to protect them against the hazards of their professions.

(g) Reincarnation

The *kra* of the ordinary sinful mortal, in which dwells the *honhom*, must be reincarnated in a descendant of the dead person's mother's family, unless during his life-time he had been entirely without sin. The child who receives his *kra* with the *honhom* may continue where his predecessor left off, and if, in his adult life, he is unable to bring it to a state of perfection, the *kra* must undergo further reincarnation before it can become wholly Nyame's in a mystic union, the final communion.

(h) The Honhom Nipadua, *the transfigured Spirits*

The *honhom nipadua* (*nipadua*, body) are the transfigured spirits or celestial beings (*osoro-fo*) who have joined Nyame, the Supreme Being, in a mystic reunion. They are the *kras* whose *honhom* has been filled with goodness. *Kra* and *honhom* are both regarded as pure, being part of the life spirit or essence of the Supreme Being. But the *sunsum* of a person may defile this purity and so hamper the development of the soul. To quote Dr. Danquah:[2]

---

[1] See also *Sacred State*, p. 86.
[2] J. B. Danquah, *The Akan Doctrine of God*, 1944, p. 85.

THE KING'S SUPPORTERS, THE ROYAL ANCESTORS

'There is never any evil stored up in the soul for the soul is part of the Source and maintains its pristine goodness or sacredness unimpaired. A soul stunted in its growth by the deprivation of acts of growth in goodness does not suddenly blossom forth into a fully matured *honhom* by a single act of confession, and the goodness, or merit, accruing therefrom. That soul returns to Nyame with its *honhom* very little filled with any consciousness of achievement, and the one act of goodness remains at bottom, just a faint glimmer of the good, a little point of a star, and not the great sun to which all souls aspire—a pure *honhom*, in glory for his achievement.'

Among the Akan goodness is regarded as an acquisition, not a gift. It is earned by each individual's own manner of life and not by the favour he obtains by uncensored grace.[1]

(*i*) The Name

The name of a person is regarded as his most special mark of identity, and a nameless being is without any rights in the other world. To preserve the identity of a dead person, it is essential that offerings be made to his *kra*; this entails the uttering of his name. Since the possession, or knowledge, of the name of a dead man can enable another person to gain power over his *kra*, the names of the founders of dynasties and other important kings of the past are usually kept secret, and others are substituted.

(*k*) The Body

The preservation of the body is the first requirement for the resurrection of the dead person in the other world, because only when the immaterial elements, the *kra*, *honhom* and the *saman*, unite with the body, does the deceased 'live'. For this reason in the past the bodies of the kings and queen-mothers were particularly cared for, and were dried or embalmed by a primitive method.[2] Today their bodies are buried for a year or longer; their bones are then disinterred and articulated with gold wire, while in some cases the eye sockets are filled with gold, the life-giving metal of the sun. The skeletons are then dressed in precious cloth and covered with gold ornaments. The coffins of the great Akan kings in the past were covered with sheet gold into which divine symbols were hammered

---
[1] ibid., p. 26.
[2] See *Sacred State*, p. 63.

(repoussé work). They were preserved in mausoleums situated in sacred groves.[1] The Akan never made statues or statuettes of their rulers, but cast their portraits in gold, either life-size or smaller. These were placed on the stools of the dead rulers in the Chapel of the Stools.[2]

2. *The Royal Ancestral spirits, the Royal Ancestors*

When a king died it was believed that his *kra* stayed in the vicinity of the palace until the fortieth day after his death when it was sent on its way to the other world in the *Werempe* ceremony, which marked the end of the royal funeral rites.[3] Then it wandered away in the likeness of the dead king and finally climbed the ladder[4] which led to the Upper Kingdom. There in the city of the Sun-god, the *kra* was received by the *nananom*, the Royal Ancestors and, after its purification, was united with theirs. The *kra* was then enstooled by Nyame, just as kings are enstooled on earth by the queen-mothers, to rule as heir-apparent of the Sun-god in the Upper Kingdom. When the dead king's *kra* appeared as king in heaven, his successor on earth received simultaneously the divine power innate in kingship in the form of the *kra* of his predecessors.

To give the dead king immortal life it was essential that the immortal elements of his personality should be united again in the body in the tomb. But in addition shrines were erected; these were the stools in the Chapel of the Stools in which the royal ancestral spirits or souls, which included all the self-existing immortal elements, could settle and unite when invoked. Offerings were made to their *kras* and were shared by the living king and the most important chiefs in the state. This had the double purpose of keeping the royal dead 'living' and of re-establishing the bond between them and their people, between whom and the Sun-god they could thus continue to act as intermediaries. When the offerings ceased,

---

[1] The ancestors of the Bono kings are said to have been buried under great tumuli. The last king of Bono, who killed himself in 1740, was buried under a small replica of a tumulus in the sacred grove at Takyiman, which is still in existence.

[2] Illustrations of two such portraits can be found in *Ak. of Ghana*, Pls. 46, 47.

[3] See Chapter VIII d.

[4] Ladders are used, according to information, only for the ascent to heaven, never for descent. If the Royal Ancestors wish to visit the sleeping king at night, they are believed to use the rainbow as a bridge between heaven and earth.

which meant that their names were no longer pronounced, they ceased to 'live', their *kra*, *honhom* and *saman*, although immortal, became nameless and thus they lost their identity.

3. The Chapel of the Stools

In the past the Chapels of the Stools (*Nkon-dwa-fieso*) were beautiful buildings. Their walls were covered with reliefs, depicting the ideograms arranged in patterns which to the Akan conveyed creation and the manifestations and powers of the gods incarnate in the Royal Ancestors. These chapels housed the shrines for the souls of the dead; these were originally leather cushions (*ate*) and later the low five-columned stools. At first the stools were entirely covered with sheet gold; at a later period they were blackened but their five columns were filled with gold dust. The stools stood in a semicircle on a platform usually along the eastern wall of the main room. The stool of the founder of the dynasty was, and in many cases still is, placed in the middle.

In ancient Bono small gold portrait masks of the deceased rulers, placed on top of the stools, identified each one but, according to tradition, the leather cushion of the founder of Bono, Asaman, was marked by a small gold model of a falcon, the *akyeneboa*, or totem, of the royal Ayoko clan. The Bosummuru gold dagger or small ceremonial sword used to rest on the stool of King Takyi Akwamo (1431–63); today it decorates the stool of the first *Omanhene* of the Bono-Takyiman state, Ameyaw Gyamfi (1748–71). At the foot of each stool stood the *kuduo*, a gold or copper vessel, filled with pieces of gold, each piece representing one year of the king's reign. On a table in the room rested the *puduo*, and in it were pieces of gold each of which symbolised a *kra* of the Royal Ancestors. Other sacred treasures were also kept in the Chapels, apart from the libation cups, water jugs, eating utensils and offering bowls. In Bono, according to the traditions, these were all of gold.

The Chapels are usually decorated with *summe* plants (*Costus sp.*) which among the Akan is the equivalent of the Egyptian lotus. Its flowers are white, the colour of purity and joy, and conically shaped; white or silver is also the colour of the moon, and the triangular cones are a symbol of the Mother-goddess. When the chapels are closed a large cloth usually covers the stools. In ancient Bono the cloth, very long, was embroidered with hammered gold thread.

4. The custodian of the Chapel of the Stools

The cult of the Royal Ancestors is the function of the king and of his 'eldest (stool) son', who, in the Bono-Takyiman state, is the *Gyaasehene*, the chief of the royal household. The *Nkondwasoafohene* is simply and solely the custodian of the Chapel in charge of the precious shrines, the stools; his title literally translated means 'Chief of the stool-bearers' (see below). Nevertheless he is regarded as *oman-ye-bosom-fo*, or 'state priest of the gods' (i.e. the Royal Ancestors). When the king sits in public on ceremonial occasions the *Nkondwasoafohene* sits behind him, robed in a white cloth, his left hand and eyelids daubed with white clay which is used for sanctification. The king is reassured by his presence since the priest, by virtue of his office, is filled with the strength and support of the royal dead. This can be transmitted by him to the king whenever the latter is in need of it. The confidence he inspires in the king is expressed in the words 'I abound in good luck when I touch you.'

The main duty of the chief of the stool-bearers and his assistants, all either brothers or sons, is to look after the Chapel with its stools, to sacrifice the bulls and rams, and to cook the food offerings on certain specified days. They also ring the bells to invite the royal spirits to take up their abode in the stools. On the day of the *Asubo* ceremony during the New Year festival they carry on the back of their necks the stools of the Royal Ancestors, as well as the silver stool of the reigning king when these are taken to the sacred river for purification. On the way the royal ancestral spirits often enter the stools, and the stool-bearers stand trembling in a trance. They are unable to move until the king descends from his palanquin and personally intercedes with the Royal Ancestors, begging them not to hamper the procession but to wait until the river is reached.

The *Nkondwasoafohene* assists the queen-mother in the presence of a few selected persons to enstool the future king in the Chapel of the Stools on the seat of the founder of the dynasty. He dresses him in the regalia, adorns him and places the Bosummuru sword in his hand. When a king has died his body is brought to the Chapel where it remains till the day of burial. When the body has been removed the desecrated Chapel is purified by the stool-bearers. The *Nkondwasoafohene* is also in charge of the *apunia* rite, the blackening of a king's stool after his death.[1]

[1] See p. 203.

13. Illustration from the Papyrus of Ani.
On the right the *Anmutef* priest wearing the leopard-skin and the sidelock, which characterise him as 'a son of a god'. On the left the scribe Ani followed by his wife.
(Reproduced by courtesy of the Trustees of the British Museum.)

14. Illustration from the Papyrus of Anhai.

Isis and Nephthys adoring the Sun-god Re at his rising. He is symbolised by the sun disk which is held up by the ankh, the symbol for Life. The dog-headed apes, the transformed openers of the eastern portals of heaven, raise their hands in adoration. (Reproduced by courtesy of the Trustees of the British Museum.)

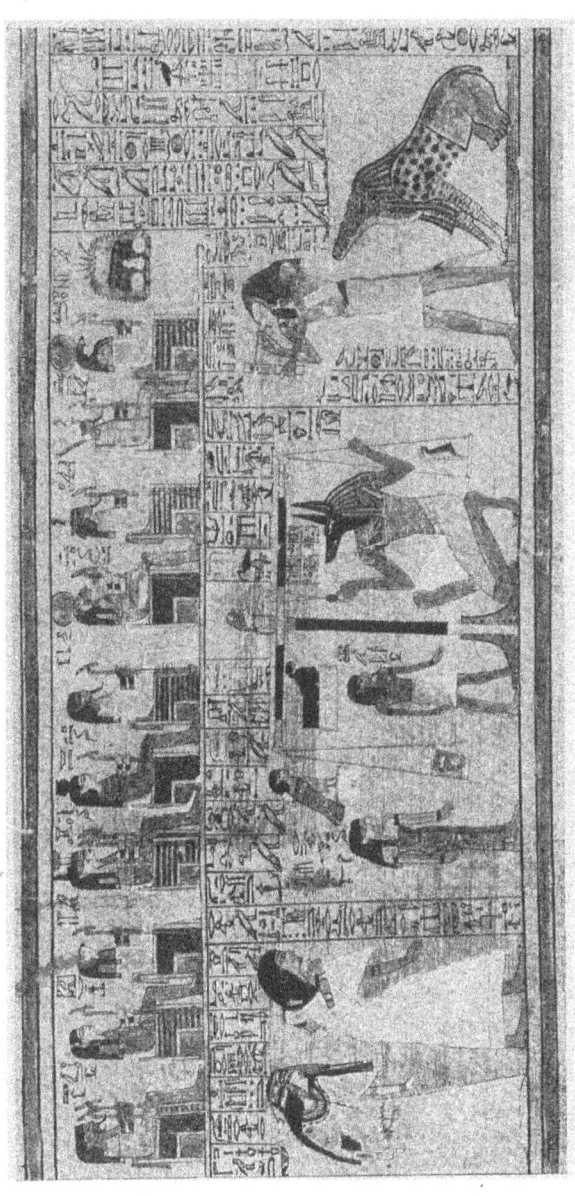

15. Illustration from the Papyrus of Ani.

The Weighing of the Heart of Ani in the Hall of Judgement. Above, the 'Great Company of the Gods' of Heliopolis who represent the divine jury. Below, centre, the jackal-headed god Anpu examines the pointer of the balance wherein the heart of Ani is being weighed against the feather, symbolic of Law, or Right or Truth. On the left Ani, accompanied by his wife, on the right the monster Amemit, the devourer of the hearts of the dead who are not permitted to enter heaven. Before her the ibis-headed god Thoth, who notes down the result of the trial. (Reproduced by courtesy of the Trustees of the British Museum.)

16. The *Ba*, in the form of a bird, visits the mummy in the Tomb. (Reproduced by courtesy of the Trustees of the British Museum.)

5. The Ritual in the Chapel of the Stools

Today in Bono-Takyiman the days reserved for the worship of the royal dead are the following in the *Adaduanan* calendar of the Akan: *Mono-* (or *Muru*) *Wukuo* meaning 'Fresh' or 'New' Wednesday, on which the *Adae* ceremony is performed;[1] *Muru-Fie* (or *Mono-Fie*) 'Fresh' or 'New' Friday; *Fo-Dwo* 'Fertile Monday'; *Fo-Wukuo* 'Fertile Wednesday; *Fo-Fie* 'Fertile Friday'; and *Nkyi-Fie* 'Hateful Friday'. These days run in a 42-day, or six-weekly cycle. On the morning of these days the king gives a bottle of rum to the *Banmuhene*, the custodian of the royal cemetery, for a libation in the Chapel of the Stools and later in the day for another libation by the king's deputy the *Gyaasehene*. Offerings are made to the *kras* of the Royal Ancestors consisting mainly of the meat, raw and cooked, of two sacrificed white rams; the lights and intestines are placed on the stools and choice morsels are roasted on skewers and placed in small bowls in front of the stools. The blood of the sacrifice is sprinkled over all the stools and some of it is cooked; when it has curdled it is made into blood sausages. The vegetable offerings are usually *eto*, boiled and mashed yams (a staple crop), some dishes prepared with palm-oil, others without; plantain beaten into *fufu*, a soft glutinous mash which is then formed into small balls; and roasted groundnuts and beans.

On the Saturday following *Fo-Fie Kese* 'Great Fertile Friday' (shortly before New Year's day on which the purification of the *kras* of the Royal Ancestors takes place) the offerings are more elaborate; four white rams of the long-legged Sudanese breed are sacrificed and a bull is slaughtered. The meat of the bull is reserved for those who have taken part in the rites on the preceding day—the chiefs of the state, elders and court officials. The meat of this animal is tabu for the *kras* of the Royal Ancestors, for the bull is sacred to Bosummuru, the god from whom they claim descent in the male line. The meat of the sacrificed rams is also distributed, except for those parts which are kept as offerings to the royal dead. The king receives the right thigh and the right shoulder and his 'eldest son', the *Gyaasehene*, the left thigh. The queen-mother is given that part of the animal containing the inner organs of procreation which

---

[1] The *Adae* ceremony is described in detail in *Sacred State*, p. 177. In Asante and other Akan states the *Adae* is also performed on every sixth Sunday (*Kwasi-Adae*).

make a woman fruitful, and the elders each receive their portion according to tradition; the stool-bearers keep for themselves the bones of the neck and the thorax.

EGYPT
1. Man's Immortal, Self-existing Elements after Death
(a) The Ka, the Representative of his Personality

The *ka* of a dead man represented his abstract personality; it was endowed with the material form of the deceased and exactly resembled him.[1] Like the Pharaoh's *ka* it probably 'rested' for a while before it hurried on to heaven.[2] It had to cross a mountain range and afterwards the Celestial Nile, then another mountain range, until at last by climbing a ladder it reached heaven.[3] Before it was allowed to make its home there, however, the dead man's life was judged by Osiris, the representative of the Royal Ancestors and of the Sun-god. His seat of judgement must have been on the Nether sun, for in the great hymn which Ramses IV set up at Abydos to honour Osiris, it is said: 'When Re appeareth daily and reaches the Netherworld to govern this land, and also the other countries, then thou (Osiris) also sittest there like him; together you are called 'The United Soul'.[4]

When the *ka* of the deceased had been admitted, it went first to 'his *ka*', meaning, no doubt what the Akan call *kra bafano*—the counterpart of one's own *kra*, or the *kra* corresponding to one's own. In other words, it returned to the planet which had given the dead man his *kra*, or in this instance, his *ka*. Like the *kra* it then moved in the cosmic circuit,[5] and was in the sky and also under the earth when the sun, moon, and stars had set in the west. But it also could wander, if it wished, from place to place on earth. Funerary offerings were addressed to the *ka* of the deceased, for it represented his personality.

[1] Wiedemann, *Doctrine*, p. 19.
[2] Kees, *Totenglauben*, p. 77.
[3] Budge, *Gods*, I, p. 171.
[4] Budge, *Book of the Dead* (Brit. Mus., 1933, p. 21). Originally Re judged the dead at sunrise.
[5] In the Pyramid texts the *kas* of the dead are often equated with the stars. Cf. Kees, op. cit., p. 78. For the dead in the cosmic circuit see Frankfort, *Kingship*, pp. 117–22, 168, 175, 183–4, 210.

(b) *The Heart, the Representative of his Emotions and his Conscience*

The *ab*, or heart, was intimately connected with the *ka*. It was regarded as the symbol of all emotions, desires, and passions, both good and evil; after death it embodied the conscience of the deceased and represented him in the 'Abode of Hearts', the Hall of Judgement. There before Osiris the deceased addressed his heart, calling it 'his mother',[1] and then identified it with his *ka*. When judgement had been given the god Thoth demanded that the (immaterial) heart should be restored to its place—that is to say in the *ka* which represented the dead man. (Pl. 15).[2]

(c) *The Ba, the Divine Soul*

The *ba* was closely associated with the *ka* and was believed to dwell in the heart; it represented the 'breath of life'.[3] After death it flew to heaven in the shape of a human-headed bird. *Ba* means 'animated' and may further mean 'manifestation', a significance easily derived from the meaning 'animated'.[4] From 'manifestation' the sense may shift to 'emanation'; the *bennu* bird was the *ba* of Re; the Apis bull, the *ba* of Osiris. Re, viewed as a creator, and the Pharaoh each had seven *bas* who, one may assume from the number, were the *bas* of the seven planets. The Pharaoh's Royal Ancestors were called the '*Bas* of Pe and Nekhen'; *ba* here is generally translated 'souls'. The European term, however, does not quite cover the Egyptian conception, which included the manifestation of the dead as 'givers of life' and 'guardians' of the Pharaoh and his people. As such they were 'souls' who were animated or 'lived'.

The *ba*, like the *honhom* of the Akan, could be either corporeal or incorporeal at will; like the *ka* it moved about freely in the shape of a human-headed bird and is sometimes depicted hovering over the body of the deceased, or descending the tomb-shaft to the burial chamber, bringing to it, or more precisely to the *ka* of the deceased, the 'breath of life' (Pl. 16).[5]

[1] *Book of the Dead*, Ch. XXX b.
[2] Wiedemann, op. cit., p. 49. The actual heart was taken out of the body before it was embalmed. It is not known what happened to it; ibid., p. 29.
[3] Budge, *Osiris*, p. 134. The heart was confused with the lungs by the ancients. Cf. V. E. Johnson, *Egyptian Science*, p. 106.   [4] Frankfort, p. 64.
[5] The vignette in the Pap. of Neb-qet proves that the breath or air, also water and food, were destined for the *ka*. Cf. Budge, *Osiris*, II, p. 129.

THE KING'S SUPPORTERS, THE ROYAL ANCESTORS

(*d*) *The* Sahu, *the Spiritualised Body*

After a favourable judgement had been pronounced on the dead man, he was transformed, through the good offices of Osiris, into a *sahu*, a shade or spirit body, and in this form passed into the netherworld.[1] The *sahu*, also immortal, was by itself an empty thing; according to an inscription on the sarcophagus of Panehenusis the '*sahu* lives on the command of the *ba*',[2] which animates it. Like the *ka* and the *ba* the *sahu* could move about at will. Those who did not pass into the kingdom of Osiris were annihilated quickly and completely, no doubt to make resurrection impossible. Personal annihilation was the lot of the wrongdoer, although his *ka* and his *ba*, being divine, could never die.[3]

(*e*) *The* Khaibit, *the Shadow Soul*

The *khaibit*, the shadow of a person in which, it was believed, resided his generative power, remained after death closely connected with the *sahu*.[4] Little is known about it. It is interesting to note that the hieroglyph for *khaibit* is a fan, which is also the symbol of the *sunsum* of the Akan, who call it the *owuo papa*, or 'death fan'.[5]

(*f*) *The* Sekhem, *the Personification of his Energy*

Sekhem means 'power' and, after death, it represented the immaterial personification of the energy or power of the deceased. Osiris and every god had its *sekhem*.[6]

(*g*) *Reincarnation*

On this point we are very badly informed. There is a reference to people in heaven, the *hemenet*, who would seem to be waiting for reincarnation; according to Budge they 'appear to have been a class of beings who either were to become, or had already been, human

---

[1] Budge, *Osiris*, II, p. 124, says that there is no information on how the *sahu*, or revivified body, was kept in existence. Among the Akan the *samanfo* were given libations of rum, gin or the blood of sacrificial victims (in the case of the Royal Ancestors); liquids were necessary to sustain them. Among the Egyptians libations poured out for the Royal Ancestors may have been destined for their *sahus*.

[2] *Osiris*, II, p. 42.

[3] Wiedemann, op. cit., p. 55.

[4] Kees, op. cit., p. 83.

[5] See p. 124.

[6] *Osiris*, II, p. 133; *Book of the Dead*, Ch. LXXIX.

beings'.[1] Further evidence of this may be that the kingly *ka* of the Pharaoh was a reincarnated *ka*—that of his Royal Ancestors, personified by Osiris; he received it at the end of the coronation ceremony at the precise moment when the late Pharaoh's *ka* was united in heaven with that of the Royal Ancestors, and he became Osiris.[2]

The idea of the transmigration of the soul was reported by Greek and Roman authors, who said that it must pass through various animals before it could again enter man. This conception may have come into being in late times when the clans had ceased to exist. Among the Akan, it will be remembered, the *kra*, except for the kingly *kra*, is reincarnated in a descendant of the dead person's mother's family.[3]

(h) The Akhu, the transfigured Spirits

The *akhu* in Egyptian texts are celestial beings who lived among the gods. They were regarded as 'Beings of Light', as the 'luminous'. They were beatified souls, transfigured spirits, who represented the imperishable qualities in man—truth and goodness. In the text that accompanies the alabaster reliefs on the sarcophagus of Seti I, the *akhu* are described as follows: 'Those who have offered up incense to the gods, and whose *kau* [plural of *ka*] have been washed clean. They have reckoned up and they are *maat* (i.e. truth) in the presence of the Great God, who destroyeth sin.' Osiris says to them: 'Ye are truth, rest in peace.' And of them he says: 'They were doers of truth while they were upon earth, they did battle for their god, and they shall be called to the enjoyment of the Land of the House of Life with truth. Their truth shall be reckoned to them in the presence of the Great God who destroyeth sin.' Then addressing them again Osiris says: 'Ye are Beings of Truth, O, ye truths. Take ye your rest because of what they have done, becoming even as those who are in my following, and who direct the House of Him, whose soul is holy. Ye shall live there even as they live, and ye shall have dominion over the cool waters of your land, I command that

---

[1] *Osiris*, I, p. 159.

[2] See p. 214.

[3] Hermann Junker, *Pyramidenzeit*, 1949, p. 109, remarks: 'Very strange is the connection of the *ka* with the ancestors and the descendants; it appears to be the member of a chain, which connects past, present and future and is anchored in the Hereafter.'

ye have your being to the limit (of that land) with Truth and without sin.'[1]

I have quoted this text so fully to show that the conceptions of the *akhu* and the *honhom nipadua* are identical. In both cases the dead had been leading a life full of truth (in the widest sense of righteousness and goodness); they had fought against sin. Their reward was 'to live with the gods' or to become one with god again (Akan). The *akhu* were sometimes identified individually, for offerings of food were occasionally made to them. Judging by Akan beliefs, this meant no more than the maintenance of the link between the living and the dead.

(*j*) *The Name*

The name was man's particular identity; a nameless being could not be introduced to the gods. To preserve the identity of the dead person it was essential that offerings should be made to his *ka*, which entailed the uttering of his name. The possession and knowledge of the name of a man could, however, enable another to do him good or evil.[2]

(*k*) *The Body*

The preservation of the body was the first requirement for the resurrection of the dead in the hereafter, for the body in the grave acted as the resting-place or abode of the immortal self-existing elements of man. Only when these were reunited did the deceased 'live'. To preserve the body embalming was practised from the earliest times. To ensure further that the mummy became a 'living soul' a magical rite was performed, the so-called 'Opening-of-the-Mouth', to enable the dead person to see, hear, speak and walk again.

The royal mummy and the royal coffin were covered with gold, the imperishable, life-giving metal of the sun:

'Thou art made perfect in gold, thou dost shine brightly in metal, and thy fingers shine in the dwelling of Osiris, the gold of the mountains cometh to thee; it is a holy talisman of the gods in their abodes and it lighteth their face in the Lower Heaven.'

To safeguard the royal mummy it was buried under a pyramid or in a rock tomb in as inaccessible a place as possible.

[1] *Book of the Dead*, Ch. CX. [2] ibid., Ch. XC.

2. The Royal Ancestral Spirits, the Royal Ancestors

When a Pharaoh died his *ka* 'rested'[1] between the time of his death and the *ka's* departure for heaven. Then it wandered off in the form of the deceased, the Sky-goddess Nut showing the way: 'Thou mountest to thy mother Nut, she takes thy hand and puts thee on the way to the horizon to the place where Re is' (*Pyr.* 356). When it, or the deceased Pharaoh, arrived at the ladder he was helped up it, usually by Horus or Set,[2] as in the case of Pepi I: 'Every spirit and every god opened his hand to Pepi when he was on the ladder.'[3] Then 'The Gates of Heaven are opened for thee, the Doors of the Cool Places are opened for thee. Thou findest Re standing, waiting for thee; he takes thy hand, he takes thee to the Dual Shrines of Heaven and places thee on the throne of Osiris' (*Pyr.* 752–64).

The Dual Shrines in heaven correspond to the Dual Shrines (*iterty*) on earth. They were the shrines of the 'Souls of Pe', the king's Lower Egyptian Royal Ancestors, and of the 'Souls of Nekhen', the king's Upper Egyptian Royal Ancestors. When Unas, last king of the 4th Dynasty, arrived at the Dual Shrines in Heaven, the text says: 'To him (Unas) come the gods, the "Souls of Pe" and the gods, the "Souls of Nekhen"—the gods belonging to heaven and the gods belonging to earth.' The 'Souls of Pe and Nekhen' then united themselves with the dead king: 'Horus has arranged with the gods (i.e. the Royal Ancestors) to unite themselves with thee, to fraternise with thee in the name of "He of Senut",[4] and not to reject thee in the name of "He of the Dual Shrines"'(*Pyr.* 575–82).

The dead king thus became an ancestral spirit, a Royal Ancestor, and only then could he be enthroned in Heaven (*Dwat*) as Osiris— the mythological form assumed by each dead Pharaoh[5]—and be established as a god by Nut: 'Nut has established thee as god because of Set, in the name of god' (*Pyr.* 575–82), and in another text:

---

[1] In the text in the tomb of Queen Meresankh III the 'resting of her *ka*' is mentioned. Cf. Frankfort, *Kingship*, p. 63 and n. 9.

[2] Instead of the ladder other means were also used: the Pharaoh could fly to heaven as a falcon (*Pyr.* 913, 891); he could climb a ramp (*Pyr.* 364–5) or he could mount a stairway (*Pyr.* 1090).

[3] Jéquier, *Pepi II*, I, p. 195; Budge, *Osiris*, I, p. 76.

[4] *Senut* was a snake whose effigy decorated two upright stelae before the Dual Shrines for added protection. Kees in *ZÄS*, LVII, pp. 120 ff.

[5] Frankfort, *Kingship*, pp. 110 ff.

'Thy mother Nut has spread herself over thee in her name of "She of Shetpet".[1] She has caused thee to be a god' (*Pyr.* 636–8).

The living Pharoah was enthroned by Isis, but Nut performed the ceremony for the dead one in heaven. At the moment when the dead king became Osiris, the divine power of kingship inherent in the late ruler was transferred to his successor on earth, for the *ka* of the living Pharaoh was the Horus *ka* of his Royal Ancestors personified as Osiris.[2] As among the Akan, the *ka* of the Royal Ancestors lived on in the reigning Pharaoh, but, to keep the Royal Ancestors immortal as persons, shrines were erected for them, the above-mentioned *iterty*, or Dual Shrines. These were the centre of their cult.

3. *The Dual Shrines*

The *iterty*, translated as Dual Shrines, were the sanctuaries in which the Pharaoh's Upper and Lower Egyptian Royal Ancestors were venerated, the 'Souls of Pe and Nekhen', the 'Gods of the Dual Shrines'.[3] The statues of the deceased rulers must have been kept in these sanctuaries for they are called at Medinet Habu 'the dead kings of Upper and Lower Egypt from the Dual Shrines'.[4] The word *itert* (singular) is related to river channel, its basic meaning being something like 'line' or 'row'.[5] Among the Akan the stools are arranged in a long row on a raised platform; in Egypt, the statues of the kings, and perhaps, in an earlier age, seats[6] representing the rulers may have been similarly arranged.

The Egyptian word *iterty* is a dual form; the pair consisted of an Upper and a Lower Egyptian shrine, called the *per-ur*[7] and the *per-nezer* respectively. The hieroglyphs for the shrines show that both were constructed, certainly originally, of reeds and matting, primitive building materials and proof of their great antiquity.

[1] This implies that the Pharaoh's Royal Ancestors were reckoned from the reign of the first Horus kings, 'the seed of Geb', who followed a Geb-Nut Dynasty, see p. 43. I could not find any explanation for *Shetpet*, it may have been the seat of the Nut queens.

[2] The rite in which the kingly *ka* power is transferred, is described on pp. 213, 214.

[3] Naville, *Deir el Bahri*, III, Pl. LX.

[4] Frankfort, *Kingship*, p. 96.

[5] A. Gardiner, 'Horus the Behdetite', in *JEA*, XXX (1944), p. 27.

[6] Statues are unknown before the time of the New Kingdom.

[7] The *per-ur* is written with the same sign as the Upper Egyptian *itert*, evidence that the *per-ur* is the same as the latter. Frankfort, p. 96.

THE KING'S SUPPORTERS, THE ROYAL ANCESTORS

There is good reason to assume that the Upper Egyptian shrine was originally situated in Nekhen. This is evident not only from the name of the 'Souls' but also from the fact that the vulture-goddess Nekhbet, who was worshipped at Nekhab, a city just across the Nile, was called the Mistress of the *per-ur*. This suggests that the goddess and her people must have been the owners of the land on which Nekhen was founded by the Pharaoh's Upper Egyptian Royal Ancestors.[1] Among the Akan the deities of people who open up a stretch of land for cultivation are recognised as the supernatural owners of the land.[2] The rites of the *Sed* festival show that in Egypt the same views were held.

The *per-nezer*, the Lower Egyptian *itert*, was presumably situated originally at Pe, as is suggested by the name of the souls. The cobra-goddess Wadjet of the adjacent city of Dep no doubt played the same part as the vulture-goddess Nekhbet in the south, for she was regarded as the Mistress of the shrine.[3] In historical times, it seems, the permanent location of the Dual Shrines was at Heliopolis.[4]

The *iterty* must have served the same purpose as the Chapel of the Stools among the Akan, for offerings were made there to the Royal Ancestors in order to give life and power to the reigning Pharaoh. In a text from the Old Kingdom the 'Souls of Nekhen' and the 'Souls of Pe' address Sahure in his temple: 'We give thee all life and happiness, all nourishment, all sacrifices which come out of the Nile, all good things which are in Upper (Lower) Egypt,

[1] Nekhbet was also called 'Mistress of the Netjeri Shema', the 'Sanctuary of the South'. This shrine is not the same as the *per-ur* (cf. Frankfort, p. 96) and the reference would appear to be to a sanctuary in which the Royal Ancestors of the kings and chiefs of the city of Nekhab were venerated. Nekhbet incidentally came from Punt (see p. 41 n. 4) and a relationship may have existed between the people of Nekhab and Nekhen, which was still remembered in later times.

[2] In some Akan states at the harvest festivals, for instance, the *asase-wura*, the chief of the people who own the land, is recognised for one day as king, to make offerings to his god on behalf of all the people who had settled on the land of his forebears.

[3] The goddess Wadjet (or Edjo) was also Mistress of a shrine called the *per-nu* situated at Dep (Buto). It was, no doubt, the shrine where the Royal Ancestors of the chiefs of the city of Dep were venerated, who gave to Queen Isis the land on which she founded Pe (see p. 48). Wadjet also came originally from Punt.

[4] Frankfort, p. 94, believes that the 'Souls of Heliopolis' denoted both the 'Souls of Pe' and the 'Souls of Nekhen'. It is, however, possible that the 'Souls of Heliopolis' represented the kings of the 5th Dynasty, who originated from Heliopolis.

living unto eternity.'[1] From other texts also it is clear that the Royal Ancestors were concerned for their successors on earth and the well-being of their former realm; their power surrounded and supported the king in every way. A variant designation, 'Guardians of Pe and Nekhen',[2] stresses this aspect. On the other hand the Royal Ancestors could give life to the Pharaoh only if they themselves 'lived'. For it was necessary for the statues, like the stools of the Akan, to constitute the focal points where the various immortal components of the personality of the deceased could be united. The statues, again, like the stools of the Akan kings, were carried in procession during the New Year festival, which centred on the god Min, presumably to be purified in a sacred stretch of water. Min, the Sky fertility-god, incarnate in the Pharaoh, was, after Horus, most intimately connected with the Dual Shrines, as is evident from the Pyramid texts 256a, 1928b, c, and 1998a.

4. *The Custodian of the Dual Shrines*

The counterpart of the *Nkondwasoafohene*, the custodian of the Chapel of the Stools, would appear to have been the *imy-khant*, for he anointed and adorned the future king in the Dual Shrines.[3] Like the *Nkondwasoafohene*, he was not an officiant,[4] this function being fulfilled by the king or his proxy;[5] too little is known about him to say more. In the funerary ceremonies depicted in the tomb chapel of Rekhmire[6] he appears together with the *Sem* priest, a reciter priest, and two female mourners.

5. *The Royal Standards*

The royal standards displayed certain divine symbols which were mounted on a bracket on the top of a pole. In inscriptions from the time of Ne-Woser-Re and Ramses II the standards were called 'the

---

[1] Borchardt, *Sahure*, II, pp. 40, 102.

[2] e.g. *Pyr.* 795. In the temple of Ne-Woser-Re 'the Guardians of Nekhen' carry the Upper Egyptian king in his litter, but the onlookers call out 'May the Souls of Nekhen give life.'

[3] Gardiner, 'The Coronation of King Haremhab', in *JEA*, XXXIX (1953), p. 26.

[4] ibid.

[5] The proxy among the Akan was generally the *Gyaasehene*, the chief of the royal household, as the 'eldest (stool) son' of the king. If he was absent the *Akyeamehene*, the chief of the royal spokesmen, took his place, or the *Nkondwasoafohene*.

[6] Ph. Virey, *Le Tombeau de Rekhmire*, Pl. XXV, bottom register.

gods, who [habitually] follow the god (i.e. the Pharaoh)'.[1] In processions they were carried after the statues of the Royal Ancestors, and it is believed that they were housed in the Dual Shrines. On the early dynastic monuments the standards display the falcon, the double falcon, the Set animal, Thoth's ibis, Upwaut's wolf, the emblem of the god Min, the royal placenta and the *hemsut* sign. In later periods the divine symbols differ widely in composition.[2]

'The gods upon their standards'[3] must have stood in a very intimate relationship to the Pharaoh and the Royal Ancestors since they were carried in such close proximity to both. This suggests that they represented ancestral deities, who in their turn represented lineages. This would explain, moreover, why there were so many more standards in later times. Each king who founded a dynasty and who was not by birth of the Horus lineage would, one may presume, add a standard representing his ancestors, symbolised by a sacred animal or emblem of the god from whom he claimed descent. Thus: the standard of the falcon surely represented the Pharaoh's descent from Horus, whose *ka* was incarnate in him; the double falcon called Neterui, the Two Gods, may have represented Horus the Elder incarnate in prehistoric times in the Pharaoh's Upper Egyptian Royal Ancestors, the 'Souls of Nekhen', and Horus of Libya incarnate in the Pharaoh's Lower Egyptian Royal Ancestors, the 'Souls of Pe'; the *hemsut* symbol, the female *ka*, seems to have represented Hathor as the divine ancestress of the Pharaohs; on a relief at Luxor she appears as the *hemsut* deity giving life to the royal child;[4] the royal placenta, always carried by the priests of Isis, would represent the Pharaoh's descent from Isis, for as king, the Pharaoh was a son of Isis; the emblem of the god Min illustrated the Pharaoh's descent from Min, the Sky fertility-god whose power was incarnate in him;[5] the wolf-god Upwaut, shown with the *shedshed* in front, guarded by the uraeus, indicated that the Pharaoh's wolf-headed Royal Ancestors were descended from him on their father's side.[6]

Close intermarriage must also have been practised between the Pharaoh's Royal Ancestors and members of the royal lineages

[1] The standards are discussed by Frankfort, *Kingship*, pp. 91–3.
[2] For illustration of standards see Pl. 17.
[3] Mariette, *Abydos*, 1870–80, I, Pl. 28d.
[4] See Pl. 10.
[5] See pp. 177 ff.
[6] See p. 45.

incarnating Set and Thoth. As outlined before, Horus princesses descended from Nephthys married Set kings or princes,[1] and the founder of the 2nd Dynasty appears to have been a Set prince, for a queen of this Dynasty is 'She who sees Horus and Set'[2] (the two ancestral gods) when she conceived the heir to the throne.[3] *Pyr.* 141d says of a Pharaoh, 'Thou art about to be born because of Horus in thee, thou art conceived because of Set in thee.'

Thoth's place in the rites depicted on the reliefs is usually the same as that of Set. We have no indication as to the period at which intermarriage in each generation between members of the royal lineages of the Horus and Thoth clans became customary. It may have had its beginning in prehistoric times when Thoth kings ruled Pnubs near Punt in Nubia.[4]

6. *The Ritual in the Dual Shrines*

No description appears to exist of the rites performed in the Dual Shrines, but these could not have been very different from those executed daily in the temples of Osiris.[5] The essential rite was to 'give life' to the deceased ancestor king, to renew the power of his *ka*, and above all to 'give life' to his body that had been torn to pieces by Set. The first was effected by the embracing of the statue that represented the dead king by the Pharaoh or his proxy, in order to transmit *ka*; the second by the 'Opening-of-the-Mouth ceremony' to restore to the dead king the powers of his physical body. The rites were preceded by fumigations in order to purify the temple and the dead, and were followed by a consecrated meal.[6] The statue was then given all the insignia of kingship to show that the king-god ruled again, with all his faculties restored.[7]

The *Adae* ceremony among the Akan, which takes place in the Chapel of the Stools, is basically much the same. The embrace to

---

[1] See pp. 48, 49.

[2] Sethe, *Beiträge zur ältesten Geschichte Ägyptens*, Leipzig, 1905, p.29 and n. 8.

[3] Among the Akan, when the king sleeps with the queen, his senior wife, after the *kra* purification rite, she is expected to see the ancestral gods and spirits, who then enter her and cause her to conceive.

[4] See p. 41 n. 2.

[5] And of the gods assimilated to Osiris.

[6] The consecrated meal seems to have been of the greatest importance, for it often symbolised the whole cult. Cf. Moret, *Royauté*, p. 165.

[7] Moret, *Rituel*, pp. 147 ff.

impart *kra*, and the 'opening-of-the-mouth' ceremony are similar, though differently handled: the king or his proxy rubs the blood of a sacrificed ram and the fat which covers its lower intestines round the centre pillar of the great stool, the stool of the founder of the lineage.[1] This is done to 'give life' to the *saman*, the spiritualised body or shade of the deceased, so that the physical powers of sight, hearing, and walking may be revived, and, through the king's personal touch or embrace, to endow the dead with *kra*. The king then places pieces of the lungs of the sacrificed animal on top of the stool to give his Royal Ancestor the breath of life, and sprinkles blood and a libation of rum over the offerings, to give him the 'fluid of life'. In the past, after victorious wars the blood of captive kings, chiefs or princes, who alone have a life-giving *kra*, was poured over the stools for the same purpose; they were beheaded over the stool of the founder of the lineage.[2] In Egypt also captives were sacrificed to Osiris, presumably because their blood revivified the deceased.[3] Cooked offerings were made in the Chapel of the Stools to propitiate the Royal Ancestors, to solicit their favour, and above all to renew the bond between the living and the dead.

[1] *Sacred State*, p. 179, and n. 1.
[2] In about 1740 the Asante conquered the Bono kingdom; the last king committed suicide and the heir-apparent was taken prisoner and later murdered. About 1810 King Kyereme Kofi of the Bono-Takyiman state and the Bono royal lineage captured in war the king of Nkoranza, whose ancestor was the cause of the ruin of Bono. He had him sacrificed over the stool of the last king of Bono, although he knew that such an action would be disastrous for his people; for, as a vassal of Asante, he should have delivered the captured king to the Asantehene for him to sacrifice over the stools of his Royal Ancestors. However, to 'give life' with such powerful magic as the blood of a divine ruler (not forgetting, of course, the element of revenge) was more important. The result of this action was that the Bono-Takyiman state was further reduced and most of its troubles today may be traced to this deed.
[3] Budge, *Osiris*, I, p. 210; according to Diodorus they were men of the colour of Typhonius (Set), red-haired men; red was the colour of Set. Set had murdered Osiris, hence it was for him to revivify the deceased with his blood, not of course forgetting the element of revenge, as at Bono-Takyiman, see n. 2 above.

CHAPTER VII

The Rejuvenation of the King's Divine and Life-giving Power on New Year's Day in Spring

AKAN

1. The Nyanku Sai *Festival, the King's Reinstatement as the lawful Ruler of the land*

In Takyiman the *Nyanku Sai* festival takes place before the *Apo* festival, which culminates on New Year's day on the *Fo-Dwo Kese*, or 'Great Fertile Monday' nearest to the vernal equinox.[1] Both centre on the renewal of kingship. The rites of the *Nyanku Sai* festival confirm the king as the lawful ruler of the land, those of the *Apo* revivify the power of his *kra*, the lunar and solar *kra* of his Royal Ancestors incarnate in him, so that he may give life to the crops, thus ensuring a good harvest and a plentiful supply of food. The two festivals are celebrated in conjunction with the rebirth of Taa Kese, Tano the Great, the city god/goddess of Takyiman, *he* being the lord of growth, and *she* the goddess of the reproductive earth.

The true owner of a piece of land is the god of the people by whom it was first cultivated, and the people who conquered the land must be acknowledged as lawful rulers, otherwise it is believed that the crops will not grow. The Bono, intruders from the north, founded their kingdom in 1295 on uncultivated land and, as it was not known to which god it belonged, Nyanku Sai, the blacksmith chief was called upon 'to open the way'. He was chosen because blacksmiths

---

[1] The festival is celebrated today at any convenient date, usually at the end of January or in February; but New Year's day is always on a 'fertile Monday', which occurs every forty-two days.

THE REJUVENATION OF THE KING'S DIVINE POWER

in the past were credited with supernatural power; they worked with, and mastered, fire. Fire is recognized as divine, for the lunar *kra*, fire, gave life to the universe and the fire of the sun keeps the earth alive. Hence they were called *atumfo* and Nyanku Sai's title was *Atumfohene*, which may be literally translated as 'Chief (*hene*) of the persons (*fo*) of power (*tum*)'.[1] The *Nyanku Sai* festival commemorates the fact that Nyanku Sai opened the land for Asaman, the first king of Bono, and a ritual fight is staged every year between the king and the *Atumfohene* of the blacksmiths, in which the king wins, to symbolise the legal transfer of power from the divine ancestor of the blacksmiths—divine because he incarnated the blacksmith god—to the reigning king.

The rites begin on the evening before the 'fertile Friday'. The king sends heralds through the streets, telling the people to go quietly to their homes since at midnight the *Atumfohene* and the blacksmiths are going to the sacred place by the river Adare where each year the black stools of the Royal Ancestors are cleansed from defilement.

Unseen by anyone the blacksmiths leave the town and silently, by the riverside, they purify their tools which are of great age and are kept in an ancient brass pan. Then the *Atumfohene* puts an egg, given to him by the king, on top of the tools and prays in a loud voice to the Royal Ancestors, asking them to continue protecting the state, to bless the crops and to bring prosperity to everyone in the coming year. The brass pan containing the tools and the egg is then thrown into the river and everybody jumps in after it; if it is found that the egg is whole this is a good omen for the new year, but if it is broken misfortune will follow and the high priest of Taa Kese must be consulted by the king as to the best means of averting disaster.

In the morning the *Atumfohene* sends invitations requesting the king, the queen-mother, the chiefs and court officials, and also the young men of the aristocracy, grouped politically under the *Mmerantehene*, to meet him at the riverside. The king therefore summons those invited to the palace. A libation is poured to the Royal Ancestors in the Chapel of the Stools and a procession is

---

[1] *Atumfo* is plural; *otumfo*, singular, is still the mode of addressing the king of Asante, equivalent to our 'Your Majesty'. *Tum* or *tumi*, meaning 'power', may have a connexion with the Egyptian god Atum, Temu or Tumu, the god of solar fire and the first king-god on earth.

THE REJUVENATION OF THE KING'S DIVINE POWER

formed, led by the queen-mother, formerly carried in her *sako* (sedan chair), the princesses, the royal daughters and the women of her state council. The king, carried in his palanquin and, like the queen-mother surrounded by *adumfo*, who guard them, brings up the rear, and the procession moves off to the sanctuary of Taa Kese opposite the palace. There the high priest of Taa Kese pours out a libation to the deity on behalf of the king and prays for the well-being of the state; he then calls on the god to give good health to the king and to support and protect him in the course of his actions on that day. The shrine of the deity is then carried outside by the shrine-bearers and the high priest under his chiefly umbrella joins the procession together with other priests carrying the shrines of their gods.

When the procession reaches the outskirts of the town the blacksmiths waylay the king and threaten him with their tools, shouting that they will not let him pass unless they receive palm-wine and gin for libations. They are driven back by the *adumfo*; the king then gives them what they demand in recognition of the services they are to perform that day for the state.

On their arrival at the riverside the king, the queen-mother, and those accompanying them seat themselves according to rank. The blacksmiths then make a fire with three pieces of *esa* wood, on which is placed a pot of yams. A brass pan filled with sacred river water is laid beside it, into which are thrown some 300 different herbs and other ingredients; the brew, when cooked, is a 'medicine' bestowing invincible powers; in former times it was used by warriors before they went into battle. When the yams are ready they are mashed (*eto*), others are pounded into a glutinous, doughy mass and shaped into balls (*fufu*). *Eto* and *fufu* are then offered to Nyanku Sai and placed in little dishes on his anvil and tools, and the rest is shared out among the participants in the ceremony.

Two snow-white rams are then sacrificed over the anvil and tools so that their blood mixes with the food offerings; their carcasses are cut up and most of the meat is distributed to the families of high-ranking chiefs. A *kra-suo*, or *kra* soup, is prepared from the rest: the top part of the breast, the lungs, kidneys, tripes and 'the part of the tail inside the animal' (*padua*). While this is cooking, the minstrels sing of the great deeds of the Royal Ancestors; the drummers beat out well-known stanzas on the talking drums which tell

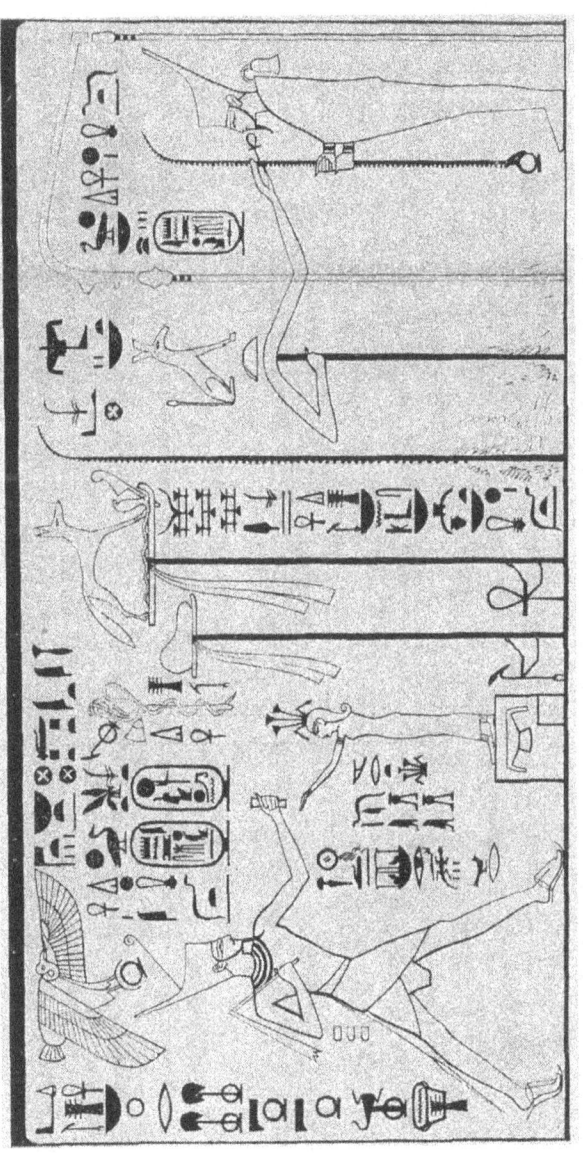

17. Two scenes from the *Sed* festival. In the first Ramses II, after his course across the field, hands the document to the goddess Mert, who symbolises the 'Beloved Land'. She says: 'King come'. Above the king's head flies the vulture-goddess Nekhbet, protecting him. Behind the goddess Mert are the standards of the Placenta and of the Wolf-god Upwaut. In the second scene the god Sed, represented by his animal, blesses the newly instated king, who holds the emblem of an infinite number of years in his hand. (Reproduced by courtesy of Messrs. John Murray, who permitted me to photograph Pl. LXIII in Wilkinson, *Manners and Customs of the Ancient Egyptians*, 1878.)

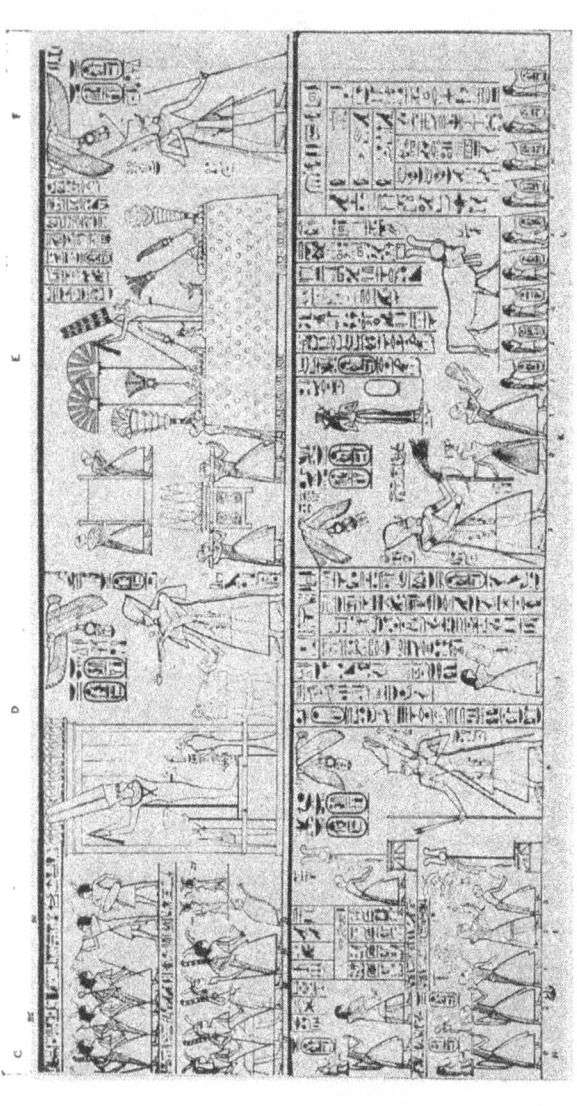

18. Scenes from the Min-Khamutef festival.

Above: (c) Soldiers and priests in the procession. (d) Min-Khamutef in his temple. Ramses III making offerings of incense to him. (e) The statue of the god is carried by priests, accompanied by the ark. (f) Ramses III walking in the procession, protected by the vulture-goddess Nekhbet.

Below: (h) Statues of the Royal Ancestors are carried by the priest. (i) The priest with the tail of the bull in his hand before the standard of the Souls of the East; 4. above him a second priest with the tail of a cow. Next to them Ramses III holding two arrows in his hand. (j) A priest reading a hymn. (k) Ramses III holding a sheaf of *emmer* and the sickle of Min. Above him the queen. Further to the right the White Bull of Min, below him nine statues of the Royal Ancestors.

(Reproduced by courtesy of Messrs. John Murray, who permitted me to photograph part of Pl. LX in Wilkinson, *Manners and Customs of the Ancient Egyptians*.)

of events in past history and the creation of the world, and priests and priestesses of Tano perform dances.

When the *kra* soup is ready the *Atumfohene* blesses it; after this the king, the queen-mother, and the great men and women of the state walk round it three times before it is removed from the fire. It is then poured over seven *fufu* balls, symbols of the seven *kra*-giving planets and the seven great clans which form the state, and is shared out among the company. Nyanku Sai receives his offering, after which everybody takes the traditional three mouthfuls. When this consecrated meal is finished, the king pours a libation of palm-wine over Nyanku Sai's offerings and the 'war medicine' to bless them; he takes a sip from the libation cup and passes it to the queen-mother who also drinks; it is then passed round so that everybody may do likewise.

The king then withdraws under the state umbrella, shielded from view by the *adumfo*, gun-bearers and sword-bearers, and takes off his regalia.[1] The *Sumankwahene*, his physician, who is also in charge of his spiritual well-being, rubs him from head to toe with the 'war medicine'. He reappears in a simple cloth which he wears in the manner of the commoners, tucked in under both arms, his shoulders bare. The *Atumfohene* is likewise smeared with the medicine; when this has been done he and the king engage in a wrestling match. Needless to say, the king must win this. Thus the land has been transferred to him anew, for he has taken it from the blacksmiths who had opened it up for his ancestor and he is acknowledged by all as its lawful ruler. This ceremonial fight is followed by a second, between the god Tano, represented by the high-priest of Taa Kese, and the *Korontihene*, the governor of Takyiman. The former's ancestor, the Fante prince Takyifiri, had founded Takyiman on land owned by the god Tano.[2] The *Korontihene*'s ancestor was a *Korontihene* of Bono-Mansu, who came to rule Takyiman about 1650. In the past the high priest in this ritual used to wear the antelope mask of the god—the black duiker antelope (*ewio*) in which Tano is incarnate; today he merely carries the shrine of the god on his head, while the *asuanifo* surround him guarding it and preventing

[1] Formerly shield-bearers, the sons of local chiefs, holding up their shields, acted in the ceremony. Royal shield-bearers, although still in service at the court of the king of Asante, no longer play a part in Takyiman.

[2] Taa Takyiwaa, the mother of Takyifiri, gave 'life' to Tano in the region of Takyiman where she settled with her followers before her son founded the town, *c.* 1600.

it from slipping off.[1] The result of the fight proclaims the *Korontihene* as the rightful ruler of the town. The fight is followed by a third between the elders, the great chiefs in the state council, and some of the young men of the aristocracy, led by the *Mmerantehene*. It symbolises the lawful transfer of power from the rulers of Takyiman to those of the former Bono kingdom, who took over the government after the foundation of the Bono-Takyiman state in 1748. When the fights are over the *Atumfohene* supplies everybody with drink, saying 'Nyanku Sai has been fed, here are drinks for your dispersal'. After this the procession returns to the town.

2. The Apo *Festival, the Rejuvenation of the King's solar* Kra

The *Apo* (*Apoo* or *Apuo*) festival at Takyiman, a state capital, centres on the divine Ameyaw Kwaakye, the ancestor king of the present dynasty, who is given new life through the rites performed over his tomb. The resurrection of his divine life-giving powers affects the reigning king, for his solar *kra* is that of his Royal Ancestors personified by Ameyaw Kwaakye. When this is renewed, so also are his own powers, and he is fully enabled to give 'life' in the coming year.

The rites begin with the *Odwira*, which means 'purification' and applies to the Royal Ancestors. The *Banmuhene*, the custodian of the royal cemetery, opens the coffins which are under his care. Assisted by his sons (his own and those of his predecessor), he takes out the royal skeletons, oils their bones and, if necessary, repairs the gold wires which hold them together. He airs and mends the cloths in which they are dressed and cleans the gold ornaments which adorn them. This takes place on the Thursday preceding 'Hateful Friday' (*Nkyi-fie*);[2] Thursday is the day ruled by Abrao, the deity of the planet Jupiter, the god of death and resurrection in the beyond.

---

[1] It is believed that when the high priest places the shrine of the deity on his head, the spirit of Tano enters into him and he becomes the god.

[2] Following Dr. J. B. Danquah I translated *Nyi-fie* (*Sacred State*, pp. 144, 150) as 'Destructive Friday' which, however, does not give the precise meaning of *nkyi*. Christaller (*Dictionary of the Asante and Fante Language*, 1933) translates *kyi* (*N* is the noun prefix) as 'to hate, loathe, abhor'; 'Hateful Friday' or 'Abhorred Friday' is a better rendering, for the day is hated because it reminds the people of the death of the king and of the fact that even the divine king is mortal.

THE REJUVENATION OF THE KING'S DIVINE POWER

In the evening of this day all the hearth-fires are extinguished in the town, a custom which otherwise only takes place when a king or queen-mother has died.[1] New fires are then lit from a fire to which the seven great clans of the state have each given a log of *esa* wood.

On the same day the sacred grove, in the centre of which is the tomb of Ameyaw Kwaakye, is also purified. The tomb is a small replica of a tumulus,[2] sheltered by a rectangular wooden structure which is covered today with a corrugated iron roof; in the past its poles were columns covered with the divine symbols and the gabled roof was thatched. The head woman of the village of Namu marks the outside corners of the structure with flowers and *summe* leaves, used for consecration. These points are important, for they symbolise the equinoctial points on which the Mother-goddess, as the ruler of the revolving universe, gives new life to the sun.

On the afternoon of 'Hateful Friday' the king, carried in his palanquin, the queen-mother, who formerly was carried in her *sako* chair, the chiefs of the state council and the chiefs of towns and villages, the priests, bearing the shrines of their gods, and the people of the capital go in procession to the sacred grove. They are received there by the *Banmuhene*, who represents the dead king in the rites. He addresses the reigning king saying 'Nana Ameyaw [Kwaakye][3] is welcoming you'. The king, the queen-mother, and the chiefs of the state council then seat themselves around the tomb of the dead king; the other chiefs, under their large umbrellas surrounded by their retinues, and the priests and priestesses sit outside in the circular grove, while the commoners, lined up along the entrance, look on. The tomb of Ameyaw Kwaakye is decorated with the insignia of kingship: three golden ceremonial state swords and three golden spokesman's staves. A libation is poured out and two snow-white rams, one given by the king, the other by the *Banmuhene*, are sacrificed over the grave. Then the offerings are cooked,

---

[1] *Sacred State*, pp. 75, 76.

[2] The ancestors of the Bono kings in Diala on the Niger and in the first Bono kingdom in Mossi are said to have been buried under large tumuli. When the second Bono kingdom was founded the Bono decided to bury their kings in temporary graves and to preserve their skeletons in coffins which were kept in a mausoleum, in order to be able to take these bones with them in case they had to move again.

[3] Kwaakye was Ameyaw's by-name. Kwaakye is a sacred name for the vulture and is symbolic of 'self-born' or 'self-created'.

while the priests and priestesses dance. When the food is ready the *Banmuhene* fills the offering bowls with his golden spoon and places them around the tomb, saying: 'King Ameyaw [Kwaakye], here is your food from Nana Akumfi Ameyaw,[1] who is giving it to you through me. I pray that you will accept it with good heart. Bless him and give him long life, wisdom and courage and a good reign, as you had.' The deceased queen-mothers all receive their share on the marked points of the four outside corners of the structure. Then the king, the queen-mother, and the chiefs of the state council, after a libation and prayer, take the traditional three mouthfuls from the 'golden bowl' (now a modern vessel), which is then passed round outside; the common people are also given a share. Then the chief spokesman of the king recites the prayer for the wellbeing of the state, and so closes the rite. As soon as this is over the queen-mother, surrounding herself with the descendants of the founders of Takyiman, gives the signal for rejoicing to begin; now everybody may sing and dance, for King Ameyaw Kwaakye and the Royal Ancestors have accepted the offerings—a good omen has been received—and there will be a prosperous and happy year in the state. Finally everybody prepares to go home and the procession leaves the grove. Soon after this the *Banmuhene*, accompanied by all his wives and children, brings the glad news of the *Apo* to town; they sing and shout that they have fed the Royal Ancestors for a year, whereupon the people join them in singing and dancing until everybody retires for the night. It is now time for the *Banmuhene* and his family to sing the sacred *Apo* songs during which they must not be disturbed.

Then follow days during which the celebrations do not start before five o'clock in the afternoon and consist solely of singing and dancing by the common people, which go on till late at night. On the next Friday after 'Hateful Friday', called *Kuru-fie*, or 'Most sacred Friday' the official celebrations are resumed. It is the great day of abuse, which is said to have been founded in the belief that grievances and evil wishes harboured secretly by one person against another endanger, in some supernatural way, the process of growth. To avert this everybody is permitted to express openly his opinion of his neighbour and can insult him without punishment; he may even insult the king, the queen-mother, and the gods. To dispel old feelings of antagonism which arose when the aristocracy of Bono came to power in Takyiman after the destruction of Bono-Mansu in

[1] The name of the present king of the Bono-Takyiman state.

1740, a battle is staged on the main road between the king and the *Korontihene*, who represents the previous rulers of the city. Both are clad in ancient battle-dress and are carried on the shoulders of their men, followed by their people. Sticks and clubs are used. After the battle the two factions forget their differences and join together in insulting the Asante who had destroyed Bono.

On the following Sunday the king, his kingship renewed for one year, appears in all his splendour in the square before the palace. He seats himself on his dais with the queen-mother on his left and, surrounded by the whole court, receives deputations which have come to greet him. The people are entertained with dances performed by the priests of Tano. The scene is most spectacular; the many golden staves of the spokesmen, the gold-hilted swords and decorated hats of the sword-bearers, the gold-plated carvings on the umbrella tops of the chiefs, and the golden ornaments and trinkets worn by them, shine and glitter in the sun. New Year's day is celebrated the following day, *Fo-Dwo-Kese*, 'Great Fertile Monday' with the rebirth of Taa Kese. This closes the triple festival.[1]

3. *The Festival of the God of the Land, Taa Kese*

The *Apo* rites in villages and towns centre round the death and rebirth of the Sky fertility-deity.[2] At Takyiman, where the festival of Taa Kese is celebrated jointly with the renewal of the life-giving power of the king-god Ameyaw Kwaakye, the death of the bi-sexual god plays no part; it is implied by his rebirth.

Taa Kese's annual birthday is on the 'Fertile Tuesday' (*Fo-Bena*) following 'Hateful Friday' (*Nkyi-Fie*), the first day of the *Apo* festival, which is dedicated to the resurrection of the powers of Ameyaw Kwaakye. On that day when dusk has fallen the king, the queen-mother, and all the chiefs of the state council seat themselves in a semi-circle round the *simpini* (literally, stairs) of Taa Kese before his sanctuary,[3] waiting for the high priest and assistant priests to come out with the shrine of the god. It is then placed on

[1] The *Apo* in Takyiman has been described in *Sacred State*, pp. 150 ff. Since then I have been able to return (1949–50) and to take part in the rites in the sacred grove, which I was not allowed to witness before. This did not alter anything in my previous description of the rites, but I was better able to understand their significance.

[2] For the *Apo* festivals in various places see *Ak. of Ghana*, ch. II, 3 (b–f).

[3] Illustrated in *Ak. of Ghana*, Pl. 36.

the stairs covered with a white cloth under the god's large umbrella. This umbrella is the symbol of kingship or chieftainship to which Taa Kese has a right, for he is Abanmu Tano, the god of the Bono-Takyiman state. The high priest then pours out a libation which is shared by the assembled company. He dances to honour the god but no offerings are made, for the god has not yet been purified from death, and his rebirth is only celebrated on the following 'Great Fertile Monday', New Year's day in spring.

On that day early in the afternoon Taa Kese's shrine is brought outside again and carried backwards and forwards three times in procession along the main road, passing the sanctuary, the palaces of the king and the queen-mother, and the houses of the chiefs. It is followed by the shrines of his many 'sons',[1] whose priests and priestesses have come to town from the nearby villages in order to take part in the rites. Taa Kese's shrine is then placed on its stairs. Priests and people dance amid general rejoicings.

When darkness is about to fall the high priest of Taa Kese and all the priests of Tano carry the shrines of their gods to the square in front of the palaces. There the king, the queen-mother, and the whole court are assembled, and one by one the priests file past to greet them. The high priest of Taa Kese then pours out a libation for the wellbeing of the state in the coming year, and finally, placing the shrine of his god on his head, falls into a trance and delivers an oracle foretelling the main events of the near future. When it is dark the priests with their shrines, accompanied only by the queen-mother, here representing her ancestress the moon Mother-goddess, go slowly, by the light of torches made from palm-leaf stalks tied together, to the sacred grove of the god. This grove is situated on the banks of the river Tano not far from the spot where it crosses the road to Sunyani. There they squat down in a semi-circle, the shrines of the gods before them resting on the circular head-pads of the priests. Tano, represented by Taa Kese and his sons, is then informed by the high priest's spokesman that he is about to be purified, whereupon all the shrines are uncovered and

[1] The most important of the Taa Kese's sons are Anikoko, Taa Atowa Yao, Taa Kuntun, and Taa Kofi who guard the northern, eastern, southern and western frontiers of the country respectively. For further details on Taa Kese see *Sacred State*, 134 ff. Tano Twumpuduo and Taa Kora are his elder brothers, not his sons. Taa Kese therefore is often called Taa Mensa, meaning Tano the third.

THE REJUVENATION OF THE KING'S DIVINE POWER

scrubbed with water and sand from the sacred river.[1] They, together with those assembled, are then blessed with river water sprinkled from an uprooted *summe* plant.

The procession then goes back to the sanctuary of Taa Kese where the priests with the shrines of their gods are greeted by Taa Kese's 'mother', the Tanohemmaa (Tano queen-mother); she is usually the mother or sister of the high priest and she cooks the deity's offerings.[2] These are already prepared and ready to be carried in. The *Abrafohene*, master of ceremonies and reciter priest, then addresses the god by all his names and titles, after which the offerings are placed on the shrine of Taa Kese as well as on those of the other Tano gods.

On the next morning, a Tuesday, Taa Kese's weekly natal day, the king and the queen-mother, accompanied by all the chiefs of the state council, come to greet the god. A ram is sacrificed and offered; the king says the prayer for the wellbeing of the state, imploring the deity to give further assistance and support in the new year. This closes the triple festival.

A week later all the Tano priests go to a place where a hole has been formed by the waters of a small river flowing into the Tano. In this hole Tano's river mother Agyentoa[3] is believed to live. A sheep is sacrificed and *eto* (mashed yams) is prepared. The offerings are shared by those assembled; the flesh of the whole sheep must be eaten there in utter silence. Then the high priest of Taa Kese pours a libation and says a thanksgiving prayer.

EGYPT

1. The Sed Festival, the King's Reinstatement as lawful Ruler of the Land

The *Sed* festival was not celebrated every year; the practice of several Pharaohs suggests that it normally took place thirty years after their accession to the throne; some monarchs, however, such as Ramses II, celebrated it repeatedly and at shorter intervals. We

---

[1] The Tano shrines consist of brass pans containing sacred objects; each is covered with a silk handkerchief.

[2] A photograph of the present high priest of Taa Kese and the god's 'mother' may be found in *Ak. of Ghana*, Pl. 6.

[3] Agyentoa was the original name of the river before it was discovered that it was the sacred abode of the god Tano.

do not know what the reasons were for staging this festival.[1] It may have been found that it was too expensive and inconvenient to have two great state festivals in one year,[2] and the Min festival, being considered the more important, received priority. On the other hand since the *Sed* festival was concerned with the land, it may have been celebrated in times when the country had suffered from a succession of poor harvests resulting in famine,[3] and it was thought desirable for the Pharaoh to reassert his dominance over the land as its lawful ruler. Thus he could renew the beneficent relations between heaven and earth which his *ka* controlled. However that may be, the rites of the *Sed* festival were coupled with rites which renewed the potency of the Pharaoh's *ka*, and which were usually performed each year on New Year's day in spring. The god who presided over the day was Nehebkau, the personification of the equinoxes;[4] he also presided over New Year's day in autumn, the culminating day of the Min-Khamutef festival. The date of the festival of Nehebkau in spring, called Khoiak, and of the *Sed*

---

[1] For a discussion on the theme see Moret, *Royauté*, pp. 258–60; Frankfort, *Kingship*, p. 79 and n. 2.

[2] At Bono-Takyiman two state New Year festivals are celebrated annually, one in spring and the other in autumn; the Asante celebrate only one. The reason given to me was that the expense was too great; moreover, in the past, when travelling was difficult, the great chiefs with their retinue of officials, and the high priests with the shrines of their gods, were absent too long from their towns, thus interrupting the administration of the country. Asante was a confederation of over thirty states before the British conquest, whereas Bono-Takyiman is only one small state where most of the sub-chiefs and high priests of the gods live no more than 15–20 miles from the capital, one day's walking distance. In the Bono kingdom horses were generally used for transport, but this was not possible in Asante which was situated in the tropical forest where horses could not live on account of tsetse fly.

[3] A high Nile which fell 30 inches below the normal meant insufficient crops and a year of hardship. A drop of 60 inches to 80 per cent normal meant that the Egyptians were faced with famine and starvation for a year. Too high an inundation was also a peril; a foot above normal would mean damage to earth embankments and would sweep away dykes and canal banks and bring destruction to the mud-brick villages. The margin between abundant life and hollow death was a very narrow one (see J. A. Wilson, *The Burden of Egypt*, 1951, p. 10).

[4] The Nile reached its greatest height on the equinox of the 22nd September (see Frazer, *The Golden Bough*, II, p. 31); in the times of Thutmosis III the equinox must have fallen at the beginning of October as it is known that the equinox of our 21st March was in those days on the 3rd April (see Brugsch, *Ägyptologie*, p. 363). In Egypt spring is in our autumn months and autumn in March–April.

festival, was normally the first day of the first month of *Piret* or spring-tide.[1] The day heralded the Season of Coming Forth, the falling of the flood waters and the subsequent sowing of barley, wheat, and sorghum in the following month.

A third festival was combined with these: the rebirth of the god Ptah-Tatjenen, the personification of nature, the 'risen land', the land of Egypt which rose out of the watery abyss at the time of the creation. Ptah-Tatjenen was the 'Lord of the *Sed* periods'[2] who caused the festival to take place at its appointed time; it was normally celebrated at Memphis, the town of Ptah-Tatjenen.[3]

The triple festival lasted twelve days, according to an inscription on a 12th Dynasty coffin at Beni Hasan.[4] To it were invited the high priests and priests with the shrines of their gods from all over the country; the governors of the *nomes*, accompanied by bearers carrying the *nome* emblems; a retinue of important officials; and many others who wished to take part in the festival. Sometimes a new temple was built for the occasion and dedicated to a deity.

Scenes from the *Sed* festival are depicted on the walls of various temples such as those at Abydos, Luxor, Karnak, and Soleb; the most detailed representations are those in the Festival Hall of Osorkon II at Bubastis, and at the Sun temple of Ne-woser-Re. Many of the reliefs have unfortunately been badly damaged; whole series are sometimes destroyed and it is not easy to reconstruct the triple festival, since the pieces remaining are not usually in chronological order. In order to put into some order the confused scenes showing details of processions, deputations before the throne, sacrifices, items of the coronation ritual, and the so-called 'dedication of the land', I intend using as a basis the spring festival of Bono-Takyiman, which, as we have seen, is also a triple festival.

The Sed *festival proper*

At Takyiman the *Nyanku Sai* festival starts with the visit of the king, accompanied by the queen-mother and the great chiefs of the state council, to the Chapel of the Stools where offerings have been made earlier to the *kras* of the Royal Ancestors. The king is then carried to the sanctuary of Taa Kese where he begs the deity to

[1] A. H. Gardiner in *JEA*, II (1936), pp. 122–4.
[2] Naville, *Osorkon*, p. 5.
[3] Gardiner in *JEA*, V (1939), pp. 192 ff.
[4] P. E. Newberry, *Beni Hasan I*, 1893.

protect him in his fight with the *Atumfohene* later in the day. The shrine of the god is taken out to be carried in the procession together with those of other gods; common people follow it to take part in the rites performed for Nyanku Sai in a sacred grove outside town.

In Egypt the ceremonies start with the visit of the Pharaoh, the queen, and the great men of the state to the *per-ur*, the Upper Egyptian shrine of the Pharaoh's wolf-headed Royal Ancestors;[1] offerings had been made there earlier, as well as to other divinities. At Bubastis Osorkon II is shown holding up the clepsydra, an instrument for measuring time, to the goddess Nekhbet, the protectress of the *per-ur*; this is perhaps to inform her that the time has come to celebrate the *Sed* festival.[2] Then in a procession the Pharaoh, accompanied by the queen, 'rested in the abode when he is going towards the pavilion (of the *Sed* festival)', according to the text at Soleb.[3] There is reason to believe that the abode, a chamber, was a temporary sanctuary of the god Amen; Osorkon at Bubastis goes to rest on a platform where he turns to the four points of the horizon before he resumes his march.[4] In Soleb and Bubastis the festival is in honour of Amen. The Pharaoh's 'resting' in the abode

[1] The inscription (Naville, Pl. II) says: 'The rising out of the *per-ur* and the departure in order to rest in the pavilion (of the *Sed* festival).' Naville, p. 10, is of the opinion that 'to rise as king' means to be crowned, which makes no sense here. Pharaoh's appearing is compared to the rising sun, that is to say, personifying the sun he became visible to the people when he left the *per-ur*. Among the Akan the shrines for the Royal Ancestors are situated in the palace grounds; the above seems also to imply that the *per-ur* was in the palace of the Pharaohs.

[2] Naville, Pl. III, p. 13. Horapollo says that on their water-clock the Egyptians engraved a crouching ape (quoted p. 9). Among the Akan the ape is a symbol of balance; possibly this was also the case in Egypt, for the ape of Thotto, the measurer of time, sits on the scales in the Judgement Hall when the life of a dead person is in the balance. Nehebkau is referred to as 'that god, secret of form, whose eyebrows are the beams of the balance'. On the days of the equinox the year hangs in the balance for the sun looks on both hemispheres equally. It is likely, therefore, that the clepsydra was an instrument used to determine the date when the equinoxes were due, and thus the date of the *Sed* festival or the festival of Nehebkau, which took place at about the same time.

[3] Naville, op. cit., pp. 12, 15. This, according to Ramses III, was situated in the 'House of the *Sed* festival' (p. 7). It is not certain where the 'house of the *Sed* festival' was, but possibly also in the palace grounds. On an *ushebti* statuette in the Leiden collection a man calls himself 'manager of the works on the *Heb Sed* House in the palace of the king' (J. H. Breasted in *ZÄS*, vol. 39 (1901), p. 91).

[4] For the significance of this rite, see below in the text.

of Amen, or on a platform, where he performs a rite connected with the state Sky fertility Sun-god, can perhaps be equated with the Akan king's visit at Takyiman to the temple of Taa Kese, where he begs for protection in the ritual fight to come. At Bubastis, however, it is said that Osorkon asked the city goddess Bastet for special protection.[1]

The procession then moved on to the place where the pavilion of the *Sed*-festival was erected. An inscription on a wall of the Sun temple of Ne-woser-Re says that it is 'behind the wall'.[2] At Memphis, where the *Sed* festival normally took place, this could only have been a sacred place, a field perhaps, or a very large artificial grove, outside the White Wall. Elsewhere too, it may have been a place outside the town where the 'houses of the *Sed* festival', reed huts in the archaic style, had been erected for the occasion to house the shrines of the various deities from all over the country. The pavilion where the throne stood and a small building in which the monarch changed his clothes and insignia, fulfilled the function of a robing chamber.[3]

Among the Bono the blacksmiths were the 'openers of the land' on which their ancestors founded the Bono Kingdom. In Egypt the wolf-god Upwaut of Siut, the 'Opener of the Ways', and the people he represented, may have played a similar part; he had a prominent role in the *Sed* festival. From his very close relationship with Osiris it would seem that it was for him and for his line of kings that he 'opened' the land of Siut for occupation, and that later he did likewise in the region where the Pharaoh's wolf-headed Royal Ancestors built their capital Nekhen. Siut was gained by the Osirians, as there is reason to assume, through the marriage of one of their princesses to the king of the Upwaut state; she seems to have been personified in the festival by the 'holy Mother of Siut' (who played such an important part in the rites, see below). The land round Nekhen seems to have been acquired through the infiltration of herdsmen of the wolf clan and their cattle into this region, if one may judge by the conspicuous part played by the 'herdsman of Nekhen' (*Bati*) at Bubastis as well as in the reliefs at the Sun

---

[1] Naville, p. 7.

[2] von Bissing-Kees, *Untersuchungen*, pp. 86, 87.

[3] The 'houses of the *Sed* festival' are believed by Moret and others to have been erected in one of the great temples. von Bissing-Kees (op. cit., p. 14) is of the opinion that they were built on an open place, which I believe to be correct.

temple of Ne-woser-Re.[1] There he is shown accompanied by two attendants wearing caps of wolf-skin with the head and tail of the animal attached, and carrying the wolf-headed *user* sceptre of Upwaut; the warlike attributes of the god, the bow and throwing stick, are carried behind them. The herdsman is depicted with his right arm raised, holding in his hand what is believed to be a sling.[2] The text says 'Back', and the presence of the 'Master of the King's Largesse' and the words in the text: 'Take it', indicate that a gift was made to him. Frankfort[3] suggests that a reward was given to the herdsman for his loyal address. But this surely is not the right interpretation, since the herdsman, his arm raised, a weapon in his hand, seems to be demanding something; moreover the command given was 'Back!' The whole scene seems to be reminiscent of the Bono blacksmiths who demand palm-wine and gin from their king in acknowledgement of the services their ancestors had rendered to the state almost six hundred years ago. Among the Akan history is recorded not only in songs and maxims beaten out on the talking drums, but also in the official recognition given to the descendants of famous men at the state festivals. Incidentally the little scene with the herdsman on the relief is followed by the singing of songs, possibly commemorating the historic role of the herdsmen. On the relief below, Nubians wearing high feathers are depicted; they represented perhaps the indigenous people of the region before they were subjugated by the warriors of the wolf-god Upwaut.

The standard of Upwaut is preceded at Bubastis by a woman called the 'divine and holy Mother of Siut'. There is no reference in the accompanying text to enlighten us as to whom she represents. She appears three times, evidence for her great importance.[4] At Soleb the divine Mother is depicted lighting a lamp in the abode of Amen; the text above the relief is too fragmentary to be translated.[5] However we know that in Egypt the ritual of lighting the lamp symbolised birth;[6] here perhaps the birth of the Osirian kingdom is depicted, since the divine Mother came from Siut and was closely connected with the wolf-god as well as with Osiris; she was the priestess of a sanctuary containing the foot of Osiris.[7] She most

---

[1] Naville, Pl. XI; von Bissing-Kees, *Re-Heiligtum*, III, Pl. XIII, block 229 and p. 34.
[2] von Bissing-Kees, *Untersuchungen*, p. 81.　　　[3] *Kingship*, p. 84.
[4] Naville, op. cit., p. 4.　[5] ibid., p. 15.　[6] Naville, *Deir el Bahri*, II, p. 16.
[7] Naville, *Osorkon*, p. 12.

probably represented the divine ancestress, the princess or queen-mother of the Osirian falcon clan people at the time of her marriage to the king of the wolf clan; as the result of such a union her son would have succeeded as ruler of a falcon-wolf confederation and thus would have become the predecessor of the last god-king Osiris; this assumption would also explain why the Pharaoh's Upper Egyptian Royal Ancestors are depicted as wolf-headed and not falcon-headed.[1] As the woman who gave birth to the Osirian kingdom, her memory would be kept alive as long as Osiris was worshipped as the Great Ancestor of the Pharaohs. It would have been only proper that she should have a prominent place in the *Sed* festival, concerned, as it was, mainly with the transfer of land once ruled by Osiris to his lawful son Horus, personified by the living Pharaoh.

When the procession reaches its destination the Pharaoh seats himself on his throne in the pavilion of the *Sed* festival. He then receives deputations from the various *nomes*, priests of the gods of Egypt, and the representatives of those who had played an important part in the early history of the country, among them the Hermopolitans, the Heliopolitans and so forth.

It is noteworthy that on the steps of the throne the *chri-nu-s* is depicted loaded with insignia, a short staff in his right hand and a switch in his left.[2] He seems to perform the same duties as the *Nsumankwahene* among the Bono and Bono-Takyiman, who in former times was always present when the king appeared in public. The king received only the great chiefs of the country, who were also his sons or those of his predecessor on the throne; everybody else had to greet him through the *Nsumankwahene*. This official was loaded with magical objects and charms designed to protect the *kra* of the king from any defilement which would diminish its life-giving power. He used to plant before the throne the *mefedua* (spear) which fulfilled the same function as a lightning conductor, namely to 'earth' the evil thoughts which some people might harbour against the king.

Offerings are made in the chapels of the various deities (in the text the word 'sacrifice' appears repeatedly), presumably after the greetings were over. Since offerings to a deity are usually shared with the living, the Pharaoh, the queen, and all those assembled

---

[1] See also p. 45.
[2] von Bissing-Kees, *Untersuchungen*, p. 78; *Re-Heiligtum*, II, Pl. XI.

may have eaten a consecrated meal, similar to that among the Bono-Takyiman. A reciter priest depicted on the walls of the Sun temple of Ne-woser-Re, says, according to the text, 'walk around'. We do not know to what these words refer, as the relief relating to the words has been destroyed; they are, however, the same as those used in the *Nyanku Sai* rites. The suggestion that the priests may have changed their positions,[1] makes no sense; moreover the relief is followed by one showing the *Sem* priest, who is in charge of sacrifices to the Royal Ancestors, taking off his leopard-skin on the steps of the empty throne, thus indicating that some rite had come to an end. At Bubastis rites in the Hall of Eating are followed by a number of confused scenes, and the 'rising of the god', which has no place here. It seems that two ceremonies belonging to different days have been combined in one representation, which is supported by the fact that two processions are shown leading up to it; one is the so-called Upwaut procession, described here, while the other celebrates the festival of Tatjenen. Among the Bono-Takyiman, it will be remembered, there are two consecrated meals; at one the offerings are shared with Nyanku Sai, at the other, with the ancestor king Ameyaw Kwaakye in the sacred grove.

We now come to the second part of the proceedings. Everywhere these are much abridged and lacking in chronological order. One of the most important rites is usually left out or, at best, merely indicated—that of the Pharaoh's ceremonial fight against a Libyan. We find it depicted on the walls of the mortuary temples of Pepi I[2] and Pepi II,[3] kings of the 6th Dynasty. Moret[4] interprets the fight —in which the Pharaoh is shown slaying a Libyan—as a human sacrifice executed by the monarch in connexion with the foundation of a temple at the time of the *Sed* festival. This interpretation cannot be correct, because in both representations the Pharaoh's action is closely connected with his course across the field, which may be regarded as a triumphant passage (see below) after battle. This rite, therefore, seems to me to correspond with the struggle between the Bono-Takyiman king and the *Atumfohene*, the representative of the 'openers of the land' and, if my assumption is correct, the Libyan personified the first comers to the lands of Upper and Lower

[1] von Bissing-Kees, *Re-Heiligtum*, III, to Pl. XI, block 27.
[2] C. R. Lepsius, *Denkmäler aus Aegypten und Aethiopen*, 1849–59, p. 116.
[3] Jéquier, *Pepi II*, Pl. 8.
[4] Moret, *Royauté*, p. 264 and fig. 88.

THE REJUVENATION OF THE KING'S DIVINE POWER

Egypt,[1] for Pepi I is shown wearing the Upper Egyptian head-dress and skirt in that scene, and Pepi II the Lower Egyptian head-dress and kilt.

It is clear that there must have been four fights altogether, for the Pharaoh receives weapons from a deity each time: from Neith of Sais, the Libyan Horus, Horus of Edfu, and Set of Ombos. Before each of them he changes his costume and insignia in the robing chamber and it would seem that at that point his feet were cleansed on the silver stone with water from the sacred lake of Horus of Edfu.[2] They were washed by 'friends' who are believed to have accompanied the ruler on his military campaigns.[3] The rite is more than a simple washing or cleansing rite (if it were nothing more it would not have been depicted at all); its purpose must have been magical, namely to strengthen the ruler's feet in battle. One may compare it with the washing and rubbing with medicines, mixed with sacred river water, of the body of the Bono-Takyiman king prior to his struggle in the sacred grove, in order to make him invincible.

The Bono-Takyiman king did not fight as a king but as a subordinate of the Royal Ancestors, which is indicated by the way he tied his cloth. The Pharaoh also does not seem to have fought as a king, for he is depicted fighting barefoot. Among the Akan a king's feet must never touch the earth in which the dead lie buried (death tabu) lest his *kra* should be defiled and his life-giving power thus reduced. For this reason he always wears sandals and when he appears in public a sandal-bearer, carrying a spare pair, walks behind him. On the Narmer Palette a sandal-bearer walks behind Narmer and, since he is the only person accompanying the king, he must be of importance and seems here to symbolise Narmer's newly won kingship of the Two Lands, particularly since Narmer is preceded by the standards of the falcon clan's Royal Ancestors. Note also that in reliefs at the Sun temple and at Bubastis, people of all ranks, including the Great Ones of Upper and Lower Egypt, are shown throwing themselves on the ground—a posture which seems to have little to do with paying homage to the monarch and is unknown except in connexion with the *Sed* festival.[4] The inscription seems to make it clear that the people invited each other to

---

[1] This is supported by archaeological finds, see p. 228.
[2] von Bissing-Kees, *Untersuchungen*, p. 77.
[3] Naville, op. cit., p. 10. [4] ibid., Pl. II, 9; XI, b;

exorcise the earth in order to protect the Pharaoh;[1] the earth, therefore, must have been regarded as a danger to him.

The rite performed in the abode of Amen at the beginning also had as its object the protection of the Pharaoh from the dangerous nature of the earth, dangerous to his life-giving *ka*. For through his *ka* the earth was joined with the sky,[2] because the sky, with its sun, moon and stars, alone gives life, and if vegetation is to grow on the earth and men and beasts are to live and multiply, it is solely due to the *ka* power of the gods derived from the planets, stars, and constellations.

Among the Bono-Takyiman the king struggles with the *Atumfohene*, the supreme chief of the blacksmiths, the openers of the land, who is a king's son and hereditary prince (not of the state, but of one of the seven great clans of the country which form the state). Although the king fights as a subordinate he cannot be touched, much less defeated, by a commoner. The 'hereditary prince' who marches at the head of the Upwaut procession[3] may have personified the Libyan in the fight with the Pharaoh, but we do not know this; nor do we know whether the *Ha'-ti-e*, who walks next to him and wears the same archaic dress as the Pharaoh,[4] took a part in one of the struggles analogous to that of the *Korontihene* in the *Nyanku Sai* festival. Nothing indicates the role he played, but it must have been a prominent one, since he is depicted three times.

The four ceremonial fights are preceded, in the reliefs of the Sun temple of Ne-woser-Re, by the Pharaoh's visit to the chapel of Upwaut, the 'Opener of the Ways', to fetch the standard of the god which accompanied the Pharaoh in all his actions in the field. The standard is carried by a 'servant of the Souls of Nekhen', who seems to have changed costume each time as did the Pharaoh; for he is shown once wearing the Lower Egyptian kilt and once in the Upper Egyptian skin-dress. Possibly in the other two fights, of which no representation is extant, a 'servant of Pe' took his place, since Upwaut was venerated as a god not only of the South but also of the North, where he seems to have opened the 'Ways' for Isis

---

[1] Moret, *Royauté*, p. 241 and n. 1.

[2] Note the presence in this scene (Naville, p. 13) of the bearers with the *ka* standard of the Pharaoh, the standard of the Sun-god Atum and the standard of the Sun-god Amen represented by the ram with the *atef* crown of Osiris.

[3] Naville, op. cit., p. 11. He holds a long stick with a hook on the end, which is a sign of command (Pl. II).

[4] Naville, Pl. II, 10-13.

and her followers, who founded the Lower Egyptian Horus kingdom; the priests and 'prophets' of the 'Souls of Pe' were also in charge of Upwaut.[1] There is much evidence for this; Upwaut, on one of the reliefs at the Sun temple and at Bubastis, is called the 'servant of the king of Lower Egypt'[2] and is styled 'Master of Egypt'[3] and 'Leader of the Two Lands'.[4]

Presumably after his first change of costume the Pharaoh went to the chapel of Neith of Sais who, at Memphis, where the festival was normally celebrated, was called, like Upwaut, the 'Opener of the Ways'.[5] In the representation of the *Sed* festival at Esne he receives from her the traditional weapons of the goddess.[6] After his victory over the Libyan the Pharaoh returns her bow and arrows to the goddess; he is depicted wearing the Blue Crown to which the *atef* crown of Osiris is attached, portraying him as the son of the Sun-god Re and of Osiris.[7] The scene indicates that the Pharaoh was assisted in his fight by the goddess, the mother of the sun and supernatural owner of the land occupied originally by the Libyans.

For his next fight the Pharaoh receives bow and arrows from the *Sem* priest, who here symbolises the Royal Ancestors, and later in the chapel of the Libyan Horus he receives the *was* sceptre, the emblem of power.[8] At Karnak the Libyan Horus appears at the head of the 'Souls of Pe', the Lower Egyptian Royal Ancestors. The Libyan Horus was none other than Horus the Elder, who in Libyan Lower Egypt became the national god of the descendants of Isis, who after death became the 'Souls of Pe'. In the procession depicted at Bubastis and on the walls of the Sun temple of Ne-woser-Re the shrine of the Libyan Horus is carried behind that of the Libyan Neith and before the goddess of Pe, the protectress of the 'Souls of Pe'. The fight, in which the Pharaoh no doubt defeated another Libyan, the representative of the former rulers of Lower Egypt, may thus have referred to the victory of Isis. The first fight illustrated the victory of the Osirian immigrants over Andjeti (or Anzti) at Busiris in the eastern delta, for the Pharaoh wears the *atef* crown of Andjeti and receives his weapons from Neith.

In the next fight he also receives bow and arrows from the *Sem* priest and weapons from Horus of Edfu, the Behdetite. We do not

[1] von Bissing-Kees, *Untersuchungen*, p. 30.
[2] ibid., p. 59; Naville, op. cit., Pl. IX, 1.
[3] Naville, p. 11.   [4] von Bissing-Kees, *Untersuchungen*, p. 32.   [5] ibid., p. 48.
[6] Kees, *Opfertanz*, p. 64.   [7] For the Blue Crown, see p. 224 n. 2.
[8] von Bissing-Kees, *Re-Heiligtum*, II, Pl. XVI, block 40.

know what role this god played in the early history of Egypt or, more specifically, in the group of falcon clan people he represented. Since the first two ceremonial fights concerned Lower Egypt, he may here represent the owner of the land situated immediately south of Nekhen, on which Edfu was built, and not the national solar god of historical times. When the Pharaoh leaves his chapel, however, he is carried by priests who represent the 'Souls of Heliopolis', the 'sons of Re' and ancestors of the 5th Dynasty.

For the last fight the Pharaoh again receives bow and arrows from the *Sem* priest and weapons from Set of Ombos,[1] the supernatural owner of the land north of Nekhab-Nekhen. Thus we have Neith as goddess of the land of Lower Egypt in pre-Osirian times, and the Libyan Horus as god of the land of Lower Egypt after its conquest by Isis and her followers. In Upper Egypt Set was the owner of the land of the Set kingdom; after the death of the king-god Osiris he became the 'Lord of Upper Egypt'; Horus of Edfu apparently once owned the land to the south of Set, but we do not know this with any certainty.[2]

The ceremonial fights or battles were followed by the Pharaoh's passage across the field touching the four points of the compass. In the course of this he is often shown carrying a document in his hand, which testifies that he is the lawful ruler of the country. An inscription at Edfu says: 'I have run holding the secret of the two partners (Horus and Set), namely the will, which my father (Osiris) has given me before Geb. I have passed through the land (represented by the field) and touched its four sides. I am running through it as I desire.'[3] He then generally hands the document to the goddess Mert, the personification of the Two Lands, Egypt.[4] She is depicted stretching out her arms in welcome, calling out to him 'Come, bring it.' She seems to be eager to acknowledge him quickly, for in the text are the words 'walk very fast' (Pl. 17).

Being thus acknowledged as a lawful ruler on the throne of Horus, Pharaoh dedicates the land, according to the inscription at

[1] von Bissing-Kees, *Re-Heiligtum*, II, Pl. XVIII.

[2] Edfu must have existed already in prehistoric times for when the 'angry' Hathor (that is to say Horus clan people) was brought back by Onuris from Punt to the kingdom of Atum (see p. 41), she was greeted in Edfu by Horus, who had been her neighbour in Punt (*Hathor-Tefnut*, p. 4). Gardiner, however, is of the opinion that Horus of Edfu was originally a Lower Egyptian god. See 'Horus the Behdetite', in *JEA*, XXX (1944), p. 23.

[3] Kees, 'Nachlase' in *ZÄS*, 52, p. 68. [4] Jéquier, *Pepi II*, p. 20.

Bubastis, to Amen.¹ The rite is depicted on the funerary monument of Pepi. There the Pharaoh is shown standing, a short sceptre in his right hand and a staff in his left, making the gesture of consecration.² Before him is a structure, usually described as a mast consisting of a long centre pole and four supporting poles, the whole forming a pyramid. Ten princes hold the ropes; two people with the ropes round their bodies are shown on each of the four supporting poles, making eight altogether. They are in archaic dress and wear feathers. The whole representation would appear to symbolise the people who had inhabited the land of Egypt before the advent of Osiris and Isis;³ the ten princes of the royal lineage may have symbolised the ten dynasties which ruled them personified by the gods and goddesses of the Great Ennead.⁴

After thank-offerings to the Royal Ancestors have been made, the Pharaoh is shown sitting on his throne in the garb of Osiris, holding the flail and the crook. This was possibly the royal dress at the time of the foundation of the Osirian kingdom, and would convey to his people that he is the lawful heir of his father as the owner and ruler of the land and its people.

2. *The Nehebkau Festival*

(a) *The Uniting of the* Kas

The rites of the Nehebkau festival, which, unlike the *Sed*, was performed annually, renewed the divine power of the Pharaoh's *ka* so that he was able to give 'life' to the land in the coming year. The kingly *ka*, as already mentioned, was the lunar and solar Horus *ka* of his Royal Ancestors, personified by Osiris, and in order to renew its potency it was necessary for Osiris, the king-god, to be reborn.

---

[1] Naville, p. 4.   [2] Jéquier, II, p. 17; Pl. XII.
[3] Jéquier, op. cit., p. 18, remarks that these people cannot be foreigners, since they show the same racial features as the princes who hold the ropes.
[4] For the Great Ennead and the significance of Horus being its tenth god see p. 38. Note also the symbolism of the so-called mast forming a pyramid, the symbol of the Sun-god, consisting of four outside poles, no doubt indicating the four cardinal points, the centre pole possibly the *ka* round which everything revolves; among the Akan the sacred black stools of the Royal Ancestors consist of five columns of which the central one is the *kra*; five is a number sacred to the Royal Ancestors; eight people on the poles; eight, among the Akan, being the number symbolic of procreation; ten princes; ten, among the Akan is regarded as twice five, two being symbolic of birth and creation, five the Royal Ancestors (*Sacred State*, pp. 94 ff.).

THE REJUVENATION OF THE KING'S DIVINE POWER

The Nehebkau festival was accordingly preceded by rites concerned with the rebirth of Osiris. They started on the 18th *Khoiak*, the last month of the year, with the watering of the Osiris beds of barley. When these seeds germinated, they were placed in his tomb, for Osiris in his form of fertility-god was manifest in barley. On the 26th the interment of Osiris was re-enacted at Memphis in the festival of Sokaris-Osiris 'the coffined one'; on the 30th, transfigured as a god, he was reborn to his mother Hathor.

The ritual that took place on that day is depicted in the tomb of Kheruef, a high official, at Thebes. In the first scene Amenophis III is shown with the *ankh* cross, symbolising him as life-giver, making offerings to the *Djed*, the emblem of the divinity of Osiris, which is here superimposed on the mummified figure of the king, who holds a crook and a flail.[1] It stands in a shrine between two altars loaded with offerings; on the left side lies a bouquet of lotus flowers. A lotus flower also grows out of the *shen* sign to the right of the *Djed*; to the left of it are three tall papyrus plants. The lotus is symbolic of the Sun-god Atum who, according to one version, was born sitting inside one at Heliopolis. The *shen* sign symbolises the eternal course of the sun, the ecliptic. The papyrus is sacred to Hathor; the *Djed* itself is in this scene an artfully contrived column of papyrus stems.[2] Lotus and papyrus symbolise Hathor, the mother of Horus and Osiris, as Hathor of Heliopolis, the mother and wife of the Sun-god; the rebirth therefore is concerned with the solar Horus *ka* of Osiris and of the Royal Ancestors.

The offerings to the *Djed* are followed by its erection; this time it is depicted in its abstract form, symbolising divinity, indicating that the rebirth of Osiris has already taken place. The *Djed* is erected by the Pharaoh, wearing the Blue Crown of Re; he is accompanied by the queen, and two *Anmutef* priests are making obeisance. As pointed out before, the *Anmutef* priest personified the Horus *ka* of the living Pharaoh. Since two are portrayed here the second may personify the Horus *ka* of the *living* Osiris. Queen Teje, a sceptre in her hand, no doubt incarnating Hathor (see below) stands behind Amenophis III; sixteen princesses walk in pairs after them.[3] In a lower register priests salute Ptah, viewed either as

[1] Fakhry, *Kheruef*, Pl. XXXIX.
[2] For Hathor manifest in the papyrus plant see Frankfort, *Kingship*, pp. 177, 178.
[3] Among the Akan the number 16 is regarded as twice 8, two being the symbol for birth, 8 the symbol for procreation.

THE REJUVENATION OF THE KING'S DIVINE POWER

Ptah-Sokaris-Osiris or as the father of the Sun-god and the Pharaoh.

In the throne scene which follows, after the various rites in honour of Ptah-Tatjenen (see next section), the Pharaoh seated on his throne wears the double diadem and the *Heb Sed* costume attributed to Osiris.[1] Hathor sits behind him on another throne; she wears the sun disk between two horns, and the uraeus with the boat-shaped lunar crescent carrying the sign of Re. She has her right arm round Amenophis III and in her left hand she holds three ribs ending in the *shen* sign, on which is a frog carrying the god Shu. The palm is a symbol of the moon and the Mother-goddess Hathor; the *shen*, on which everything rests, is the eternal sun; the frog is the symbol of birth. Shu is here represented as the god who has lifted up the heavens with the sun and stars and supports them with both arms above the earth. Queen Teje stands behind Hathor, a lotus in her hand. The dais on which the thrones stand is decorated with lotus and papyrus. The scene clearly expresses the conception that, not only has Osiris been reborn to Hathor, but the Pharaoh also (he is in the garb of Osiris) in whom the divine lunar and solar *ka* of his Royal Ancestors operates. In a following scene the Pharaoh, still in the *Heb Sed* costume of Osiris, leaves the palace; he is wearing the Upper Egyptian crown which has the Horus falcon in front of it with the uraeus on its head. Thus Nehebkau reunited the rejuvenated *ka* of the Royal Ancestors, personified by Osiris, with that of the living Pharaoh.

(b) *The Rebirth of the Sun-god incarnate in the King*

From about the 18th Dynasty onwards, Nehebkau also united the *ka* of the state god Amen-Re with that of the Pharaoh after the rebirth of the god—he was a Sun Sky fertility-god—on New Year's day in spring. The rites are depicted in most detail at Soleb; on the walls of the Festival Hall of Osorkon II at Bubastis they are but imperfectly indicated.

The 'rising' or rebirth of Amen-Re is announced at Soleb as follows: 'The appearing (of the king) in the Hall of Eating in order to cause the rising of His Majesty the venerable god Amen-Re, the Lord of the Throne, and his resting in his place in the Hall of the Sed festival.'[2]

The Hall of Eating at Soleb seems to have been identical with the

[1] Fakhry, op. cit., Pl. XL.   [2] Quoted by Naville in *Osorkon*, p. 17.

House of Amen, which Ramses III took pride in having reconstructed for the festival,[1] and with the sanctuary at Bubastis.[2] It was erected in the Hall of the *Sed* festival, which was either in the palace or in the hypostyle hall of one of the great temples. Judging from the hieroglyph it consisted of a covering supported by a single pole[3] and was, apparently, originally a tent which housed the shrine of the god.

The name 'Hall of Eating' applied to Amen's sanctuary suggests that the main rite was a consecrated meal shared by all present—that is, by Amen-Re, the gods gathered outside in the Hall of the *Sed* festival, the Pharaoh, the queen and all those who were entitled to attend the festival. Naville speaks of a banquet,[4] but this is surely a European conception; among the Akan each person receives only the ritual three mouthfuls; and parts of the sacrificed animals are usually sent to the houses of the chiefs so that their families, who have not been invited, may have their share. At Soleb and Bubastis, where the victuals were so plentiful, a similar custom may have been practised.

One may compare the Hall of Eating, a tent at Bubastis, and a small pavilion at Soleb, with the wooden structure, formerly also a pavilion, in the sacred grove at Takyiman where offerings are made to the sun-king Ameyaw Kwaakye, the ancestor king of the present dynasty. A consecrated meal is eaten not only by those assembled in the pavilion—the king, the queen-mother, and the great men of the state—but also by the town and village chiefs, the priests with their gods, and the common people, sitting or standing outside in the grove. Offerings are also made to the equinoctial points, their places marked for the occasion on the four outside corners of the structure. These offerings are destined for the deceased queen-mothers, who personify the moon Mother-goddess, the giver of birth to the sun on the day of the equinox; *summe* leaves, the equivalent of the Egyptian lotus, are placed there in the morning.

At Bubastis the astronomical instruments of Heliopolis receive offerings from the Pharaoh,[5] an indication that the course of the sun with the equinoxes and solstices had been discovered at Heliopolis. Again the Pharaoh is offered the clepsydra by the *Sem* priest. Naville remarks that the instruments and the clepsydra had some reference to the astronomical meaning of the festival and to its

[1] ibid., p. 7. [2] ibid., p. 4. [3] ibid., p. 17. [4] ibid., p. 18. [5] ibid., Pl. IX.

THE REJUVENATION OF THE KING'S DIVINE POWER

coincidence with the date of the calendar.[1] There can be no doubt, since Nehebkau presided over the day, that the reference was to the equinox, a day on which the sun rises due east, facing equally towards the two hemispheres, and therefore a day eminently suitable for the rebirth of a Sun-god. Besides this, special offerings were made to Thoth, the god of astronomy, science, and calculation.

A curious scene is depicted behind a shrine (Amen's?) in which Osorkon II pours water on the hands of priests. For the lower ones water pours out of his hands, for the upper ones a stream of water is represented as running from behind him and falling on them. Naville asks whether there was a spring or fountain in the temple.[2] The scene, like so many others, is purely symbolical and seems intended to show that Amen-Re has been reborn in the divine ruler, who is now able once again to give 'life' from the sky. With reference to the land, this 'life' means rain. The accompanying inscription for the lower scene reads 'making purification twice four times'. Making purification four times is a funerary rite connected with the royal dead; here it is an indication that the Pharaoh can only give 'life' with his *ka*, the Horus *ka* of his Royal Ancestors, if it is purified by him with sacred water. At Takyiman the same idea is expressed by the *apupuo* head-dress worn by the king in the rites in the grove. *Apupuo* means 'Creator of Water' who is dispossessed of water by mankind';[3] the king incarnating a Sun Sky fertility-god has to give 'life' in the form of rain and sun to mankind; it is his *raison d'être*.

In another scene the Pharaoh stands in front of a shrine which is shown to be a funeral chamber.[4] Twelve priests carrying the standards of their gods and goddesses are depicted before the Pharaoh, and in an upper row men carry statuettes in the form of mummies. The twelve dieties would seem to represent dynasties, for they are: Atum, Tefnut, Shu, Geb, Nut, Horus (the Elder), Osiris, Isis, Set, Nephthys, Re (5th Dynasty), and the *ka* standard of the Pharaoh (Horus), the historic line. The statuettes in the form of mummies probably represented the dead kings of his dynasty. The Pharaoh is offered a lotus bud. The significance clearly is that the Sun-god is

[1] ibid., Pl. IX and pp. 22 and 24.   [2] ibid., Pl. XI, p. 24.
[3] The *apupuo* is a river mussel which remains filled with water for several days after being taken out of the stream; hence the mussel is believed to create water. On the king's head-dress the *apupuo* are cast in gold, symbolic of the sun. Illustrated in *Sacred State*, Pl. 15.
[4] Naville, op. cit., Pl. X, p. 25.

now reborn in him and he is recognised once more as the divine ruler. In a register above, the Pharaoh, alone inside a sanctuary, receives the homage of a god.

After the rebirth of the Sun-god and the Pharaoh in whom he is incarnate, the boat-shaped shrine of Amen-Re is carried out of the Hall of the *Sed* festival and round the building and probably also through the main streets of the town where the New Year's day was celebrated; the Pharaoh and the queen march before the shrine. This showed the people that the god had risen and the Pharaoh's divine power had been fully restored.

3. *The Festival of the God of the Land, Tatjenen*

The festival of the god Tatjenen, the personification of the 'risen land' at the time of creation, was the third that was generally celebrated in conjunction with the *Sed* and the Nehebkau festivals. At Bubastis the representations start with a procession, but those taking part are very different from those who marched in the so-called Upwaut procession to the *Sed* pavilion. For they are mostly women—royal daughters holding sistrums, priestesses, wives of peasants and labourers as well as Nubian women. At Takyiman the *Apo* is also dedicated to women, since they are regarded as the representatives of the Mother-goddess,[1] who alone can give rebirth and bring new life to nature and mankind.[2] As in Egypt, this is a spring festival.

In the reliefs at Bubastis, of which unfortunately a great many have been destroyed, women mainly sing and dance. In one important scene women are depicted in pairs turned towards each other in

[1] The proclamation of Osorkon also makes it quite clear that the festival is dedicated to the women; it reads: 'In the year 22 on the first day of the month Khoiak the issuing (of the King) out of the sanctuary of Amen in the Festival Hall resting on his throne: the beginning of the consecrating of the harem of Amen (i.e. the priestesses of the god), and of consecrating all women, who are in this city, and who act as priestesses since the day of the fathers . . .'

[2] This is evident from the *bo-me-tuo-* custom. During the dances that take place on the festival days in the streets any young man may go up to any girl and say *bo-me-tuo*, literally 'fire a gun at me'. The girl is then expected to throw off her cloth and reveal herself naked, except for the little red cloth between her thighs. The original formula would have been 'shoot an arrow at me'—namely a life-giving moon-ray, like those shot by the moon Mother-goddess into the universe. The girl, in fact, impersonates the goddess and the young man is asking to have his life-force re-vitalized by her. See also *Sacred State*, p. 70.

THE REJUVENATION OF THE KING'S DIVINE POWER

curious attitudes. They shout words aloud and accompany them with extraordinary gestures, while others clap their hands or beat their drums.[1] Likewise in the tomb of Kheruef, women, including Nubian women from the oases, shout and beat their tambourines or clap their hands. At Takyiman the same thing takes place on the eighth day of the *Apo*; women as well as men shout insults at each other, while others standing round them incite them further by clapping their hands or beating the small *dono* drums, singing abusive songs. The object of this is to rid the people of their pent-up grievances and their secret evil designs against each other, for it is believed that bad feeling endangers the process of growth. The queen-mother suffers with the rest, for delegations of women beleaguer her and reproach her in no uncertain terms for her wicked acts during the year.[2]

At Takyiman, where members of the ruling class are intruders, the king is fetched from his palace, insulted, and engaged in combat in the street, in order to relieve the bitter feelings of those who have been ousted from power. His adversary is the *Korontihene*, the governor of the town, whose ancestors founded it and once ruled it as chiefs. The king, dressed in the war-dress of his ancestors, is carried on the shoulders of one of his men, as is the *Korontihene*; both are armed with clubs and a shield. The men who follow them take part in the fight and belabour each other with their fists, sticks or clubs. This battle not only relieves the ill-feeling of one section of the population but also serves to commemorate a historical event.

In Egypt it seems to have been much the same. In the tomb of Kheruef men are shown fighting with their fists or with papyrus stalks. At Bubastis the Pharaoh is shown leaving his palace without the insignia of royalty, accompanied only by one man; the corresponding inscription says: 'returning, retracing his steps'.[3] This seems to refer to the past, going back to the beginning of the history of the Two Lands, perhaps to the time when Menes made Memphis his capital, depriving the Memphis chief of his power. The rite which would illustrate the words is missing, and we can only

[1] The description is taken from Naville, *Osorkon*, p. 27 to Pl. XIV.

[2] Plutarch (*De Is.* sec. 59) says that the Egyptians at certain festivals 'both speak and think words of most wicked and lewd meaning, even of the gods themselves', which shows that the Egyptian custom was the same as that of the Akan.

[3] Naville, op. cit., p. 22 to Pl. XIV, is uncertain whether this translation is correct, but in fact the words make perfect sense.

assume that the Pharaoh fought a ceremonial battle, since women abusing each other are depicted in the reliefs near by.

The rites of abuse are followed at Bubastis, by the 'adoring of Tatjenen': 'Hail to the festival, the festival of Tatjenen takes place'; the renderings are unfortunately much abridged. The 'adoring of Tatjenen' probably corresponded to the 'adoring' of Taa Kese at Takyiman, whose purification, following his death and rebirth, is celebrated on the 'Great Fertile Monday', New Year's day.

At Bubastis the last scenes are concerned with the rebirth of the city goddess Bastet.[1] The triple festival ends with Osorkon II sitting in shrines raised on platforms, one representing Upper Egypt, the other Lower Egypt. He has all the emblems of Osiris, showing to his people that the Horus *ka* of Osiris, his Royal Ancestors, is active in him again. The text says: 'Horus rises, he has received the two plumes (i.e. he has been crowned anew), he is the King, Osorkon living eternally.'[2]

[1] The rite (Naville, Pl. XXIII and p. 34) is curious; there is nothing in Akan ritual with which to compare it, but one can easily interpret it. Six poles with a broad base arranged in a line receive offerings; the text says, not to the 'holy Six' but to 'the holy circle of Bastet'. Naville asks (p. 34), 'How does this number constitute her circle or orbit?' Among the Akan six is the number symbolic of death and rebirth. Bastet's orbit therefore is that of perpetual death and rebirth. She was the 'Lady of the East' and as such a daughter of Re, representing the beneficent powers of the sun, reborn each day in the east. The poles may have been gnomons, with which the ancient Egyptians determined the hours of the day. [2] Naville, op. cit., Pl. XXI.

CHAPTER VIII

The Rejuvenation of the King's person on New Year's Day in Autumn

AKAN

1. *The* Aferehyia Dwaree, *the King's Death and Rebirth*

The *Aferehyia Dwaree*, the great annual purification ceremony of the king's *kra* and *ntoro* spirit, is still performed at Takyiman. It takes place on New Year's day in autumn, on the nearest Thursday to the autumnal equinox.[1] On this day the king 'dies', for he is deprived of his kingship, but after his *kra* and *ntoro* spirit have been cleansed from all defilement and their full strength restored, they are resurrected in him and he is enthroned again.

Early in the afternoon the king, the queen-mother, the chiefs of the state council, the royal wives,[2] the stool-sons of the king's predecessor and his own stool-sons,[3] assemble, all dressed in white, in a palace room which serves on that day as *Kra Fieso*, and wait for the *Akrafohene*, the 'bearer of the king's *kra*', and *akrafo*. When the *Akrafohene* enters, the king rises to greet him and offers him his throne seat. The regalia is then brought, and the king himself invests the *Akrafohene* with it, since in the rites which follow the *Akrafohene* impersonates the king.

When the *Akrafohene* has been robed the king gives him his

[1] The 'Great Fertile Thursday' of the *Adaduanan* calendar, which ends the *Sanaa Kese* festival, lasting twenty-four days. The festival is described in full in *Sacred State*, pp. 164–71.

[2] Members of high-ranking families, heiress princesses to the stools of the great clans.

[3] Stool-sons are those sons of the king who occupy hereditary posts in the state council, at court, and in the provinces. See p. 87.

'Silver (Moon) Stool';[1] he then takes one of his golden-hilted state swords and, standing before the *Akrafohene* in the guise of a sword-bearer, a mere commoner, he hands over to him and the *akrafo* two snow-white long-legged rams, as well as four cocks, seven yams, and eight eggs, which must be taken to the sacred river for purification. Then he steps aside and announces: 'the king is coming' and, walking ahead of the *Akrafohene*, he halts at the entrance to the palace. There the palanquin-bearers, the bearers of the large state umbrella, the bearers of the black stools of the Royal Ancestors, the sword-bearers, gun-bearers, and drummers are waiting for them, and a procession is formed.

At its head walk the queen-mother's stool-carriers bearing the low white stools for the royal wives and the offerings; they are followed by the royal wives. After them, beneath one of the state umbrellas, walks the *Sanaahene* or chief treasurer, the son of a former king, who carries the *puduo* in the *sanaa* bag. The *puduo* consists of gold nuggets separately wrapped, each of which represents the *kra* of one Royal Ancestor; on top of them lies Bosummuru's gold sword. The whole collection, still in the *sanaa* bag, is placed in a brass basin and covered with a white sheet. Behind this official, under a smaller umbrella, walks the *Akyeamehene*, chief of the royal spokesmen; he is followed by the silver stool, which is carried by the chief stool-bearer; another stool-bearer is entrusted with the white stool for the *puduo*. Behind them the *Akrafohene* is borne in the king's palanquin—a long basket-shaped litter flanked on either side by the *akrafo* holding scimitars with hilts decorated in white and gold. Next come the stool-sons, many of them weeping to see their father, the king, thus deprived of his kingship. They are flanked by gun-bearers, and the drummers with the huge state drums bring up the rear.

On arrival at the sacred river Adare, the *Akrafohene* seats himself on the silver stool; the brass basin containing the *sanaa* bag is placed before him on the white stool, and he is shaded by the state umbrella. The *akrafo* sit in two rows on the ground in front of the *Akrafohene*, and the stool-sons form a semi-circle round him and the *akrafo*. A little apart from this group sit the royal wives. Another basin is now filled with sacred river water by an *okrafo*; the *Sanaahene* uncovers the *sanaa* and uses the leaves of a *summe* plant,

---

[1] An illustration of the regalia worn by the *Akrafohene* is given in *Sacred State*, Pl. 15.

uprooted on the riverside, to sprinkle this water on the *puduo* and on Bosummuru's sword. He also sprinkles the *Akrafohene*, thus purifying and blessing him; he then does the same to the stool-sons, one after the other; and finally to the royal wives. No speech, is made, however, nor is any libation poured. When the rite has ended, the *sanaa* is covered up again with the white sheet, and everybody shouts '*Asubo*', 'Cleansed, cleansed', and '*Aferihyia pa o*', 'We wish you a good year'; the state drums are beaten, and the gun-bearers fire into the sky in four directions. Three eggs are left on the river bank as an offering to the river-god, after which the procession forms up again and returns to the town, where crowds of people are awaiting it.

At the southern end of the town the queen-mother and elders, sitting in a semi-circle, are also waiting for the procession to arrive. The *Akrafohene* dismounts and sits down on the king's throne seat on the right of the queen-mother. The *Sanaahene* then steps forward and purifies and blesses all the assembly, including the common people who throng around, with sacred river water which has been brought by them.[1] The queen-mother then makes a speech, thanking the chiefs of the state council and the people for all they have done for the state during the past year. She is followed by the *Akrafohene*, who speaks as if he were the king. Guns are fired again, drums are beaten and the procession, which now includes the queen-mother and the elders, returns to the palace. The king, still disguised as a common sword-bearer, is waiting at the entrance gate and humbly greets the *Akrafohene*. The same group of people who congregated in the *Kra Fieso* earlier that afternoon assemble there again. Everyone sits down, the *Akrafohene* taking the silver stool, slightly in front of the queen-mother, who is next to the *Gyaasehene* (the chief of the royal household, here acting as the eldest stool-son); the king, however, takes his seat far in the background, next to the royal wives. The *sanaa*, together with the Bosummuru gold sword, are placed on the table before the *Akrafo-*

[1] When the Bono kingdom was at the height of its power, the sacred water came from the source of the Tano River. All sons of the reigning king and of his deceased predecessors, who were chiefs and sub-chiefs, and all vassal kings whose mothers had been daughters of a Bono king, would form a line stretching from the source of the river to the south end of the town and from there to the *Kra Fieso* in the Bono-Mansu palace. They would pass a golden basin containing the sacred water from hand to hand; all participants were on horseback. It was a scene of great splendour and showed the people how immensely powerful their kingdom had become.

hene and uncovered. The queen-mother now rises and purifies the *puduo* and the Bosummuru sword by sprinkling them with sacred water; she then sprinkles the assembly. She utters the prayer for the well-being of the state in the new year, and implores the Royal Ancestors to help their people yet again and make them prosper.

Meanwhile yams and eggs, purified at the riverside, have been cooked and brought in. The yams are mashed by the *akrafo*, kneaded into balls, and placed on a dish; pieces of hard-boiled eggs are sprinkled over them. The *Akrafohene* takes an *adwera* leaf, which is floating in the sacred water, puts it into his mouth and spits the water from it three times over the food, saying 'Blessing: let my *kra* take this food from my heart'; he then eats the traditional three mouthfuls. When the *eto* has been divided into three portions, the first is offered in a small bowl to the *kras* of the Royal Ancestors and placed before the *puduo*; the second, offered to Bosummuru, is placed next to his gold sword; the whole assembly shares the third. If any *eto* remains in the dish it is placed on the *puduo* and the sword.

Next a fowl is brought in and held by the *Akrafohene* before one of the offering bowls. He says: 'If no misfortune is destined to befall the new year, then take this fowl.' If thereupon the fowl pecks three times at the consecrated food, the Royal Ancestors are held to have accepted the offerings. Everybody now shouts 'We thank you, we thank you', and the fowl is sacrificed. If, however, it refuses to eat, this is regarded as a bad omen and a sheep must be sacrificed to avert disaster.

After a while, everybody moves into the audience courtyard, where the *Akrafohene*, still impersonating the king, sits on the royal dais. The others arrange themselves according to rank. Two rams which have been purified at the riverside are brought in and sacrificed by the *Sanaahene*, who pricks their throats; four cocks are also killed. A fire of three logs of *esa* wood is lighted, and while another sacred meal, the *akra suo*, is being prepared, minstrels recite the great deeds of the Royal Ancestors. The talking-drums then play their part, the drummers beating out the rhythm which interprets great historical events, and which all present understand. There is dancing to the rhythm of the drums until the meal is ready. The *akra suo* here consists of a soup made from the flesh of the rams and cocks which is poured over seven *fufu* balls, prepared from mashed yams, and offered by the *Akrafohene* to the Royal

Ancestors and to Bosummuru. On top of four offering bowls thus filled are placed pieces of the rams' hearts, livers, and tails and a cock's head and legs, heart and liver; a sausage made from the rams' blood is also added. The *Akrafohene* blesses the bowls, over which he pours a libation of gin; he does the same to the *akra suo* soup eaten by the assembly. Women and children of the palace who wish to share the consecrated meal may send in small bowls. The rest of the meat (uncooked) is then sent to the houses of the chiefs of the state council along with their share of the gifts sent to the king by Tano's (Taa Kese) high priest.

When the meal is over the *Akrafohene* calls for palm-wine, and while the assembly is drinking it, he slips quietly away to a room near by, takes off his borrowed regalia and walks home, accompanied by the *akrafo*. The king withdraws equally quietly to another room, where he resumes his regalia and reappears as king. In former times the king of Bono, representing the risen sun, wore only gold on this occasion. His body would be greased and powdered with gold dust; he would put on a square loin-cloth of gold thread, and, wearing many gold ornaments round his neck, arms, wrists, knees, legs and ankles, as well as golden sandals, would seat himself on the Golden Stool. When homage had been paid to him, he would withdraw with his senior wife, the queen, into the *Nyame Dan*, a sanctuary dedicated to Nyame. He would spend the night there with her so that the Royal Ancestors, led by Bosummuru, might enter her and cause her to conceive. Three white rams were sacrificed to Nyame on the threshold of their bed-chamber.

In the past also the white bull of Bosummuru was sacrificed by the *Akrafohene* for the king, probably during the rites at the sacred river. Thus the god died and was reborn in the king when the latter appeared in all his splendour seated on the Golden Stool. The black cow of the goddess was sacrificed by the queen-mother or her proxy, the *Akrafo-ba-panyin*, about a week earlier. Today the queen-mother's *kra* is purified in the same manner as that of the king but the rite is performed not on the 'Great Fertile Thursday' but on the preceding 'Great Fertile Friday'. She also is divested of her royal status and reinstated.[1]

[1] The shrine of the goddess Bosummuru is not a sword but the *aforo* box filled with precious beads, the red *bota* and *bodom*, which symbolise blood and therefore lineage, and pieces of silver and gold; silver symbolises the moon and the queen-mother's predecessors in office; gold, the kings, the Royal Ancestors,

THE REJUVENATION OF THE KING'S PERSON

In Asante, however, the rites for both the king and the queen-mother were differently performed. There, on a '*Nwona*' or 'Shielded' Sunday, the king suffered 'death' in the royal cemetery at Bampanase, just outside the capital. His regalia was taken from him in a humiliating way by the *Banmuhene*, the grave-priest and custodian of the royal mausoleum, and he was given instead a strip of bark-cloth, the garb of the poorest slave in the realm. His feet were then bathed in the blood of a human sacrifice to rejuvenate his person.[1] After this his regalia was returned to him and he was again acknowledged as king. His first act was to offer the first-fruits of the season to the *Odwira Suman* of Osei Tutu, the founder of the kingdom, a minor deity who had presided over the rite.[2] On the following '*Nkyi*' or 'Hateful' Monday the king sacrificed the white bull of Bosummuru in front of his palace with the sacred sword of the god.[3] On the day after '*Kuru*' or 'Most Sacred' Tuesday, the god's birthday, or day of rebirth, the king made a public sacrifice to purify the sword that had been defiled by death. Identical rites were performed for the queen-mother who sacrificed the black crouching cow (*Apafram*) of the goddess Bosummuru on the 'Fertile' Monday at the beginning of the festival.

the sons of the moon queen-mothers. I do not know whether the black cow was sacrificed with a special sword belonging to the goddess or with the silver *Nkerante*, the queen-mother's state sword. Only one elder at Takyiman remembered the sacrifice of the bull and cow; all the others, including the *Omanhene* of Bono-Takyiman, rejected it as a detestable custom of the Asante. These animals ceased to be sacrificed when Bono was dismembered and the small Bono-Takyiman state came under the overlordship of Asante (1740), the king of Asante, as great king and the Asante queen-mother having the sole right to the great sacrifice.

[1] It is exceptionally difficult to get information on this rite, partly because to speak of the humiliation of the king is tabu, partly because the last time the rite was performed it had very unpleasant repercussions, as it ended in a police investigation by the British Government which had abolished human sacrifice. Moreover, it spoilt the people's joy at the return of King Prempeh I from exile in the Seychelle Islands (1925) where he was sent by the British in 1896 as a prisoner of war.

[2] In Takyiman permission to harvest is given by the king and queen-mother on the preceding Wednesday, which is celebrated as the first New Year's day. See *Sacred State*, pp. 168–9.

[3] For greater detail see *Sacred State*, p. 174.

EGYPT

1. The Min-Khamutef Festival, the King's Death and Rebirth

The Min-Khamutef festival fell at the beginning of the harvest season and lasted for twenty days.[1] The death and rebirth of the Pharaoh and the god whom he incarnates, in this instance Min-Khamutef, were celebrated on New Year's day, when the moon was full at about the time of the equinox in March, the culminating day of the festival.[2] It depicted in all its splendour on the walls of the Temple of Ramses III (20th Dynasty) at Medinet Habu.[3]

The festival has been discussed in the greatest detail by Gauthier[4] and Jacobsohn,[5] but much is left unexplained owing to the Egyptian habit of combining in one representation rites and ceremonies which were not likely to have been performed on the same day. One is also hampered by the lack of particulars in the accompanying text. To remedy this I attempt here to reconstruct the sequence of events in what I believe is the right order, using my knowledge of the corresponding Akan festival, the *Aferihyia Dwaree*.

The Pharaoh on the reliefs at Medinet Habu (Pl. 18) is depicted five times, wearing a different crown three times. He wears the Blue Crown firstly in the procession to the temple of Min and secondly in the rite which he performs in the temple of the god. One may assume that these two incidents, depicted next to each other, are connected and probably took place in the morning of the same day. Next he appears wearing the Lower Egyptian crown in

---

[1] Brugsch, *Ägypt.*, pp. 191, 363.

[2] Egyptologists do not agree as to the date of the festival. I am inclined to follow Brugsch (*Rel.*, p. 358), who is of the opinion that the festival fell generally in the month of *Pachons* (our 17th March–15th April) and that the main rites fell on a full moon day in that month. On full moon day the moon and sun can be seen simultaneously from a raised place; under normal circumstances the opposition moon-sun occurs on the 14th day, sometimes on the 12th or 16th day, of the calendar month (cf. F. X. Kugler, *Astronomische historische Vorunrersuchungen*, I, p. 15). The March equinox in Thutmoses III's time fell on the 3rd April (Brugsch, *Ägyptologie*, p. 363). See also 'The Lunar Dates of Thutmosis III and Ramesses II' by J. B. MacMinn in *JNES*, XVI (1957).

[3] H. H. Nelson, et al., *Medinet Habu*, Chicago, 1932, IV, Pls. 196–217. The earliest representations of the festival are on the pylons of Amenophis III's temple at Luxor and in the temple of Karnak.

[4] Gauthier, *Fêtes*, pp. 20 ff.

[5] Jacobsohn, *Dogm. Stell.*, pp. 37, 38.

the scene of the 'Going Forth of Min to the Stairs' and the rites performed there; the evidence suggests that it took place in the afternoon and evening. The fourth time he is adorned with the Great Crown of Upper and Lower Egypt completing the rites at night-time on the same day, certainly New Year's day. The fifth time he is seen again with the Blue Crown in ceremonies that closed the festival, probably on the following morning.

In the opening scene the Pharaoh is depicted in his palanquin, accompanied by his sons,[1] priests, musicians, and soldiers of his bodyguard, being carried to the 'house of his father Min'. On arrival he is greeted by a priest who, according to the text, has already made the libations and offerings. The Pharaoh then offers incense to the god, almost certainly in order to invoke Min and to induce him to take up his abode in the statue;[2] in the text, significantly, Min is addressed as 'Amun-Re-Khamutef'.

According to the text programme this rite took place on a day that was under the 'Protector of the Moon'.[3] Among the Akan this would be a Monday, which is ruled by the *kra* progenitor (*akragya*) of the planet moon, the protector or guardian deity of those born on that day. It is interesting to note that in this rite the Pharaoh wears the Blue Crown, symbolic of the deities of the sun and the moon; the reference here must be to the solar Amun-Re and the lunar Min-Khamutef.

In the afternoon, presumably, since the Pharaoh now wears the Lower Egyptian Crown, the statue of Min is carried out of the sanctuary and Min's reciter priest is shown greeting the god. A procession is formed in which the queen now takes part. The statue is carried by twenty priests, while bearers of whisks and fans stride along beside it; other priests follow, carrying the box with the lettuces of Min. The Pharaoh is shown walking before the statue;

[1] For the dominant part played by the sons of the Pharaoh in the procession see Gauthier, op. cit., p. 126. For the role of sons of the king in the corresponding Bono festival see p. 172.

[2] Wilkinson, *Customs*, III, p. 414, says that the Pharaoh 'addressed the god before whose statue he stood with a suitable prayer to invoke his aid and favour; he begged him to accept the incense he presented'. Among the Akan to invoke a god is to induce him to take up his abode in the stool or other shrine provided for the deity; only there is he able to accept the prayers and food, or libations offered to him.

[3] Gauthier, op. cit., pp. 62, 63, says that the term 'Protector of the Moon' is otherwise unknown and it is therefore not certain whether the translation is correct.

in front of him marches the white bull of Min,[1] adorned with the two feathers and other insignia of the deity. The queen does not walk in the procession, but is depicted above it, in front of the bull, and amidst the text. This is an indication, perhaps, that the rites which are about to be performed are for the benefit of the Pharaoh's *ka* but not hers; the text reads that the Pharaoh is 'going forth to the stairs of Min to sacrifice to his [own] *ka*'. The bull in its turn is preceded by bearers with offerings, bearers of the royal standards and of the statues of the Royal Ancestors; here again priests, among them the 'negro of Punt',[2] musicians, and soldiers accompany the procession.

The destination of the procession was the 'Stairs', a base with steps in front of it on which the statue was placed.[3] This could not have been far from the sanctuary, since the Pharaoh and the queen are shown walking to it. It may have been situated in a sacred grove near by. There, according to the text, Min rests on the stairs; the Akan would express this by saying that the god entered the statue, his shrine, to rest before taking part in the rites to come. Min on the stairs 'caused His Majesty to perform the great sacrifice to his father Min-Khamutef' (the distinction made between Min the father and Min-Khamutef should be noted).

The great sacrifice is not depicted but it is obviously the central rite and closely connected with the rebirth of the god, which is celebrated later. In the Book of the Dead (chapter 17) the 'Going Forth of Min' is equated with the birth of the god, that is, in the sense of rebirth. But rebirth implies that death has taken place. The great sacrifice[4] the god caused the Pharaoh to perform must have been the killing of the mortal incarnations of the deity. These were three and therefore the death of Min-Khamutef is, as we shall

---

[1] Wilkinson, op. cit., p. 306, says that 'White Bull' is specified by the same character used to denote silver or, as the Egyptians called it in their inscriptions, 'white gold'. Silver, among the Akan, is symbolic of the moon, gold of the sun.

[2] See p. 32.

[3] Among the Akan the 'stairs' (*simpa*) are usually not transportable and are situated just outside the sanctuary of the god. On them is placed the shrine of the god on his birthday and also on other days of the New Year festivals. Taa Kese's 'stairs' consist of three rounded steps (see *Ak. of Ghana*, Pl. 36);

[4] What is sacrificed is not mentioned, no doubt on account of the tabu on the word 'death' in connexion with the gods and the Pharaoh. For the same reason the 'great sacrifice' is also not depicted but is only implied. It could not have been merely an ordinary sacrifice, as egyptologists in general suggest.

see, a triple one; he dies firstly as the god of vegetation, represented by the *emmer* wheat in which he was incarnate; secondly as the god of procreation in the animal world, represented by the white bull in which he was incarnate; and thirdly as the god of procreation in man, represented by the Pharaoh in whom he was incarnate.

The death of the god was preceded by the singing of praises to him, to the Royal Ancestors, and to the living *ka* of the Pharaoh, but these were cut short by the appearance of a priest, or officer of the palace. According to the text he hands the Pharaoh a sickle fashioned of black copper and inlaid with gold, and a sheaf of *emmer* wheat. The Pharaoh cuts the sheaf in two with the sickle while the *shemayt* (an untranslatable female title) who must have been the queen, walks round, or entwines herself about him, uttering a spell seven times. This must surely have been a magical rite designed to protect the god, here personified by the Pharaoh, and to ensure his rebirth. The queen here personified Isis 'great of magic', 'Isis the Great' called at Edfu 'the Divine Mother Shemanut, who protects Min on the Stairs'.[1] Also Isis is the only one of Min's mothers who is connected with his rebirth, and the white bull on the relief at Medinet Habu carries on his left side the red steamers sacred to Isis.[2] The expression to 'entwine herself around' suggests that the queen walked round the Pharaoh in a spiral, which is the symbol of Min, and, it would seem, also symbolised birth in Egypt.[3] The Pharaoh in this rite wears the crown of Lower Egypt, that of his Lower Egyptian Royal Ancestors descended from Isis, with the spiral projecting from it. Seven is a life-giving number, symbolic of the seven planets and their *kas*.

When this rite is completed the Pharaoh, according to the text, takes the sheaf of *emmer* wheat and holds it to the nose of the

---

[1] Gauthier, p. 98.

[2] ibid., p. 193. Apart from Isis, the goddess Sekhmet was the only other goddess to whom this ornament belonged. Sekhmet is another name for Tefnut (see p. 41 n. 4) and Tefnut was the supreme Mother-goddess of Punt. Sekhmet was sometimes depicted like Min, with lifted arm and ithyphallic (Budge, *Fetish*, pp. 159, 160). In the temple of Khonsu at Karnak it is difficult to decide whether Min is portrayed with the head of a lioness or Sekhmet with the ithyphallic body of Min.

[3] Frankfort, *Kingship*, chapter 15, n. 28, suggests that intercourse took place between Pharaoh and the queen at that point of the festival. The sacred marriage between the Pharaoh, incarnating Min-Khamutef, and the queen incarnating the wife of the Khamutef, took place (see below in the text) but not, I should imagine, at this stage of the festival.

THE REJUVENATION OF THE KING'S PERSON

white bull of Min, presumably to tell the divine animal that it also must die; a priest then places it on the ground before the statue of the god and cuts off an ear which he presents to the Pharaoh. This small gesture seems to indicate the Pharaoh's approaching death, or more precisely, the death of his kingship, the renewal of which we find celebrated with so much joy in the last sentences of the text.

The sickle of Min seems to be analogous to the sword of Bosummuru, which is the shrine of the god. Min, a lunar god, has a sickle, a crescent-shaped weapon used for peaceful purposes such as the cutting of grain; Bosummuru, whose planet is Mars, has a golden sword. The sickle is fashioned of black copper inlaid with gold; black symbolises Min as the Lord of the night sky (moon); copper, among the Akan, is symbolic of blood animated by the *kra*;[1] in Egypt this may also have been so, for gold among both peoples symbolised the sun with its immortal life-giving *kra* or *ka*. The white bull of Bosummuru could only be sacrificed by the king, with the weapon which served as the god's shrine; the sickle of Min in the hand of the Pharaoh may have had the same significance.

The cutting of the *emmer* wheat is followed by the killing of Min's white bull, which, however, is not depicted. Only a priest holding a bull's tail is shown; an identical priest, also with a tail in his hand, is shown above the first. Since the upper priest is on a level with the figure of the queen shown above the procession, this tail in the priest's hand may have belonged to 'the daughter and mother who gave birth to her begetter',[2] who was almost certainly incarnated in the black cow of Min.[3] Among the Bono and the Asante the sacrifice of the black cow of Bosommuru by the queen-mother took place about a week before the killing of the white bull.

The priests holding the tails are not those of Min but priests

[1] The water jugs used in the *kra* purification rite at Takyiman are, for this reason, of copper.

[2] This is said of Mut of Thebes, the mother and wife of Amun-Khamutef (cf. Kees, *Götterglaube*, p. 352). In the representation at Karnak Amun-Re-Khamutef is accompanied by Amaunet in her form of female Khamutef (Jacobsohn, p. 38).

[3] For the black cow of Min see p. 79. There is no direct assertion that the female Khamutef was incarnate in a black cow, but how else can one explain the second tail? These tails, moreover, are curved as if taken from a living animal, and are not to be confused with the straight tail worn by the Pharaoh in certain rites.

serving the Pharaoh. They are here surnamed the 'Satisfied' or 'Satiated', no doubt because the Pharaoh has performed the 'great sacrifice' which will renew his kingship and give it fresh vigour. These priests—their title Gauthier was unable to explain[1]—seem to correspond to the *adumfo* of the Akan, who in the past slaughtered the white bull and the black cow of Bosummuru; the king and queen-mother in Asante, the *Akrafohene* for the king in Bono and the *Akrafo-ba-panyin* for the queen-mother, only pierced the throat of the animal three times. The priests in the reliefs are portrayed looking backwards, possibly at the corpse of the bull (or the cow) to draw attention to their sacrifice. Gauthier, however, believes that they are looking back at the *imy-khant* priest behind them.[2] The *imy-khant* was in charge of the Dual Shrines of the Royal Ancestors, so that this could be interpreted to mean that the act of killing the bull was performed for the Royal Ancestors, whose vigour was also renewed through the rite, since their *kas* were identified with that of the living Pharaoh.[3]

While the Pharaoh's priest shows the tail of the sacrificed animal to the assembled company, bearers bring out the standards of the 'Souls of the East', which are fixed before the statue of the god, but with 'their faces turned backwards'. The 'Souls of the East' may have represented the first kings or chiefs who incarnated Min in Punt and who would thus naturally be regarded as ancestors, or predecessors, of the Pharaoh.[4] Following the text the Pharaoh then 'comes out' of the stairs of Min and, looking towards the north, proceeds to walk round them. It is improbable that the stairs had a chamber inside, but possibly in the rite they were hidden by the screen named 'the shadow of the god' which was carried in the

[1] Gauthier, op. cit., pp. 106, 107.

[2] The priest above the other actually looks back to the statues of the Royal Ancestors.

[3] The relevant passage in the text (second hymn) is: 'the same was done to the living *ka* of the king together with the Royal Ancestors'.

[4] The 'Souls of the East' seem to correspond to the 'Souls of Pe and Nekhen' who were worshipped in the Dual Shrines. 'The Souls of the East' would seem to have been venerated in the *Sn.w.t.*, for Min's title is 'Lord of the *Sn.w.t*'. The meaning of the word is unknown and it has been interpreted in various ways. Kees, *Das Felsheiligtum des Min bei Achmin, Recueil de Travaux*, vol. XXXVI, p. 121, translates the term as 'Doppelhaus', because in the Pyramid texts the *Sn.w.t* are treated as parallel with the Dual Shrines (*Pyr.* 1830). Also on the Palermo stone it is said that the king appears in the *Sn.w.t.* during the accession rites, no doubt acclaimed there by Min and the 'Souls of the East' as he is acclaimed by the 'Souls of Pe and Nekhen' in the Dual Shrines.

procession.¹ The 'shadow of the god' was his mortal soul, his personality embodying his generative force, by contrast with his *ka* which was immortal.² The Pharaoh, personifying the god, may have been divested of his regalia behind the screen before he encircled the stairs in order to induce the Mother-goddess, Isis, to give him rebirth; the full moon is at its highest in the north. The 'Souls of the East' look backwards (towards the Pharaoh and not to the assembly); this, one may assume, is to protect the Pharaoh and the god in their present vulnerable state.

Two hymns are recorded, which may have their place here;³ unfortunately they have come down to us in a very mutilated state. The first urges the god to rise, to appear, assuring him that he has been justified before the tribunal of Re-Atum. He then seems to appear, for he is hailed: 'Hail to thee Min, who impregnates his mother; how mysterious is that which thou hast done to her in the darkness.' The embrace with his mother has rejuvenated his *ka* and his power of fertility, he is reborn; the hymn once more proclaims that Min has been justified and has been pronounced free and pure. A long passage which follows has been almost completely destroyed, only these words remain: 'he brings you the crown' and 'Ramses III sees the crown', meaning that Min, now in renewed strength, has been able to return the crown to Ramses, who has thus regained his kingship.

In the second hymn the Pharaoh is assured that 'Pe and Dep do not reject you' (i.e. the Lower Egyptian Royal Ancestors and the goddess of the crown, Wadjet). Min, here called Min-Horus, the Vigorous, then sends messages from his mother Isis. From the text, therefore, it is clear that not only the god's powers have been

---

¹ C. J. Bleeker, *Die Geburt eines Gottes*, 1956, p. 76, doubts whether it was a building but cannot find another explanation, The Akan god Ntoa, a Sky fertility-god of the Min type, 'dies' in the sacred grove at Seseman-Nkoranza not far from his sanctuary. The rites are performed by the high priest, protected from view by a line of shield-bearers, who, their shields raised, form a wall (see *Ak. of Ghana*, p. 76) while the people dance in a frenzy around him. Also at the Min Khamutef festival dancing took place at this point, see n. 3.

² See p. 81.

³ The word 'hymn' or 'song' is combined with a word that means 'dance'; that is to say, while they were sung or recited by the priests, others danced. Note the dances performed while Ntoa 'died' in the sacred grove (n. 1). The significance of the dance is to create sexual desire and thus stimulate the god and goddess in heaven to perform the sacred marriage so that rebirth can take place.

resurrected, but also those of the Pharaoh. Moreover, in the accompanying scene the Pharaoh is shown with all the insignia of kingship, wearing the double crown, while four birds are released to carry the following proclamation to the four corners of the earth: 'Horus, the son of Isis and Osiris, has assumed the Great Crown of Upper and Lower Egypt; King Ramses III has assumed the Great Crown of Upper and Lower Egypt.'

The relief shows a further scene which might be entitled 'after the rebirth'. The Pharaoh is again depicted wearing the Blue Crown, holding the sickle and a sheaf of *emmer* wheat. The text says: 'to harvest *emmer* for his father so that he is given life'.[1] *Emmer* is then placed on the ground 'before this god'. In other words, Min is offered the first-fruits of the season which had been cut with the sickle, the instrument no doubt having been purified from the defilement of death.[2] Among the Akan, only after the gods, the ancestral spirits, and other non-human spiritual powers, have been offered the new crops may the king and the nation eat of them.

The white bull, disregarding the priest who holds up some ears of grain, walks away out of the picture. Among the Bono and Asante a white bull calf from the sacred herd of the king, born on New Year's day, replaced the old bull. Behind the bull and again above, amidst the text, is the queen. This indicates perhaps the sacred marriage, performed between the Pharaoh, personifying Min-Khamutef, or Amen-Re-Khamutef and herself, the 'wife of the Khamutef', either Isis, Hathor or Mut.[3] Below the bull are

[1] No egyptologist seems to have realised that the cutting of *emmer* wheat has been performed twice; first to indicate the death of the god manifest in vegetation—we only know this through the text programme—and second the rebirth of the god, who gives to his people a plentiful harvest. Bleeker, op. cit., p. 74, complains that the text programme and the representation of the scene, with the accompanying text, differ from each other; sure evidence that the rite must have been performed twice with different meanings, unless one wishes to assume that the Egyptians were inaccurate, which is unlikely on a relief in a royal temple.

[2] One can assume this as the Bosummuru sword which killed the god's white bull in Asante was publicly purified; for greater detail see *Sacred State*, p. 174.

[3] Gauthier, *Fêtes*, p. 100 (1), suggests that she pays homage here to the white bull. This would not be reason enough to depict her in a representation of rituals which are given in shorthand, so to speak, and where everything is symbolic. Frankfort (p. 390 n. 28) suggests the sacred marriage but does not seem to realise that the *shemayt* of the text programme and in the last scene performs two different rituals; in the first she is the protecting mother, in the second the wife.

depicted nine statues[1] of the Royal Ancestors; an adjacent scene shows the Pharaoh making offerings to Min, whose statue is back in his temple. Over it the words are written: 'I give you all the praises of Re, I give you all joy and strength.' There is no further text so that we cannot tell the sequence of events.[2]

Among the Bono the god Bosummuru and the king die and are reborn on the second New Year's day (Thursday); at nightfall the king appears in all his glory and then withdraws with the queen to perform the sacred marriage. On the first New Year's day a great number of snow-white rams are sacrificed and offerings are made to the Royal Ancestors and Bosummuru in the Chapel of the Stools (*Adae* rites). In the afternoon the king, queen-mother, princes and princesses appear in public, surrounded by the court. The *sanaa* is brought out and shown to the people as a signal to begin the harvest. There are great rejoicings. Among the Asante the death and rebirth of the god and the king were performed (on a Monday and Tuesday respectively) before the *Adae* which ended the festival (Sunday). The sacred marriage took place after the great purification ceremonies on the previous Friday.

[1] Nine statues may have been chosen because they symbolise at the same time the 'nine gods'. The 'nine gods', called thus in a liturgy to Min-Horus, the Vigorous, from a 12th Dynasty memorial stone at Abydos, can only be those of the Ennead of Heliopolis who, I maintain, represented nine prehistoric royal lineages which preceded the dynastic one, the *summa summarum* of the Pharaoh's Royal Ancestors.

[2] Bleeker, p. 62, is surprised that there is no indication of celebrating crowds. There are none among the Akan either, as the common people are not allowed to witness the 'death' and rebirth of the king.

CHAPTER IX

The King's Death

AKAN

1. The King's Death

The death of an Akan king was regarded as one of the greatest misfortunes which could befall a state, for it was believed that once the king had died chaos must prevail, because the established order of the universe, embodied in the king's person, was destroyed by his death. If it was necessary to speak of it this was done indirectly—'a great tree has fallen', or 'the fire has died',[1] or simply 'he has gone to his village to cure himself'.[2]

When a king of Bono (or Bono-Takyiman) was ill, he was nursed by the *Ahenemahene*, the chief of the royal sons, whose mothers were commoners. He was assisted by the heir-apparent of the *Daberehene*, the chamberlain; the heir-apparent of the *Manwerehene*, the keeper of the king's clothes and personal effects; the heir-apparent of the *Sodohene*, head cook and supervisor of the royal kitchen; and the heir-apparent of the *Nsafiesohene*, the chief of the cup-bearers and stewards. All these personages were sons of the king or of his predecessor. The *Ahenemahene*, normally the only person permitted to enter the king's bed-chamber when the latter was present, would give him medicine, prepared by the *Sumankwahene*, the king's physician. When all hope of recovery was gone, the *Korontihene*, the governor and administrator of the state, was called in to witness the king's death, as also were the *Daberehene*, the

---

[1] A fire symbolising the *kra* of the king, that of his Royal Ancestors, was maintained and guarded by his senior wife and was never permitted to go out as long as he lived. When he died it was extinguished by her. The senior wife of the succeeding king kindled a new fire. See also *Sacred State*, p. 75.

[2] In the past whoever said plainly that the king was dead, was killed.

Manwerehene, the *Sodohene* and the *Nsafiesohene*. When the king was at the point of death, the four household officers arranged themselves in the form of a cross around his bed, one behind him, one on either side of him and one at his feet. They lifted him slightly, for a king must be carried with his head resting on the chest of the one behind him, while the *Ahenemahene* gave him water for the last time, saying, 'Receive this water and do not permit an evil thing to come whence you are setting out.' The king then expired.

If it so happened that he was incurably ill and dying by slow degrees, the *Banmuhene*, the custodian of the royal cemetery and mausoleum,[1] was summoned by the *Korontihene* to hasten his death. In the past, owing to the death tabu, the king was never allowed to see the *Banmuhene* when he was not well, for it was feared that if he did so he might die. When the king himself, and those who surrounded him, wished that he should die, however, the *Banmuhene* was permitted not only to come into the royal presence, but to touch the king gently from head to foot, saying at the same time, '*gyako*'—'I sympathise with you.' It is said that whenever this took place the king died soon afterwards.

Whether the *Banmuhene* was present at the king's death or not, the *Korontihene* officially informed him of it secretly through a messenger, on the fifteenth day after it took place, telling him at the same time to come immediately to the palace to take charge of the body. (This had been washed and cared for in the preceding fourteen days by the *Banmuhemmaa*, usually the mother or sister of the *Banmuhene*, and the other old women of her family.)[2] Meanwhile other messengers of the *Korontihene* had informed the *Gyaasehene*, the chief of the royal household and palace, who immediately summoned all the stool-sons of the late king, who lived

---

[1] The mausoleum of the Bono kings and queen-mothers was burnt to the ground before the Asante entered Bono-Mansu, the capital, after their conquest of the country in 1740. The mausoleum of the kings and queen-mothers of Bono-Takyiman at Takyiman was destroyed in 1877 when the king, the queen-mother and all the chiefs of the state and their families left their country to continue the war with the Asante from Gyaman. A photograph, showing the mausoleum of the Asante kings (demolished by the British when they entered Kumasi in 1895 after a victorious war) is reproduced in the *Sacred State*, pl. 98.

[2] The intestines of the royal corpse were given an infusion, the ingredients of which are now forgotten, which had the effect of making the body stiff and the flesh dry; decomposition was thus prevented so long as the body was exposed to the air. See also *Sacred State*, p. 63.

THE KING'S DEATH

in the capital. Furthermore the *Adumfohene*, the chief of the executioners, was ordered to surround the palace with a number of *adumfo*. Meantime rumours were spread by the heralds that 'Nana is not well', or 'Nana has gone elsewhere to cure himself', with the object of preparing the people for the catastrophe.

In addition to these the *Akyeamehene*, the chief royal spokesman, was also given the news. Thereupon he, together with the chief stool-bearer and his assistants, removed the Golden Stool (the enthronement stool of the kings of Bono)[1] and the sacred black stools from the Chapel of the Stools. This was done, on the one hand, so that the king's body could be placed in the Chapel which would become desecrated through contact with death, and on the other to prevent any prince from usurping the throne by enstooling himself. The stools were taken secretly at night to the house of the *Werempehene*, the chief of the *werempefo*, a body composed of selected members of the royal lineage and sons and daughters of a king, heirs to the *Gyaase* and *Koronti* stools. The stools were returned to the Chapel the night before the enstoolment ceremony of the new king. While the stools were in the *Werempehene's* house, the *Akyeamehene* poured a libation to the *kras* of the Royal Ancestors each day, while the *Sodohene* poured a daily libation in the front room of the Chapel of the Stools. The *Sodohene* was chosen for this duty, because he was regarded as the 'wife' of the *kras* of the black stools; he cooked the offerings to the Royal Ancestors and cooking is regarded as a female occupation. Owing to the desecration of the Chapel only libations were poured out; food offerings were not made until the funeral was over. The significance of the libation was to tell the Royal Ancestors that they would receive offerings again when a new king had been enstooled.

The first to come into the presence of the corpse, besides the *Banmuhene*, was the *Adiakahene*, the chief of the Adiaka clan, a descendant of the kings who once ruled the Dia-Mo kingdom.[2] He

---

[1] It is not known what has happened to the Golden Stool; the Golden Stool now in the possession of the queen-mother of Asante is believed by the Bono-Takyimanhene to be the stool that the last queen-mother of Bono, Dwambara Akenten, had made for herself but was not permitted to use on official occasions. The queen-mother's stool was the silver stool.

[2] The Dia-Mo or Djomo kingdom, once situated in the furthest north-west corner of the Northern Territories of Ghana (Gold Coast), was destroyed c. 1330 by the Mossi. The last king, Adu Kodjo, with his followers, sought refuge in Bono.

was given *ntoasie* by the *Ahenemahene* (that is to say, a payment in advance for things promised); in olden days this was gold dust and a bottle of rum to pour a libation before the corpse of the deceased king. After the libation the *Adiakahene* placed the *adiaka-duro*, a bowl filled with water and medicinal herbs, in front of the body; this was to enable the king to cure himself of the disease which had caused his death and so be able to enter heaven, the Upper Kingdom, in good health. He then took a piece from the king's white cloth and wrapped it round a staff (*adiaka-pomum*) the shrine of the god Damankama, the *obosom* of the Adiaka clan. This staff had to remain near the king's body till its burial. The *adiaka-pomum* still exists today; it is said to be a short, thick stick plated with gold; all the pieces of material tied to it, taken from the cloths of dead kings for several centuries, have made it large and unwieldy.[1]

By the second day the *Banmuhene* had finished treating the royal corpse, which he had rubbed and rubbed again with alcohol; he also poured gin or rum down its throat to prevent its decomposing too soon. If necessary he took it to the *Banmu* to drain it of all liquid. On the third day the *Gyaasehene* and the stool-sons came to take the body to the bathing house in the palace to wash it ritually. This was done with lime or lemon juice, applied with a sponge made from the bark of the plantain tree.[2] The juice was used to dry and perfume the skin, whereas water might have hastened decomposition. During this procedure the dead king was seated on a new stool that he had had made for himself for this purpose; this stool was later blackened and preserved in the Chapel of the Stools; his feet rested on elephant tusks.[3] As each stool-son came forward to play his part in the rite, the attendant he had brought with him was strangled by the *adumfo*, with the words '*Kogya wo Nana*'—'Walk before your king' and 'carry his cloths, his pillows, his boxes' and so forth. The bathing ritual was preceded by the sacrifice of two beautiful girls and during it the king's senior wife and his *okra* (the bearer of his *kra*) were killed, after they had performed all the rites, so that they might go with him into the other world.

When the stool-sons had left, the *Banmuhene* and his assistants dressed the dead king's body in his most costly cloth and adorned it

[1] It is impossible to say whether this staff is the original one or a copy made at a later time.

[2] The lime or lemon here symbolises the sun; the plantain, a recognised phallic symbol, the fertility of the sun personified by the king.

[3] The elephant is a royal emblem.

with the gold ornaments he had worn during his life. In earlier times the corpse was then set up in state on the *asipim* throne chair in the Chapel of the Stools; later the corpse was laid out in state on its left side, with legs slightly drawn up; the left hand was placed under the left cheek, while the right hand and the head rested in bowls filled with gold dust. Gold dust was poured into the ears of the dead king, so that he could hear; it was also strewn over his eyes and eyebrows so that he could see, and his bare right shoulder was covered with it. Little bags filled with gold dust were attached to his wrists; this was the money (*kra sika*) believed to be necessary for his *kra* to use on his journey into the other world. The *Banmuhemmaa* sat at the head of the corpse to drive the flies away; an elder woman from her house sat behind her, to take over her task when she fell asleep from exhaustion. This was done for nine days. Only the *Banmu* people were allowed to enter the room in the Chapel where the king lay in state, with the exception of the *adumfo*, who brought in the victims for the human sacrifice each day. These unfortunate people were caught in the street, their heads were cut off, shown to the dead king, then placed in brass basins before the bed for a day or two. Their bodies were thrown into the bush at night in a place called Bogyawea—'there is blood all the time'.

Food offerings consisting of the favourite dishes of the king also stood in little bowls in front of the bed. Sheep caught each day in the streets by the *Banmu* people provided the meat for these. The king's most important wives sat in the neighbouring room during the nine days; defiled by death, they sat on the floor with legs stretched out, wailing and weeping. Formerly on the night of the burial they were sacrificed; they could choose either to be poisoned or strangled by female *adumfo*, so that they might follow their husband to Nyankopon-kurom, the city of the Sun-god.

From the day when the *Adumfohene* was secretly told of the king's death, the executioners guarded the palace, and everybody who entered its gates was taken aside and asked to which clan and family he belonged. If he was a prince of the royal lineage he was hidden and his family was allowed to 'buy his head' by paying a fine; if he was a commoner of the royal Ayoko clan a thin, sharp stick was rammed down his throat.[1] All the king's sons, whether

---

[1] One informant said that ceremonial chewing sticks, decorated with divine symbols, were used for this purpose. For illustrations see *Sacred State*, Pl. 46, and *Ak. of Ghana*, Pl. 44.

stool-sons (chiefs or heirs to chief's stools) or *ahenema* (commoners) could return unmolested; everybody else was taken to the room where the king lay in state and executed on the spot. All persons employed in the palace who were not royal sons were seized and sacrificed, unless they managed to flee to a sanctuary.[1]

At last, four days after the secret announcement of the death, the news was made public. This was done by the *adumfo*. Early in the morning they appeared in a body in the streets, their faces blackened with charcoal; their drummers beating the *atopre* drum, the signal that killings were to take place. They were soon joined by those sons of the king who served in the royal bodyguard, and others who cared to follow them. Maddened with grief, they roamed the streets, killing everybody who crossed their path. In the markets they 'turned over things', a custom called *dwabum*. Since the lord of the land was no more chaos prevailed. Looting took place; the executioners were allowed to enter the houses of the chiefs and to seize their *asipim* chairs. The slaughter and pillage went on everywhere for the nine days during which the king's body lay in state, except in the main street outside the palaces of the king, the queen-mother, and the chiefs of the town. It was realised that no outside disturbances should interfere with the rites and ceremonies which were being performed there daily until the night of the burial.

A few hours after the *adumfo* had cleared the streets, a procession was formed in front of the queen-mother's palace. A bearer carrying the state sword was at the head, followed by *mpintin* drummers.[2] Then came the daughters and sisters of the king, the queen-mother and the heiress-apparent and other female members of the royal lineage. They were followed by the sons of the king, the great chiefs of the state, the princes and finally the heir-apparent, all of them throwing ashes over their heads, wailing and weeping and rending their garments. Male and female *adumfo* surrounded them

[1] The nearest sanctuary was the temple of the state god, situated opposite the king's and queen-mother's palaces. (In Bono the king's palace was situated behind that of the heir-apparent and co-regent.) If the people who wished to save themselves, which always included royal wives who had been secretly warned by their eunuchs, managed to hold on to the cloth of a sacred person— the high priest of any god, the custodian of the Chapel of the Stools, the *Akrafohene*, for instance—they were pardoned by the new king and, after a purification ceremony, were free to live where they liked.

[2] The *mpintin* is a kind of tabor, tabret, tambourine or timbrel, which had been introduced into Bono by refugees from the Mande-Wangara country in the reign of Berempon Katakyira (1564–95).

with drawn swords and knives. They walked three times from one end of the main road to the other, the stretch between the two sacred trees of the town on either side of the *gya dua kra*[1] before the palace, then they returned to the square in front of the palace.

Before each stool-son a stylised figure of the king, the so-called *adosowa*, was carried. Every one of these had been constructed with loving care by the wives of the stool-sons to comfort and honour their husbands in their great grief, for on the night of the burial their mothers had to sacrifice themselves. The body of the figure was made with a hoe and a pillow; the shoulders of a stick;[2] a *nsaa* blanket[3] was wrapped round to hold the whole together. It was then dressed in precious *kente* cloth,[4] which also formed the rectangular head supported by the blade of the hoe, and was adorned with a gold chain which only the king had the right to wear; the arms were made from silk handkerchiefs. The *adosowa* was then placed in a brass basin and covered with white cloth. Each one was carried by a young woman, the *adosowa suani*, literally the disciple of the *adosowa*.[5] Before the figure walked the two most beautiful girls of the stool-son's lineage, called *adosowa adagya*, the 'naked *adosowa*'; the girls wore nothing but a loin-cloth, the *mma ntan*. Their bodies, however, were covered with fine, intricate designs in all colours of the rainbow, consisting of heavenly symbols. They wore precious beads round their necks, arms, and legs. Their hair was cut short and shaved in a design of four half-moons.

When the procession had returned to the square in front of the palace the *adosowa* were put down; each one was placed on a *nsaa* cloth, and a jug of water with a brass basin was placed in front of it. The naked girls sat down next to their *adosowa*. Then a sister of the deceased king approached and, wailing, poured some of the water on the ground, placing a stone each time on the spot where the water had been spilt.[6] In the evening another procession was formed

[1] See p. 217 n. 2.
[2] In other places these shoulders are more usually made with the scales used for weighing gold dust.
[3] The *nsaa* blankets are still imported into Ghana from the Timbuktu region. Their designs are identical with those on North African Berber rugs and are composed of triangles, lozenges and squares which, among the Akan, symbolise the various aspects of their deities.
[4] The *kente* is locally woven and consists of a number of strips of cotton-cloth sewn together. See illustration, Pl. 19.
[5] For the *adosowa* custom in Asante see *Sacred State*, p. 71.
[6] I was unable to get an explanation for this rite but it seems to be the same as the one in which the priest of a clan rubs the blood of the sacrificed totem

and the *adosowa* were again taken from one end of the main street to the other. They were then carried into the Chapel of the Stools and left for the night near the body of the dead king.

The next morning and the following days until the burial the *adosowa* were not carried through the street but set down straight away on the square before the palaces. The *adosowa adagya* girls changed their loin-cloths and beads every day. The women kept up the weeping and wailing until the ninth day, the twenty-eighth day after the king's death.

On the morning of that day the *adosowa* were again carried in procession three times from one end of the main road to the other, but this time the stool-sons walked before their *adosowa*, firing guns (arrows in early days). No facial marks were worn by the mourners, for on the morning of that day the *Korontihene* had sent heralds through the streets informing the people that the fast was over, and had sent a sheep to the queen-mother, thus indicating that the 'time had come for washing', i.e. for washing off the facial marks. The queen-mother then appeared with her retinue before her palace, in order to encourage the people to follow her example. Apart from brief outbreaks of wailing, the atmosphere gradually changed from one of deepest mourning to happiness, even merrymaking. For on the night of that day the king's body was to be buried; he would be on his way to heaven to join his ancestors and from there he would give life, as well as support and protection, to his people on earth. Guns were fired continuously to encourage the dead to shoot life from the sky; the *adosowa adagya* danced before their *adasowa* and ate publicly from the dishes of food set before them. This had been cooked by the wives of the stool-sons to encourage others to break the fast. Drink was liberally supplied by the stool-sons to all those concerned with the making of their *adosowa*, and to the people in their households.

To comfort their mourning husbands their wives placed gold chains (*asisiada*) round their husbands' necks on which hung little bags containing gold dust; they thus showed publicly their love and sympathy for them in the loss of their mothers during the coming night. Some of the wives also placed small dishes of ripe pawpaw before their *adosowa* as a symbol of the softness or kindness which the dead king had shown towards them; some, on the other hand,

animal or its substitute into the sacred tree of the god and then quickly pours a libation of palm-wine over it to undo 'death', so to speak.

placed dishes of pepper to indicate how cruelly he had treated them; this was to give public expression to their feelings, so that no bitter memories of the dead should remain. In the end everybody drank and danced in order to forget their unhappiness; they danced with relief also, for after that night the human sacrifices would cease until the funeral ceremonies started about fourteen days later.

In the evening the *adosowa* were again carried in procession, after which they were taken back to the stool-sons' houses and were then destroyed, but not before the husbands had given a considerable amount of gold dust to their wives, and had made presents to all those who had helped in making the effigies. The pillows and hoes were thrown on a refuse heap in the bush, and the cloths, gold chains, and silk handkerchiefs were returned to their owners.[1]

2. The King's Burial

While the people slept in exhaustion the king's body was laid in a coffin by the *Ahenemahene* and the sons of the king in whose presence he had died. The act was supervised by the *Gyaasehene* as the eldest of the stool-sons. The coffin had been made by the *Banmu* people from the wood of the silk cotton tree; it was finely carved with the divine symbols. The body of the king was laid in it, resting on the left side, the legs slightly drawn up and the head lying in a bowl filled with gold dust. When the coffin was closed the *Sodohene* poured a libation in the Chapel of the Stools with liquor supplied by the chiefs of the state council. The coffin was then placed in the king's palanquin and covered with precious cloth. A procession was formed, composed of the *Gyaasehene*, the *Ahenemahene* and the victims for sacrifice, who included a son and daughter of the king both of whom he had loved dearly.[2] Each section of the royal household had to supply one victim to serve their lord in the Upper Kingdom; each section of the palace personnel, sword and shield-bearers, palanquin and umbrella carriers, stool-bearers, sandal-bearers, drummers, blowers of the state horns, and so forth, in-

[1] Information for this and the following sections was supplied by the *Ahenemahene* Kwasi Twi, the *Gyaasehene* Yaw Atoa, the *Banmuhene* Kwame Twi, the *Adumfohene* Kofi Fofie, the *Abrafohene* of the *Adumfo* Kwasi Wusu, the *Akyeamehene* Kwaku Ankoma, the *Sumankwahene* Kwaame Boto, the *Nkondwasoafohene*, the *Adiakahene* Kwaame Kra, the *Sodohene* Yaw Duro, the chronicler Kwaame Nyame, the *Akwamubaa-panyin* of the queen-mother Yaa Anaa and the oldest woman of the *Werempehene*'s house.

[2] During their life-time these wore the golden *kra* disk like the *akrafo*.

cluding an *odumfo*, had also to give one member. In addition a large number of captives, criminals, and slaves, besides others who of their own free will wished to follow their king into death. In this procession also went the *Korontihene*, who had to witness the burial on behalf of the state. *Adumfo* with drawn knives and swords preceded and flanked the procession and killed everybody, without exception, who set eyes on it.

While the procession moved to the *Banmu Kese*, the royal cemetery, the king's wives in the harem went to their death. They had had permission from the queen-mother to go home and bid farewell to their families, after which they decked themselves as if for a ceremonial feast, and put on all their jewellery. They were given wine, or rum to drink themselves into a state of semi-consciousness, and were then strangled by women *adumfo*. A wake was kept by the queen-mother and the chiefs and head women of the king's and the queen-mother's state councils in which drumming and drinking figured prominently.

When the procession arrived in the *Banmu Kese* the grave had already been prepared by the *Banmuhene* and his sons. In the morning the *Adiakahene* and his group had marked the spot with the claw of an *apatan* (aardvark), the totem animal of his clan. The grave consisted of one large chamber for the coffin and a small one for the offerings and the toilet articles and favourite objects of the dead king. Before the coffin was lowered and placed in position, with the king's head pointing west, his feet east and his face turned to the south, the human sacrifices were strangled with leather thongs and so dispatched to serve their lord in the other world. Their bodies were laid in rows in the grave forming a truncated pyramid, the base for the coffin. The chamber was then closed with a finely carved door made from the wood of the silk cotton tree. The neighbouring chamber was filled with a little table on which were arranged the favourite dishes of the king, water in earthenware jugs, and some of his personal effects laid on mats. It was then closed with three trunks placed across the opening so that no earth should fall on the contents. Then the grave was filled and the surface smoothed over. Only the *abusua kuruwa*, an earthenware vessel with the stylised portrait of the dead king, marked the spot.[1]

---

[1] In Asante the potteress who was to make the *abusua kuruwa* (a woman from Aboakwa, about six miles from Kumasi) was summoned to the palace when a new king was enstooled. She had to look at him well to memorise his

It contained the nail parings and hair of the king, which were cut off when the corpse was bathed by the stool-sons. On the next day a hut was built over the grave, which remained closed for a year until the completion of the funeral ceremonies. During that time no food was offered to the dead king in his grave.

On the anniversary of the king's death, the *Adumfohene* and the *adumfo* were commissioned 'to see how the corpse was', a custom called *adafa*. They marched like soldiers through the town, preceded by dancing female *adumfo*, singing and merry-making to attract as many strangers as possible. When they reached the *Banmu Kese*, the *adumfo* seized them and sacrificed them before the grave was opened by the *Banmuhene*. Hence the name *adafa*, which means 'to decoy', 'allure', or 'entice'. The coffin was then opened and the *Banmuhene* inspected the body to see whether all the flesh and tissues had rotted away, a process that had been hastened by cutting holes in the bottom board of the coffin, thus letting in ants and other insects to gnaw away the flesh. If all was satisfactory the king's skeleton was taken away to be cleansed by the *Banmu* people. The bones were then rubbed with grease perfumed with fragrant oil from the *bedewonua* tree[1] and articulated with gold wire; pieces of cast gold closed the hollow of the eyes. The skeleton was beautifully dressed and adorned and placed on its back in another coffin plated with gold into which the divine symbols were hammered. The coffin was then carried to the royal mausoleum, the last resting place of the kings, which was situated in the precincts of the *Banmu Kese*.

3. *The King's Funeral Rites*

The first stage of the funeral rites ended with the burial of the king. In the days which followed the successor to the throne was elected and enstooled by the queen-mother. The first act of the new king was to arrange the *Ayikeseada*, the performance of funeral ceremonies by each of the principal chiefs or state elders, lasting

features as she was not allowed to see him again. When the king died the *Gyaasehene* sent her a present of rum, a sheep, and a large brass pan. This pan she had to fill with water and then gaze at it till she could see the image of the deceased king. After that she modelled his figure on the *abusua kuruwa*, which was finally placed before the coffin in the mausoleum at Bantama.

[1] The name *bedewonua* is said to mean 'desire your sister', a name which no doubt has a reference to the king. He must be viewed in this context as the incarnation of Bosummuru, who married the goddess Bosummuru, his female twin.

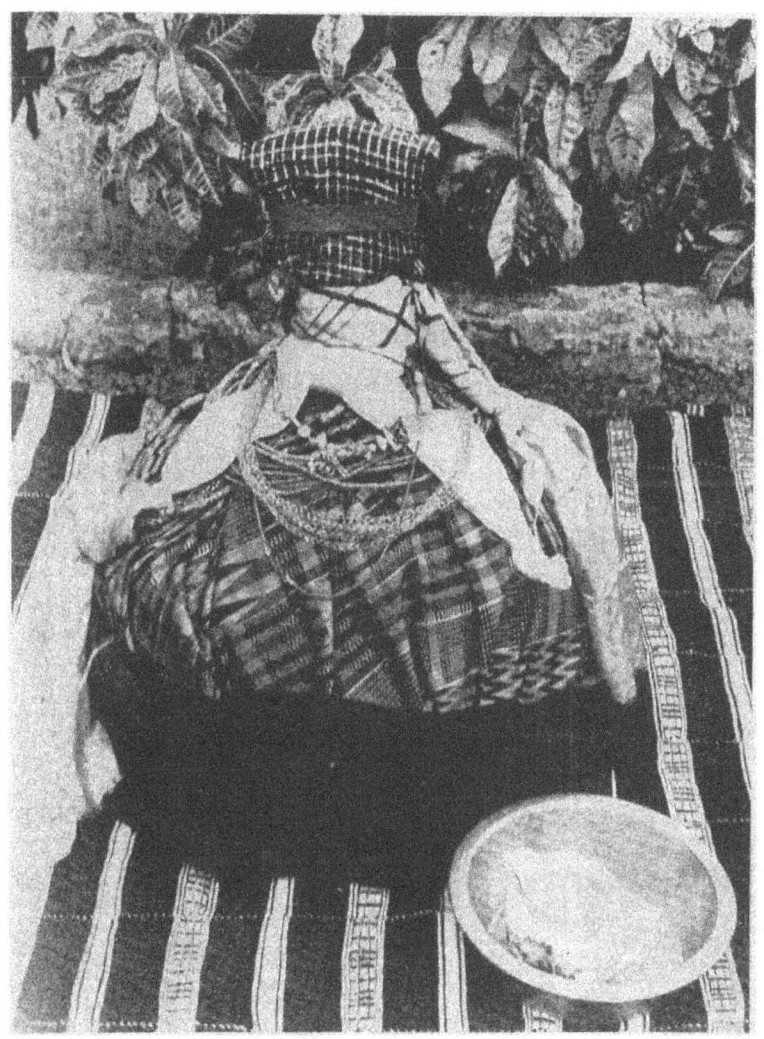

19. *Adosowa*, the effigy of a deceased Akan king.

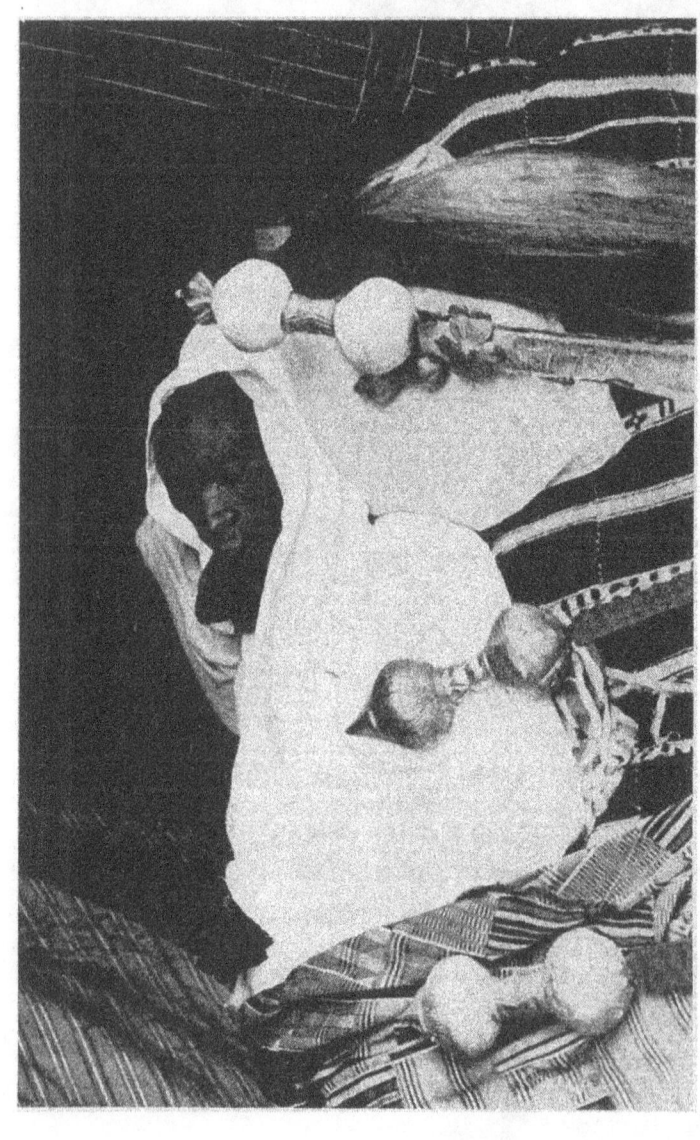

20. The Brother of Nana Akumfi Ameyaw III, lying in state, a cola nut, the symbol of life, closes his mouth. The two state swords symbolise his royalty, the *kra* sword his divine *kra*.

seven days and ending on the fortieth day after the late king's death. The ceremonies had to begin on a Tuesday, the day of Abena (planet Mars), the god of fierce strength, or a Wednesday, the day of Aku (planet Mercury), the leader of dead souls, the Royal Ancestors, or a Thursday, the day of Yaw (planet Jupiter), the god of death and resurrection in the beyond. Once the day was fixed messengers, accompanied by bearers carrying drink, were sent to all the chiefs in the state and to kings of neighbouring countries, inviting them to come to the capital to take part in the ceremonies. They were expected to arrive with their followers a day before the funeral started. It was a day of quiet mourning, on which everybody in the town shaved his hair as a sign of grief; this hair was then tightly packed into bundles and desposited by the *banmu* people behind the late king's grave. Some of it was strewn along the road from the palace to the grave. Hair had the significance of money which the dead man needs on his way to the netherword.[1] On the evening of the same day, after sunset, the funeral was announced by the firing of guns, drumming, and the blowing of the state horns. Men and women rushed to the square before the palaces, wailing and weeping, to take part in the mourning vigil throughout the night. At about 10 o'clock next morning the new king and the queen-mother, accompanied by the whole court, seated themselves in a large open place just outside the town, ready to receive the guests from other countries and the chiefs of the kingdom or their representatives. In a long procession the visitors filed past, followed by their retinues and bearers carrying gifts. These consisted as a rule of kegs of gunpowder, gold dust, slaves destined for sacrifice, and cattle, sheep, and chickens for offerings. When the greetings were over the chiefs and sub-chiefs of the country were led into the palace and into the room in the Chapel of the Stools where the late king had lain in state. His bed was still there, but his body was replaced by an effigy, or simply by a pillow. Before this figure, or symbol, each chief had to swear an oath as follows: 'I swear *Wukuoda*, *Yaaoda* and *Tainso*, that if you had been killed in war I would have joined you in death.[2] But a natural

[1] Note that *kra sika* or *kra* gold was given to the dead king, personified by his *kra*, to use on his way to the sun in the Upper Kingdom; hair was given to his *saman*, or shade.

[2] The reference is to a lost battle that took place at Tainso on a Wednesday (*Wukuoda*) and Thursday (*Yaaoda*) in a war against the Nsawkaw people in the last century.

death has taken place, which nobody can prevent.' The chief then pointed to the shackled human victims who had accompanied him and said: 'Nana, here is somebody to serve you', whereupon an executioner stepped forward and cut off the heads of the unfortunate men. The heads were gathered in brass pans and placed before the bed, and the bodies carried away and thrown into the bush in the place called Bogyawea.[1] Some of the skulls and jawbones were taken to decorate war drums and horns. When the chiefs returned they were greeted by the king and sat down and were offered liberal amounts of drink. They were entertained with drumming and dancing by the *adumfo* women and salvoes in memory of the dead ruler were fired continuously by the hundreds of men of the *Korontihene*. At sunset a procession was formed and everybody returned home, but the state drums boomed throughout the night and the wailing and weeping started anew.

Each of the following days was assigned to one of the great chiefs of the state council in order of seniority, to honour the dead king in the same way as the *Korontihene* had done, with processions, firing of muskets, drumming and dancing,[2] the men wearing the wardress of their ancestors. On the seventh, the last day, it was the turn of the new king, assisted by the *Gyaasehene* and the stool-sons, to honour his predecessor.

In the morning of the preceding day the *Korontihene* had sent bearers to all the important chiefs, asking them to prepare themselves for the funeral feast and the ceremonies on the following day. A number of sheep were sent to the foreign visitors and their retinues. The king's performance started at about 10 o'clock in the evening with a night-long vigil on the square before the palace. Drinks were served to all those present, while state drums were beaten incessantly.

Before the ceremonies began the following morning the king, the queen-mother, and all the chiefs ate in their own houses dishes prepared from the meat of animals sacrificed early in the morning in the Chapel of the Stools. About 2 p.m. people thronged the square to watch the procession leaving for the site just outside the town where the funeral ceremonies were again to take place. In this procession was carried, in a palanquin, the *abusuwa kuruwa*

---

[1] See p. 190.
[2] The purpose of the shooting at funerals is to induce the deceased to shoot 'life' from the sky; the dancing is to induce him to bestow fertility.

which had been fetched from the *Banmu*. Before it sat the *Awusu*, a boy under the age of puberty, who personified the *kra* of the late king;[1] he wore the king's war-dress covered with charms, the sacred dress of the Royal Ancestors. The palanquin was carried by stool-sons and canopied by the double state umbrella. The new king followed on foot preceded by the royal insignia and surrounded by soldiers of the royal bodyguard, firing guns. When the procession reached its destination, the *abusuwa kuruwa* was placed on an *asipim* throne chair set on a dais and the *Awusu* seated himself before it. Below the dais in two rows sat the *akrafo*, dressed in white, holding their *kra* swords, and the state sword-bearers. On the right of the dais, but farther forward, sat the new king under a state umbrella, surrounded by his retinue; a little farther away sat the queen-mother with her women weeping and wailing. Opposite were arrayed the tables heaped with offerings and the rams which would be sacrificed in the night to purify the Chapel of the Stools. All the treasures of the state were displayed.

The *Gyaasehene* with the *gyaase* and his numerous followers, performed the ceremonies in much the same way as the chiefs had done on the preceding days. Marching in procession they filed past the king, the queen-mother, and the chiefs of the country, each seated under an umbrella (the sign of his rank) and accompanied by his followers. Guns were fired continuously. After a time the king returned the greetings of the *Gyaasehene* and his people and those of the chiefs, going from one to the other. Drinks were served liberally; there was much drumming and dancing, especially by the *adumfo* women, who fell into trances, often brandishing knives. Towards the end of the afternoon the *Abrafohene*, the master of ceremonies and minstrel of the *adumfo*, took his seat next to the king on his *asipim* throne chair and sang into his ear tales of the great deeds of the Royal Ancestors. Meantime the king's eyes moved wildly round the assembled company and from time to time he pointed towards someone whom he wished to follow his predecessor into death. The people were then taken away and sacrificed by the *adumfo*. At last a man, helplessly drunk, was brought to the king. His neck was broken by the *adumfo* and people then danced in a

---

[1] The *Akrafohene* personified the *kra* of the living king; the *Awusu* that of the deceased king who had not yet been resurrected in heaven. He had been chosen by the late king when still alive; when the boy reached maturity, another, whom the king loved, took his place.

THE KING'S DEATH

frenzy around the corpse. He was the last victim and it was believed that without him the dead king would not be able to enter the Upper Kingdom. Then all the chiefs got up and shouted '*gya wo kwan*', 'we have sent you off', meaning the dead ruler. Drink-bearers appeared and placed pots containing palm-wine before the king and the chiefs. A royal spokesman then asked for a libation to be poured out so that 'Nana can go away now'. As he passed each of the important chiefs he poured a little from each cup onto the ground. When they had all finished drinking, the spokesman began singing '*agyani yee*', and the chiefs answered in chorus three times '*yee*'. Then the spokesman said, 'You whose name should not be mentioned, we have sent you off.' Thereupon the chiefs drew back their chairs three times and rose as one man. Slowly and quietly everybody walked home. The king returned to his palace, carried on the shoulders of his men, followed by the *fontomfrom* state drums.[1] Only the *Awusu*, seated below the *abusua kuruwa*, remained with the *akrafo*, the state sword-bearers, and the princes of the royal lineage to keep watch till dawn. *Adumfo* and *ahenema* of the king's bodyguard kept guard.

Late in the evening the *Werempefo* (see next section) assembled and went in procession to the royal cemetery (*Banmu Kese*) to take part in a rite to enable the late king to transfigure himself in heaven and become one with the *nananom*, the Royal Ancestors.

4. *The King's Ascension and Transfiguration*

(The *Werempe* ritual as it is still performed for the king and the queen-mother at Takyiman.)

The *Werempe* custom was introduced into the Bono kingdom by Gyamfi Kumanini (1669–84) at the command of the state god **Tano**.[2] The ritual is carried out by a body of people (*Werempefo*) which still exists at Takyiman and consists of elderly princes and princesses of the royal lineage and *adehye*, heirs of both sexes to the *Gyaasehene's* and the *Korontihene's* stools, who are sons and daughters of the late king or one of his predecessors. The *Werempehene* or chief of the *Werempe*, who is a member of the State Council,

---

[1] See *Ak. of Ghana*, Pl. 4. This photograph was taken by me during the funeral ceremonies performed by the Bono-Takyimanhene for his brother, who was generally regarded as the heir-apparent, in November 1949. See also this vol., Pls. 20 and 21.

[2] *Ak. of Ghana*, ch. V, p. 17.

represents the commoners at the rituals.[1] The *Werempefo* have two duties after the death of a king: to seize all the black stools in the Chapel of the Stools in order to prevent any prince from usurping the throne by enstooling himself, and to assist the late king to become transformed into a god in heaven, so that his *kra* may become divine power in his successor.

In the evening following the last funeral custom, the *Werempefo* from the houses of the *Gyaasehene* and the *Korontihene* daub their faces with a mixture of gin and gunpowder to enable them to see the spirit of the deceased king; those of the princes and princesses who take part in the rite are daubed with *ntwuma* (ochre, the symbol of grief) by a woman from the *Korontihene's* household, who is entitled to charge a fee for this service. Everybody is given bunches of leaves or branches of a tree, which they carry in order to console those who are watching, for 'if the branches of a tree have been cut down, this is not the end; new life springs from the nodes' (i.e. if a king has died, another from the same family will succeed).

When the *Werempefo* are ready they gather in the *Korontihene's* house in order to cover the stool of the late king with *nsaa* cloth;[2] they sew the ends together so that it cannot become displaced and reveal the stool. The stool is the one on which the naked corpse of the king was bathed. A state sword is then placed on top of it and a libation to the Royal Ancestors poured over it three times before it is carried out. A procession is then formed by the *Werempefo*; the stool is borne under a state umbrella by the *yereba*, the first-born of the favourite wife of the late king,[3] who is believed to have been the most beloved of his children. *Ahenema*, the royal sons and daughters, join the procession led by the *Ankobeahene*, the chief of the royal bodyguard (always the son of a king)[4] and the wives of the late king, who carry staffs of elephant grass to symbolise their loss.[5]

[1] His title as chief of the commoners is *Asonkohene*. In other Akan states the *Werempefo* are chosen from different sections of the population, see *Sacred State*, p. 65.

[2] The Chapel of the Stools was still desecrated—the late king had lain in state there before his body was taken to the burial place. Till it had been purified all the black stools and the white stool of the late king were kept in the *Korontihene's* house, where the *Akyeamehene* poured a daily libation to the Royal Ancestors.

[3] The 'favourite wife' is a title applied to an heiress princess from the *Gyaasehene's* house, the mother of a future *Gyaasehene* 'the eldest son'.

[4] The *Ankobeahene* is also the teacher and trainer of the royal sons; see p. 218 n. 3.

[5] Formerly, of course, the royal wives were sacrificed, except for those who managed to escape in time.

Adumfo, the executioners, dance around it, brandishing their swords and firing guns; women *adumfo*, armed with knives, fall into trances. The procession moves to the *Banmu*, the royal cemetery, and nobody is permitted to enter the town all night. The *Werempefo* have the right to seize any sheep and fowls they may come across on the road.

It was explained to me that the carrying of the late king's stool to the *Banmu* means 'to see his spirit off so that it can join the Royal Ancestors in heaven, to become one with them'. The *Werempefo* watch the stool, which is placed on an offering table from the Chapel of the Stools, throughout the night until they see 'the dead king return as spirit'. In order to keep awake, they cook and eat the sheep and fowls they have seized as well as the three rams the new king has given them.[1] They drum and dance and leap round the stool to keep themselves awake, while guns are fired incessantly. To induce the late king (that is to say, his *kra, honhom* and *saman*) 'to settle in the stool' libations of gin, given by the new king, are poured out three times—once when the stool is placed in position by the *Banmuhene*, the custodian of the royal cemetery, once at midnight, and once at daybreak. When, shortly after this, the late king 'is seen', transfigured into a Royal Ancestor, all guns are fired simultaneously. The guns are answered by the acclamations of the hundreds of women and young girls who are present. The stool, now charged with divine power, is then taken in triumph to the new king 'to bring him his power'. He has sat all night in the audience courtyard, weeping most of the time and chewing a tuft of *bahama* grass to signify his intense grief, while the *ntumpane* (talking drums) have been proclaiming the brave deeds of the Royal Ancestors. The stool is placed beside him for a while; later in the morning it is carried out and, still covered up, is displayed before the palace gates under a state umbrella. This is to tell the people that their ruler is now endowed with divine power. In the evening the stool is taken to the Chapel of the Stools to be blackened.

In the Bono kingdom the stool of every deceased king was blackened from the time of Gyamfi Kumanini onwards (1669–84); earlier the stools were plated with gold.[2] The blackening of a king's stool

---

[1] No offerings, however, are made to the late king.

[2] This emphasised a theological change from the theory of *kra*, or disembodied power, to that of *saman*, ghost or shade, resurrected, transfigured in heaven.

came to be regarded as the greatest honour that could be conferred on a ruler; for this reason in many Akan states only the stools of kings who had proved to be true 'life-givers' were blackened. This is still so today.

The blackening of the stool (*apunia*) is done in the courtyard of the Chapel of the Stools in the presence of the *Gyaasehene*, who must witness the rite as the state's representative. The actual work is done by the *Nkondwasoafohene* and his assistant stool-bearers; as the custodian of the Chapel he is in charge of all the black stools. The *Nsumankwahene*, the priest of Bosummuru, guardian of the spiritual and physical welfare of the kings, is responsible for providing the materials used in this process; what these are must be kept secret and all present have to swear an oath to keep silent. Also present are the *Adumfohene*, the chief executioner of the human sacrifices and the guardian of kings, as well as a number of selected state elders. The king again sits in the audience courtyard weeping and drinking to bring him solace because 'the same will happen to his stool when he dies'. When the blackening is completed the stool is carried into the Chapel, which had been purified the night before, and is placed in position. It is by then about eleven o'clock in the evening, and the king retires to his bed-chamber, where the *Gyaasehene* goes to him and gives him a nugget of gold. After a small rite the king returns it to him and he places it in a *kuduo*, a vessel cast in gold, which is deposited in the Chapel of the Stools. This rite signifies the beginning of the new king's reign, each year of which is symbolised by a nugget of gold. When the king dies the one first placed in the *kuduo* is taken out and given to the queen-mother, who keeps it for use in the same rite when it is performed at the beginning of the reign of the succeeding king.[1]

On the following morning the king calls all his chiefs and elders to go with him to the Chapel of the Stools. He touches the newly blackened stool three times, then places a little bag containing gold dust and precious beads on it. Next a libation of rum is offered to the late king, white rams, long-legged and short-haired, are sacrificed, both those presented by the king and the many others he has received as gifts from the families of his predecessor's wives and from others. Offerings are made to all the Royal Ancestors. Then the king seats himself on his *asipim* chair in the audience courtyard

[1] See *Ak. Trad.*, pp. 30 ff.

where he receives deputations from all over the country in order to accept the people's good wishes and gifts.

EGYPT

1. *The King's Death, Burial, and Funeral Rites*

A Pharaoh's death was regarded as a disaster of the greatest magnitude, for on his life-giving *ka* the welfare of the land depended. Once he was no longer at the head of the divinely ordered universe, chaos prevailed; moreover the death of each one was a reminder to the Egyptians of the murder of Osiris; so vivid was this episode in their minds that it was translated into the perennial mythological form of Osiris's murder by Set.

The death of a sovereign, therefore, was a subject too painful to be spoken of. He did not die, he was 'ill', or 'tired', 'he departs' or 'he has gone to join his *ka*'; it was never admitted that a Pharaoh really experienced death as other men do.[1] The physical fact of his death could not be ignored, however, and the 'Opening-of-the-Mouth' ceremony was devised to restore the deceased from apparent death to immortal life.

Owing to this attitude towards the divine ruler's death we know little of what really happened when he died. The main outline of events can be adduced to some extent from the text of Ikhernofret[2] and the Mystery Play of the Succession.[3] Ikhernofret, finance minister under Senusert III (12th Dynasty), records the festival of Abydos, which commemorated the death of Osiris, when a play was performed, re-enacting the funeral procession and burial of Osiris; it was the prototype, it would seem, of the royal funeral and burial rites. The Mystery Play of Succession, which was enacted at the accession to the throne of Senusert I (12th Dynasty), shows that the royal funeral ceremonies, which ended with the removal of the king's body to the place of embalming, preceded the coronation of the new ruler, who then arranged for the burial of the mummy and the transfiguration of his predecessor from a mortal to a god.

Ikhernofret, who organised the Abydos festival, said in this connexion on his stela that he had 'the duties of an eldest son (*sa-mer-f*) of Osiris'.[4] Since in the festival the funeral procession and burial of

---

[1] cf. Frankfort, *Kingship*, p. 211.
[2] In Schäfer, *Mysterien*. Discussed by Frankfort, *Kingship*, pp. 203 ff.
[3] Sethe, *Dram. Texte*, II. Discussed by Frankfort, op. cit., pp. 123 ff.
[4] Schäfer, p. 15.

21. The *Gyaasehene*, Nana Yao Atoa of Bono-Takyiman in funeral cloth and head-dress.

22. Nana Akumfi Ameyaw III performing a ritual dance in honour of the Royal Ancestors.

Osiris were re-enacted, it must, then, have been the duty of an 'eldest son' of a prehistoric king to be in charge of his father's funeral rites and ceremonies.[1] In late periods it was still the duty of the son to bury his father and to provide for him liberally in the hereafter. One may safely assume, therefore, that in historical times also the physical son of the Pharaoh with the title 'eldest son' was entrusted with the arrangement of all the rites which concerned the royal corpse. It is highly unlikely that, as has been suggested, the heir-apparent or a prince in the line of succession purified, dressed, and adorned the corpse, placed it in the coffin and accompanied it to the tomb, since the successor, as a rule, was not a royal son.[2] Moreover, death was tabu for the Pharaoh and so also for his

[1] *Sa-mer-f* (eldest son) is sometimes translated 'beloved son'. Among the Akan the eldest child is always regarded as the most beloved.
   The duties of the 'eldest son' among the Akan and the ancient Egyptians seem to have been similar. Ikhernofret, 'the eldest son' of Senusert III, prides himself that 'he knew the secrets of the Two Crowns and ... placed the crown on the head of Horus, the Lord of the Two Palaces', when the latter appeared in the throne chamber for a meeting (Schäfer, p. 37). Among the Akan, the 'eldest son', the *Gyaasehene*, is in charge of the regalia and the royal insignia; he also dresses the king in the sacred robes of his ancestors during the enstoolment ceremony.
   Ikhernofret furthermore prided himself that 'he possessed the secret of the words of the gods'. The gods can only, in this context, be the Royal Ancestors and if he knew their 'words' he must have officiated for the Pharaoh in the Dual Shrines, as the *Gyaasehene* officiates for the Akan king in the Chapel of the Stools; the crowning of the Pharaoh took place in the Dual Shrines.
   Ikhernofret was also in charge of the decision of all 'difficult things' (p. 38). The 'difficult things' on which the *Gyaasehene* as 'eldest son' has to make decisions relate to quarrels between the king and his wives or with his children; if his verdict should be unfavourable to the king, this would indeed be 'difficult'. In Egypt the 'eldest son' may likewise have been charged with this difficult task; it is unlikely that it refers to political matters as Schäfer suggests, although occasionally these also may have played a part.
   Schäfer, p. 15 n. 2, believes that the title 'eldest son' is a priestly title, because a row of graves of priests from Esne who held this title has been found. But priests, if they were high priests, would have had their own 'eldest sons'. Among the Akan, for instance, the high priest of Ntoa at Seseman has the same important officers as the king, including a *Gyaasehene* with all the duties of an 'eldest son'.

[2] Matrilineal succession among the Akan means that the queen-mother's son or grandson, and not the king's, succeeds to the throne. An exception is when a queen-mother's husband becomes king at the time when a new dynasty is founded; but it is still her son who succeeds; that he is the king's son is of no account. In Egypt, too, the sons of kings succeeded if they were sons of the occupant of the female throne, but in general the king's sons were barred from the succession. The word 'father' has not the same meaning as among

successor. For the same reason, among the Akan, it is that son of the king, or of one of his predecessors, who is the eldest son among those who occupy chiefly stools, who is in charge of the ritual washing of the king's body and the funeral and burial rites. But the *Banmuhene* prepares the body for burial and adorns it. In Egypt the *Sem* priest assisted the 'eldest son'.[1] His duties seem to have been similar to those of the *Banmuhene*.[2]

The text of Ikhernofret, of which the important lines are quoted here, is followed by my own comments, which differ in many respects from those of Schäfer and Frankfort.

Line 1. 'I arranged the Procession of Upwaut when he went to champion his father.'

Line 2. 'I repelled those who rebelled against the Neshemet and overthrew the enemies of Osiris.'

Line 3. 'I arranged the Great Procession and accompanied the god on his way.'

Line 4. 'I caused the divine boat to sail, and Thoth guided the journey.'

Line 5. 'I adorned the boat named "He who shines forth in Truth, the Lord of Abydos" with a deckhouse and put on him (Osiris) beautiful jewelry when he went to the locality of Peqer.'

Line 6. 'I directed the path of the god to his tomb in Peqer.'

Line 7. 'I championed Unnefer (Osiris) on that day of the great conflict and overthrew all his enemies on the banks of Nedyt.'

Line 8. 'I made him embark in the ship. She carried his beauty.'

Line 9. 'I made the hearts of the deserts of the East great for joy and brought jubilation to the hearts of the deserts of the West when they saw the beauty of the Neshemet boat.'

Line 10. 'She landed at Abydos and brought Osiris, the Chief of the Westerners, the Lord of Abydos, to his palace.'[3]

Europeans, because it often means no more than predecessor; it is a title like 'eldest son'; both have their roots in religious conceptions.

[1] Budge, *Osiris*, II, p. 5.

[2] The position of *Sem* priest could never have been held by an hereditary prince as Wainwright maintains ('Seshat and the Pharaoh', *JEA*, XXVI (1940), p. 37), since death was generally tabu for the Pharaoh and the princes (see p. 209 and n. 1). We know that Ikhnaton 'hated the *Sem* priest' (Wainwright, loc. cit.).

[3] Translated by J. A. Wilson, cf. Frankfort, *Kingship*, p. 203.

THE KING'S DEATH

Line 1. The word 'champion' is interpreted by Frankfort as 'avenge' or 'support'.[1] 'Avenge' does not make any sense in this context; 'support' is more likely unless its meaning is not 'to sustain' or 'uphold' but 'to carry' or 'defend'. Among the Akan, it will be remembered, the funeral procession took place at night and everybody who tried to see it was killed, because it was feared that any evil wishes on the part of the onlookers might make difficulties for the deceased on his journey to heaven. In this sense the king's sons, who carried the royal coffin, also 'championed' or 'defended' the royal dead.

If the funeral procession here is called the Upwaut Procession, one may presume that its members were royal sons whose mothers in the time of Osiris belonged to the Upwaut clan.[2]

Line 2. The Neshemet boat was a sledge shaped like a ship on which the coffin was placed when the procession reached the desert on its way to the necropolis.[3] Osiris was murdered and the Set people were his enemies; any effort on their part to interfere with the dead god's journey to heaven had therefore to be repelled.

Line 4. 'Thoth guided the journey.' Both Upwaut and Thoth were closely connected with Osiris, historically and mythologically; they both supported Horus and thus 'avenged' Osiris.

Among the Akan only two high officials direct the funeral procession and the burial of the dead king—the *Gyaasehene*, as 'eldest son', and the *Korontihene*, as the governor and administrator of the state. Upwaut and Thoth possibly represented the two high officials who were in charge in Egypt: Upwaut the 'eldest son' and Thoth the vizier (*t'ate*). The vizier, like the *Korontihene*, was 'the second after the king in the court of the palace';[4] he also, like the *Korontihene*, belonged to a different family from that of the king. Both, apart from being the chief executive of the king and the administrator of the state, were also ministers of war and both tried civil cases concerned with land and inheritance.[5] Thoth in

---

[1] loc. cit.

[2] See p. 45, and Schäfer, p. 22, for Upwaut being regarded as the son of Osiris, which he considers remarkable.

[3] This burial ceremony is depicted in the tomb of Tut-ankh-Amon; see *The Shrines of Tut-Ankh-Amon*, ed. N. Rambowa, trans. Alexandre Piankoff, Bolingen Series XL, 2, 1955, Pl. 6.

[4] Erman, *Life in Ancient Egypt*, 1894 (translated), pp. 87, 88.

[5] Frankfort, p. 53.

THE KING'S DEATH

mythology was the administrator of the moon and ruled it for the lunar givers of life, above all Horus incarnate in Osiris.

Line 5. Ikhernofret, then, as 'eldest son', adorned the sledge and the body of Osiris for its journey to the grave (as does the *Gyaasehene*).

Line 6. The tomb of Osiris at Peqer is depicted as a mound among trees, a sacred grove.[1] At Bono-Takyiman the tomb of the last king of Bono, Ameyaw Kwaakye, is a conical mound in a sacred grove. His predecessors were all buried in a mausoleum, also situated in a sacred grove outside the town. After this was destroyed during the conquest of the country by the Asante, Ameyaw Kwaakye, the ancestor king of the succeeding dynasty, was buried in the earlier form of tomb.

Line 7. The day of the great conflict and the overthrow of the enemies of Osiris on the banks of Nedyt must, one may presume, refer to the day when the death of Osiris and, in later times, the deaths of his successors, became known. Among the Akan this is the day of the *dwabum* custom, literally the 'turning or throwing things over' (in the market), to illustrate chaos. People were killed in the streets and looting was prevalent.[2]

Lines 9, 10. After the burial of a Pharaoh his transfigured divine spirit, that of Osiris, returned from the tomb to the palace and became the *ka* of the new ruler.[3] 'Chief of the Westerners' implies here that the transfiguration of Osiris had taken place.

The Mystery Play of the Succession exists in the form of a 'script' for a play that was possibly performed at some time during the accession ceremonies of each Pharaoh, to convey to the people that their dead king had become a Royal Ancestor and thus a god. It consists of an undifferentiated sequence of scenes with no subdivisions, no emphasis, no connexion between actions more closely interrelated than others, and no transition. Moreover, apart from the actions which are indispensable for the performance, such as the bringing of insignia for the king, there are others which are symbolical, or which constitute mythological situations; this often makes it difficult to envisage what actually happened after the death of a Pharaoh, assuming of course that the play was based on the actual rites.

The play starts with the equipping of the royal barge and the

---
[1] Schäfer, p. 29.
[2] See p. 191.
[3] For details, see p. 214.

THE KING'S DEATH

barges for the 'royal children', the princes and princesses, certainly those in the line of succession.[1] Various sacrifices are also made; the king has died (scenes 1–7). Then the royal insignia, sceptre and mace, are brought out for the coronation of the 'king who will rule' (scene 8). This is followed by preparations for the coronation which are interspersed with allusions to the death of Osiris at the hand of Set, the defeat of Set at Letopolis, and the ascension of Osiris to heaven (scenes 9–11). The *Djed* pillar of Set[2] appears to have been erected on the stage and mock battles took place to illustrate the fighting that broke out after the death of Osiris between the 'Children of Horus' and the 'Followers of Set' (scenes 12–15). The Set pillar was then taken down again, no doubt after the victory of the 'Children of Horus', and the 'royal children', princes and princesses, enter the barges on the Nile which have been prepared for them. It is not clear from the text at what stage the 'king who will rule' embarked.

The sequence of the scenes so far seems to indicate that the king's death was kept secret so that the barges could be prepared and the coronation arranged. It was announced publicly by the erection of the *Djed* pillar of Set, an indication that chaos prevailed. Among the Akan the *dwabum* custom announced to the people the death of their king and was the signal for the large-scale slaughter of people in the streets by the *adumfo* and those of the king's sons who did not occupy high offices. In Egypt the mock battles in the play staged by the 'Children of Horus' and the 'Followers of Set' may in fact have been real battles between the Pharaoh's sons holding minor positions at court and people they met in the streets and killed.

---

[1] Sethe (op. cit., p. 106) speaks of the king's children and grandchildren; Frankfort simply of 'royal children', by which he means the princes in the line of succession. If 'king's children' is the correct translation from the Egyptian, it must have been a loose term, as it is among the Akan. There the king is regarded as the father of his own children, who are not eligible for the stool, as well as of the princes and princesses who, like himself, are the descendants of queen-mothers). In Egypt it was the same since matrilineal succession was the rule. Moreover, in the play a distinction is made between 'the royal children' or 'king's children' who go to live on barges during the funeral rites, and the 'Children of Horus', who clearly represent the king's own children, especially the sons, see below in the text.

[2] Sethe is of the opinion that the *Djed* pillar is that of Set (p. 156). Frankfort (p. 128) believes that it is the *Djed* of Osiris, 'and probably serves as a symbol of rebirth and resurrection'. Since the transfiguration of Osiris has not yet taken place it cannot be that of Osiris; moreover the *Djed* here symbolises the victory of Set. Other gods too are known to have had a *Djed*.

Among the Akan order was restored when the royal body was removed at night to the burial place. In Egypt the succeeding scenes in the play show that the state of chaos ended with the removal of the dead king's body to the 'Beautiful House', the 'Place of Embalming'.[1]

Scenes 19–32 deal with further preparations for the coronation of the 'king who will rule' and with the ceremony itself. The coronation is followed immediately by a number of scenes (33–5) in which the new king gives 'life' to his predecessor. On the mythological plane the locality given is Pe, the town of the Pharaoh's Lower Egyptian Royal Ancestors, descended from Isis; in reality, the corresponding ritual which effected the transfer of 'life' seems to have been staged first at the entrance to the tomb and then in the mortuary temple.[2] With reference to the first the text says: 'Horus speaks to Geb: I hold in my embrace this my father who has become tired until he becomes quite strong again.'

'To be tired' means here 'to be dead'; 'until he becomes quite strong again' refers to his transfiguration when he is reborn as a god.[3] The embrace is no mere sign of affection but signifies that Horus (or Pharaoh) imparts *ka* to the dead at the crucial moment, no doubt, when the mummy is carried away to be interred in the tomb. Until this moment the *ka* of the deceased 'has rested';[4] now

---

[1] 'The Beautiful House' is mentioned in the stage directions of the play. Sethe suggests (p. 128) that the 'Beautiful House' may have been a chapel on the royal barge. This is quite out of the question owing to the death tabu for the divine king; moreover the place of embalming must have been situated outside the king's town for the same reason. It would have been impossible for the new ruler to be in a town which harboured the corpse of his predecessor before it was immortalised. It is, however, more than likely that while the mummy was taken away for interment the king re-entered his barge until his predecessor was transfigured and, as a Royal Ancestor, entered the Dual Shrines.

[2] From the Middle Kingdom onwards, the tomb of the kings in the Valley of the Kings is distinct from the mortuary temple built on the left bank of the Nile.

[3] See Frankfort (p. 136). The last sentence may also be read 'may he become quite strong again'. I selected the first reading because it is more relevant.

[4] In the tomb of Queen Meresankh III we find two dates: first the date of her death, when her body was taken to be embalmed, and, second, the date of her burial in the tomb. The first is called 'the resting of her *ka*—her departure to the mortuary workshop'; the second 'her departure to her beautiful tomb'. See J. A. Wilson, 'Funeral Services of the Egyptian Old Kingdom', in *JNES*, III (1944), p. 202, n. 5. The *ka* of the queen had stopped to rest after death and wandered off as soon as the mummy was carried to the tomb. The *kra* of the Akan 'rests' or hovers around the house for 40 days after death, see p. 121.

it wanders off to heaven and needs support in the form of life until it is united with that of the Royal Ancestors.

The embrace was part of a ritual in which the *Sem* priest, proxy for the Pharaoh, donned the *qeni* stomacher which covered his chest and back.[1] This was an object in which the immortal powers of Osiris were believed to be immanent. He gave 'life' or *ka* to the mummy, probably by pressing the cloth in which it was to be wrapped against the *qeni*. This rite is far from clear, for two mummy cloths play a part, one identified with Set and one with Osiris. The scene is explained in the following words: 'This means Horus speaks to Osiris when he embraces him who embraces him, and who says that he (Osiris) must cling to him (Horus).'[2]

These rites, which take place after the coronation of the new ruler, seem to correspond to the second funeral rites of the Akan king, when the new king and his people give 'life' to the late king by shooting guns, and finally send his *kra* off to heaven. While the *kra* is on its way, and until it is transfigured, the *Awusu*, personifying the late king's *kra*, keeps watch till dawn, surrounded by the princes of the royal lineage, royal sons, and *akrafo*.

According to Herodotus and Diodorus the whole period of mourning lasted 70 or 72 days. Of these Diodorus assigns only 30 days to the embalming process; from Genesis i. 3, however, we learn that 'forty days were fulfilled' for Jacob, as was customary for those who were 'embalmed'.[3] According to Wilson the embalming period between death and burial alone took 70 days.[4] Among the Akan, it is interesting to note, the period between death and resurrection lasted 70 days. This included the 15 days in which the king's death was kept secret, as well as another four days during which the elders and chiefs were notified so that they could make arrangements for the funeral and discuss the succession. In Egypt, if the scenes in the Mystery Play of the Succession have been rightly interpreted, the king's death was also kept secret for a short period; how long we do not know. Among the Akan the king's death was made public on the 19th day and the announcement was followed

---

[1] In the funerary rites for Seti I the *Sem* priest is shown donning the *qeni* stomacher; owing to the death tabu it is most improbable that the Pharaoh took any part in funeral rites. In the text of the play it is said 'It happened that a *qeni* stomacher was brought by the recitation priest. That means Horus (Pharaoh) embracing his father.' Frankfort's references to the *qeni* stomacher and its significance are on pp. 134, 136.   [2] See Frankfort, p. 137.
[3] Wilkinson, *Customs*, III, p. 443.   [4] Wilson, 'Funeral Services', p. 201.

by nine days of wailing and deepest grief on the part of the people. During this time they threw ashes on their heads, beat their brows, tore their garments, marched in procession through the main street while the funeral rites were performed; meanwhile the king's body lay in state in the Chapel of the Stools. All the temples were closed; sacrifices, including those offered to the Royal Ancestors, were forbidden; there was a general fast and no festivals were celebrated. Diodorus (i. 7, 2), with reference to Egypt, reports exactly the same (he makes no mention, however, of the Pharaoh's body) but seems to believe that this went on during the whole period of mourning, which seems unlikely, since the coronation took place between the death of the Pharaoh and his burial. Among the Akan, on the 28th day after the death of the king his body was buried; 14 days later (42 days after the death)[1] the new king, having been enstooled, moved into the palace and announced the time of the second stage of the funeral rites. These lasted a week and culminated in the transfiguration of his predecessor. This last but all-important rite took place 28 days later (a full 42 day period after the burial and 70 days after his death).[2] From then on the king's death was commemorated every 42 days by wailing and lamenting on the part of the women, drumming in his honour, with the talking drums recalling his deeds and those of the Royal Ancestors, and a generous provision of drink to the people for libations. On the anniversary of his death the *aferinhye da* was celebrated, bringing the funeral rites to an end.[3]

We have no information as to how soon after the Pharaoh's death in Egypt the new king was crowned, or exactly when the burial and transfiguration rites took place within the period of 70 or 72 days.[4] Among the Akan the above-mentioned dates with their symbolical meanings were not always adhered to; difficulties in

[1] The *Adaduanan* calendar of the Akan, literally the 'Forty Days', consists of 40 or 42 day periods, it depends upon how one calculates it, for it has 4 ten-day periods, or 6 seven-day periods. See *Sacred State*, p. 143.

[2] 28, of course, symbolises the whole lunar cycle. For the symbolism of the other numbers, the days have been most carefully chosen, see *Sacred State*, p. 94 f. No doubt 70 is a 'great seven', 14 the full moon on which the new king is enstooled.

[3] Today an Akan king's death is made public at once and he is buried within a few days. The second funeral rites, instead of lasting seven days, are usually cut down to four. Other features are modernised also.

[4] The Egyptians like the Akan had a ten-day period; 70 therefore was 7 ten-day periods. 72 was symbolic of the Sun-god.

connexion with the succession often made it impossible, and sometimes it was found more convenient to have the second funeral rites at a later date. In Egypt, no doubt, the circumstances were often similar.

The divine kingship in ancient Egypt was an institution involving two generations after the introduction of the cult of the king as the son of the Sun-god, and so it is among the Akan. There can be little doubt that until recently the Akan of Ghana performed, and in some areas continue to perform, royal funeral rites which had their origin in ancient Egypt.

2. *The King's Ascension and Transfiguration*

The rites which transfigure the late king from a dead mortal to an immortal ancestral spirit (Osiris), and the transfer of his divine power to his successor, are also known to us from the Mystery Play of the Succession (scenes 36–41). They start with the command of Horus to Thoth: 'Go and seek my father.' On the stage then appear the 'spirit-seekers', Children of Horus, to whom is given the duty of finding the spirit of the late king. The rites performed by them would seem to correspond basically to those performed among the Akan by the *Werempefo*, sons and daughters of the late king. One may also call them 'spirit-seekers', for they paint their faces in the transfiguration rite with a magical fluid in order to see the spirit of the royal dead.

The *Werempefo* go to the burial place of the late king in the royal cemetery bearing his stool, which is to be the shrine of his spirit. During the night they invoke the Royal Ancestors with the aid of libations and beseech them to allow the newcomer, represented by his *kra*, to unite with them. When the union has taken place, and the deceased is thus transfigured into a god, the spirit is seen and acclaimed by the princesses and daughters of the late king. It then enters the stool, which is brought in triumph to the new king in the palace and, after it has been blackened, to the Chapel of the Stools.

In Egypt the 'spirit-seekers' may have gone to the 'beautiful tomb';[1] the locality is not given.[2] Instead of the stool they carry the

---

[1] See p. 210, n. 4

[2] From other sources we know that, at the entrance to the tomb, mummers wearing conical head-dresses reminiscent of the *atef* crown enacted a ritual called 'the dancing of the people of Pe' (Kees, *Totenglauben*, pp. 358 ff.). The *Werempefo* may also be regarded as mummers.

statue of the late ruler referred to as Osiris by Horus (scene 37). They then build a sort of heavenly ladder and invoke Nut, asking her to take her son to heaven (scene 38). When Osiris is 'found' or 'seen', the dead king, who has become Osiris after the union with the Royal Ancestors, is acclaimed by Isis and Nephthys who are called here 'wailing women' (scene 39).[1] The spirit of the late ruler, one may assume, enters the statue which then seems to have been carried to the 'Gold House'[2] where a rite is performed, supervised by the Master of [the king's] Largesse[3] (scenes 40, 41). The statue is then brought into the palace and erected in the Dual Shrines (scene 42), while the new king is praised (scene 42), possibly at the moment when he embraces the statue. In a relief on the shrine of Tut-Ankh-Amon the new king is shown, followed by his *ka*, embracing the statue of his predecessor who had become Osiris.[4] Compare the scene in the Chapel of the Stools when the new Akan king touches the blackened stool of the late king three times and places gifts on it.

Then follows a consecrated meal in which all the great of the land took part (scene 43). Among the Akan shares of the offerings made to the Royal Ancestors in the Chapel of the Stools are distributed to the houses of the chiefs to be eaten later by them, their families, and visiting chiefs. In the Egyptian play it is simply said 'the Great shall eat'.[5] The play ends with the bringing in of

---

[1] We have to imagine that the late king is 'seen', as no mention is made of it in the text; it is indicated by the acclamations of Isis and Nephthys who here personify the princesses and daughters of the king.

[2] Sethe, *Dram. Texte*, pp. 233 and 156. In the 'Gold House' the cult statues were made and the 'Opening-of-the-Mouth' ceremony performed over them to give them 'life'.

[3] For the Master of the King's Largesse see A. H. Gardiner in *JEA*, XXIV, pp. 83 ff., 'The Mansion of Life and the Master of the King's Largesse.' His duties seem to have been the same as those of the *Sodohene* among the Akan. He supplied the food for the royal household and presided over the king's meals. He was also in charge of the gifts given by the king and the victuals offered in the Chapel of the Stools and the *Kra Fieso*. The Master of the King's Largesse in this scene supervises the rite, no doubt because a bull's thigh, identified with Set, is offered. He would have supplied the bull. Since this official presided over the rite the statue of the late ruler must have been 'fed' with the thigh of Set, perhaps smeared with the blood of it before it was plated with gold. It was the first 'Opening-of-the-Mouth' ceremony performed over the statue, which must have differed to some extent from those usually performed. Blood was used in the blackening of the stools.

[4] Rambowa, *The Shrines of Tut-Ankh-Amon*.

[5] Sethe, p. 236. Oil to anoint the great (scene 44) also plays a part. He has

ingredients destined for the purification of the late ruler (scenes 45, 46). Among the Akan numerous rams are slaughtered and their blood is made to spill out over the late king's stool. The blood is regarded as food to sustain the *saman*, the spiritualised body of the deceased, and so to rid him of, or purify him from, the last traces of defilement brought about by death.

The transfiguration of the Pharaoh's predecessor having been completed, the *ka* of Osiris is now immanent in his successor. He has become a truly divine ruler who is able to give 'life' to the Royal Ancestors and men and bring prosperity to his country.

_{no explanation to offer for the rite (p. 238) and there is nothing in Akan rites in the way of 'anointing' the chiefs. Frankfort, pp. 138, 139 interprets the scene on the mythological plane.}

CHAPTER X

The Royal Succession

AKAN

1. The Selection and Enstoolment Rites (as practised in Bono-Takyiman)

The new king is chosen from among the princes of the royal lineage and is usually enstooled 42 days after the death of his predecessor.[1] He is one of three candidates selected by the *Gyaasehene* and the *Korontihene* in consultation with the queen-mother and the *Werempehene* as chief of the commoners. The latter's judgement as to whether the prince will be acceptable to the people is important. He is assisted by the *Werempefo*, a body constituted, as already mentioned, of elderly male and female members of the royal lineage, as well as the sons and daughters of the late king or his predecessor, and the heirs (*adehye*) to the *Gyaase* and the *Koronti* stools. The three chosen candidates are then introduced by the *Asonahene*, the chief of the Asona clan,[2] to an assembly presided over by the queen-mother and the elders of the state. Should this assembly accept the three candidates, three sticks, each representing a candidate, are then sent to the priests of the great gods so that they may consult the oracles of their deities and make their choice. The prince who has the majority of votes is elected king.

Before the answer is received from the priests the *Werempehene* announces a date for a meeting to take place before the *ahemfie* or palace to which the whole town is invited. When, on the stipulated day, the crowd has assembled and has greeted the queen-mother

[1] A whole period of the *Adaduanan* state calendar.
[2] The Asona was the most important clan in ancient Bono after the royal clan Ayoko and the affiliated Anana clan.

and the elders, the *Werempehene* introduces the future ruler and invites the people to show either their pleasure or displeasure at the choice. If they show pleasure, the chosen candidate pretends to be overcome with emotion and runs away to seek refuge in a relative's house near by. The young men run after him and, when they have caught him, carry him shoulder-high back to the assembly. They hand him over to the queen-mother,[1] who embraces him and cries '*osei yee, osei yee, osei yee*'. All the great women of the state do likewise. This custom is known as *awaa awaa atun*, and is said to signify that their future king is their child (*atun* from *turu* to carry a child). The candidate is then carried on the shoulders of the palanquin-bearers from 'one end of the town to the other', along the stretch between the three sacred trees of the town which are planted in the main road.[2] The trees are decorated with white cloth; women are waiting below each one to greet him and cheer him. He is then carried back to the queen-mother and the great women of the state. As the future king's feet must not again touch the ground,[3] he is then carried to his own house in the town. The palanquin-bearers receive from him a fixed sum of money; this is his first expenditure as a future king.

On the following morning the chosen candidate is visited by the elders, who ask him to prepare himself to pay *aseda*, thanksgiving money, a custom which is equivalent to putting a seal to a document. The prince must also give them two cases of gin or rum when he enters the Chapel of the Stools for the first time. This he does in the company of the queen-mother and the elders of the state, when he is shown the black stools of the Royal Ancestors by the *Nkondwasoafohene*, the custodian of the Chapel. The drink is used for the first libation which he, as future ruler, pours out over the stools of his predecessors.

From that day forward the prince's body is the object of much

[1] This rite is reminiscent of the *akyeneboa*, or totem animal, which is caught on New Year's day and brought for sanctification to the king and queen-mother. See *Ak. of Ghana*, pp. 39, 40.

[2] Each town has generally three sacred trees; one, the *gya dua*, in front of the palaces, planted before the town was founded and under which a human sacrifice was buried (see *Sacred State*, pp. 72, 121, 186–7, and *Ak. of Ghana*, p. 27); one at the north end of the main road which passes the palaces, and one at the south end planted at the same time. The last two are sacred to deities of clans whose people played an important part in the foundation of the town.

[3] A king's feet must never touch the ground, for in the earth the dead are buried and death may defile the life-giving powers of his *kra*.

attention; it is repeatedly cleansed and his *kra* is purified;[1] he is given special food to fatten him 'to make him look noble'. On the night before the enstoolment the queen-mother and the *Korontihene* examine his body for leprous spots, or any other disease or deformation which he may have concealed from them.

The enstoolment ceremony which is performed at night is preceded by a visit to Taa Kese, the bi-sexual city god/goddess of Takyiman. There in the presence of the queen-mother and a few chosen elders the future king touches the shrine of the goddess three times, asking her to accept him as her child, and begging her protection and help.

Ahensi, the enstoolment ceremony, takes place in the presence of five people: the queen-mother, the *Gyaasehene*, the *Ankobeahene*, the *Sanaahene* and the *Nkondwasoafohene*. The *Gyaasehene* here acts as former 'father' to the prince;[2] the *Ankobeahene* as his former educator.[3] The *Sanaahene*, the royal treasurer, is present because he is responsible for the *puduo*, the sacred gold pieces that symbolise the *kra* of the Royal Ancestors, the *Nkondwasoafohene* as custodian of the Chapel with its sacred black stools. The ceremony begins with the undressing of the prince; all his clothes are taken from him and his body is examined for the second time. If everybody is satisfied with his physical condition the queen-mother leads him, naked, to the black stool of the founder of the Bono-Takyiman state.[4] She and the *Nkondwasoafohene* then place him three times on the sacred stool, which is believed to be charged with kingly power.[5] Each time they say '*tena so*'—'sit down' and '*sore*'—'arise'. Then the queen-mother hands him over to the *Gyaasehene*, saying 'here is your king'. The *Gyaasehene* thereupon dresses him in the ancient war-dress and cap of his ancestors which are covered with charms and believed to have magical properties. He next hands him the

---

[1] It is purified either by the priest of the god who has chosen him or by the priest of a god to whom the prince is especially devoted.

[2] An elderly prince is in charge of the princes; the *Gyaasehene* is their 'father' in so far as he acts as the intermediary between them and the king.

[3] He is always the son of a king and is elected. His mother is usually from one of the great families of the state. In the past he was also the chief of the royal bodyguard which was entirely composed of royal sons whose mothers were commoners.

[4] Nana Ameyaw Gyamfi, a nephew of the last king of Bono, who came to the stool as first king of the Bono-Takyiman state in 1748.

[5] When the Bono kingdom was in existence the prince sat each time for a moment on the Golden Stool used in the enstoolment ceremonies.

bodua, the tail of a bull, mounted in gold.[1] The *Gyaasehene* then briefly exhorts the new king to be a good and just ruler. The queen-mother finishes his speech for him by saying in so many words: 'You are no longer a member of the royal clan; now you belong to the whole nation.'

The Bosummuru sword, the shrine of Bosummuru, the divine ancestor of the kings in the male line, is then taken from its place on the stool of the founder of the kingdom, and put into the king's hand. Standing before the stool and pointing the tip of the blade towards it, the king swears the oath of allegiance to the state. He says: 'Should I ever neglect my duty to the state, may the spirits (*nananom nsamanfo*) of the black stools (i.e. the Royal Ancestors) kill me';[2] and then continues 'and in the same spirit in which my ancestors have ruled over this country, so shall I rule'. So ends the enstoolment ceremony which gives the king power to rule over the land; the divine power to give life and maintain life in the state, is given to him at the close of the *Werempe* ceremony after the completion of the funeral rites for 'his father' the late king, as described in the previous chapter.

On the morning after the enstoolment ceremony a deputation from the commoners calls on the *Korontihene* and asks to see the king. The *Korontihene* thereupon sends a messenger to the queen-mother telling her of this. The queen-mother immediately sends back a message saying that she will introduce the new king to all the people in exactly seven days; since, however, he is at present in her house, the deputation may greet him in private that same day. The elders are then summoned to a small informal gathering. While drinks are served the new king meets the deputation and receives congratulations from all those present. Finally the king gives the commoners a small present of money to buy gin for use as a libation; he also gives money to the elders for a sacrificial ram. After this the guests begin to argue with the queen-mother, demanding that their king should be given to them tomorrow; she, however, remains firm, saying that she cannot possibly be ready so soon; they must, she says, wait for seven days. She does, however, give the elders permission to visit the king daily in his own house

---

[1] Bosummuru is incarnate in the bull and the king. The *bodua* is therefore an emblem of royalty.

[2] The *kras* of the Royal Ancestors give life; the *saman*, the spiritualised body, has the personality or *sunsum* of the deceased and therefore can kill.

in the town to discuss state affairs. During these seven days the king is not allowed to go outside, and he is fed with very rich foods, so that when he finally appears he looks 'like a new man'.

Early in the morning on the seventh day the king is anointed by the *Sumankwahene*, the priest in charge of Bosummuru, with the oil of the shea-butter tree mixed with special ingredients (*nkuan*).[1] Dressed in a white cloth (white is the colour of purity and joy) he is then taken to the Chapel of the Stools. There he swears on one of the golden state swords the oath of allegiance to the queen-mother and the elders of the state, affirming that he will undertake nothing without their concurrence. Afterwards he presents the elders with gin, referred to as *nsuasa*—'swearing drink' or oath fees. On the following morning he sacrifices a ram to the *kras* of the black stools.

A day or two later the queen-mother introduces the new king officially to the elders and all the state chiefs in the audience courtyard of the *ahemfie*. The king's official name is proclaimed; this has been determined by the high priest of Taa Kese, after consultation with the oracle of the deity.[2] It is then the turn of the elders and the chiefs to swear an oath of allegiance to the king in the courthouse. They promise to serve him as faithfully as they did his predecessor. People throng the place to see their king, and are afterwards received by him in the audience courtyard. The elders and chiefs are presented with a case of gin; this represents oath fees and is paid for by the king.

Later in the day, or sometimes on the following day, the *Gyaasehene* shows the king the so-called stool property: the crown lands, the palace, and all the treasures of the state. The paraphernalia and regalia are handed over to him before witnesses in the Chapel of the Stools. Nowadays the stool property includes the wives of the late king; formerly they were sacrificed. Should the senior wife, or queen, please the new king, she retains her status; if not, she is sent back to her family, as are the other wives whom the king

[1] The *Sumankwahene* is also the priest of minor *abosom*, which have their shrines in the courtyards of the palace. Besides this he is the physician of the king and supplies the medicines for him, the queen-mother and her children and the royal wives. The kings of Bono are said to have owned a large zoological and botanical garden, from which the *Sumankwahene* could choose the ingredients he required for medicines and pomades (lion fat) or poisons.

[2] Sometimes another method was used: the king was blindfolded in the Chapel of the Stools and led before the stools of the Royal Ancestors. The stool he touched determined his name in so far as he then took the name of the king whose repository it was.

does not like, and the queen-mother selects a wife for him, a young girl, an heiress princess usually of the Asona clan. Since she becomes a member of his harem the marriage takes place secretly on the next *Fo*-Thursday, the day set aside in Bono-Takyiman for the worship of the kingly *kra*. The rite formerly took place in the *Nyame Dan*, a room dedicated to the worship of Nyame, the Supreme Being, so that the Royal Ancestors may enter the body of the queen.

The day after the handing over of the stool property the king usually sacrifices a ram. When he arrives at the Chapel of the Stools guns are fired and the royal drums are beaten. The king is then allowed to move into his palace. On the next day the king appears for the first time in his full regalia before his elders and assembled chiefs. The audience courtyard is thronged with people eager to congratulate him. After a while he leaves the palace and, amid great jubilations, is carried for the first time in a palanquin to the temple of Taa Kese, in order to pour a libation and to thank the deity for her help; at the same time he prays for further protection and assistance. Then he is carried three times from 'one end of the town to the other' amid the cheers and greetings of his people. The sacred trees of the town are hung with pieces of white cloth; the women standing under them invoke Nyankopon in his form of Sky fertility-god:

> '*Osei yee, osei yee, osei yee,*
> *Tweduampon, EE,*
> *Ye dase o. Amen.*'

'Hail, hail, hail,
Lord of the Tree (on whom we lean and fall not),
We thank you. Amen (He of Saturday).

At the south end of the main road he finally dismounts in order to thank the queen-mother, elders, chiefs, and assembled people for having chosen him. In the afternoon of that day the first state council takes place, presided over by the new king. His first act of state is to arrange the date of the funeral ceremonies of his predecessor; the second was, in the past, to elect the heir-apparent.

Not only the living, but also the Royal Ancestors, acclaim the new king. When the present Bono-Takyimanhene appeared for the first time as king before his people shouts of *osei yee* were heard from the tomb of the ancestor of the dynasty, the last king of Bono, which is not far from the palace. It also rained during the preceding night; this was considered a lucky omen, for it meant that the choice of the new king was heartily approved by the Royal Ancestors.

EGYPT

1. *The Accession and Coronation Rites*

The most important sources for the coronation ritual of the Pharaohs are the inscriptions at Deir el Bahri and the accompanying scenes on the temple reliefs; these are the oldest and most detailed. There are also the inscriptions at Abydos and those on the statue of Haremhab at Turin, as well as the Mystery Play of the Succession. None of these, however, gives us an idea of the whole procedure; they merely represent what the ancient Egyptians regarded as the most significant features of the coronation. From them we gather, nevertheless, that the whole ritual was divided, as among the Akan, into two parts: the accession, culminating in the coronation, which gave the future ruler his secular power as the 'son of Isis', and the rite, following the transfiguration of the late king, which gave him his divine power.[1]

In ancient Egypt the fiction was maintained right through the ages that the Pharaohs were chosen by a god. In the Middle Kingdom this choice usually lay with the state god Amen, although occasionally with a minor deity. Thutmosis IV owed his throne to the Sphinx Harmakhis,[2] and Haremhab to the special favour of Horus of Cynepolis.[3] Among the Akan the future king is also a divine choice.

In Egypt the coronation rites invariably started with the purification of the royal candidate, usually by the gods of the four quarters.[4]

---

[1] Frankfort, *Kingship*, p. 102, says: 'The succession to the throne involved two stages which are not always properly distinguished: we may call them "Accession" and "Coronation".' From the Akan ritual, however, it is clear that 'Accession' and 'Coronation' form the first part, and the deification of the ruler the second. Frankfort, although referring to the latter on pp. 136–8, disregards this most important ritual in his chapter dealing with the Royal Succession.

Moret, *Royauté*, ch. III, also does not seem to have been aware of the significance, in connexion with the succession to the throne, of the rite which gave the Pharaoh his divine power. This may have been due to the fact that this rite cannot be found depicted on the reliefs which record the coronation of the various kings; it may have been classed as a funerary rite since it refers to the deceased sovereigns. We only know of this rite from the Mystery Play of the Succession.

[2] G. Maspero, *Histoire ancienne des peuples de l'orient classique*, Paris, 1895–7, vol. II, p. 294.   [3] ibid., p. 343.   [4] Moret, op. cit., p. 77.

This act is represented on the supernatural plane. Among the Akan the *kra* of the future king is purified by the priest of the state god, or by the priest of the god who had chosen him, or by the priest of the god to whom the prince is especially devoted.

The purification rites in Egypt were followed immediately by a rite which enthroned the prince and made him king. It is only described on the statue of Haremhab, the founder of the 19th Dynasty.[1] According to the inscription it was performed in the Dual Shrines, the *per-ur* and the *per-nezer*, not at Pe and Nekhen but in a room of a temple in the town where the coronation took place.[2] The *imy-khant* priest, whose duties seem to have corresponded with those of the *Nkondwasoafohene* (the custodian of the Chapel of the Stools) adorned and ornamented the future king.[4] The uraeus, however, of the goddess Edjo (Wadjet), the protectress of the Lower Egyptian Royal Ancestors, 'established herself on his (the future king's) forehead', while the Divine Ennead, the Lords of the *per-nezer*, 'showed exultation at his glorious arising, Nekhbet, Edjo, Neith, Isis, Nephthys, Horus, Set and the complete Ennead that presides over the Great Seat'.[5] Among the Akan the queen-mother and the custodian of the Chapel of the Stools enstool the king, but the Egyptian queen never appears in the coronation ritual;[6] it would, however, have been quite unthinkable that she, a sovereign, should not be the central figure in the ceremony. The *imy-khant*, after all, represented the Royal Ancestors in his official capacity only, and it seems reasonable to assume that in the Dual Shrines the queen personified Edjo, called 'Great of Magic, the noble daughter of Amun', and enthroned the future king, the 'son of Isis' on the 'throne of Horus'. The uraeus was the most essential element of all the various crowns, the personification of the power of royalty immanent in the crown.[7]

Haremhab was then taken by Amen to the palace where he

[1] A. H. Gardiner, 'The Coronation of King Haremhab', in *JEA*, XXXIX (1953), pp. 21 ff.

[2] ibid., pp. 22, 25.

[4] ibid., p. 26.

[5] ibid. For the gods of the Ennead as representatives of prehistoric dynasties, see p. 38.

[6] Moret mentions the queen of Haremhab, Moutnozmit (p. 80) which Gardiner (p. 19) shows is wrong.

[7] Thutmosis III in a relief on the temple walls at Semne (LDIII, 51a) seems to be depicted wearing the uraeus only on a golden circular headband (Fig. 9 in G. Steindorff's, 'Die blaue Königskrone' in *ZÄS*, 53 (1918), p. 65).

placed the Blue Crown on his head, decorated with the uraeus.[1] The Blue Crown characterised the king as the 'son of Re'.[2] Haremhab only speaks of the Blue Crown but, since the Red Crown of Lower Egypt and the White Crown of Upper Egypt are sometimes referred to as the Blue Crown, we may assume that he also received these.[3] Then his royal names and titles were proclaimed.

Hatshepsut, who ruled as queen as well as king, recorded her coronation as co-regent of her father Thutmosis I and as king on the throne of Horus, on the temple walls at Deir el Bahri. In the first coronation ritual she is purified by the gods Amen and Horus, who pour water over her.[4] She is then introduced by Amen to all the gods of Egypt, which means that she travelled through the country to visit all the shrines of the important gods and to be acclaimed and embraced by them.[5] Among the Bono the royal candidate is introduced by the *Werempehene* to the court and the people; the queen-mother and the women, personifying the Mother-goddesses of the clans, acclaim and embrace him.[6] In ancient Bono the future co-regent also toured the country to be acknowledged by the people.[7]

Amen then invested Hatshepsut with the Nebti diadem in which was immanent the power of Edjo and Nekhbet, the two goddesses who protected the Royal Ancestors and the king. This ritual took place in the palace in front of 'the nobles of the king; the notables, the friends, the attendants of the palace and the chiefs of the people'. After that her royal names and titles were proclaimed.[8] The new titulary was devised by a priest of rank, the *kerhebu* in the 'House

---

[1] Gardiner, op. cit., pp. 15, 27.

[2] Steindorff, op. cit., p. 69. The Blue Crown became very important in the New Kingdom (p. 74). If it was very old, as Steindorff suggests, then it must originally have characterised the Pharaoh as the solar Horus, the son of the lunar Isis. I deduce this from the circles with which the crown is covered. Steindorff is at a loss to explain these, but realises their importance. The Blue Crown of Ramses II (p. 59, fig. 1, 2) has circles with a dot in the centre, surrounded by a larger circle, that of Amenophis II and III (figs. 4, 5), a smaller circle within a larger one. Among the Akan the circle with the dot in the centre symbolises the solar *kra* (in Egypt the name of Re is written thus); when surrounded with a larger circle it indicates that the solar *kra*, or the Sun-god, is the son of the moon Mother-goddess; a smaller circle within a larger one refers to the path of the sun and the path of the moon, see *Sacred State*, pp. 109–10, fig. A–M.

[3] Steindorff, op. cit., p. 69.   [4] Naville, *Deir el Bahri*, Pl. LVI, p. 1.
[5] ibid., Pl. LVII, p. 3.   [6] See p. 217.   [7] See below in the text.
[8] *Deir el Bahri*, Pls. LXI–LXIII.

of Life', where religious books were compiled and interpretations given. It was then made known by rescript to the officials throughout the land, for the oath was administered by the 'life' of the king, who had to be named.¹ This may be compared with the Akan custom, where the proclamation of the name of the king as determined by the high priest of the state god, is followed by the oath of allegiance sworn by the assembled chiefs and elders in the audience courtyard of the palace.²

All the scenes preceding Hatshepsut's investure with the Nebti diadem have been erased, but one may assume that she first, like Haremhab, had the uraeus fixed on her brow in the Dual Shrines. The Nebti diadem may have been the proper crown for the co-regent, for the Blue Crown³ and the Red and White crowns she received from Amen in a ritual which followed at a later date, no doubt when she was crowned as king.⁴

Again, the purifications come first: then Hatshepsut is blessed by the gods who represent East and West, the two halves of the sun's course, symbolising that the new king is a son of Re. The coronation itself takes place in a wide hall, the Hall of the Festival of *Seshed*, in which two pavilions are erected, the so-called Dual Shrines. In the first Horus and Set crown her with the White Crown of Upper Egypt and in the second with the Red Crown of Lower Egypt.⁵ Hatshepsut is then seen leaving the hall in full regalia, with the double crown on her head, the crook and flail in her hands. Henceforth she is the rightful occupant of the throne of her fathers. Here again the whole ritual is depicted on the supernatural plane, for gods take the place of men. Among the Akan the *Gyaasehene*, acting for the queen-mother, hands over to the new king in the Chapel of the Stools the regalia and insignia of which he is in charge, in the presence of all those who have enstooled him.⁶ In ancient Bono the *Nkondwasoafohene* robed the king and adorned him with the golden crown surmounted by the parrot and with the golden triangular breastplate, the symbol of royal authority.⁷ In

---

¹ ibid., p. 7.
² See p. 220.
³ The investiture with the Blue Crown, Hatshepsut records on her obelisk (LD III, 23). See also Steindorff, op. cit., p. 63.
⁴ *Deir el Bahri*, p. 9.
⁵ ibid., Pl. LX IV, p. 8.
⁶ See p. 220.
⁷ This is still worn by the king of Asante. See *Sacred State*, Pl. 1.

ancient Egypt, as is evident from the text on the stela of Amenemes II, the *imy-khant* crowned the Pharaoh with the White and Red Crowns;[1] he may have been assisted by a royal son with the title 'eldest son', for he seems to have been the 'priest of the royal crown' and 'who knew the secrets of the two crowns'.[2]

In Egypt as well as among the Akan the coronation was followed by the public appearance of the king, who afterwards visited the god to whom he considered he owed his accession. During his visit he gave thanks to the deity, and at the same time asked him for further assistance and protection. At Takyiman the king is then carried three times 'from one end of the town to the other'; the Pharaoh at Memphis made the circuit of the walls four times.[3]

The first act of rulership for an Akan king is the arrangement of the second funeral rites for the late king. Only when the latter has been established in heaven can his successor receive the kingly *kra* which makes him divine and gives him the power to give 'life'. In ancient Egypt the same action took place as described in Chapter IX, E. 2.

The second act of the new king in ancient Bono was the election of an heir-apparent. It is not certain when the institution of the heir-apparent, who acted as co-regent, was first introduced into Egypt. The 12th Dynasty kings all had co-regents, and it is known that there were many in the 18th and 19th dynasties. The reason for the institution of co-regency among the Bono was, as mentioned previously,[4] to leave the king free to concentrate as much as possible on his divine task of giving 'life' to his people. In Egypt, no doubt, the same idea prevailed.

Simpson[5] is of the opinion that many difficulties must have arisen as a result of having two rulers. The history of Bono suggests that there this was not so. The king, revered as a god, lived in seclusion, but everything down to the smallest detail was reported to him and

---

[1] Gardiner, op. cit., p. 26.

[2] See p. 205 n. 1.

[3] Moret, *Royauté*, pp. 96, 97, is of the opinion that when Memphis ceased to be the capital the so-called circuit of the walls was executed in a room behind the hall where the coronation had taken place. Akan ritual suggests that it may originally have had a practical purpose, namely to give the people the opportunity to see their king and acclaim him.

[4] See p. 87.

[5] William K. Simpson, 'The Single-dated Monuments of Sesostris I, an Aspect of the Institution of Co-regency in the 12th Dynasty', in *JNES*, XV (1956), No. 4, p. 214.

THE ROYAL SUCCESSION

he made all the final decisions. His co-regent, on the other hand, was much in evidence in public where he appeared in full royal splendour. He sat in the State Council, received foreign visitors, and travelled and held court in the provinces.[1] The queen-mother also had her heir-apparent and co-regent. She lived in complete seclusion though, like the king, surrounded by hundreds of attendants at Amona, beyond the Yaya river a few miles north of Bono-Mansu, the capital.

[1] The king and the co-regent were completely identified with each other. I had the greatest difficulty, when I collected the historical traditions, in distinguishing between the two, which was essential, particularly when it came to the destruction of the Bono kingdom for which the co-regent and not the king was entirely to blame. And yet no distinction was made till I pointed out that the king could not possibly have been murdered when he was held captive by the Asante, since he had committed suicide when the Asante entered the capital and his tomb is in Takyiman. Only then they began to speak of the co-regent, but were surprised that I found it important to separate the actions of the two, since the king was responsible in every respect for the co-regent.

CHAPTER XI
Diffusion

The matrilineal ancestors of the founders of the Bono and Asante kingdoms are believed by their descendants to have been a 'white people' who originally lived in the north in the 'country of the sand'. The 'white people', we may deduce, were predominantly Saharan Libyans and others descended from the Libyans of North Africa and the Fezzan.[1]

In *The Akan of Ghana*, Chapter VI, it is shown in great detail that the Akan religion has much in common with that of the Libyo-Phoenicians of North Africa. The Carthaginian deities Tanit and Baal Hamman can in every respect be equated with the Akan Nyame and Nyankopon. The Libyan Tanit (Nit with the Berber feminine prefix *ta*), on the other hand, almost certainly had the same origin as the Libyo-Egyptian Nit, Net or (Greek) Neith, and the ram sun and Sky fertility-god Baal Hamman was the same as the Egyptian Amun, Amen or (Greek) Amon.[2]

The goddess Neith was one of the oldest supreme deities of Egypt; this is confirmed not only in the texts of dynastic times but also by archaeological evidence, for Libyans have been credited with the introduction of the first civilisation (Amratian or Naqada I) in early prehistoric times;[3] it was they who laid the foundation of the great civilisation of ancient Egypt.

[1] See 'The Akan and Ghana' in *MAN*, LVII (1957), pp. 82–8.
[2] Amen was also worshipped by the Libyans in his two forms as a Sky fertility-god in the oasis of Shiwa and as a sun Sky fertility-god in Carthage. The Romans equated the latter with their god Saturn.
[3] Petrie, *Making of Egypt*, p. 15. There is good reason to believe that the preceding Badarian civilisation also had the same origin. Remains of this age have been found in the region of the Tibesti Mountain range in the eastern Sahara which since earliest times has been the home of Libyan peoples. A. J. Arkell, *A History of the Sudan to A.D. 1821*, 1955, p. 34.

The crown of Neith, which in a later age became the crown of the kings of Lower Egypt, was found depicted on a potsherd at Naqada,[1] the southern town of Nubt in Upper Egypt. This suggests that the ancestors of the kings and queens of Lower Egypt originally ruled in the region of Nubt in the south.[2] The delta at that date may still have been too swampy for habitation; certainly no remains of the first civilisation have as yet been found there.[3] Moreover, the crossed arrows, the emblem of Neith, are of the Gerzean or Naqada II type which was widespread in Lower Egypt.[4]

Naqada I and Naqada II (and the preceding Badarian) ceramics are rich in symbols which are still common among the Akan[5] and decorate the cloths of kings and chiefs, their gold ornaments and those of the queen-mothers and princesses, as well as ceremonial utensils and gold weights. They are neither Akan nor Egyptian in origin, and would appear to have been invented by the aboriginal matriarchal inhabitants of western Asia, to serve as ideograms or ideographs to express their religious beliefs. Among the Akan the knowledge of what they represent has survived to some extent, so that there seems some justification for using their symbolism to interpret that of Egypt. It is quite evident that in the course of time different meanings were occasionally substituted, particularly

[1] G. A. Wainwright, 'The Red Crown in Early Prehistoric Times', *JEA* (1923), 26ff.

[2] The people of Nut (Nit or Neith) came from Punt (see p. 42 and wandered up the Nile valley. Possibly they stayed first in the Naqada region before they ousted Shu at Memphis-Hininsu. When a Horus king in turn usurped the throne of Geb, the Geb-Nut people, a prince and princess with followers, may have settled in Lower Egypt and founded Sais. The Set people in the Naqada region probably came after the people of Neith, for Neith became the 'wife of Set'; also the Set people had the pig or boar in common with Osiris, that is to say, they originated from the same state (see p. 73 n, 3, i.e. Syria, not Punt; also in various texts Set is called the 'brother' of Osiris.

[3] Robert P. Charles, 'Essai sur la chronologie des civilisations prédynastiques de l'Egypte', *JNES*, XVI (Oct. 1957), No. 4.

[4] Baumgärtel, *Cultures*, p. 47.

[5] See *Sacred State*, ch. VI. Some of the names of the symbols still indicate what they mean; in former times it was the craftsmen who applied them and knew their significance, and today only someone who is of the old craftsmen families in the service of kings. Some are only known to the women of royal lineages, others by families or heads of clans, who 'own' these symbols but keep their true meaning secret and let the people substitute other meanings for them. It was extremely difficult to get information on them and in many cases it was only possible to interpret them from the manner in which they are applied.

when the original meaning had been forgotten[1] or its sense altered owing to the development of religious ideas.[2] But I think we come nearer to the truth if we use the Akan interpretation rather than relying on explanations based on a European concept. Petrie tried to do this, to interpret a painting on one of the Naqada I potsherds. He says 'No. VI, 6 shows a long-haired man in successful combat with a taller man; the suggestion of motion of the legs by a zig-zag line between them is an interesting convention. So far as we know, this is the earliest interpretation of fighting.'[3]

I cannot agree with this, for it leaves unexplained some other items, such as the cone below the men and the tree standing beside them. To me the scene seems to describe the whole cult of the Sky fertility-god who dies annually to be reborn to the Mother-goddess. Here the taller man with arms raised could portray the god, and the long-haired man joined to him (see Fig. 9) could be the priest-king or his proxy, who personified the god in the rite. Both have triangular-shaped bodies, which characterise them as being part of the Mother-goddess—that is to say, her sons who rule the sky and earth on her behalf. She gave 'life', or *ka*, to them with fire symbolised by the zig-zag lines between their legs; the Egyptians envisaged the nature of the *ka* as a flame. The arms of the god are raised as in the *ka* symbol, indicating that it is the *ka* of the god which joins that of the goddess to be re-animated by her. Two arrows seem to be shot into his head; arrows in particular transmitted *ka*, even in late times. The emblem of Neith was two arrows. The arms of the priest-chief or his proxy seem to be bound behind his back, which may convey the idea of a sacrificial victim, or may mean that his body is mortal in contrast to that of the god, who in

---

[1] An example of this is the lunar creation symbol (*Ak. of Ghana*, Fig. 2) which is now taken as meaning 'One should not bite one another'; or when the swastika is described as a 'cock's foot'.

[2] An example of this is when '*nyansa pow*', 'knot of wisdom' is translated as 'the wise man's knot' and regarded as male, whereas the original meaning is still preserved, for the sceptre of the queen-mother (see Fig 7.) is called thus; it has the knot of wisdom in its centre to indicate that 'all decisions taken in her council will hold fast' (literal translation of the explanation given to me). Among the Egyptians Isis was the goddess of wisdom, showing that originally wisdom was regarded as a female characteristic. Also among the Greeks Athene, whom they equated with Neith, was the goddess of wisdom.

[3] *Making of Egypt*, pp. 15, 16; M. Murray, 'Burial Customs', *JEA*, XXXXII (1956), believes these figures to be female, performing a ritual dance; the zig-zag lines along the legs she interprets as a kind of skirt.

the early period was pure *ka*. This concept seems also to be conveyed by the 'little flames' which shoot out of his extremities and the lower part of his body; these are lacking in the other figure. Between the two figures, and far below them (indicating perhaps that they are on their way to heaven), is depicted the triangular cone of the goddess, decorated with lines which may represent stairs leading to the sky-world, the equivalent of the ladder of later times. Next to the priest-chief we find the sacred tree of the god, the shrine for his *ka*, and next to it a two-forked pole to which six triangles are attached; the number two among the Akan is the symbol for birth, and six is the symbol for death and rebirth. Three lines encircle

Fig. 9

Painting on a potsherd from the Naqada period. Petrie, Making of Egypt, Fig. VI, 6

the rim of the pot or vase; three symbolises the goddess as the ruler of sky, earth, and underworld.

Assuming that the symbols on the Naqada I and II ceramics mean the same as they would among the Akan, we conclude that the prehistoric Libyans worshipped the deities of Cult Type II of the matriarchal or matrilineally organised peoples. As this volume shows, the religious beliefs of Cult Type II, the cult of the Sky fertility-deities (Venus), remained in existence till the end of the

Egyptian civilisation. It was, however, further developed in some cases, when the cult of the king as the son of the Sun-god (Cult Type III) was introduced and the concept of the soul was further enlarged.

The most frequent symbols or ideographs painted on prehistoric Egyptian ceramics were: the *crux decussata* and the triangle of the Mother-goddess, the cross of the Sky fertility-god; the spiral and double spiral, the circle and double circle, the zig-zag line and the wavy line, the square and the crossed lines, stars and the tree symbol. The combination of these conveyed ideas connected with the deities. The ideographs appeared first in western Asia in a number of places, where they are ascribed to the First and Second Aeneolithic Periods.[1]

The early prehistoric matriarchal peoples who created the culture of the First Aeneolithic Period and diffused it in western Asia are so far unnamed, but their descendants in Africa, in the Nile valley, the eastern Sudan, the Sahara and North Africa, would seem to have been the so-called Libyans. The name 'Libyan' has been derived from the Greek 'Libu', Egyptian Lebu or Rebu, a tribe that had settled along the North African coast adjacent to Egypt. Archaeological evidence shows that the early Libyans were small and dark-haired like the early inhabitants of Mesopotamia and Elam, the so-called Proto-Elamites. Speiser[2] terms these people 'Japhetites' because elements in their speech based on extant philological material cannot be included with those of the Semites, Hamites, Indo-Europeans or other well-defined groups, nor can they be located elsewhere. On the other hand the Libyans on the Egyptian monuments of the 5th and 19th Dynasties are portrayed as fair-skinned and tall. Rodd has identified them as Libyan nomads, whom today we call Tuaregs;[3] their racial appellation is Ilam or Lamta (also Iram or Aram in various Sudanese dialects)[4] which recalls Elam and Elamtu. They were also originally matrilineally organised.[5]

---

[1] Baumgärtel, *Cultures*, shows Egyptian symbols next to western Asiatic ones right through her book.

[2] E. A. Speiser, *Mesopotamian Origins*, Philadelphia, 1930, p. 16 et passim.

[3] F. R. Rodd, *The People of the Veil*, 1926, p. 194. In *The Times*, 30th March 1928, he pointed out the striking similarity between the names of certain Libyan tribes described in Egyptian records of the 5th and 19th dynasties and certain extant and recent Tuareg clan names.

[4] Sir Richmond Palmer, *Bornu, Sahara and Sudan*, 1936, pp. 140, 141, 157, 166.   [5] Rodd, op. cit., pp. 103, 148; today the Tuaregs are Moslems.

DIFFUSION

The culture of the Second Aeneolithic Period is believed to have been introduced into Syria, Palestine, Mesopotamia and Elam by the Hurru, Hurri or Hurrians, a people originating in the Caucasus region, who from the 5th millennium onwards spread all over the ancient East.[1] Their great Mother-goddess in Mesopotamia became known as Ishtar, in Syria Ashtart, which is the same name (prefix *A* instead of *I* and with the west Semitic feminine ending *t*);[2] her name in Palestine was Ashtoreth (vowel change from *a* to *o*) and in other regions Ashirat. She was bi-sexual and in this form survived into historic times—the 'bearded Ishtar' and the 'bearded Ashtart'. More generally her male aspect was personified as a god, called Athar in southern Arabia as well as Ashir; Asher, Ashur, Assur or Aththur became the national god of the Assyrians in historic times.

It is interesting to note that the name Ḥr, Hor or Her, in Greek Horus, is obviously the same as Athar or Asher without the prefix; his mother Hathor, or Athor, was the Greek Athyr. More than one scholar has already connected the name Asar (Greek Osiris), the son of Hathor, with the Babylonian god Marduk, whose secret (that is, true) name was Asar, and with the Assyrian Marduk, who was called Asar or Assari.[3] From this one may deduce that the falcon clan people of Horus and Hathor were originally Hurri,[4] who had formed a clan among the people of Punt in southern Arabia with whom they migrated into Nubia to found a second Punt. The people of Osiris or Asar, who came from Syria into Egypt, seem to have been Hurri, who had allied themselves with Semites.[5] If so this would explain the Semitic element in the Egyptian language.

Whereas Cult Types I and II, the cult of the Mother-goddess and the cult of the Sky fertility-deities, were diffused from Asia into Africa, Cult Type III, the cult of the king as the son of the Sun-god, evolved in Egypt and was diffused from that country into various parts of Africa. The diffusion probably took place as it did with the

[1] E. A. Speiser, *Introduction to Hurrian*, American School of Oriental Research, 1941, p. 137.

[2] S. A. Cook in *Cambridge Ancient History*, I, p. 208.

[3] S. Smith, 'Marduk, Ashur and Osiris', *JEA*, VIII (1922), pp. 41–4; A. Erman, 'Zum Namen des Osiris, *ZÄS* (1910), pp. 46, 92–5; Budge, *Fetish*, p. 188. It is interesting to note that among the Akan the name Asare is common; most of the kings of the Akyerekyere kingdom had this name. *Ak. Trad.*, p. 135.

[4] Suggested by Mercer, *Horus*, p. 91.

[5] Speiser, op. cit., p. 155, says that 'up to the present there is a lack of relevant sources with regard to the interrelations between Hurrians and Semites, but further excavations in Syria might furnish the necessary material'.

Akan. A queen-mother or princess, or a prince and a princess, accompanied by followers, left their home to settle elsewhere, usually after their country had been conquered in battle or, equally often, after a succession quarrel, for civil war among 'brothers' was not approved of.

In Egypt, apart from invasions and revolutions, each new dynasty must have produced emigrants of the royal lineage who, discontented with the state of affairs, sought new homes in adjacent regions.[1] Unfortunately nothing is known of the history of the Libyan states in North Africa, the Sahara and Sudan before the beginning of our era and equally little since. Delafosse[2] believes that the Sudanese titles for king—Fari, Farima, Farhama, Faran and so forth—are derived from the Egyptian Para' o, or, as we say, Pharaoh. In the early Middle Ages there also existed in the Senegal region the kingdom of the Faraoui, whose royal lineage may originally have had an Egyptian origin.

The cult of the king as the son of the Sun-god among the Akan is evidently derived from the Middle Kingdom, for their Sun-god Nyankopon has all the characteristics of Amen-Re of Thebes. Both are essentially Sky fertility-gods who had been fused with a creator Sun-god and both are incarnate in the ram; Nyankopon's secret name is Amen. Amen-Re was regarded as one with Ptah Tatjenen, and Nyankopon was one with Odomankoma whom one can equate with Ptah. Both had an aspect not pronounced in other gods—they were wind gods.[3] In demotic texts Amen was made to represent the breath of life (*pneuma*); Nyankopon's soul was the breath of life (*honhom*). A maxim says: Amen-Re was also worshipped by the Pharaohs as Amen-Re-Khamutef, the ancestor and begetter of kings; Nyankopon is fused with the *Ntoro* god Bosummuru, the ancestor and begetter of kings; *Ntoro* and *Khamutef* represent the same ideas.

The old material civilisation of the Akan peoples was far from uniform. The Bono, whose chief clanspeople were the Agwana (now called Anana), descendants of Saharan Libyans, wore the tunic, often richly embroidered, and built their houses on a rectangular base (two-storied for the nobles, three-storied for the king) with

---

[1] See also W. J. Perry, *The Children of the Sun*, p. 19.
[2] M. Delafosse, *Haut-Sénégal-Niger* (1912), Série I (II), p. 21.
[3] W. Spiegelberg, 'Amon als Gott des Luft oder des Windes', *ZÄS* (1911) pp. 49, 127–8.

a flat roof surrounded by a parapet and a staircase leading up to it. The walls were broader at the base than at the top; the front of the house was decorated with the divine symbols. The Akan from the Kumbu kingdom, who settled from about 1500 onwards in the forest region, wore the Roman toga, patterned with designs in bright colours, which became the national dress of the Asante and is now generally worn by all Akan. Their houses, also on a rectangular base (two-storied for the nobles, higher for the king) had a thatched roof and colonnades, pillars, arches and friezes, the arrangement and proportions of which were exactly like those used by the Greeks and Romans in North Africa. Their fronts and the walls in the courtyards were richly decorated with mural designs or reliefs consisting of the same divine symbols, but more often arranged in patterns; they also had perforated fretwork designs.[1]

This is not the place to show how much the Akan, among other Sudanese peoples, have preserved from the various nations which once colonised North Africa; suffice it to say that the Akan state organisation, religion, and much of the material culture is of non-negro African origin. The Akan civilisation, nevertheless, has an identity and a distinctive quality of its own.

[1] *Sacred State*, pp. 189 ff.

APPENDIX

The Problem of Similarities and Differences in the Cult of the Divine King in Ancient Egypt, Mesopotamia and among the Akan

Modern social scientists on the whole deny that a common pattern underlies the cult of the divine king in the ancient civilisations and among primitive peoples. They maintain that the concept of a divine life-giving king stems from the common ground of human experience and emphasise that among each people it was determined and derived meaning from certain fundamental values prevalent in their culture. It is my contention that the theory of the diffusion of this particular cult, namely the divine kingship from the Near East and Egypt, has nowadays been discredited because the concept of what constitutes the divine kingship, has been so ill defined.

Professor H. Frankfort in his Frazer Lecture (1950) *The Problem of Similarity in Near Eastern Religions*, basing his judgements on the findings of the social scientists, denies a common pattern underlying Mesopotamian and Ancient Egyptian divine kingship. He asserts that 'Pharaoh was a god incarnate, but in Mesopotamia the king was a *man* who was sometimes, during one short period about 2000 B.C., deified'.[1] If, however, we examine the evidence more carefully we find that the Pharaoh in early dynastic times was the incarnation of the gods Horus and Min, of which the first can be classed as a clan god and the latter as a Sky fertility-god, by which I mean a god of vegetation who received his life-giving power from the sky. From the time of the 4th Dynasty onwards the Pharaoh

---
[1] See p. 9.

APPENDIX

became in addition the incarnation of the Sun-god Re and claimed to be his son on earth. From the 18th Dynasty onwards the Pharaoh was also regarded as the incarnation of Amen-Re-Khamutef (or Min-Khamutef). The king embodying several gods is one of the principles in the dogma of the divine kingship.[1]

In Mesopotamia in the period Professor Frankfort refers to, the king was not merely a man deified but was, as in Egypt, the incarnation of the-Sun god. The great king Hammurabi said of himself, 'I am the sun-god of Babel, who causes light to rise over the land of the Sumerian(s) and the Accadian(s)'.[2] The Sun-god of Hammurabi was Marduk, like the Egyptian Min a god of vegetation, who received his life-giving power fire as from the sky; in the cult of the divine king he was made to be a Sun-god, to be more precise a Sun-Sky fertility-god.[3] The Pharaohs of the 18th Dynasty adopted the Sky fertility-god Amen of Thebes, the god of their dynasty, as a Sun-god and personified him as Amen-Re. The Akan kings in turn chose their Sky fertility state god Nyankopong (his secret name was Amen) to be the Sun-god of the divine king. The Sun-god Re was immortal and everlasting, but the Sky fertility Sun-gods, be it Amen-Re or Marduk, died at each New Year festival to be reborn, and so did the kings, who were their incarnation.

To show further the great gulf that existed in the cult of the king in Mesopotamia and ancient Egypt Professor Frankfort gives as an example the treatment of the king in the Babylonian New Year rite—'the king offering atonement for his own and his people's sins, was subjected to an indignity unthinkable in Egypt. He went to the temple where his insignia were taken from him and he was struck in the face by the High Priest!'[4]

Among the Akan we find that whereas the Bono kings suffered their annual 'death' to be reborn anew without humiliation, the Asante kings on the other hand were humiliated almost as much as the Babylonian. The Bono king himself handed over to the *Akrafohene*, 'the bearer of his divine life-giving soul', the regalia and the royal insignia in a chapel of his palace—an act which symbolised the death of his kingship, and which made the king a commoner. The

[1] A. M. Hocart, *Kingship*, 1927, p. 20.
[2] Ivan Engnell, *Studies in Divine Kingship in the Ancient Near East*, 1943, p. 23.
[3] Like the Egyptian Min and Amen-Re *Khamutef* the white bull was the incarnation of Marduk and played the same role in the New Year rites.
[4] See p. 12.

APPENDIX

king's divine soul was then purified at the sacred river and the king was reinstated in the night of that day.[1] In the old Asante kingdom the king was deprived of his regalia and the royal insignia by the *Banmuhene*, the royal grave priest in the royal cemetery, and had to dress himself in barkcloth, the garb of the poorest slave in his realm. After he had propitiated a minor deity which presided over the rite as a war lord, the symbols of his kingship were returned to him.[2] In the evening the king and certain people of his capital Kumasi went to a special spot to atone there for their ancestors' sins. The great sin which the predecessor of the Asante kings, Kwabena Amenfi, had committed was the murder of the priestess queen-mother Awo, who had 'given life' to Kumasi, and also the murder of her reigning brother Otumfi Bi and all their kinsfolk (c. 1630). To kill a divine king, and worse a divine queen-mother, was regarded as one of the greatest crimes which could be committed.

Here we have two examples from among one people of the ritual death of the king in the New Year rite. The gulf seems to be as great as that between the Babylonian and the Egyptian rite, and yet the Bono and Asante kings shared the same ancestors and were the incarnation of the same clan and Sky fertility-god. Moreover the cult of the divine king as the son of the Sun-god was introduced into Asante by Opoku Ware who had conquered Bono in 1740. He made the captive heir-apparent of the last Bono king teach him the cult and he took all the important palace officers of Bono, who were familiar with the details of it, into his service. The Asante king therefore accepted the cult but changed, among other items, the ritual connected with the symbolic death of the king in order to atone for a crime that could never be forgotten or forgiven. The Babylonian ritual may have had a similar origin. In Egypt the usurper of the throne married an heiress princess and his position was thus legalised. In Mesopotamia, as the Babylonian rite suggests, some of its conquerors may have shed the divine blood of their predecessors.

The Bono and Asante rites teach us how careful one has to be in evaluating the differences that are apparent in the ritual. Among the Akan not only each state but each town and village has its own

---

[1] See p. 175.

[2] I am unable to say whether this was all that happened as it was impossible to get information on this subject. The Asante New Year festival called *Odwira* is described in *The Sacred State*, pp. 171 ff.

APPENDIX

form of New Year ritual. The concepts are the same, the local differences are largely due to two factors—important historical events which left their mark on the form of the ceremonies, and uneven diffusion of the religious ideas of later periods (Cult Types III and IV). In *The Akan of Ghana* I described the New Year rites centring on the death and rebirth of the god Ntoa as practised in three towns situated not far from one another. In Wankyi the ritual is that of the earliest period (Cult Type II); the life-giving power of the goddess Ntoa, personified by the queen-mother or her substitute, who is her incarnation, is still more important than the life-giving power of the god Ntoa.[1] At Asueyi both the god and the goddess are equally important.[2] At Seseman-Nkoranza the goddess plays no part, all the emphasis is on the god as procreator (Cult Type IV) but he is still reborn by the moon Mother-goddess as in Cult Type II.[3]

---

[1] See pp. 59 ff.   [2] See pp. 63 ff.   [3] See pp. 73 ff.

Index

Aahmes, King of Egypt, 53, 54, 55
Aahmes, Queen of Egypt, 56
Aahmes Nefertari. *See* Nefertari
Aahotep I, Queen of Egypt, 53, 76
Aardwolf, 73 n. 3, (fig. 7), 74
Aat Nebes, 41
Ab (the heart), 131 and nn. 1, 2, 3
Abaama, deity, 83. *See also* Children
Abosom. See *Obosom*
Abrafo, 63, 83. *See also* Priests: reciter priests
Abrafohene (Master of Ceremonies), 151, 199
Abrao, deity of Jupiter, 146
Abuse, Akan traditional, 148–9, 169 and n. 2, 170
Abusua kuruwa, 195–6, 195 n., 1, 198–9, 200
Abydos, 44 n. 2, 55, 116 n. 4, 185 n. 1, 222
   festival at, 204
   temple of Osiris at, 46
Accession ceremonies, Egyptian, 208–9, 222 ff. *See also* King, Akan: enstoolment
Adaduanan calendar. *See under* Calendar
Adae rites, 117 n. 1, 129 and n. 1, 140, 185
Adafa custom, 196
Adare, sacred stream, 107, 143, 172
Adehye, 200, 216
Adiaka-duro, 189
Adiakahene, 188–9, 195
Adiaka-pomum (a staff), 189 and n. 1
Adosowa, 192–3, 194
   adagya, 192, 193
   suani, 192
Adu Gyamfi, 99 and n. 4

Adu Kodjo, King, 188 n. 2
Adumfo (executioners of human sacrifice), 144, 145 and n. 1, 182, 188, 189, 190, 191–2, 195, 196, 200, 202, 209
   female, 190, 195, 196, 198, 199, 202
Adumfohene, 188, 190, 196, 203
Adwera leaves, 104, 107, 108, 174
Aeneolithic Period I, people of, 232
   Period II culture, 233
Aethiopians, Eastern, 32
Aferihyia Dwaree (New Year autumn purification ceremony), 118, 171–176, 177
Aferinhye da, 212
Agriculture, Sky fertility-deities and, 29. *See also* Land
Agyentoa, 151 and n. 3
Ahenema (royal children), 94, 191, 200, 201
Ahenemahene, 186
   death of the king and, 186, 187, 189, 194
Ahemfie (palace), 216, 220
Ahensi. *See* Enstoolment
Ahoboa, 27
Akan, the, 23–30, 59–64, 71, 78, 85–90, 98–100, 103–9, 121–30, 142–51, 156, 171–6, 186–204, 216–22, 234, 235
   animals and, 37, 51
   chiefs, 95
   civilisation of, 16, 235
   falcon and, 35
   goat and, 74 n. 4
   goodness and, 125
   houses and dress of, 235
   name, 26 n. 3
   plants and, 51

INDEX

Akan, the—*contd.*
  religion derived from Egypt, 15, 16, 17 *et passim*
Akhmin, 79, 101
  stele from, 81
  title of chiefs of, 79
Akhu (transfigured spirits), 133–4
Akomfo, 63, 79 and n. 4, 83. See also Priests
Akra suo (sacred meal), 174, 175. See also Meals
Akrafo (*kra* or soul-bearers), 106, 107, 108, 109, 115, 171, 172, 174, 175, 199, 200, 211
  female, 108
Akrafo-ba-panyin, 106–7, 175, 182
Akrafohene (chief of the soul-bearers), 106–9, 115, 117, 171, 173 ff., 182, 199 n. 1, 237
  king impersonated by, 106, 108, 109, 171–5
  leopard-skin cap of, 115
  regalia of the king and, 108, 109, 117, 171–2, 179 n. 1
Akragya (*kra* progenitors), 60, 66, 72, 80, 103, 104, 113 and n. 1, 178
Akua Dapaa, Bono-Takyiman queen-mother, 57 n. 4
Akuaba, statuettes (fig. 6), 69
Akumfi Ameyaw II, King of Bono, 106
Akyeamehene (chief royal spokesman), 138 n. 5, 172, 188, 201 n. 2
Akyeneboa (totem animal), 27–8, 60, 61, 62, 217 n. 1
  kra and, 30, 61
  obosom incarnated in, 27
Akyerkyere Kingdom, name Asare among, 233 n. 3
Amen, Creator-god, 53, 85, 92, 101, 120, 154, 155, 160, 163
  Pharaohs and, 222, 223–4, 225, 237
Amenemes I, King of Egypt, 97
Amenemes II, King of Egypt, 226
Amenemhet, founder of the 12th Dynasty, 96
Amenhotep I, King of Egypt, 53, 54, 113
Amenhotep III, King of Egypt, birth scenes at Luxor of, 112
Amen-hotep IV. See Ikhnaton
Amenophis I, King of Egypt, ritual of, 101
Amenophis III, King of Egypt, 164, 165
Amen-Re, 92 and n. 3, 93, 165, 166, 237
  Hatshepsut and, 96
  Nyankopon and, 234
  rebirth of, 165 ff.
  shrine of, 168
Amen-Re-Khamutef, 234, 237
Ameyaa Kese, Bono Queen-mother, 24
Ameyaw Gyamfi, *Omanhene*, 127, 218 n. 4
Ameyaw Kwaakye, 147 n. 3, 149, 158, 166
  Apo festival and, 146, 147–8
  tomb of, 147, 208
Amon, Amen. See Amun
Amona, 90, 227
Amosis I, King of Egypt, 96
Amtes, Queen of Egypt, 57
Amun (Amen, Amon), bull moon-god, 101 and n. 5, 102, 228 and n. 3
  sacred marriage of, 101–2
  statues of, 101
  Thebes ram-god, 101
  three forms of, 101 n. 5
Amun-Apet, sky fertility-god, 101
Amun-Re, 67 n. 2, 101, 178
Anana (Agwana) clan, the, 88, 234
Ancestors, ancestral spirits, Royal, 23, 45, 48, 51, 86, 88, 99, 126–7, 131, 135 ff., 135 nn.
  dead Pharaoh and, 135–6
  offerings and libations to, 109, 137, 141 *et passim*
  statues of, 136 and n. 6, 138, 185 and n. 1
  stools and, 128
  See also *Ka*; *Kra Nananom*; Nekhen; Ntoro cult; Pe; *Saman*; Stools: black
Andjeti. See Anzti
Anhai, Papyrus of, 77, 78
Animals, 37, 51
  gods represented by four-footed, 70 n. 4
  mummification of sacred, 37
  See also *Akyeneboa*; *Padua*; Sacrifice; and animals by name
Ankh sign, 112, 164
Anmutef, priest of the Pharaoh's *ka*, 114–15, 164
  leopard-skin of, 114–15
  significance of, 114
Ankobeahene, 201 and n. 4, 218 and n. 3
Ankyeo Nyame, Princess, 24
Antelopes:
  bongo (*otromo*), 86
  mask of, 145
  otromo, tail of, 78 n. 1
  oryx, 74 and n. 6. See also *Ewio*

INDEX

Antubam, Kofi, 17
Anzti, ram-god, 44 and n. 3, 161 kings, 51
Apafram, 99, 176
Apatan (aardfark), 195
Ape, the, 41 n. 2, 154 n. 2
Aphroditopolis, 31 and n. 1, 43
Api, hippopotamus-goddess, 112
Apis bull, 77 and nn. 6, 8, 78 and n. 3, 81, 90, 131
   cloth and, 77
Apis, Bull-god, 76-9, 76 n. 2, 79 n. 4
Apis, Sky fertility-god, 46
Apo festival, 118, 142, 146-9, 149 nn. 1, 2, 168
   kra and, 146
   songs of, 148
Apunia rites, 128, 203. *See also* Stools
Apupuo, Akan royal head-dress, 167 and n. 3
Arrows, crossed, 229
   Sa and, 112 and n. 6
   symbolic, 230
Asah or Asaman, Prince of the falcon clan. *See* Asaman
Asaman or Asah, King of Bono, 24, 63, 64, 127, 143
Asante, the, 16, 23, 185
   war between the Bono-Takyiman and, 23, 25, 187 n. 1, 208
Asante (Ashanti) Kingdom, 23, 26, 56, 152 and n. 2, 175 n. 1, 176
   emblem of, 51
   mausoleum of royalty, 187 n. 1
Aseda (thanksgiving money), 217
Asiakwa, city state, 24
Asipim (throne chair), 108, 190, 199, 203
Asisiada, 193
Asona clan, 216 and n. 2
Asonahene, 216
Asramenta, 123
Ass, the, 74 and n. 5
Assyrians, Aththur god of, 233
Astronomical instruments, 91, 166-7
Asuanifo (disciples), 145-6
Asubo ceremony, 87, 128
Asueyi, 239
Ate (leather cushion), 127
Athena (Athene), 71, 230 n. 2. *See also* Neith
Aththur, Athar, god, 233
'*Atoapoma*', 'Ever-ready shooter', 27, 86, 103
atofo, 123
Aton, 93

Amen-hotep IV and, 92-3
Atum, ichneumon god, 37, 38, and n. 2, 39, 40, 41 and n. 4, 41, 77 n. 6, 90 n. 1, 90-3, 164, 145 n. 1
   cult of, 39 n. 2
   Shu succeeds, 42
   Sun-god, as, 90, 93
   'throne of Atum', 39, 90. *See also* Re-Atum
Atumfohene, 143 and n. 1, 145, 146
   ritual fight with king of, 143, 145, 154, 158, 160
Awaa awaa atun custom, 217
Awo, priestess queen-mother, murder of, 238
Awusu, Akan king's funeral rites and, 199 and n. 1, 200, 211
Axes, 75-6, 75 n. 5
   golden, 75-6
   triangular, 75, 76
Ayikeseada, 196 ff.
Ayoko clan, 23, 127, 190
   totem of, 23

Ba, the (divine soul), 77, 96, 122 and n. 1, 131, 132
   Osiris, of, 46, 77
   Pharaoh, of, 131
   Ptah, of, 77 n. 5. *See also* Souls of Pe and Nekhen
Baal Hamman, ram-god, 82 n. 4, 228
Badarian civilisation, 228 n. 1
Bampanase, 176
Banmu Kese, 195, 196, 200, 202
Banmu people, 189, 190, 194, 197, 238
Banmuhene (cemetery priest), 107, 109, 129, 176, 195
   Apo festival and, 146, 147, 148
   king's death and, 187, 189, 202, 206
Banmuhemmaa (cemetery priestess), 187, 190
Barley, 38, 164
   Osiris and, 164
Bastet, goddess, 119, 120 n. 1, 155, 170 n. 1
   rebirth of, 170
   solar goddess, 119
bayi-fo, 122
Beads, *bota* and *bodom*, 99, 175 n. 1
Bear (arcturus), the, 59
Bedewonua tree, 30 n. 3, 196 and n. 1
Bee, the, 51, 82 and n. 4
Bee clan, 42
Begetter, cult of the:
   Akan, 98-100
   Egyptian, 100-2

INDEX

Bempomaa, 24
Ben-ben stone, 90
bennu bird, 90–1, 96, 131
Berbers, 26. See also Gbon; Libyans
Bes, god, 112
Birth, 112, 156. See also Death and rebirth
Blacksmiths, 142–3, 144, 155, 156
   Atumfohene of, 143 and n. 1, 145, 146
   tools of, 143
Bleeker, C. J., 183 n. 1, 184 n. 1, 185 n. 2
Blood sausage. See Bonsua
Bodua, 219 and n. 1
Body, the king's, 125–6, 134, 217–18
   ritual washing of dead, 189
   See also King, Akan; Sahu; Saman
bogya (blood), 103, 104
Bogyawea, 190, 198
bo-me-tuo, custom, 168 n. 2
Bona or Gbona, Kingdom in French Ivory Coast, 24
Bono, the, 63, 118, 147 n. 2, 148, 149, 155, 224, 234–5
   co-regency among, 226
   houses of, 234–5
   king and, 87, 88–9, 126 n. 1, 227 n. 1
   kra ritual of, 106–9
   mausoleum of royalty, 187 n. 1, 208
   totem of, 26. See also Bono-Takyiman
Bono Kingdom, 16, 23, 24, 25, 26, 56, 61–2, 63, 64, 142, 152 n. 2, 173 n. 1, 200, 227 n. 1
   Asante conquest of, 141 n. 2. See also Asante
   deity of, 26, 62
   emblem of, 51
Bonohemmaa Gyaasewaa, 89
Bono-Mansu, 63
Bono-Takyiman (Tekyiman-Brong), the, 16, 129, 160
   wars with Asante of, 23, 25, 187 n. 1, 208
Bono-Takyiman State, 23, 35, 41 n. 3, 62, 141 n. 2, 146, 152 n. 2, 153, 218 n. 4
   deity of, 150
   See also Takyiman
Bono-Takyimanhene, 188 n. 1, 221
   Kra Dware ceremony and, 109
Bonsua (blood sausage), 108, 123 n. 1, 129, 175
Book of Am Duat, 118, 119 n. 1
Book of the Dead, the, 73 n. 3, 119 and nn. 2–5, 133–4, 134 n. 1, 179
Bosummuru, Ntoro god, 98, 99, 129, 174, 175, 181, 185, 196 n. 1, 219, 234
   gold dagger or sword of, 99, 127, 128, 172, 173, 174, 176, 181, 184 n. 1, 219
   priest of, 203
   shrine of, 175 n. 1
   three forms of, 101 n. 5
Breastplate, golden, 225
Bronzes, Egyptian, 76
Bubastis, 154, 155, 163, 166, 168–9, 170
   Festival Hall of Osorkon II at, 153, 154, 156, 158, 159, 161, 165
Budge, E. A. Wallis, 75 nn. 4, 5, 77 n. 8, 132–3, 132 n. 1, 141 n. 3
Bull, the, 77 and n. 6, 82 n. 4, 90, 92, 100
   Geb and, 42–3
   horns of, 83
   kings incarnated in, 75 n. 1
   Min's, 84
   Set and, 75 and n. 1
   tail of, 78 and n. 1, 181
   thigh of, 214 n. 3
   white, 63, 77–8, 80, 99, 102, 175–6, 179, 237 n. 3
   See also under Sacrifice
Burial, Akan royalty and, 125–6, 126 n. 1, 147 and n. 2
   Apis bull, of, 78 and n. 3
   See also Funeral rites
Buru, Bull-god, 63–4, 82 n. 4
Buru, Sky fertility-god, 101 n. 5
   maize and, 100
   Ntoro cult and, 98–100
   shrine of, 99
Buru, mouse-god, 82 n. 4
Buru-kung, Mother-goddess, 101 n. 5
Busiris, 44, 74 n. 4, 161
Buto, 48, 51

Cabiri, the, 71
Calendar, 90, 119
   Akan Adaduanan, 79, 119, 129, 212 n. 1
Catfish, Tano personified by, 61
Ceramics, Egyptian, symbols on, 232
Cerny, J., 31 n. 1, 37 n. 2
Chapel of the Stools (Nkon-dwa-fieso), 88, 89, 126, 127–30, 153, 185, 188, 197, 198, 210 n. 2, 203, 217, 220
   custodian of, 128
   ritual in, 129–30
   stool and kra of king in, 89 and n. 2
   See also Nkondwasoafohene; Stools
Charms, 78, 124, 157, 218

244

INDEX

Chenemhetep, Satab, wife of, 54 n. 2
Chester Beatty Papyrus, No. 1, 48, 73 n. 3
Children, *kra* and, 104, 124
  royal, 209 n. 1: see also *Ahenema*
  Sky fertility-gods and, 62
Chri-nu-s, 157
Circle, black, 78
  dot and, symbolism of, 224 n. 2
Circumpolar stars, seven, 59, 65, 66, 71 n. 3, 72
Clans, Akan, 28, 41 n. 3
  chiefs of, 98
  deities of, 37, 40
  seven, 47, 63, 145, 160
Clepsydra, 154 and n. 2, 166
Cones, 36, 62, 70 n. 5, 84, 127
'Contending of Horus and Set', 48
Copper, 71, 107, 181
Co-regents, 54, 57, 224, 226–7, 227, n. 1
Coronation of Akan king, 225, 226
  Pharaoh, of, 117, 133, 209, 210, 222, 223
Co-rulers, 55 and n. 3, 56, 57. *See also* Co-regents
Cosmic order and time, 65, 72, 93, 113
Costume, 159, 160, 163, 234–5
  Heb Sed, 165
Cow, the, Apis and, 76
  black, 63, 80, 99, 175 and n. 1, 176, 181 and n. 3
  goddesses, 40 n. 4, 113
  Hathor incarnated in, 34–5, 57
  Nut as, 43
  See also Hathor; Sacrifice: cow
Creation of the World, Odomankoma and, 59
Crime and trial of Akan queen-mother, 57 and n. 4
Crocodile, the, 73–4, 74 n. 1
  Horus incarnated in, 73
Crowns, Egyptian, 51, 165, 177–8, 180, 224, 225, 229
  atef, 69, 161, 164
  Blue, 161, 164, 177, 178, 184, 224 and n. 2, 225 and n. 3
  double, Upper and Lower (fig. 3), 36, 184
  Neith, of, 42, 229
  Red, 226
  White, 51, 53–4, 117
Crux decussata, symbolism of, 78, 107, 111, 232
Cult periods:
  Cult Type I, 103, 233

Cult Type II, 60, 61, 63 n. 1, 65 n. 8, 103, 231, 233, 239
Cult Type III, 60, 85, 233, 239
Cult Type IV, 239

Daberehene (Chamberlain), 186–7
  heir-apparent of, 186
Damankama, god, 189
Danquah, Dr. J. B., 17, 124–5
Dead, the, Hathor and, 34
  mother-goddess of, 27
  Osiris judge of, 130, 131, 132
  See also Ancestors; *Dwat*; *Ka*; *Kra*; Netherworld; *Saman*; *Saman-fo*
Death:
  king, Akan, and, 186–94. *See also* King, dead Akan
  Moon Mother-goddess and, 27
  Odomankoma and, 60–1
  Ptah and, 66, 67
  tabu on Akan royalty from, 105, 106, 159, 187, 206, 217 n. 3
  tabu for Pharaoh, 205–6, 206 n. 2, 211 n. 1
Death and rebirth, 30, 62, 68, 69, 71, 72, 78, 102, 119, 163 ff., 185, 237
  Apo rites and, 149–50
  ka and, 109
  king, Akan, and, 30, 87, 89, 171–6, 237–8
  kra and, 105, 121–2
  Min and, 179 ff.
  Ntoro god and, 99–100
  pharaoh and god incarnated by, 177–85
  serpent and, 118 n. 4, 119
Deer, 82 n. 4
Deir el Bahri, 55, 66, 112–13, 112 n. 1, 222, 224
Deities, bi-sexuality of, 29, 30, 34, 36, 60, 61, 72, 98, 101 n. 5, 233
  Egyptians and, 37–8, 42, 159
  forty-two, 119
  kra of, 36
  land and Akan, 137 and n. 2, 142
  matrilineal, 31
  stars and, 75 n. 4
  state, 62
  twelve, 167
Delafosse, M., 234
Denderah, 34
  birth temple at, 112
  relief on tomb at, 68–9
Dep, 137
  per-nu shrine at, 137 n. 3
Dia or Dja, the, 25–6

INDEX

Dia or Dja Confederation. *See* Diadom
Diadom, Djadum, 23, 24 and n. 1, 26,
  dynasty of, 23–4
Diala, 24 and n. 1
Dia-Mo kingdom, 188 and n. 2
Diana, 24 and n. 1
Diodorus Siculus, 52, 94, 141 n. 3, 211, 212
Djed object, 68–70, 164
  symbolism of, 164
Djed pillar, 209 and n. 2
Djenné, 24 n. 1
Djoser, king, 50, 90
  pyramid of, 90
Dog, the, 63
Double descent system, Akan, 100, 102
Drake, Apis and, 77
Drums, 198, 200
  atopre, 191
  dono, 169
  state, 172, 173, 200
  talking, 64, 144–5, 156, 174, 202, 212
Dual Shrines, 101, 135 and n. 4, 136–41, 182 and n. 4, 205 n. 1, 214, 223, 225
  ritual in, 140–1
Dwabum custom, 191, 208, 209
Dwambara Akenten, Bono Queen-mother, 188 n. 1
Dwat (land of the dead), 116 and n. 2, 135. *See also* Netherworld

Edfu, 55, 116 n. 4, 162 n. 2
  sacred marriage at, 35
Edjo (Wadjet), goddess, 51, 223, 224. *See also* Wadjet
Eggs, symbolism and, 35, 65 and n. 8, 143, 173
Egypt, and religion of, 15, 16, 17, 31–58, 64–84, 90–7, 100–2, 130–141, 151–70, 177–85, 204–15, 222–7, 234
  Akan religion and, 15, 16, 17 *et passim*
  dynasties of, 38
  Lower, 43
  Lower and Upper (Two Lands), 49, 51, 53, 162
  map of, 33
El Khab, 36
Elder Woman, 28–9, 106. See also *Akrafo-ba-panyin*
Elders, 38 n. 3, 108, 146, 203, 216, 217, 219, 220 *et passim*

city states and, 38
Eldest son, 204–5, 204 n. 1, 205 n. 1, 206, 226. See also *Gyaasehene*; *Sa-mer-f*
Elephant, the, 189 n. 3
  tusks of, 189
Embalming, 134
Ennead, gods of the, 223 and n. 5
Enstoolment and its ceremonies, Akan, 86, 88, 128, 196, 212–22, 218 n. 5, 222 n. 1
Equinoxes, rites and, 54 n. 2, 118, 119, 120 n. 8, 152 and n. 4, 154 n. 2, 166, 167
Esa wood, 108, 144, 147
Esne, *Sed* festival at, 161
Eto (mashed yams), 108, 129, 144, 151, 174
Ewio (duiker antelope), 61
  Tano incarnate in, 145
Exogamy, clan, 28, 32, 55

Falcon, the, 34, 44, 50, 70 n. 5, 127, 139
  burial and mummification of, 37
  crouching and upright, 35, 37
  double, 139
  falcon gods, 36–7
  Hathor incarnate in, 32, 34
  Horus and, 35–7, 84
  Osiris as, 44
  Soker as, 46
  statue of, 79
  totem as, 23, 26, 127
Falcon clan, 45, 50, 82 n. 4
  Horus, god of, 49
  kings of, 48, 51
  Upwaut's production of Horus and, 45
Falcon clan people, the, 23–6, 31, 35, 233
  map of migration of, 25
  Min and, 79
  totem, as, 26
  standards of, 159
Fante, the, 61
Faraoui, Kingdom of the, 234
Feathers, two, 81 and n. 1
Fertility, 62
  Sasabonsam and, 70
  symbols of, 61, 77
  See also Procreation; *Tuobo* custom
Fire, 86, 112, 115, 122, 143
  Apo festival and, 147
  kra and, 115, 143, 186 n. 1
  Ptah and, 64 and n. 3
Fish, Set and, 74 and n. 3

246

INDEX

Five-figured hand, as symbol, 71 n. 3
Flame, symbolism of, 112. *See also* Fire
Fluid of life. See *Sa*
Fo, or 'Fertile Thursday', 106, 221
Fo-Bena, 'Fertile Tuesday', 149
Fo-Dwo-Kese, 'Great Fertile Monday', 142, 149, 150, 170
Fo-Dwo, 129
Fo-Fie, 'Fertile Friday', 129
Forty days, Akan and, 78-9, 212 and n. 1
  royal succession and, 216 and n. 1
Frankfort, Henri, 16-17, 51, 66 n. 3, 94, 110, 116 n. 2, 130 n. 5, 137 n. 4, 156, 180 n. 3, 184 n. 3, 207, 209 nn. 1, 2, 211 n. 1, 222 n. 1
  divine kingship and, 236, 237
Friday, 60, 61, 185
  'Fertile Friday,' 129, 143
  'Fresh Friday,' 129
  'Hateful Friday,' 129, 146 and n. 2, 147
  'Most Sacred Friday,' 148
Frog, the, 165
Fufu, 129, 144, 145, 174
  symbolism of, 145
Funeral rites:
  Akan, 86, 125-6, 128, 197 and n. 1. See also King, dead Akan
  Egyptian, 204-13. *See also* Pharaoh, dead
  Osiris, of, 46, 204-5
  purification and sacred water and, 167. See also *Ayikeseada*; Burial

Gara or Kora, the, 26
Garamantians, the, 26
Gauthier, H., 79 and nn., 81 and n. 4, 83, 177, 178 nn. 1, 3, 182, 184 n. 3
Gban or Gwan. *See* Gbon
Gbon, or Gwon, the, 24, 26. *See also* Bono
Gbon-Dja (Gonja), 24
Geb, deity, 37, 38, 41-3
  character of, 42
  earth-god, 42
  goose or bearded man, as, 42
  Horus and, 45
  kings and, 43
  'Seed of Geb,' 45
  Shu and, 40-1
  'throne of Geb,' 42, 45
Goats, 74 n. 4
  bush, emblem of Tano, 61
Gold, 50, 127, 181
  Akan kings and, 89, 125-6, 127, 175 and n. 1, 196, 203
  gold dust, 89, 190, 193, 194
  metal of the Sun, 50, 89, 96, 125, 134.
  weights, 70, 112
  See also *Puduo*
Goose, 43, 92 n. 3
  Geb as, 42
Goose clan, 42
Great Bear, Set and, 75 n. 2
Gun-bearers, 172, 173
Guns, ritual firing of, 173, 193, 198, 199, 201
Gya dua kra (sacred tree), 192 and n. 1, 217 n. 2
Gyaasehene (eldest son), 128, 129, 138 n. 5, 173, 187, 189, 194, 195 n. 1, 198, 199, 201 and n. 3, 203, 205 n. 1, 207, 216
  enstoolment of king and, 218-19, 218 n. 2, 220, 225
Gyamfi Kumanini, 200, 202

Hair, Akan funeral rites and, 197 and n. 1
Hammurabi, as Sun-god, 237
Haremhab, King of Egypt, 96, 222-3, 224
  queen of, 223 n. 6
  statue of, 222, 223
Harendotus, deity, 43
Harmakhis, Sphinx, 222
Harvest festival of Min Khamutef, 118, 152, 177 and nn. 1, 2, 3, 177-85
Hathor, Moon Mother-goddess, 31-2, 34-5, 36, 55, 74 n. 3, 102, 112 n. 1, 113 n. 3, 164 and n. 2, 165, 233
  Behdetite, the, 49
  clan of, 31-2
  Cow-goddess and incarnated in cow, 34-5, 39, 47 n. 2, 49 n. 2, 56, 67 n. 3, 80, 113, 114, 115, 233
  Egyptian queen incarnation of, 55, 102
  'Golden One,' 50
  head depicted, 84
  Heliopolis of, 55, 164
  hemsut deity, as, 139
  Horus and, 49 and n. 2, 73
  Horus as male aspect of, 35
  Isis, incarnation of, 52, 53
  ka and, 112
  'Lady of the Flame,' 34, 47 n. 2
  moon-goddess, as, 35
  'Mother of the Dead,' 34
  Onuris and, 162 n. 2
  Pharaoh and, 117
  rebirth of, 56
  sons of, 50
  Sun and, 34
  Venus aspect of, 55

247

INDEX

Ha'-ti-e, 160
Hatshepsut, Queen of Egypt, 56, 57 and n. 2
  Amen-Re and, 96
  birth scenes of, 66, 102, 112–13
  co-ruler and heir-apparent, 56, 57
  coronation of, 224, 225, and n. 3
Hawk, mummified sacred, 37
Head-dress, 86, 88
  golden helmet, 88
  Min and, 81 and n. 1
  See also *Apupuo*
Heb Sed costume, 165
Heirs-apparent, 186, 205
  to king, 56–7, 87, 226, 238
  to queen-mother, 90, 56–7, 227
Heket, birth-goddess, 112 n. 1
Heliopolis, 39 n. 4, 91–2, 96, 137, 166
  Great Ennead of, 38, 45, 48 n. 3, 163 and n. 4, 185 n. 1
  'Souls of Heliopolis,' 137 n. 4
He-Maat-hap, 56
Hemenet, 132
Hemsut (female *ka*), 34, 66 and n. 3, 72, 113
  sign of, 111, 139
Hephaistos, god of fire, 64, 71
Herher, King of Egypt, 55
Herodotus, 71, 73 n. 3, 76, 211
Heru-Shu-Onuris, deity, 36
Hierakonpolis, reliefs at (figs. 2–4), 36
Hieroglyphs, 111, 112, 115, 132, 136
  ka.t, 111
  See also Ideograms
High priests, 57, 82–3, 116 n. 3, 145–6, 146 n. 1, 183 n. 1, 225
  Min, of, 82, 83
  See also under Ta Kese
Hippopotamus, the, 74 and n. 3
Honhom (breath of life, divided soul), 104 and n. 2, 122 and n. 2, 124, 125, 131, 234
Honhom Nipadua (transfigured spirits), 124–5, 134. See also *Akhu*
Horapallo, 71, 91, 154 n. 2
Horses, 152 n. 2
  white, tail of, 78 n. 1
Horus, the Elder, Son of Hathor, 31, 35 ff., 43, 44 ff., 47, 48 nn. 1, 3, 49 n. 2, 68, 72–3, 101, 114, 115, 161, 207, 222, 224, 225, 233, 236
  Behdetite, the, 49, 161
  children of, 213
  Edfu, of, 73, 162 and n. 2
  falcon and, 35–7, 47, 50, 84

  forms of his personality, 72–3, 74 and n. 6
  Geb and, 45
  Hathor, mother-wife of, 55
  Heru-Nub, 36
  'Horus of Gold,' 50
  Horus *ka*, 114, 115
  moon-god, as, 36
  Pharaoh incarnation of, 35, 37, 38, 46–7, 49 ff., 139
  Re and, 92
  reliefs of (figs. 2, 3, 4), 36
  Set and, 42, 43, 48
  son of Isis, 47 ff.
  throne of, 52, 54
Horus kings and kingdom, 43, 48
  royalty, married to Set royalty, 140
Horus-Anmutef, 114, 116 and n. 3
Horus name, 37, 100, 113
Horus-Shu-Onuris, (fig.) 36
Hurrians, 233 and n. 5
Hyebea, 104 and n. 3

Ichneumon, and clan of, 39 n. 2
Ideograms, 77, 127, 229
Ideographs, 232
Ikhernofret, text of, 204, 205 n. 1, 206–7
Ikhnaton (Amen-hotep IV), 92–3, 206 n. 2
Immortality, 136
  Akan kings and, 126
  Sahu and, 132. See also Death and rebirth; Resurrection
Imy-khant, 138, 182, 223, 226
Ishtar (Ashtart), Mother-goddess, 233
Isis, goddess, 44, 47–8, 47 n. 2, 49, 52 ff., 55, 66 n. 3, 74, 80 and n. 3, 112, 113, 139, 160–1, 214 and n. 1, 230 n. 2, 249 n. 2
  Horus and, 31, 52, 53, 139
  incarnate in the divine queen, 52–8
  legend about Set and Thoth and, 47
  Min and, 180
  Nefertari and, 53
  Pharaoh and, 50, 136, 222
  Thoth clan and, 47
Iterty (Dual Shrines), 51, 135, 136. See also Dual Shrines
Iusaaset, goddess, 40 and n. 4

Jacobsohn, H., 177
'Japhetites', 232
Junker, Hermann, 31 n. 2, 133 n. 3
Jupiter, 59, 60, 73, 116, 146, 197

INDEX

Ka, the, 34, 37, 66 and n. 3, 69, 70, 113 and n. 4, 131 and n. 5, 132, 133 and n. 3, 136, 160, 230
    Aton and, 93
    concept of, 109 ff.
    dead king Osiris, of, 69
    Horus, of, 37, 111
    ladders and, 130, 135 and n. 2
    luck and, 110
    Nehebkau and, 118–20
    Nehebkau festival and, 163 ff.
    Neith and, 111
    personality and, 130
    Pharaoh, of, 92, 110, 111 ff., 133, 135, 160, 167
    Pharaoh's fourteen *kas*, 113 and n. 2, 120
    planets and, 110, 130
    Ptah and, 72
    purification rites for, 115, 116–17
    representation of, 111
    Royal Ancestors, of, 111–12, 113–14, 118, 182, *et passim*
    standard of, 167
    symbol and, 113
    uniting of, 163–5
    See also *Hemsut*
Kakau (Kaiekhos), king of Egypt, 76
Karnak, and reliefs at, 55, 66, 102, 161, 180 n. 2, 181 n. 2
Kente cloth, 192 and n. 3
Kerhebu, 224–5
Khaibit (shadow soul), 66, 81, 132
    sunsum contrasted with, 81
Khamutef and cult of, 100–2, 101 n. 5, 234
Kheruef, tomb of, 70, 164, 169
Khetiu, Prince, tomb of, 65 n. 1
Khnum, craftsman Creator-God, 112 and n. 1
Khoiak festival, 152
King, the:
    death and rebirth, 30, 87, 89, 171–6
    divine, and cult of, 29–30, 45, 76, 102, 236 ff.
    duty and tabus of, 105–6
    incarnation of gods by, 75 nn. 1, 2
    life and life-giving power of, 86, 87
    priesthood of, 29, 88
    royal ancestors and, 23
    sacred marriage of, 62
    sacrifice of, 30 and n. 2
    son of the Sun-god cult, 111–12, 233, 234
King, Akan, 23, 53 n. 3, 99, 110, 128
    akrafohene impersonates, 171–5
    anointing of new, 220
    Atumfohene's ritual fight with, 143, 145, 154, 158, 159, 160
    body of, 125–6, 134, 217–18
    bull and, 77–8
    children of, 88, 194, 200, 209 n. 1
    coronation of, 225, 226
    enstoolment ceremony of new, 86, 88, 128, 196, 212–22, 218 n. 5, 222 n. 1
    feet and sandals of, 159, 217 and n. 3
    fount of all, and his authority, 87
    heir-apparent of, 56–7, 87, 226, 238
    Korontihene's fight with, 149, 159, 160, 169
    Kra of: see under *Kra*
    kra power and ritual death of, 106
    land and, 142, 145
    moon Mother-goddess and, 87, 128
    new king, 197, 198 ff., 202–3, 212 ff.
    preparations about, and body of, 217–18
    name of, 220 and n. 2
    stool property of, 220–1
    ntoro cult of, 98, 99
    Nkondwasoafohene and, 128
    public appearance of new, 226
    queen-mother and, 30, 87
    regalia and insignia of, 108, 109, 117, 147, 171–2, 172 n. 1, 176, 221, 225, 237, 238
    sons of, 87–8, 94–5, 190–1, 194, 207, 209
    standards of, 138–9
    state council, 29, 87, 221
    stool of living, 86, 189
    stool-sons of: *see* Stool-sons
    Sun and Sun-god incarnated in, 85 ff., 88–90
    daily life of, 88–9
    sexual life of, 88
    tabu on death for, 105, 106, 159, 187, 206, 217 n. 3
    wives of, 62, 87, 88, 140, n. 3, 170, 172, 173, 175, 186 n. 1, 189, 190, 191 n. 1, 192, 193, 195, 207 and nn. 3, 5, 220–1
King, dead Akan, 176
    ascension and transfiguration of, 200–4, 212
    body, after death of, 187 and n. 2, 189–90, 193, 194–6, 210
    chiefs and, 197–8, 200
    coffin of, 89, 125–6, 194, 196
    funeral rites, 196–200, 207
    second, 211, 212 and n. 3, 226

R

INDEX

King, dead Akan—*contd.*
  human sacrifice and, 189, 190–2, 194–200, 209
  immortal life for, 126
  stool of, 89, 201 and n. 2, 202, 213, 214
konkom dua kom, 68
Koma (the heart), 122
Koptos, 79, 101, 102 n. 2
Korontihene (elder of the Omanhene and Governor of the State), 38 and n. 3, 145, 216
  fight with king, 149, 159, 160, 169
  fight with Tano of, 145, 146
  king's death and, 186, 187, 193, 195, 198, 201, 207
  new king and, 219
Kra, the, 27, 29, 30, 34, 37, 66, 70, 80, 109–10, 121 ff., 141
  akyeneboa and, 30, 61
  bi-sexuality of, 103, 105, 111
  clan-goddess of, 30
  concept of, 103–9
  death and, 105, 121–2
  deities of, 36
  king's, 29, 30, 87, 89, 105–9, 126, 157, 226
  king's lunar, 29, 85, 98, 111
  king's solar, 85, 86, 87, 98, 108, 111, 146, 223
  ladders and, 121, 126 and n. 4
  life-giving power of, 29, 30 *et passim*
  lucky, 110
  moon and, 103
  moon Mother-goddess of, 27, 30
  name and, 125
  nananom, of, 86, 106 107 and n. 3, 108, 109, 111, 115–16, 129 *et passim*
  Nyame and, 59, 104, 126
  Nyankopon and, 30, 85, 88
  obosom and, 60
  okra and, 30, 106, 115, 189
  personality and, 121–2
  planets and, 60, 103, 110, 113, 122, 130
  purification of royal, 106, 107–9, 129, 223
  queen-mother's, 28–9, 89, 105, 106–7, 111, 175
  queen-mother's lunar, 29, 105
  reincarnation of, 133
  representation of, 104, 111
  shrines for, 123
  solar and lunar, 105
  sunsum contrasted with, 60

Sun and, 30
Sun-god and, 61
kra bafano, 109–10, 122, 130
Kra Dware, 107–9, 107 n. 2
Kra fieso (house of the *Kra*), 107, 109, 115–16, 117, 171, 173
kra sika (money), 190, 197 n. 1
kra suo (a soup), 108, 144, 145
Kuduo (metal vessel), 127, 203
Kumasi, capital, 238
Kumasi State, 25
Kuru or 'Most Sacred' Tuesday, 176
Kuru-fie, 'Most Sacred Friday, 148
Kus, 43
Kwabena Amenfi, 238
Kyereme Kofi, King, 141 n. 2

Labour, Akan communal and Egyptian slave, 95
Ladders, 121 n. 2
  Ka and, 130, 135 and n. 2
  Kra and, 121, 126 and n. 4
'Lady of the Flame,' 34, 47 n. 2
Land, the, 137 n. 2, 142, 153, 155, 157
  Akan kings and, 142, 145
  deities and, 137, 142
  Geb and, 42, 142
  Pharaoh and, 42, 162–3
  See also Nyanku Sai festival; Sed festival
Leopard, the, skins of, 114–15, 158
  symbolism of, 86, 115
Letopolis, 43
Lettuces, 82 and nn. 1, 2, 178
Libations, 109, 123, 129, 132 and n. 1, 137, 141, 143, 144, 145, 188, 194, 202, 217
Libyan North Africa, analogies to Akan beliefs in, 228 ff.
Libyans (Berbers), the, 26, 43, 161, 228 and nn. 1, 3, 232 and n. 3, 234
  deities of, 231
  Nubian, 26
  Pharaoh's fight with, 158, 159, 160, 161, 162
Libyo-Phoenicians, Akan religion and, 228
Life and life-giving power, 54–5, 86, 87, 219
  Akan queen-mother and, 51, 52, 54, 55
  Pharaoh and, 51, 57, 163 ff., 167
Lion, 32 n. 11, 41, 43, 73 n. 3
  lion-god, 39–40
  symbolism of, 86
Lion clan, 32 and n. 10, 40, 41 n. 4

250

INDEX

Lioness, 82 n. 4
  Hathor as, 32
  Tefnut as, 34, 82 n. 4
Lotus flowers, 164, 167
Luxor, reliefs at, 112, 113, 139

Maat, 65, 94, 113, 133
  feather of, 113
  goddess, 94
  Pharaoh and, 93–4
  Ptah and, 65
Maize, 64, 99, 100
Manatee or sea-cow, the, 63, 82 n. 4
Mande, the, 24
Manetho, 48, 64
  lists of gods and kings by, 38
Manwerehene, 187
  heir-apparent of, 186
Marduk, god, 233, 237 and n. 3
Marriage:
  Akan, 55, 56 n. 2, 99
  Egyptian royal brother-sister, 59
  Egyptian royal intermarriages, 139–140
  patrilocal, 100. *See also* Sacred marriage
Mars, 59, 60, 61, 63, 73, 99, 181, 197
Maspero, G., 54
Master of the King's Largesse, 156, 214 and n. 3
Mast, 163 and n. 4
Matrilineality, 15, 31, 40, 49, 94, 228, 231, 232
  clans, 37, 39
  state, 47, 55
  succession, 205 n. 2, 209 n. 1
  system of, 52
Meals, consecrated or sacred, 108, 117, 140 and n. 7, 145, 158, 166, 174–5 214
  Nehebkau festival and, 166. See also *Akra suo*
Medinet Habu, temple at, 80, 102, 136, 177–8, 180
Mefedua (spear), 157
Memphis, 35, 41 and nn. 4, 5, 43, 46, 70, 71, 78, 79, 153, 155, 161, 164, 169, 226 and n. 3
  Memphis-Hininsu, 51
  prehistoric, 41 n. 8
  state god of, 46
  temples at, 46, 76
Memphite Theology, 45, 48, 65 n. 2, 66
Menat, 44
Menes, King of Egypt, 48, 49, 50, 76 n. 2, 169

Mentu-Hetep III, temple of, 55–6
Mercer, S. A. B., 39 n. 5, 48 nn. 1, 2, 49 and n. 2
Mercury, 59, 60, 197
Meren-Re, 119
Meresankh III, Queen of Egypt, 135 n. 1, 210 n. 4
Mert, goddess, 162
Mertitefs, Queen of Egypt, 56
Mesopotamia, 238
  cult of the divine king in, 236, 237, 238
Metternich stela, 47
Min, Bull-god, 79–84, 82 n. 4, 92, 101, 138, 179, 180 n. 2, 236, 237
  bee-god, as, 82 n. 4
  death and rebirth of, 179 ff.
  emmer wheat and: See Wheat
  festival of, 32, 80, 82, 138
  head-dress of, 81 and n. 1
  Pharaoh as incarnation of, 84, 101, 102, 139
  sanctuary of, 83
  shadow of, 81
  sickle of, 181
  sky fertility-god, 80
  stairs of, 179, 182, 183
  statue of, 80–1, 178, 179, 185
  titles of, 79
Min-Horus, 31, 32
  'negro' at festival of, 32
Min Khamutef, 177
  death of, 179–80
  rebirth of, 102, 179
Min-Khamutef festival, 118, 152, 177–85, 177 nn. 1, 2, 3, 183 n. 1
  two hymns of, 183–4, 183 n. 3
Mmerante (Queen-mother's state swords), 89
Mmerantehene, 143, 146
Mmoatia (ugly dwarfs), 70
Mnevis bull, 77 n. 9, 90
Mo, the, 24
Mock battle:
  See King, Akan: *Atumfohene*'s ritual fight with; and *Korontihene*'s fight with; Pharaoh: ceremonial fight
Mock-king. See *Okra*
Monday, 60, 61, 80, 178, 185
  'Fertile Monday,' 142, 176
  'Great Fertile Monday,' 142, 149, 150, 170
Mono-Wukuo (Wednesday), 129
Moon, 59, 60, 65 n. 8, 75 and n. 2, 78
  cow-goddesses and, 113

INDEX

Moon—*contd.*
  eggs and, 65 and n. 8
  Egyptian beliefs about, 52
  Horus and, 73
  Kra and, 103
  Min and, 80
  obosom and, 27-8, 29
  Thoth and, 208
Moon-goddess, 34, 35, 61
  Akan queen-mother daughter of, 89. *See also* Neith
Moon-gods, 29, 36
  Egyptian kings incarnate, 90
  Horus as, 36. *See also* Amun
Moon Mother-goddess, 26 ff., 29, 76, 105, 166, 168 n. 2
  Akan queen-mother incarnates, 30, 85, 89, 111
  Apo and, 168
  Atoapoma, as, 27, 103
  death and, 27
  falcon and, 35
  king's descent from, 87
  kra and, 27, 30, 106
  male aspect of, 29
  Odiawuono, as, 27
  Sun and, 147
  symbolism of, 78
Moret, A., 114, 116 n. 3, 155 n. 3, 158, 222 n. 1, 226 n. 3
Mossi, the, 24
Mother-goddess, 233
  Sky fertility-god and, 230. *See also* Moon Mother-goddess; Nut
Mound, the, 62, 70 n. 5, 82 n. 4, 83-4
Mouse, the, and mouse clan, 63, 82 n. 4
Mpintin, 191 n. 2
  drummers of, 191
Muru-Fie, 'Fresh Friday', 129
Mut, goddess, 53, 101 and n. 5, 102 and n. 2, 181 n. 2
  incarnation of, 55
Mystical embrace, 113 n. 4, 117
Mystery Play of the Succession, death of a Pharaoh and accession ceremonies, 204, 208-10, 210 n. 1, 211, 213-15, 222 and n. 1

Name, 125-7, 134, 225
  kra and, 125
Nampranee tree, Buru and, 64
Nananom (royal ancestors), 86, 99, 121, 123, 126, 213 *et passim*
  king and, 89, 105, 107 and n. 2, 126, 200, 219
  kra of: See under *Kra*

stools of: *See under* Stools
Naqada, 229 and n. 2
Naqada civilisation:
  I, 228, 229, 230, (fig. 9), 231
  II, 229, 231
  III, 232
Narmer, King of Egypt, 84, 159
Narmer Palette, 49, 84, 159
Naville, E., 56 and n. 2, 166, 167, 170 n. 1
Nebt-hetep, cow-goddess, 40 n. 4
Nebti diadem, 224, 225
Nefert, 54 n. 2
Nefertari, Aahmes, Queen of Egypt, 53 ff.
  life-giving and cult of, 54-5
  regency of, 53 and n. 3, 54
  statue of, 55
  titles of, 53-4
Negroes, 32 and n. 7, 82 n. 4
  Punt, from, 79 n. 5, 179
  Sudanese, 26
Nehebkau, 118-20, 119 n. 1, 120 nn. 1, 6, 152, 154 n. 2, 167
  emblem of, 119 n. 1
  kas and, 118-20, 163 ff.
  serpents and, 118-19, 118 n. 4
Nehebkau festival, 118, 163-8
Neith (Nit, Net) goddess, 2, 42, 51, 82 n. 4, 161, 162, 228, 229 n. 2
  crown of, 42, 229
  emblem of, 111, 229, 230
  ka and, 111
  'Opener of the Ways,' 161
Neit-Hotep, Egyptian Queen, 50, 53
Nekhab, 137 and n. 1
Nekheb, 41 n. 4. *See also* El Khab
Nekhbet, vulture-goddess, 41 n. 4, 50, 51, 117, 137 and n. 1, 154, 224
Nekhen, 36, 137, 155. *See also* Hierakonpolis
Nekhen: 'Souls of Nekhen', 45, 51, 114. *See also* Souls of Pe and Nekhen
Nephthys, goddess, 38, 44, 47 n. 2, 48-9, 48 n. 3, 50, 214 and n. 1
Neshemet boat, 207
Netherworld or underworld, 27, 66, 99, 115
  Nehebkau and, 119. *See also Pa Dwat*; *Samandow*
Ne-Woser-Re, Sun temple of, 43, 138 n. 2, 153, 155-6, 158, 159, 160, 161
New Year Festival, 56, 62, 63, 237, 238-9
  Akan, 100, 128, 148-9, 152 n. 2
  Babylonian rite, 237

252

INDEX

Egyptian, 114, 118, 138
Thebes, 92. See also *Odwira*; and festivals by name
New Year's day, 77, 80, 89, 102, 115, 118, 120, 129, 142 and n. 1, 149, 150, 152, 165, 168, 171, 176 n. 2, 177, 178, 185
Nkondwasoafohene (custodian of the chapel of the stools), 128, 138 and n. 5, 203, 217, 218, 223, 226
king and, 128
Niger river, 64, 99
Nile river, 77, 152 nn. 3, 4
Nkerante (queen-mother's state sword) 175 n. 1
nkosuano, 65 n. 8
Nkrabea, 104 and n. 1
Nkwan Suo (water of life), 104, 112
'*Nkyi*' or 'Hateful' Monday, 176
'*Nkyi-fie*', 'Hateful Friday', 129, 146 and n. 2, 147
nomes (city states), 31 n. 1, 42, 79, 95, 96, 157
nome chiefs, 95
Ptah-Tatjenen festival and, 153
Nsaa blanket and cloth, 192 and n. 2, 201
Nsafiesohene, 187
heir-apparent of, 186
nsana berry, 64
Nsuasa, 220
Nsumankwahene, 157, 203
ntr, neter, netjer, 75 and n. 4, 76
Ntoa, Bono bi-sexual deity, sky fertility-god, 62, 63, 75 n. 2, 81 n. 6, 183 nn. 1, 3, 239
sanctuary at Seseman-Nkoranza of, 83 n. 6, 239
sanctuary at Wankyi, 83 n. 6, 239
tobacco sacred to, 89
Ntoasie, 189
Ntoro cult, 98–100, 102, 234
gods, 100
procreative power and, 100 and n. 4
spirit, 98, 99, 104
Ntumpane. See Drums: talking
Ntwuma (ochre), 201
Nubians, 156
Nub-Kha-Es, 54 n. 2
Nubt (Ombos), 43
temple at, 73
Numbers, sacred, and symbolism of, 82 n. 2, 163 n. 4, 164 n. 3, 170 n. 1, 212 and n. 2, 231
seven, 180
six, 170 n. 1, 231

three, 231
two, 78, 163 n. 4
Nun, Creator-god, 40 n. 4, 68
Nut, Mother-goddess, 31–2, 38, 43, 82 n. 4, 214
cow, as, 43
deceased Pharaohs and, 43, 135, 136
incarnation of, 43
Sun and, 91
Nyame, Supreme Being, 30, 59, 74 n. 6, 78 n. 1, 83 n. 7, 86, 113, 124, 125, 175, 221, 228
honhom and, 122
kra and, 59, 104, 126
Nyame Amowia, 65 n. 8
Nyankopon as male aspect of, 30, 85, 88
praise name of, 86
Nyame Dan, 175, 221
Nyame-dua, 83 n. 7
Nyamkomaduewuo, Akan Queen mother, 24
Nyankopon, Sun-god, 61, 85–6, 121, 221, 228
Amen-Re and, 234
Nyame and, 30, 85, 88
titles of, 86
See also Sun; Sun-god
Nyankopon-kurom, 88, 121, 190
Nyankopon Kwaame, 85
Nyankopong, sky fertility state god, 237
Nyanku Sai, blacksmith chief, 142, 143, 144, 145, 158
title, 143
Nyanku Sai festival, 142–6, 153–4, 158, 160
'medicine' at, 144, 145, 159

Oba Panyin (Elder Woman). *See* Elder Woman
Obosom, 27, 59, 62
kra and, 60
Moon, personification of, 27–8, 29
shrine of, 62
Odabeni (chief of the royal bed-chamber), 56 n. 3, 88
Odiawuono, 'Killer Mother', 27
Odomankoma, Bore-Bore, Creator-god, 59–61, 63, 65 n. 8, 66, 72 n. 1, 103, 234
Akan maxim on, 71–2
death and, 60–1
Ptah and, 65, 72
Odumfo. *See Adumfo*
Odwira, 146, 238 n. 2

253

INDEX

Odwira Suman, 176
Ohemmaa, 28, 52, 59, 106. *See also* Queen-mother
Okomfo. *See Akomfo*
Okra (mock-king), 30 n. 2, 106 and n. 2 king's *kra* and, 30, 106, 115, 189 *See also* Sacrifice: human
okrabiri, 105–6, 123
Okrafo. *See Akrafo*
Omphalos (conical mound), 83–4
Onuris, 41, 81 n. 1
  Hathor and, 162 n. 2
Onuris-Shu-Horus, 81
Opening-of-the-Mouth Ceremony, 67–68, 134, 140, 141, 204, 214 nn. 2, 3
Opet, Beautiful Festival of, 59
Opoku Ware, King of Asante, 25, 238
Oracle, and consultation of, 220
Orion, 77 and n. 3
Osei Tutu, King of Asante, 25, 99 n. 4, 176
Osirian kings and kingdom, 44 ff., 50, 51, 77 n. 6, 156–7
  Apis bull and, 78
  deification after death of, 46
  moon-god, as, 46
  royal dress of, 163
  Set and, 46
  See also Osiris
Osiris, god, 31, 37, 38, 44–7, 44 nn. 1, 2, 3, 68, 73 and n. 3, 77 n. 3, 115, 116, 141, 155
  akhu and, 133–4
  amulet of (fig. 5), 68
  dead judged by, 130, 131, 132
  death and resurrection of, 69, 163 ff.
  'Entrance of Osiris into the Moon' festival, 46
  funeral procession and festival of, 46, 204–5
  gods incarnated in, 46
  Horus incarnate in, 44
  moon-god, as, 46, and n. 1
  Pharaoh as, 113–14, 135, 136, 214, 215
  rebirth during Nehebkau festival of, 163 ff.
  representations of, 44
  Set and death of. *See under* Set.
  son of Hathor, 47
  tomb at Peqer of, 208
  Upwaut incarnate in, 114
Osiris-Soker. *See* Sokaris; Soker
Osofo-okomfo (prophets), 83 and n. 3
Osoro Ahemman ('Upper Kingdom'), 121, 123

Osorkon II, 154, 155, 167, 170. *See also* Bubastis
Otumfi Bi, murder of, 238
Owuo Papa (the Death Fan), 124, 132
Oxyrhynchus, Set's sanctuary at, 75 n. 5

Pa Atemt. *See* Pithom
Pa Dwat, 115–17
  rites of, 114, 115–17, 115 n. 2
Padua, 108, 144
Palermo stone, 76 n. 2, 182 n. 4
Palm-trees, symbolism of, 34
Panehenusis, 132
Panopolis, 80
Papyrus plants, 164 and n. 2
Parrot, the, as emblem, 51, 88
Patrilineality, 40, 98
Pe, city, 48, 137 and n. 3, 210
  goddess of, 161
  Souls of, 45, 48, 51, 79 n. 4, 136, 137–8, 137 n. 4, 139, 161
Pepi I, Pharaoh, 57, 119, 135, 158, 159, 163
Pepi II, Pharaoh, 158, 159
Per Sui, 47
Per-nezer, 136, 137, 223
Persea tree, 74
Per-ur, 136 and n. 7, 137 and n. 1, 154 and n. 1, 223. *See also* Dual Shrines
Petrie, W. M. Flinders, Naga potsherds and, 230, 231 (fig. 9)
Phallic symbols, 99
Phallus sheath, 42
Pharaoh, 50, 52, 133
  accession and coronation rites, 222–7, 222 n. 1
  Amen and, 222, 223–4, 225, 237
  Amen-Re and, 92
  ba and, 131
  ceremonial fights with a Libyan of, 158, 159, 160, 161, 162
  coronation of, 117, 133, 209, 210, 222, 223
  death and rebirth, ritual of, 102, 165, 177–85
  descent of, 139
  divinity of, 215
  gods incarnated in, 45
  Hathor and incarnations of, 49–50, 55 n. 2, 236–7
  Horus and incarnations of, 35, 37, 46–7, 49 ff., 114, 139
  'Horus of Gold' and, 50
  Isis and, 50, 136, 165

INDEX

ka symbol and Horus name, 37, 100, 113
king of Upper and Lower Egypt, 57 *et passim*
  land and, 42, 162–3
  life-giving of, and maintaining life in the state, 51, 57, 163 ff.
  Maat and, 93–4
  Min incarnated in, 84, 101, 102, 139
  moon-god, as, 35
  mother of, 52
  name of, 35
  Nebti title of, 50, 51
  Onuris-Horus as, 43
  Osiris and, 50, 113–14, 116, 135, 136
  Osiris, king-god and, 46
  Pa Dwat and, 115–17
  placenta and, 94
  priesthood of, 51
  Re and, 51–2, 67 and n. 2, 96–7
  royal ancestors of, 48, 51. *See also* Ancestors
  'Son of Isis', 50, 222
  sons of, 94 and n. 3, 95, 178 and n. 1
  'Sons of Re', 51–2, 92, 93, 225
  standards of, 138–9, 167
  Sun incarnated in, and son of the Sun-god as, 43, 67, 93–7, 111–12
  daily life of, 94
  tabu for death for, 205–6, 206 n. 2, 210 n. 1
  'throne of Geb' and, 42, 45
  titulary of, 51–2
  Upwaut and, 139
  washing of feet of, 159
  wives of, 94 and n. 3
Pharaoh, dead, 67 n. 3
  ascension and transfiguration of, 213–15
  children of, 209 and n. 1
  death of, and rites after, 204–13
  'eldest son' of, 205
  Mystery Play of the Succession and. *See under* Mystery Play
  Ptah and, 67–8
  statue of, 140, 214 and n. 3
  transfiguration of, 208
Philae, bas-relief at, 65–6
Piesie, 31
Pig or boar, the, 73 n. 3, 229 n. 2
Pithom (Pa Atemt), 39 and n. 2, 40
Pkharti, 42
Pipes, queen-mother's ceremonial smoking, 89
Placenta, the, 94 and n. 3, 139
Planets, seven, 59–60, 61, 72, 75 n. 4, 180

akragya and, 66, 72
bas of, 131
divinities of, 113
ka and, 110, 130
kra and, 60, 103, 110, 113, 122, 130
Plantain, the, 188 and n. 2
Plants, incarnation of deities in, 81–2
Pliny, 76, 78, 91
Plutarch, 48, 52, 73 n. 3, 74 n. 3, 76, 169
Pole, the, 83 and n. 7, 170 n. 1
Pole star, the, 59, 72
  Ptah, and, 65, 67 and n. 3, 72
Porcupine, the, as emblem, 51
Portraits of Akan rulers, 126 and n. 2
  portrait masks, 127
Prempeh I, King, 176 n. 1
Priest-chiefs, 39, 230
  Atum and, 90
Priestesses, 29, 34 n. 1, 55–6, 56 n. 2, 62, 63, 145, 156
  Akan, 83, 147
  Egyptian royal marriages and, 55–6
Priesthood of Egyptian queens, 54–5
Priests, 62, 63, 144, 147, 153, 157, 162, 167, 181–2, 205 n. 1, 225
  Akan succession and, 216
  Apis, of, 78, 79 and n. 4
  Bosummuru, of, 203
  Heliopolis, of, 91, 92
  Isis, of, 139
  Min, of, 82, 178, 179, 181–2
  Ntoro cult and, 100
  Ptah and, 64 and n. 3
  reciter, 63, 83, 151, 158, 178
  Sem, 158, 161, 206 and n. 2, 211 and n. 1
  See also *Akomfo*; *Anmutef*; *Banmuhene*; *Imy-khant*; Tano: priests
Primeval water, 68
Procreation, 74, 81, 82
  god of, 76, 93, 180
  Ntoro cult and, 100 and n. 4
Tano and, 61
Ptah, Creator-god, 41 n. 4, 46, 64–72, 64 nn. 3, 4, 5, 67 and nn. 2, 3, 164–5, 234
  deceased Pharaohs and, 67–8
  emblem and worship of, 64, 71 and nn. 3, 4
  fire and, 64 and n. 3
  Khnum and, 112 n. 1
  name, 64
  Odomankoma and, 65, 72
  Pole star and, 65, 67, 72

INDEX

Ptah—*contd.*
  representations of, 70 and n. 5
  resurrection of, 66-7
  statuette of, 70 and n. 5
  Sun and, 91
  time and order and, 65 and nn. 4, 5.
    See also Cosmic order
Ptah-hotep, precepts of, 110, 111
Ptah-Soker, 70, 71
Ptah-Soker-Osiris, 46, 70, 165
Ptah-Tatjenen, deity, 153, 234
  festival of rebirth of, 153
  rites for, 165
Puduo (gold nuggets), 127, 172, 173, 174, 218
Punt I, Arabia, 31, 32, 233
Punt II, Nubia, 31, 32, 42, 79, 82 n. 4, 233
Purification rites, 115, 116-17, 167, 171, 222-3. See *Aferihyia Dwaree*
Pyramid texts, the, 39 40, 39 n. 5, 43, 44, 45, 46, 47, 48, 58 n. 1, 67 and n. 3, 73 n. 3, 75 n. 4, 90 n. 1, 96, 97, 101, 110, 111, 112, 113-14, 119, 120, 130 n. 5, 135 and n. 2, 136, 138, and n. 2, 140
Pyramids, 96 and n. 8
  building of, 95
  symbols, as, 96

Queen-mothers, 62
  abuse and, 169
  deceased, 166
  house of, 80
Queen-mothers, Akan, 23, 47 n. 3, 54 and n. 2, 57, 89, 99, 106, 147, 175, 193, 195, 197, 200, 203, 220, 223, 227
  Aferihyia Dwaree and, 173 ff.
  Buru and, 98-9
  council of, 29-30
  crimes and trial of, 57 and n. 4
  deceased, 148
  divinity and incarnation of, 28-9
  enstoolment and choice of new king and, 128, 216, 217, 218, 219
  heir-apparent and, 56-7
  king and, 87
  kra of, 28-9, 89, 105, 106-7, 111
  life-giving power of, 52
  procreative power of, 98-9
  royal ancestors of, 23
  sceptre of, 28, 29, 230 n. 2
  silver and its symbolism for, 76, 89 127, 175 n. 1
  silver stool of, 172, 173, 188 n. 1

Queen-mothers, Egyptian, 38-9, 42, 47, 52-8, 154
  Min-Khamutef festival and, 178, 179
Queens, Akan, 175
  senior queen's Venus aspect, and sacred marriage of, 62
Queens, Egyptian, 42, 52-8, 154
  coronation of, 224, and 225 n. 3
  coronation of Pharaohs and, 223
  divinity of, and incarnation of Isis in divine, 52-8
  life-giving of, 51, 54, 55
qeni stomacher, 211 and n. 1
Quertet, snake-god, 39 n. 2

Races, Egyptians and, 32 n. 3
Rainbow, Akan king and, 89
Ram, 82 n. 4, 92, 234
  Mendes, of, 78 n. 5, 81
  white, 86. See also under Sacrifice
Ram-gods, 101. See also Anzti; Baal Hamman
Ramses II, 39 n. 1, 151, 224 n. 2
Ramses III, 154 n. 3, 166, 183, 184
  daughters of, 53 n. 3
Ramses IV:
  hymn of, 130
  legitimate ruler, as, 50
Re, Sun-god, 37, 47, 50, 67 and n. 2, 91, 112, 118, 237
  Ba and, 131
  cult of, 92
  daughter of, 94
  dead, the, and, 130 and n. 4, 135
  Ikhnaton and, 93
  Nehebkau and, 120
  Pharaoh incarnation of, 67 and n. 2, 96-7
  Pharaoh 'Son of Re', 51-2
  shrine of, 90
  See also Amun-Re; Aton; Gold: metal of the Sun; Nyankopon
Re-Atum, god, 90-2
  cult of, 39 n. 4
Rebirth, annual, 163 ff., 230. See also Death and rebirth; Resurrection
Regalia of Akan king. See under King, Akan
Re-Harakhte, temple of, 56
Reincarnation, 124, 132-3
Rekhmire, tomb chapel of, 138
Resurrection, 68, 134, 136
  body, the, and, 125. See also Death and rebirth; Immortality
Rice, Tano and, 62
Rodd, F. R., 232 and n. 3

INDEX

'Royal Kinsmen', Egyptian, 94
Royal Standards:
  deities and, 139
  Pharaoh, of, 138–9, 167
  Upwaut, of, 156, 160

Sa, fluid of life, 112, 141
  sa-ankh, 117
Sacred Groves, the 29, 36, 62, 147, 150, 154, 158, 159, 166, 179, 183 nn. 1, 3, 208. *See also* Trees, sacred
Sacred marriage, the, 30 and n. 3, 35, 55 and n. 2, 56, 62, 63, 101–2, 183, n. 3
  Akan and, 55, 99
  Amun, of, 101–2
  Egyptian, 180 n. 3, 184 and n. 3, 185
  Hathor and Horus, of, 35
Sacred water, 107, 117, 167, 173, 174. See also *Sa*
Sacrifice, 30 and n. 2, 128, 151, 174, 176, 209, 212
  Akan king and, 30 and n. 2
  animal, 30, 166, 175 n. 1, 198
  bull, 63, 77–8, 83, 102, 129–30, 175, 176, 182
  cattle, 80
  cocks, 174
  cow, 56, 63, 175, 176, 182
  geese, 92 n. 3
  goat, 74 n. 4
  great sacrifice, 179 and n. 4, 182
  human, 106 and n. 2, 123 and n. 1, 124, 141 and nn. 2, 3, 158, 176 and n. 1, 217 n. 2
    Akan king's death and, 189, 190–191, 192, 194–5, 196, 197, 198, 199–200, 209
  Ntoro cult and, 100
  pig, of, 73 n. 3
  ram, of, 86, 92, 106, 108, 123 n. 1, 129, 141, 144, 147, 151, 174, 175, 185, 199, 203, 215, 219, 220, 221
  sheep, of, 151, 174
Sahu (spiritualised body), 117, 132 and n. 1
Sahure, 137
Sais, 42, 43, 51, 229 n. 2
Sako (sedan chair), 144, 147
Saman (spiritual body), 60, 107, 123 and n. 1, 124, 141, 197 n. 1, 202 n. 2, 215, 219 n. 2
Samandow (other world), 60, 123. *See also* Netherworld

Saman-fo (departed spirits), 60, 123, 124, 132 n. 1
Saman-tenten, 123
Sambehdet, 49 and n. 1
Sa-mer-f (eldest son), 204, 205 and n. 1
Sanaa bag, 172, 173, 185
Sanaahene (chief of the treasury), 172–3, 174, 218
Sankofa bird, 91, (fig. 8) 91
Sannaa Kese festival, 118, 171 n. 1
saru (men's council), 38 and n. 3
Sasa or *Sesa* (personification of energy), 124
Sasabonsam, Akan demi-god, 70
Sat-Amen, 53 n. 3
Saturday, 60, 61, 85
Saturn, 59, 60, 61, 73, 85, 228 n. 3
Scarab, the, 71
Sceptre, *Nyansa Pow* (fig. 1), 28, 29, 230 n. 2
Schäfer, —, 205 n. 1
Scorpions, goddesses and, 47 n. 2
seven, 47
Sed festival, the, 43, 45 n. 3, 91, 118, 137, 151–63, 166–7
  houses of, 155 and n. 3
  pavilion of, 155, 157
  scenes on reliefs of, 153
Sedge, the, 51
Sekhem, 132
Se-khentneb-Ra, 53
Sekhmet, lioness-goddess, 41 n. 4, 119, 120 n, 1, 180 n. 2
Sem-Anmutef, 115. *See also* Priests: Sem
Semites, 233 and n. 5
Senusert I, King of Egypt, 204
Senut, a snake, 135 and n. 4
Serpents, 96, 118–19, 118 n. 4, 120 n. 1
  symbolism of, 119
Seseman-Nkoranza, sanctuary of Ntoa at, 83 n. 6, 239
Set, god, 38, 48 and n. 1, 73–4, 73 n. 3, 74 nn., 141 n. 3, 162, 225
  birthplace of, 73 n. 3
  contending with Thoth of, 48
  death of Osiris and, 46, 74 nn. 1, 3, 4, 5, 117, 140, 141 n. 3, 162, 204, 207, 209
  drowning of, 46
  incarnations of, 73–5, 73 n. 3
  Isis and, 47
  Ombos, of, 162
  Osirian kingdom and, 46
  sanctuary at Oxyrhynchus, 75 n. 3
  sky fertility-god, as, 75

257

INDEX

Set—*contd.*
  standard of, 74
  state god of Nubt, 43
Sethe, K., 209 nn. 1, 2, 210 n. 1
Seti I, 118, 133
Seven-day week, 59–60, 72
Seventy days, Egyptian funeral rites and, 212 and nn. 2, 4
Shadow:
  Min, of, 81
  procreation and, 81 and n. 4
  See also Khaibit; *Sunsum*
Shedshed, 45, 139
Shemayt, 180, 184 n. 3
Shen sign, 164, 165
Shield-bearers, 145 n. 1, 183 n. 1
Shrines, 62, 70, 84, 99, 126, 144, 150–151, 151 n. 1, 153, 154, 155
  Re, of, 90. *See also under* Ntoa; Taa Kese
Shu, god, 38, 40 and n. 3, 41, 42, 165
Shu, lion clan, 51
Sickle, the, 181
  Min-Khamutef festival and use of, 180, 181, 184
Silver, Akan queen-mother, and symbolism of, 76, 89, 127, 175 n. 1
Simpini (stairs), 149, 179 and n. 3
Simpson, William K., 226 and n. 5
Siut, 44, 45, 155
  'holy Mother of Siut,' 45 n. 3, 155, 156–7
Sky, god of night, 35
  goddess of the night, 34, 55
Sky fertility-deities, 29, 61–4, 77, 98, 237
  Akan, 81, 84
  cult of, 231–2, 233
  Egyptian, 76–7, 81–2
  incarnation of, 62
  rebirth yearly to the mother-goddess, 230
  vegetation and water and, 62
Snake, the, 39 n. 2, 70 and n. 5
Sodohene (head cook), 214 n. 3
  heir-apparent of, 186
  king's death and, 187, 188, 194
Sokaris-Osiris, festival of, 164
Soker or Sokaris, falcon-god, 46, 70 and nn. 3, 5
Soleb, 154, 156, 165
  Hall of Eating at, 165–6
Souls:
  'Souls of the East,' 182 and n. 4, 183
  'Souls (or *Bas*) of Pe and Nekhen,' 112, 131, 135, 182 n. 4
  See also under Heliopolis; Nehken; Pe

Speiser, E. A., 232
Spiral, the, symbolism of, 83, 180
Spokesman, royal, 148, 200
  staff with falcon of, 35
  See also Akyeamehene
sraman, 76
Staff, golden, falcons on, 35 and n. 1
Stag, the, Min incarnate in, 82 n. 4
Standards, 156, 160
  royal, 113, 138–9, 167
Star, five-pointed, 115, 116 n. 2
State umbrellas, 108, 145, 150, 172, 199, 201
Statues:
  Amun, of, 101
  Ancestors, royal, of, 136 and n. 6, 138, 139, 185 and n. 1
  falcon, of, 79
  Haremhab, of, 222, 223
  Min, of, 80–1, 178, 179, 185
  Nefertari, of, 55
  Pharaoh, deceased, of, 140, 214 and nn. 2, 3
Steindorff, 224 n. 2
Stone-borer, Ptah and, 64 and n. 3, 71
Stools, the Akan, 87, 88, 126, 127 ff., 136, 138, 141, 172
  black, 127, 128, 143, 163 n. 4, 188, 201, 202–3. *See also Apunia*
  cloth over, 127
  dead king's, 89, 201 and n. 2, 202, 213, 214
  Golden, 175, 188 and n. 1, 218 n. 5
  hereditary offices and, 87
  king's, 86, 189
  silver, 172, 173, 188 n. 1
Stool-sons of the divine Akan King, 128, 171 and n. 3, 172, 173, 187, 189, 191, 192, 193, 194, 198
Succession, royal, 216 ff.
  Akan, 216–22
  Egyptian, 102, 205 n. 1, 222–7
Sumankwahene (king's physician and a priest), 145, 186, 220 and n. 1
Summe plants, ritual use of, 127, 151, 166, 172–3
Sun, 30, 59, 60, 67, 72, 92, 119
  Hathor and, 34
  Horus and, 73
  Moon Mother-goddess and, 147
  Nut and, 91
  Ptah and, 65 and n. 8
  rising of, 118
Sunday, 129 n. 1, 149, 185
  '*Nwona*' or 'Shielded', 176
Sun-god, 35, 67, 72, 237

258

INDEX

Egyptian Sun-gods, 90 ff.
king, as, 72
king as son of, 85–6 ff., 111
Nehebkau and, 120 and n. 1
Pharaoh and, 43
See also Nyankopon; Re
Sunsum (generative force), 30, 60, 61, 63, 66, 72 n. 1, 80, 81, 124, 132
Bosummuru, of, 99
kra and, 60
Swords, state, 147, 172, 201, 220
symbolism and, 99 and n. 1
See also Bosummuru: Gold dagger or sword; Mmerante; Nkerante
Symbolism:
Akan, 229–30, 229 n. 5, 230 ff., 230 n. 1, 232 n. 1, 235
Egyptian divine, 138, 139
Syria, 31, 44, 73 n. 3

Taa Kese, 61, 142, 149–51, 149 n. 1, 170, 218
festival of, 149–51, 155
High Priest of, 143, 144, 145, 150, 151 and n. 2, 220
shrine of, 144, 149–50, 153–4, 221
sons of, 150 and n. 1
Taa Kofi, 61, 149 n. 1
Taa Kora, 61, 149 n. 1
Taa Takyiwaa, 145, n. 2
Tabus, 105–6, 107
Takyi Akwamo, Bonohene, 98, 127
Takyifiri, Fante prince, 145 and n. 2
Takyiman, 107, 142, 145 and n. 2, 146, 149 and n. 1, 167, 168, 169, 171, 226
See also Nyanku Sai festival
Tanit, goddess, 82, n. 4, 228
Tano, sacred river, 61, 62, 150, 151 and n. 3, 173 n. 1
Tano, state god-goddess of Bono Kingdom, 61–2, 63, 145 n. 1, 150–1, 200. See also Taa Kese
antelope mask of, 145
Korontihene's fight with, 145, 146
priestesses of, 145
priests of, 145, 149, 150, 151
Tano Twumpuduo, 61, 68
Tanohemmaa, Tano queen-mother, 151
Tatjenen, god, 68
festival of, 158, 168–70. See also Ptah; Ptah-Tatjenen
Ta-urt, hippopotamus-goddess, 74 n. 3
Tefnut, lioness-deity, 34 and n. 1, 38, 40, and n. 3, 41 and n. 4, 42 and n. 4, 47 n. 2, 82 n. 4, 180 n. 2

Teje, Queen, 164, 165
Tekyiman-Brong. See Bono-Takyiman
Thebes, 55, 71
New Year festival at, 92
Thoth, 41 and n. 2, 47, 48, 70, 131, 140, 167, 207–8
kings and, 140
moon and, 208
Thoth clan, 47
Thursday, 60, 116, 146, 171, 197
'Fertile Thursday,' 106, 221
'Great Fertile Thursday,' 171 n. 1
Thutmosis I, King of Egypt, 57, 224
Khamutef cult and, 100
Thutmosis II, King of Egypt, 56, 57
Thutmosis III, King of Egypt, 57 and n. 2, 96, 111 n. 2, 223 n. 7
Thutmosis IV, King of Egypt, 222
Tobacco, 89
Totemism, 27–8, 37. See also Akyeneboa
Trees, sacred, 62, 64, 68, 69 and n. 2, 192, 217 and n. 2, 221, 231
Djed and, 69
Moon Mother-goddess and fig-tree, 29, 35
obosom and, 62. See also Gya dua kra
Triangles, 232
symbolism of (fig. 6), 69, 76
Tuaregs the, 24, 26, 232 and nn. 3, 5
Tuesday, 60, 61, 63, 151, 185, 197
'Fertile Tuesday,' 149
Tuobo custom, 62, 78 and n. 5, 81
Tut-Ankh-Amon, tomb of, 207 n. 3, 214
Twemma, 79–80
Two Lands, union of, 48, 49. See also Egypt: Lower and Upper

Unas, King of Egypt, 135
Uni, Queen Amtes and, 57
Upper Kingdom. See Osoro Ahemman
Upwaut, wolf-god, 44, and n. 4, 45 and n. 3, 114, 139, 155, 156, 160, 161, 207 n. 2
clan, 207
'Opener-of-the-Ways', 44, 45
Pharaoh and, 160
Procession, 158, 160 and n. 3, 207 and n. 2
standard of, 156, 160
Uraeus, 165, 223, and n. 7, 224, 225

Vegetation, deities and, 80, 81, 236, 237

INDEX

Venus, 29, 30, 59, 60, 61
   Hathor, as, 34
   senior queen's Venus aspect, 62
Vizier (*t'ate*), 38 n. 2, 207
Vulcan, god, 64
Vulture, the, 71, 72

Wadjet, cobra-goddess, 48, 50–1, 117, 137 and n. 3
Wainwright, G. A., 83–4, 206 n. 2
Wankyi, 83 n. 6, 239
Was sceptre, 43, 161
Wednesday, 60, 176 n. 2, 197
   Fo-Wukuo, Fertile, 129
   Mono-Wukuo, 129
Werempe, ceremony, 126, 200–4, 219
Werempefo, 188, 200, 201 and n. 1, 202, 213 and n. 2, 216
Werempehene, 188, 200–1, 216, 217, 224
Wheat, *emmer*, 82, 180–1, 184 and n. 1
White, 109, 127
   ritual use of, 109, 128, 220, 221
   symbolism of, 107
Wilkinson, Sir J. G., 178 n. 2, 179 n. 1
Wilson, J. A., Egyptian embalming period and, 211

Wind-gods, 234
Wives:
   harem, 56 and n. 3
   royal: *see under* King; Pharaoh

Wolf, the, 114
   wolf-god: *see* Upwaut
   wolf-skin, 156
Wolf clan people, 44, 155
Women, 100
   Apis bull and, 78
   Apo festival and, 168 and nn. 1, 2, 169
   festival of Tatjenen and, 168–9, 170
   matrilineal system in Egypt and, 52 ff.
   queen-mothers and, 54 and n. 2.
   See also *Tuobo* custom

Yaa Takyiwaa, Fante Queen-mother, 61
Yams, ritual use of, 62, 100 n. 2, 144, 174
Yereba, 201

Zagha, 25–6. *See also* Dia

www.ingramcontent.com/pod-product-compliance
Lightning Source LLC
Chambersburg PA
CBHW060114170426
43198CB00010B/885